SORCERY AND SOVEREIGNTY

TAXATION, POWER, AND REBELLION
IN SOUTH AFRICA,
1880–1963

SEAN REDDING

SORCERY AND SOVEREIGNTY

OHIO UNIVERSITY PRESS   ATHENS

Ohio University Press, Athens, Ohio 45701
www.ohio.edu/oupress
© 2006 by Ohio University Press

Ohio University Press books are printed on acid-free paper ∞™

14 13 12 11 10 09 08 07 06   5 4 3 2 1

An earlier version of chapter 2 appeared in *Journal of Southern
African Studies* 22 (1996): 249–70 (http://www.tandf.co.uk).
Chapter 7 is a revised form of the article "Government Witchcraft: Taxation, the
Supernatural and the Mpondo Revolt," *African Affairs* 95 (1996): 555–79, and is
published by permission of Oxford University Press.

Cover image: "Woman Plowing, Transkei, 1949." Transkei, South Africa. Black and
white photograph by Constance Stuart Larrabee, 1949. Image no. EEPA 1998-061342, Eliot
Elisofon Photographic Archives, National Munseum of African Art, Smithsonian Institution.

Library of Congress Cataloging-in-Publication Data
Redding, Sean.
  Sorcery and sovereignty : taxation, power, and rebellion in South Africa,
1880–1963 / Sean Redding.
    p. cm.
  Includes bibliographical references and index.
  ISBN-13: 978-0-8214-1704-1 (cloth : alk. paper)
  ISBN-10: 0-8214-1704-5 (cloth : alk. paper)
  ISBN-13: 978-0-8214-1705-8 (pbk. : alk. paper)
  ISBN-10: 0-8214-1705-3 (pbk. : alk. paper)
  1. South Africa—Politics and government—1836–1909. 2. South Africa—Politics
and government—1909–1948. 3. South Africa—Politics and government—
1948–1961. 4. South Africa—Colonial influence. 5. Blacks—South Africa—Politics
and government—19th century. 6. Blacks—South Africa—Politics and government—
20th century. 7. Taxation—Political aspects—South Africa—History. 8. Government,
Resistance to—South Africa—History. 9. Witchcraft—Political aspects—South Africa—
History. 10. Power (Social sciences)—South Africa—History. I. Title.
  DT1798.R44 2006
  968.05—dc22

2006017574

CONTENTS

ILLUSTRATIONS

Figures

Tables

Maps

PREFACE

In the time I have taken to research and write this book, South Africa has changed dramatically. The project that I undertook as South Africa was loosening the grip of the apartheid state in the early 1990s has emerged in the postapartheid world that finds the country struggling with the legacy of its troubled past. My own slow work habits aside, the project changed in part as a reflection of later events. While resistance to colonial rule and the apartheid state is still a significant element in the story, the broader cultural meanings of resistance and violence have become more prominent.

Studying beliefs in witchcraft and their impact on people's actions has become trendy. In writings about South Africa, topics that used to be confined to ethnographies have become part of the academic mainstream. While there is a danger that witchcraft beliefs may be used to explain too much, there has been a real benefit in taking spiritual beliefs seriously as historians and other scholars confront difficult questions about how colonized people ordered and interpreted the world and their political options. Recognizing that spiritual beliefs are not a simple handmaiden of material frustrations or desires creates the potential for a richer description of people's lives and for a more complete explanation of events.

I did not start this project with the idea that tax payments as a ritual of rule had a connection to beliefs in the supernatural. But as I engaged with my sources I came to think there was such a connection. There were certainly plenty of dry documents reporting the rate of tax payments and detailing down to the last shilling who owed back taxes and how best to get them to pay up. But there were other kinds of documents—including court transcripts and transcripts of meetings as well as the proceedings of various commissions—where Africans testified, often eloquently, about taxes and about their relationships with state officials. Magistrates' reports and letters expressed official unease about the same topics and speculated why Africans were or were not paying their taxes and why they had suspicions about state officials' intentions. The words of African officials—headmen and chiefs, clerks and translators—also appear in the archives at various moments, often in an official capacity, to explain the actions or beliefs of their peers. Missionaries left letters and reports of their own, many of which contain observations and concerns about African supernatural beliefs and their connection either to acceptance of the political order or unrest. These writings and archives have formed the bulk of my sources, and they provide evidence for the persistence of beliefs among many rural Africans in the supernatural generally and in the workings of witches and other malevolent actors in particular to shape events both in their personal lives and in the broader political and social realm.

I also encountered mentions of witchcraft beliefs when I interviewed people in various Transkeian districts in 1990. The Xhosa name for the poll tax, or General Rate, that virtually all the informants used was *irhafu yempundulu* (lightning-bird tax), a reference to the mythical lightning bird, which can be sent by witches to harm their enemies via lightning strikes or by sucking blood. (Govan Mbeki, a leading figure in the ANC in the 1950s and 1960s who wrote the first account of the revolt that took place in the Transkei at that time, also notes that name for the poll tax.) This direct association of a particular tax with a supernatural being caused me to delve more deeply into the archival sources for additional evidence to support the broader claim that many rural Africans commonly associated colonial rule with whites' supposed abilities to manipulate supernatural powers. The works of anthropologists—especially Monica Wilson's very important *Reaction to Conquest*, based on research conducted in the 1930s—also provide quotations from various African informants that directly link witchcraft practices to the exercise of colonial power. These materials and sources were more than suggestive of a critical role being played by supernatural beliefs in the routine assumptions many Africans made about the state. They provide ways into the worldviews and beliefs of people who both helped to build a particular version of colonial rule in the Transkei and then tried to tear it down.

Let me provide a quick note on spelling of African words and names in the text. In general, I have used the commonly accepted written version of various place names and people's names, although there are often two or more versions of a single name (for example, the older version "Umditshwa" and the more correct spelling "Mditshwa," or the older version "Gangelizwe" and the more correct spelling "Ngangelizwe"). I have allowed the spellings in original sources to remain as they are in the original, and hope this will not cause too much confusion.

It is my pleasure to acknowledge the numerous intellectual debts I have incurred in the course of this project. Amherst College provided me with the financial support to conduct the research for the project and the time to write it. My colleagues in the history department were also extraordinarily supportive, and I have learned a great deal by talking to them and teaching with them. My fellow African studies colleagues in "the Happy Valley" have also taught me a great deal and extended my horizons beyond the boundaries of South Africa. Various scholars have read drafts, provided comments, and occasionally forced me to see the error of my ways. First on the list is Catherine Higgs, who read the whole manuscript and gave me invaluable suggestions. Mitzi Goheen has also been a kind but incisive critic of the chapters she has read at various stages. William Beinart read an earlier version of some of the material and provided excellent criticisms. Jeff Peires generously helped me and discussed the project when I came to Umtata in 1990 to conduct interviews in the Transkei. My research assistant (who asked for anonymity at the time) in the Transkei in December 1990 was extraordinarily helpful and conscientious as he assisted me with interviews. Archivists in the Cape Town, Pretoria, Pietermaritzberg, and Umtata archives depots, as well as those in the Cullen Library, were always knowledgeable and gracious. Detailed comments were provided by anonymous reviewers, including those who read the whole manuscript for Ohio University Press, and those who read the earlier versions of the individual chapters that were published as journal articles. Gillian Berchowitz, the press's senior editor, also gets my thanks for taking on the project, for sharing her own comments and suggestions, and for her elucidations of other people's comments.

I also thank Harrison M. Wright, now professor emeritus of history at Swarthmore College, for initially teaching me not only about South African history, but also about doing research and for instilling in me a real interest in digging out information wherever it leads. He also introduced me to Joan Broster, whose vocation was the documentation of African rural life in the Transkei. During my first visit to the Transkei in 1979, she took me around the countryside, introduced me to people, and shared her knowledge, all of which made me see African rural life as more than a question of material resources and population migration. In that same vein, I have an enormous debt to the numerous Africans, often unnamed, whose lives and testimonies I have found in the archives and have used in the writing of this book.

My debts to my family, including my husband, Peter Siegelman, and my son, Dan, are boundless. They have enriched both my life and this book.

CHAPTER 1

SORCERY AND THE STATE

Taxation, Rituals, Witchcraft, and Colonialism in South Africa, 1880–1963

"A word is like a morsel of honey," advised one African chief in an 1894 meeting with his local government official, the resident magistrate, on the subject of newly imposed taxes and regulations. The morsel of honey he and his headmen provided to the magistrate was that the new taxes proposed by the colonial state were oppressive and would eventually turn the largely peaceable district of Idutywa, in the rural southeast of South Africa, into a breeding ground of political dissent and poverty.[1] The sweetness of their words did not mask the bitterness they felt at the government's repeated refusals to listen to their warnings.

By the 1950s the words being offered to the South African state were much less honeyed. For many rural Africans in South Africa, taxes had become the work of witches and other evil supernatural beings that stalked ordinary people and sucked their blood at the command of white government administrators and those African chiefs who collaborated with them. The imposition of new taxes and other regulations caused wave upon wave of violent unrest in many rural areas. As a pamphlet produced by some members of the African National Congress noted, Africans suspected the South African prime minister and the leading architect of grand apartheid policy, Hendrik Verwoerd, of planning to "suck in oppression the warm blood of the Natives who have been made the sacrificial lamb to feed the families of the Europeans. . . . The [collaborating] chiefs will compel the people to pay more taxes than they are able to bear; they will compel the people to go out to work in the mines and on the farms, where a man is worked until he becomes as thin as a bark and receives in payment a paraffin tin of mealie meal [a kerosene can—or a small measure—of corn-meal]; they are going to force the people to limit their stock [cattle] so that they become perpetual slaves."[2] In response to this threat, Africans widely refused to pay their taxes in the 1950s; they sabotaged various government projects; and rebels set the homes of collaborating chiefs on fire, hoping to kill them in the way that witches had historically been executed.

Taxes have been at the root of much political violence in South Africa. White-controlled colonies and republics expanded and consolidated their control over the South African black population into the easternmost part of what is now South Africa from 1878 through 1894 and usually were quick to impose taxes. Africans disliked being ruled and taxed by colonial authorities, and dissent occasionally erupted into outright rebellion. In many areas, including regions of the current Eastern Cape and KwaZulu-Natal Provinces, revolts broke out shortly after the institution of white rule, and over the next century that rule was periodically called into question by African organizations and individuals. Distrust of the colonial regime reached a new peak in the late 1940s through the early 1960s, when revolts blossomed across a wide area of rural South Africa. All these revolts were rooted in part in grievances over taxes; at the same time rebels frequently invoked supernatural powers to assist them and accused government officials, particularly Africans who worked for the state, of using witchcraft to enrich themselves and to harm ordinary people. Beliefs in witchcraft and supernatural powers were just below the surface of much of the political rhetoric, and the system of taxation—with all its prescribed interactions between ruler and ruled—was intimately connected to these supernatural beliefs.

African reactions to colonial taxation and governance were not one unbroken chain of violent resistance, however. Any consideration of the connections between taxes, resistance to taxation and the colonial state, and supernatural beliefs has to take into account the long periods of relative political quiet among Africans. Decades of historical and other forms of scholarly research have indicated that most Africans did not believe the colonial state to be legitimate, so African quiescence in the face of white rule did not result from a sense that they were being properly represented and governed by the state.[3] Yet Africans did have an ongoing association with the state that was enacted and reinforced on a yearly basis with the complicated and highly personalized ritual of tax payment. The intersection of taxation, political attitudes, and supernatural beliefs among Africans speaks directly to some of the most significant issues in the history of colonized Africa: What bonds existed between African colonial subjects and the white-controlled states that ruled them? What meanings did Africans and whites attach to their interactions, and how did those meanings inform their construction of and reactions to the state?

Tax collection and taxpaying were opposite sides of the same interaction. The yearly payment of these taxes meant that each adult African man or his stand-in came into regular contact with state officials. Dealing personally with either the magistrate or his clerk, each man paid the money owed and walked away with an itemized receipt. While this might seem a clear-cut monetary transaction, the cultural understandings and assumptions behind that transaction were far from straightforward. Magistrates collected taxes because the state needed money. Yet state officials had interests other than monetary ones bound up in tax collection, and they often saw compliance with tax payments as an indication of the acceptance of colonial laws in general. Africans had their own reasons for paying taxes: out of a need for farmland, to which the magistrate could deny access if taxes were not paid; out of fear of the police, although the police were few in number and often reluctant to be involved in the dangerous duty of rounding up tax defaulters; and out of a deeply ingrained understanding of the fusion between the material world of money, taxes, and laws and the spiritual world of the ancestors and witchcraft. These attitudes can be seen in the narratives people constructed around taxation and the state, and these narratives can, in turn, help to explain both the timing and the nature of violent resistance as well as the occasionally long periods of seeming acceptance of colonial state authority. Both the words of honey and the rhetoric of blood sucking came from people's experiences of the colonial state and its demands for taxes and other forms of obedience and submission.

PRECOLONIAL STATES AND TAXES

Africans in the southeastern part of South Africa, once known as the Transkei and now the easternmost part of Eastern Cape Province, will provide the bulk of the evidence for this study. Africans in the Transkeian region were brought within the colonial state between 1876 and 1894. They came largely from decentralized, scattered chiefdoms like the Thembu or the Mpondo, where one chief had a higher ritual and social status than others but often had little power to enforce his authority. There was little precolonial bureaucratic administration, and the power of chiefs and their subordinates (headmen) typically stemmed from their ritual authority and the goodwill of their subjects.

Most Africans had experience with taxes and other levies imposed by their chiefs. These levies frequently took the form of gifts presented to the ruler on certain occasions, such as at his marriage or during the harvest, or of fees paid to chiefs for services provided, such as hearing a court case. Rarely were precolonial levies as regular or as bureaucratized as colonial taxes would become, and few chiefs had access to significant military or police power to enforce their demands. The power that individual chiefs did have was also limited by the fact that they faced competition for the loyalty of followers from neighboring chiefs or from other claimants to the title, with the result that an unpopular or overly demanding chief could easily find himself either with few followers or else dead.

Chiefs did have claims to other kinds of power, however, as precolonial chiefs claimed both paternalist and supernatural foundations for their rule.[4] A Wesleyan missionary in this region commented in 1826 that "a naked Chief is reverenced and loved by his people as a Father . . . and his people style themselves his Dogs."[5] The Xhosa word for chief—nkosi—expressed a paternalistic relationship. Anthropologist Monica Wilson quotes a saying among the Mpondo people in the 1930s: "Nkosi nguyise wabantu (a chief is the father of his people). He stands to all his people in the same relation as does the head of an umzi [homestead] to the occupants of an umzi."[6] Although a proverb of this kind too easily glosses over the stresses and rivalries common to any society, it expresses the ruling ideology of the chiefs— that they were hereditary elders in a broader social family. Chiefs communicated with the ancestors to boost the fertility of the land and livestock and to bring rain.[7] They protected the community from malevolent witches by employing diviners, who could mobilize supernatural powers to name wrongdoers and by punishing those who were accused of using witchcraft. Chiefs also had access to potentially destructive witchcraft powers themselves, which they could use to build up their own wealth and power or to harm their enemies and rivals. A Mpondo chief had his own supernatural medicines that he used "to give himself an isithunzi (shadow), that is to make himself awesome, to protect him against medicines used by other chiefs, and to attract followers."[8] Zulu chiefs also reputedly had such medicines, according to the Reverend Henry Callaway in 1868: "There are medicines which give chiefs strength and presence; a common man, who is neither a chief nor a doctor, cannot touch this kind of medicine," for fear of being harmed by it.[9] Supernatural and political power were complementary and survived the colonial annexation even as the white magistrates usurped many of the chiefs' functions.

COLONIAL RULE AND THE IMPOSITION OF TAXES

In 1880, shortly after the Cape Colony took over the largest segment of the Transkeian region, there was a rebellion against colonial rule that, although short-lived, did make white rulers cautious about the kinds of laws they imposed. The rebellion, known as the Mpondomise Rebellion, or Hope's War, also prevented widespread expropriation of land to be handed out to white settlers (the common practice elsewhere in southern Africa) because colonial officials were wary of generating additional unrest.[10] The initial defeat of African resistance in 1880 impressed on Africans the futility of military combat against the white-controlled state, but that was not the only reason that over the next several decades Africans did not actively rebel. In the aftermath of the 1880 rebellion Africans dynamically incorporated the colonial state and its officials into their own, existing worldviews, and together, white officials and African subjects engaged in an ongoing—if antagonistic and lopsided—contest over the nature and substance of colonial rule.

Africans were not, however, "colonizing themselves" or making the jobs of white officials necessarily easier. The colonial world in South Africa was a complicated mixture of *baaskap* (a crude white supremacy), paternalism, rampant and aggressive capitalist exploitation of resources, a long-standing relationship between rural Africans and agriculture, and complex social, economic, and cultural changes. Africans, no matter what choices they made or what actions they took, had limited resources with which to realize their ambitions, and they frequently found their options further limited by the erosion of social networks through religious conversions and the disintegration of families. But Africans did take an active part in shaping certain aspects of white rule by interacting with state officials. These interactions were often scripted in the sense that both Africans and officials played formal "roles" as subjects and rulers respectively. These roles tended to circumscribe the actions, if not necessarily the thoughts, of colonized Africans. Interactions between rulers and ruled usually occurred in specific places at specified times: for example, an African man went yearly to the magistrate's office to pay taxes shortly after his sheep had been shorn and their wool sold, or an African father used the magistrate's court to sue his daughter-in-law's family for the return of bridewealth—a payment made to the bride's family at the time of the marriage—if his son's marriage had fallen apart. Paying taxes and using the courts required that Africans accept at least outwardly a particular relationship to the state.

There were also "hidden transcripts"—to use James Scott's term for hidden interpretations and agendas—that contradicted and delegitimized the "public transcript" (or role playing) of submission to colonial authority.[11] Most Africans were not pleased to be colonized subjects, even when they strategically used the colonial state to achieve certain goals. That discontent with colonial rule deepened for a variety of reasons with passing years. The idea of hidden transcripts may help to explain the eruption of rebellion in the 1940s and 1950s. However, we should not discount the significance of the public transcript or of the fact that colonial rule was relatively untroubled by active unrest for several decades.[12]

Africans found ways to coexist with colonial control. The content and scope of that control developed over time as white officials discovered that, in the interest of social and political stability, they had to allow Africans to interpret colonial power in their own ways. Writing of the Tswana colonial experience, Jean and John Comaroff observe a similar phenomenon they term "the colonization of consciousness," although they make it clear that this type of colonization worked both ways as Africans and Europeans borrowed ideas and cultural forms from each other. The borrowed cultural forms created a common, if contested, political vocabulary that was necessary to sustain colonial rule over the long term: "Modern South Africa is built upon a long history of symbolic struggle, a bitter contest of conscience and consciousness."[13]

The Comaroffs have discussed consciousness as emerging from myriad daily actions, including modes of dress and address, choice of language and names, the delineation of space within the African household, the uses of medicines and rituals, and the power of literacy.[14] Christian missionaries worked hard to change the consciousness of Africans when they required their converts to dress "modestly" and to farm with the plow as well as to learn the Apostles' Creed and to take Communion.[15] Regardless of the missionaries' intentions, however, African converts often used their Christian beliefs and identities to protect their worldly interests and expand their political options. Thus, while superficially conversion might seem a capitulation to Western culture, at a deeper level, Christianity and adherence to certain Western norms could legitimate resistance to unpopular state actions and corrosive social trends and could, in certain circumstances, support—and indeed provide the language for and the morality behind—rebellion.[16]

The connections between Africans' beliefs in the supernatural, the power of the white-controlled colonial state, and taxation are analogous to the case of religious conversion and its political effects. Immediately after the colonial takeover and for several decades thereafter, Africans managed to develop and maintain their own social networks and cultural forms that existed largely outside the scrutiny of the state. Effectively, rural Africans "bought" this autonomy from the state through the medium of taxpaying. Africans thus participated in the ritual of taxpaying and helped to write the public transcript of submission to authority as a way to fend off the powers of the state that existed both in the form of demonstrated military might and, in the eyes of many Africans, in the ability of state officials to manipulate supernatural powers. At the same time, in the first decades of colonial rule, Africans kept their access to farm land and to markets that allowed a small group of farmers to profit significantly and allowed a larger group to maintain at least partial economic and social autonomy. These complex interactions created a resilient, if occasionally clumsy, system of administration that functioned at least until the late 1930s and early 1940s, although the system was constantly under stress and changing. By the 1940s two long-existing trends approached their crisis points and began to corrode the system irreparably.

The first trend was a state-created shortage of agricultural land for African farmers. The amount of land available to Africans was strictly limited by the state from the 1880s onward. The African rural population increased steadily, so that by the 1920s in some districts and by the 1940s in almost all the Transkei's districts, few young adult Africans could realistically hope to farm enough land so that they could set up an independent rural household.[17] Acquisition of land was key to becoming a "social adult," a status that carried with it respect and authority. The loss of this older, land-based method of achieving the status of a respectable, mature adult was not replaced by a new method as Africans who moved to the urban areas increasingly found their wages limited and their social identities infantilized by colonial law. Although increasingly impoverished, families were often able to hold onto a small household in the rural areas because of the efforts of migrant laborers, who took jobs in the major industrial cities and used their wages to heavily subsidize rural incomes. However, by the 1940s even urban wages were frequently not enough to support a rural household, and influx control laws prevented Africans from migrating permanently to the urban areas, thus preventing them from achieving or enacting social adulthood in the cities.[18] When the state tried to raise taxes paid by Africans in the 1950s, it sparked a revolt that was partly about an inability to pay the additional taxes and partly about a much broader range of political, social, and economic issues. Africans concluded that the state's power was at the heart of their problems and that tax payments, which provided the money to support the state and which were also a ritualized expression of Africans' subordination to the state, had to stop.

A second trend that corroded state authority by the 1940s was the increasing intrusiveness of state officials into the daily lives of those Africans who did still have access to farmland. In the 1930s, after the findings of the 1930–32 Native Economic Commission were published, the South African state began aggressively to draw up plans to make the "Native Reserves" (including the Transkei) become agriculturally productive areas for a class of "native peasants." These plans were an attempt to provide a small minority of Africans a viable way of supporting a household in the rural areas but lacked any real discussion of how the vast majority of Africans was to raise enough food to survive in the rural areas.[19] Called betterment schemes, the plans imposed principles of scientific management on African agriculture in a misguided effort to make it more productive.[20] The outbreak of World War II stalled the implementation of the plans until the late 1940s, but official enthusiasm remained keen. The creation of economically self-sustaining Native Reserves fit into the developing ideology of the apartheid state after the National Party was elected to power in 1948. In grand apartheid terminology, the Transkei and other reserves would become quasi-"independent" states, so that Africans could be denied political rights within the larger "white" South Africa. But the grand apartheid ideology was very unpopular among Africans and the rehabilitation and betterment schemes were equally unpopular. As officials implemented these schemes in the 1950s and 1960s, they found that a fair bit of brute force and petty harassment was necessary because the schemes relied heavily on unpopular policies such as cattle culling and fencing. As officials became more and more abusive, Africans became more and more bitter toward all state policies, resulting in a very deep pool of resentment from which rebels in the 1950s would draw.

Thus Africans who paid their taxes, at least through the mid-1930s—and a very high proportion of them did so—bought two very important things with their money. One was access to farmland, under the official formula of no tax, no land. The other was the right to be left alone by the state. When, by the 1950s, tax payments no longer bought these things, Africans began to evade them, and they also began more overtly to resist the state and its policies.

The relationship between rural Africans and the state that was embodied in the payment of taxes was not a simple exchange of money for benefits, though. When the various precolonial chiefs in the Transkei came under colonial rule in the 1870s and later, they did not have a contract with the state specifying that tax payments bought a certain type of relationship with the state. Rather, that relationship developed out of a historical process that combined what Africans understood to be the function and power of the state deriving in part from their precolonial experiences, with what white state officials chose to impose and had the ability to enforce. White officials had to compromise their own ideas about the colonial mission with African ideas about the nature of their rulers' authority. This compromise brings us back to the intertwined concepts of political and supernatural power common to precolonial African chiefs.

BELIEFS IN THE SUPERNATURAL AND CHANGES
IN THE COLONIAL PERIOD

Any discussion of African political beliefs in the precolonial period usually involves a discussion of the supernatural, including beliefs in witchcraft, a category of beliefs about the ability to harm someone else or to augment one's own fortune or power through the magical manipulation of substances or through supernatural beings.[21] However, historians focusing on twentieth-century South Africa have only recently engaged with this topic, often borrowing heavily from the extensive anthropological literature on witchcraft beliefs.[22] Historians' reticence has partly resulted from a lack of sources. Because the colonial state officially outlawed witchcraft accusations, beliefs in witchcraft tended to go underground, leaving few public discussions or written sources to which the historian can refer.[23] It is very difficult to get a broad sense of the specific content of witchcraft beliefs at any given moment or of the change in witchcraft beliefs over time. The earliest detailed account by a formally trained anthropologist of supernatural beliefs held by people living in the Transkei dates from the 1930s, forty years after the colonial takeover and twenty-five years before the widespread outbreak of violence directed against the state in the region.[24] The historian can catch glimpses of witchcraft beliefs in various kinds of official records: court cases spanning the entire period as African witnesses testified in civil and criminal trials, magistrates' reports on social trends in their districts, and the testimony of African witnesses to various state commissions. However, all these sources have been filtered or, perhaps more accurately, distorted through the lens of those who translated and recorded the evidence and testimony. The nature of these records has often made historians nervous about relying on them.

The elusive quality of historical sources on witchcraft is in contrast to the well-documented decline in African incomes, particularly in the rural areas as the twentieth century progressed.[25] Many historians have underemphasized witchcraft and beliefs in the supernatural in favor of detailed discussions of the hard material reality of African life.[26] This strategy, however, ignores the problem that people's actions are based not only on their material circumstances but also on their own interpretations and explanations of those circumstances. Many Africans, as well as whites, believed in the existence of supernatural forces—a category that includes both witchcraft and Christianity. White mis-sionaries and colonial officials often expressed the opinion that a Christian god supported colonial rule; some Africans agreed, but many more saw selfish and evil supernatural forces behind the power of the colonizers, and that belief informed their actions. Leaving out a discussion of people's beliefs runs a real risk of making their actions seem almost inexplicable.[27] The rhetoric of the supernatural was part of the local idiom of power.

More recently historians working on South Africa have recognized the importance of supernatural beliefs to the interpretations and actions of people, and anthropologists have also been expanding the historical scope of their studies. Many of these discussions have focused on witchcraft beliefs particu-larly as they affected outbreaks of political violence or interpretations of destructive social and economic changes.[28] While these studies have illumi-nated the political consciousness of various African populations, they often do not provide an account of the ways in which supernatural beliefs may have—over long stretches of time—actually worked in favor of continued colonial rule. The colonial state's ability to rule over a newly subjugated African popu-lation was not simply a result of sly white administrators adopting the politi-cal camouflage of African culture and making strategic public appearances to make white rule more acceptable.[29] It was also the daily, monthly, and yearly rituals of rule, in particular the ritual of tax collection, that reinforced and reenacted the subordination of Africans to the colonial state.

Particularly after the defeat of the 1880 Mpondomise Rebellion, Africans in the Transkei saw state officials as people who had supernatural powers, and therefore it made sense to participate in rituals that would appease state officials and make their use of those powers more predictable. The payment of taxes can be understood as such a ritual, with the tax receipt being used as an object that incorporated the potency of that ritual to ward off malevolent state powers.[30] A widespread African belief in witchcraft and in the ability of state agents to manipulate supernatural means to attain selfish ends became part of the ongoing interaction between officials and African subjects. Monica Wilson, an anthropologist who investigated supernatural beliefs, among other topics, in the 1930s in part of the Transkei known as Pondoland, noted that whites "are believed to be possessed of powerful materials for sorcery." Quoting an unnamed informant, she elaborated: "'All *ubuthi* [material for sorcery] comes from Europeans. They are the real *amagqwira* (witches or sorcerers).' . . . Informants, when asked, replied that store-keepers and individual Europeans in Pondoland did not kill Pondo by witchcraft or sorcery, but 'It is that European, the Government, who *ukuthakatha* [does harm by witchcraft or sorcery].'"[31] Witchcraft beliefs were not uniformly held across the African population, nor were they unchanged by the experience of white rule; but, as a category, beliefs in witchcraft and the existence of supernatural powers survived with some continuity and they affected people's actions.[32] These beliefs were "traditional" in the sense that they had roots that stretched into the remote past; but people often remade and altered witchcraft beliefs, just as they did other elements of traditional culture.

One of the most significant reasons for changes in supernatural beliefs was the extensive contact Africans had with another set of supernatural beliefs— Christianity. The first mission stations had been founded in the Transkeian region by Wesleyan missionaries in 1828. Although missionaries did not have extensive followings until after the consolidation of colonial rule, they did create a solid connection between particular supernatural ideas and the power of whites. Missionaries invoked the Christian god as a force who continually acted in the world and who was not a remote creator.[33] Christians used prayer and ritual to affect natural forces and heal disease in much the same way that non-Christian Africans used sacrifices made to the ancestors.[34] Christianity's influence went well beyond the church: missionaries ran virtually all the schools in the Transkei well into the 1950s, and Africans widely recognized the usefulness of literacy even if they doubted the advantages of conversion. Missionaries and early Christian converts were also often the first people in the region to take advantage of newly available farming technology, such as the ox-drawn plow, and of consumer goods, such as metal cooking pots, cotton blankets, and coffee and tea. Christian converts were also more likely to side with colonial forces in frontier conflicts, and they often benefited if their side was victorious.[35] Many of the white men who staffed the local colonial administration after 1880 were the sons of missionaries, and African converts educated in mission schools were frequently their clerks, further cementing the connection between political power and the supernatural power that Christianity conferred.

Christian missionaries, like colonial administrators, were hostile to beliefs in witchcraft and they tended to emphasize the harmful effects of witchcraft accusations. But just as with the case of colonial laws that forbade witchcraft accusations, mission rules that discouraged beliefs in witchcraft did not always have their intended effect. Missionaries, magistrates, and Africans who testified before the 1881–83 Native Laws and Customs Commission noted the routine nature of beliefs in witchcraft in this period immediately after the imposition of colonial rule.[36] The beliefs remained routine even if they could not be openly expressed once laws were in place criminalizing both witchcraft accusations and the practice of divining witches. The criminalization of these accusations, however, tended to make people believe that the state was shielding witches, and that combined with other administrative procedures to make magistrates themselves look very suspicious (see chapter 2).

African converts who wished to stay in good standing with their white missionaries typically had to obscure the extent to which they believed in witchcraft and the powers of the ancestors. Other converts chose a different route and went into separatist (African-led) churches that were usually far more tolerant of these supernatural beliefs.[37] In the 1930s, though, it was still common for African Christians (sometimes referred to as school people) to continue with certain customs held over from their non-Christian families, including beliefs in witchcraft. A 1936 Church of England inquiry into witchcraft noted that Africans believed that all practices of witchcraft and sorcery were increasing and that "the number of witchdoctors [diviners—people trained to determine who might be a witch or might be using sorcery] is on the increase, in particular the number of women witchdoctors." The report also noted that people still respected and feared diviners and their own ancestors; and an estimated 90 to 100 percent of Christian Africans believed in sorcery and the efficacy of various charms. Finally the report stated that "it is rather humiliating to find that Europeans [living in the Transkei] have been known to resort to the witchdoctors for such things as charmed sticks to ward off hail from their crops."[38] Monica Wilson, in her many interviews with African informants in the 1930s, found that a number of Christians believed not only in sorcery but also in the magical beings (known as familiars) thought to assist witches. She quoted one Christian woman: "The (witch's) baboon and all these things exist. People ride their baboons at night, and go about naked bewitching others; I swear it on the Cross."[39]

In the 1950s, beliefs in witchcraft and sorcery were still common. Anthropologist Philip Mayer commented, "The witch myth has been adapted to labour migrancy exactly as the beliefs about the ancestors have been: social nearness remains essential, but physical distance can be transcended with the greatest of ease." The beliefs also incorporated new elements to accommodate new circumstances. "It was sometimes said that the witch herself can fly to town in a 'cage,'" similar to the cage—a form of elevator—that transported mineworkers underground. And witches used familiars that could make themselves look like expensive consumer goods so as to better target their victims: "The familiar's appearance changes into that of some attractive-looking object—a ring, money, a piece of cloth, a fountain-pen." Ultimately, according to Mayer, "Witches . . . work 'from envy.' Among the special objects of their envy are a thriving family and a thriving herd [of cattle]."[40] While it may have always been true that witchcraft was a product of envy, this targeting of rural wealth in the 1950s was directly related to the declining fortunes of most African farmers at this time.

Witchcraft accusations were also associated with social anxiety. Both Wilson and Mayer suggest that allegations of witchcraft were not necessarily attempts to destroy wealthy people, nor were the poor more likely to be accused of witchcraft. Instead, by the 1930s and developing into the 1950s there was a broad belief among people in the rural areas that their society was changing for the worse and becoming immoral.[41] Evidence of this immorality might be the unexplained death of a child, or persistent crop failures, which could then be directly tied to the practice of witchcraft or the neglect of the ancestors. Throughout this period, people consulted diviners—even though it was illegal to "smell out" a witch—to find the cause of their problems. If the diviner named a witch then that person was driven out, by force if necessary. If the person named as a witch went to the magistrate to complain, both the diviner and those people who employed the diviner were liable to be charged with a criminal offense, sometimes leading people to kill "witches" outright—often by burning down their huts while they slept within—so that there would be no one to complain.[42]

In the precolonial period chiefs had presided over certain rituals and used their own considerable supernatural powers to protect their followers and help them prosper. Once the magistrates replaced the chiefs as the local rulers, they also imposed their own rituals that for a time seemed to perform some of the same functions. But over the course of the twentieth century, the rituals of the magistrates impoverished Africans and exposed them to the malevolence of witches rather than making them prosperous and protecting them.

TAXATION AS A RITUAL OF RULE

The discussion of tax payments as a ritual and as allied with beliefs in the supernatural may seem to exoticize an obligation that most people find mundane and dull. In general, taxation does have a mundane purpose: it is a method of raising revenue to support state projects and officials. In this sense, every state is predatory because it survives by extracting money from the ruled.[43] However, calling the state predatory can obscure the extent to which the ruled participate actively in the process of paying taxes. Beyond their money-raising aspect, taxes perform a complex function by tying together the rulers and the ruled in a ritual of interaction that makes them partners, even if very unequal partners, in the maintenance of state control.[44] Taxation became part of a ritual of rule that bound Africans to the white-controlled state.[45]

Taxation involved Africans paying tribute in cash to the state, at a place—the magistrate's office or his traveling camp—that was the local residence of the state, on a yearly basis, usually June through September, following the harvest of crops and the shearing of sheep. As agricultural people, precolonial Africans had always associated a good harvest and healthy livestock as partly a product of the supernatural intervention of the chiefs, and the chiefs had some claim on the harvest. When the colonial state took over, the magistrates did nothing to dissociate themselves from beliefs that they had taken over the chiefs' role in promoting good agricultural years. The ritual of taxpaying thus reconstituted and reenacted an older ritual of paying homage to the state and was a symbolic acknowledgment of the chief's, and then the magistrate's, use of supernatural powers to promote the well-being of his subjects.

After the imposition of colonial control in the Transkei, Africans were governed by the Department of Native Affairs of the Cape Colony, and later by the same department in the South African government.[46] All the magistrates and assistant magistrates in this period were white, but in the rural areas many of their clerks were African. A magistrate and his clerks were responsible for maintaining order in a district populated by twenty thousand or more Africans; yet through the 1940s a district often had only three regular policemen. Most of a rural district's daily administrative and police work was performed by chiefs and headman, all of whom were African. African officials translated the words and the ideas of the state into the local Xhosa language, and they provided an African voice, albeit a limited one, at local centers of administrative power. Ultimately, however, that power was controlled by whites, and one element in the maintenance of that power was the imposition and collection of taxes.

Taxes collected in the Transkeian Territories were principally of three types: hut taxes, poll (or head) taxes, and livestock rates. The earliest tax imposed was the hut tax, payable by all married men. The state imposed additional taxes from 1895 through the 1920s, including the General Rate, commonly called poll or head tax, and livestock rate, sometimes called dipping or tank tax.[47] With the passage of the Native Taxation and Development Act of 1925, all men over the age of eighteen, whether or not they were married or owned livestock, become taxpayers, as they all became obligated to pay the General Rate (poll tax).[48] From 1926 to 1958 the tax burden for most Africans remained the same, although some taxes were extended to districts in which they had not previously been collected. In 1958, with the enactment of the Native Administration and Development

FIGURE 1.1. "Hut Building: The First Coat of Plaster," Western Pondoland.
Photograph by Mrs. Fred Clarke, n.d. (probably 1920s–1930s). The Campbell
Collection of the University of Kwazulu-Natal.

Amendment Act, the General Rate increased by 75 percent (from one pound to one pound fifteen shillings).[49]

The colonial state required that Africans pay the taxes in cash, and this innovation itself tended to reinforce the state's hegemony. Minted with the image of the current British sovereign on one face along with writing (in Latin) that was frequently indecipherable, and therefore mysterious, even for people literate in English, the coins used to pay taxes may well have appeared to be magical objects in themselves, self-referential and unnatural fetishes with which the state required Africans to live on intimate terms.[50] Africans widely recognized the usefulness of money, but they were also grimly aware of how whites, including shopkeepers and employers as well as magistrates, occasionally cheated them when using cash. To be taken advantage of in this way demonstrated the material disadvantage suffered by Africans in the colonial world, and whites' ways of reckoning with cash enhanced their reputation for malevolence.[51] In pulling together the official lists of taxpayers, state officials also needed to know from African taxpayers the names of their wives (if married), their places of residence, the number of livestock they owned, and other personal information. In return for the tax payments and information, the state gave taxpayers receipts that themselves had value, both as proof of payment of taxes but also as proof of marriage, of rights to land, and of ownership of livestock. This pattern, in which the state conferred value on money, some of which then had to be returned to the state in a yearly ritual of tax collection, was the foundation for two ongoing narratives constructed by Africans and whites about taxpaying and tax collecting and state power in general.

AFRICAN NARRATIVES OF TAXATION AND POWER

African ideas about taxation showed a great deal of variety. Some of that variation resulted from differences between regions, but much resulted from changes in the relationship between people and the state over time. As we shall see in the next chapter, in 1880 a brief armed rebellion (the Mpondomise Rebellion, or Hope's War) broke out among many Africans in this area as a response both to new demands for taxes and to the supernatural and military threat posed by colonial state. Colonial forces, with some African allies, managed to quell the rebellion quickly but at a cost that officials were not eager to repeat. Thus for some years after the rebellion officials were unwilling to coerce Africans to pay their taxes or to do anything else for fear of provoking another revolt.

Paradoxically, after the revolt even those Africans who had rebelled largely complied in making the tax payments demanded of them.[52]

In the early decades of colonial rule in the Transkei (roughly until 1910 or 1915), there were high levels of quasi-voluntary compliance with the tax laws; at the same time people tended to be deferential to state officials. Examples of that deference can be seen in how people, even chiefs, spoke to the magistrates, routinely addressing them as *nkosi,* a word meaning both chief and "father."[53] In 1881 several Africans testified before the Cape Native Laws and Customs Commission. Chief Mgudhlwa stated to the white commissioners, most of whom were government officials, "We hope Government will, from time to time, send persons to explain matters to us. We are Government children, and a child must be advised every day." A Mfengu headman, Mendela, remarked, "Your children are glad to see you. You gave them bread and land also. You also gave them magistrates, who are dealing well with them."[54] These elaborate shows of deference may have been strategic and even cynical, but even so they reflected a real respect for the authority wielded by the magistrates.

Many Africans at this time believed that the state's authority extended beyond the material realm of agricultural land and jail time to a more dangerous collusion between white magistrates and African witches and sorcerers. The suspicion of this collusion derived from several different causes. First, white officials banned witchcraft accusations. While the intent of this ban was to prevent individual Africans from being accused of and punished for an "unreal" crime, Africans widely interpreted the law as proof that the state was protecting witches and was therefore benefiting from the supernatural powers of its protégés.[55] In 1880 a missionary in one district of the Transkei noted that, with the ban on witch finding, "the people in their ignorance believe that they have now no protection against the wicked practices of the 'Umtakati' [witches or sorcerers]."[56] Second, the imposition of the hut tax required a population census. As magistrates asked questions about a man's wife or wives and the number of children, Africans worried about what the state would do with that information. Witches and sorcerers needed such personal information to kill a man or injure his family, and among Africans themselves there were taboos about speaking the names of family members and making such intimate information broadly known.[57] Finally, the coins used to pay the taxes were themselves somewhat "unnatural." On the one hand, the image of the British ruler on the coins personified and personalized the state in the same way the magistrate did, thus making it more intimate. On the other hand, the coins were perhaps the familiars—in a supernatural sense—of the state, able to do its bidding at a distance, as well as maintaining supernatural surveillance over the sovereign's subjects. Thus tax collection and the use of cash were not only symbolic of the state's secular authority, but they also provided the state and white magistrates with the information and opportunity to exercise supernatural powers over their subjects.

Yet in these first few decades of colonial rule, many Africans may have seen the potential supernatural threats posed by the state as manageable. Most Africans were able to continue their rural lives with relatively little interference from the state as long as they paid their taxes. Rural society was certainly undergoing changes during this period, some of it the result of rapid industrialization elsewhere in South Africa. Much of the early impact of industrialization was a boon to the continuation of agriculture in the Transkei, however, at least until after the South African War.[58] African farmers had more and larger markets for produce; the gold and diamond mines paid African men relatively high wages that they then reinvested in agriculture or rural families; and arable land, although becoming progressively scarcer because of population increases and the official limitation of land available for African occupancy, could still have its productivity enhanced through more widespread use of plows, fertilizer, and improved seed.[59] Moreover, Africans living in the Transkei and the Cape generally remained in a better position to retain agricultural land than did Africans living elsewhere in South Africa post-1913: the 1913 Natives Land Act severely restricted the ability of Africans to own land in South Africa's other three provinces, but the act could not be implemented in the Cape Province for constitutional reasons.[60] Having access to land gave Africans, at least in the short term, greater economic security in the rural areas.

Many Transkeian Africans, like Africans elsewhere on the colonized continent, succeeded in incorporating the cash economy and migrant labor into the rural world they esteemed and over which they felt they had some control.[61] As the resident magistrate for Engcobo District noted in 1887, "The natives now thoroughly understand that the hut tax in each year falls due when they have harvested their maize and kaffir corn [sorghum] crops which is usually in the month of June."[62] The same magistrate noted four years later that he would tell all tax defaulters that "unless their hut tax is paid by next plowing season they will not be permitted to cultivate their gardens."[63] The latter remark was an expression of the official policy of no tax, no land. Paying their taxes allowed Africans to continue farming and to control the more threatening powers available to state officials.

By 1915 the high levels of quasi-voluntary tax compliance were beginning to be punctuated by occasional sharp drops. Simultaneously, intermittent rural opposition movements developed that mobilized people on both spiritual and

FIGURE 1.2. "Mr. Moodie, Magistrate of Ladysmith, Natal, collects hut tax, 1879." Wood engraving, Illustrated London News. The Campbell Collection of the University of Kwazulu-Natal.

material planes. Although these movements rarely lasted more than a couple of years, they show the changing nature of rural Africans' relationship to various state officials and rituals. In 1908 the state imposed increasingly coercive veterinary quarantines and restrictions related to the cattle disease East Coast fever (see chapter 3). These restrictions included the frequent dipping of cattle in chemical baths (to rid them of the ticks that spread East Coast fever), a procedure that over the years became one of the most hated policies the state ever imposed. Further, regional quarantines stopped the marketing of Transkeian cattle in the wider Cape Provincial and Union markets, thus depriving Transkeian stock owners of higher prices and the benefits of bringing in new cattle for breeding. These restrictions sparked intermittent resistance, including the destruction of dipping tanks, in some districts of the Transkei from 1914 through 1916, and a decline in tax payments across a broader range of districts; tax defaults were then made worse by the poverty induced by the Spanish Influenza epidemic of 1918, the decline in world market prices in goods after World War I, and localized droughts from 1919 through 1922.

In contrast to the ways in which taxation and resistance played out in the Transkei in this period, in Natal and Zululand the imposition of a poll tax in 1905–6 sparked an outright rebellion, led by the minor chief Bambatha (see chapter 4). In its initial motivation, the Bambatha Rebellion had much in common with the Mpondomise Rebellion in 1880. Spurred by the imposition of the new poll tax in Natal and Zululand, rebels invoked both the military history of the Zulu state and the will of the ancestors as inspiration for their cause. The repression of the Bambatha Rebellion by Natal authorities was grim and bloody, as the Natal colonial military engaged in wave after wave of repression and retribution against any people thought to be rebels and set fire to entire districts. But, just as in the Transkei in the wake of the Mpondomise Rebellion, the rebellious districts following the Bambatha Rebellion began paying their taxes. The Bambatha Rebellion contrasts with the relative political quiescence of Africans in the Transkei in the early part of the twentieth century, but Africans in the Transkei watched the Bambatha Rebellion with interest and saw the violence perpetrated by the colonial state there as a lesson about the likely outcome of violent resistance to taxation. Interestingly, many of the rumors that swirled around the outset of the rebellion, about the necessity for Africans to "prepare for war by killing their pigs, and destroying utensils of European manufacture," presaged similar rumors that emerged in the 1920s in several Transkeian districts.[64]

In the Transkei in the 1920s tax increases combined with falling agricultural prices to stimulate political unrest that focused on the rumor that Americans would intervene on the side of Africans by bombing the white-controlled state out of existence (see chapter 5). An African named Butler Wellington or Wellington Buthelezi proposed to end taxes as a way of severing the link between Africans and the state.[65] Breaking the hold the state had on Africans was a preparation for a coming bloodbath: "forces are coming, armies coming from America to drive away the white people from Africa."[66] Wellington's converts believed that the expected Americans were all black followers of Marcus Garvey, the Jamaican-born black nationalist who built the Universal Negro Improvement Association in Harlem, and that they would fly airplanes overhead and drop burning coals. These coals would cause all pigs to burst into flames and set their owners and the owners' property alight.[67] Not surprisingly, Wellington's followers frequently killed, sold, or drove away their pigs and in addition paid the fee of one to two shillings per person to belong to his organization, actions that would protect members from the burning coals. Those who registered also received membership cards that people assumed had the same protective powers as the old hut tax receipts, providing protection against imprisonment by the magistrate for defaulting on their taxes and also against the malevolent witchcraft of the state.[68] An African court interpreter explained the widespread belief that the "Imperial [British] government promised to give the American Negroes this country for services rendered in the Great War. The natives who to some extent resent the increased taxation, firmly believe this man's [Wellington's] saying and look to a happy time of release from European rule which the American Government will bring. . . . The natives firmly believe in all Dr. Wellington says. . . . They believe he has the great magic powers and that the white men fear him."[69] When the prophesied American invasion did not occur, and when the state asserted its ability to control Wellington by trying and convicting him of fraud, his movement gradually fell apart. His followers, still unhappy with the state but respectful of its power, began to pay their taxes again.[70]

Wellington's movement operated in tandem with other political organizations in both rural and urban South Africa. These movements were evidence of a broader current of unrest generated by industrialization, population shifts, cultural changes, and deepening rural poverty. While Wellington seemed to be weaving fantasies about magical international intervention on behalf of Africans, he spoke to the heart of the state's relationship with the African population. Both taxes and supernatural powers were components of the state's control over its African subjects, particularly in the rural areas, and to undermine that control a political movement had to attack both the system of taxation and the supernatural powers reputedly wielded by colonial administrators.

Rural Africans in the 1920s found themselves increasingly disadvantaged by various state policies. The rural land shortage was made worse by the state's influx control policies that hindered the movement of Africans from the rural areas to cities and towns. Those Africans who did migrate legally went to town as wage-earners and employees. After the implementation of the 1923 Natives (Urban) Areas Act in the major cities of South Africa, Africans who migrated had the legal status of "temporary sojourners": that is, people who could not legally establish permanent residence in the urban areas which were designated "whites only" by the Act.[71] Without their families in the urban areas, Africans could not live as social adults under the older, rural definition of an adult as someone with a spouse, children and a thriving homestead.[72] If migrants brought their families with them to the urban areas, their illegal presence often promoted greater social insecurity, as well as multiplying the difficulties of survival in the harsh urban conditions.[73] As a result, adult African men, even those without access to farmland, often had to leave their families in the rural areas when they migrated to town to get a job. By the 1930s and

1940s many families were crowded on small homesteads with little land to farm, and often without adult men in residence (see chapter 6).[74] Within this context, the direct and indirect effects of tax policies on African women in the rural areas is very significant, as women had no personal legal liability for taxes but frequently faced the burden of paying their husbands' taxes if they wanted to retain what little land they had in the countryside.

Women were caught in a significant economic and social bind. Historically, women had done the bulk of the agricultural work that involved raising crops, but men were supposed to take care of the livestock, particularly the cattle. By the 1940s, however, there was relatively little agricultural land available to women on which to grow crops for their families, but they did have common grazing land available to them. Many families invested the earnings of family members who were migrant laborers in livestock, particularly cattle.[75] The ownership of cattle was a sign of adulthood and economic autonomy, as well as being the most acceptable currency for the payment of bridewealth (a marriage payment made by the groom's family to the wife's family). But as more and more people invested in livestock, the grazing land deteriorated, degrading the health of the livestock and devaluing their worth. This trend eventually eroded the income and wealth even of those families who did have access to farmland as well as grazing land. This economic crisis, many decades in the making, not only pitted Africans who had no arable land against those who did but also set the stage for a new round of state interference in the lives of individual Africans and their families.[76] Women, trying to hold rural families together at a time of expanding poverty, often found themselves the targets of witchcraft accusations from in-laws who blamed them for whatever disasters befell their families. Widowed and unmarried women faced even more overt suspicion for causing social and family-related disasters, and sometimes they were harassed and threatened with death from Africans desperate to enact a moral social and economic order.

The developing discontent of the 1948–63 period eventually resulted in a complete breakdown of the tax system (chapter 7). This breakdown was again a product of both economic hardship and spiritual concerns; many people evaded taxes as a way of severing the material and ritual connections between themselves and the state. This time, however, the unrest erupted into armed attacks on state officials. People revolted in the 1950s because the South African state raised taxes, began to delegate more power to appointed chiefs who were widely viewed as sell-outs, and interfered in people's daily lives, lives that had already been disrupted by state policies: the supernatural powers of the state had taken a more destructive turn.

As part of the proposed geographical and political partition known as grand apartheid, the state implemented the Bantu Authorities Act of 1951. Under that act, chiefs, despite their widespread reputation for corruption, took over many administrative functions, including presiding over most court cases. In addition, later in the decade taxes went up to pay the costs of new administrators, and magistrates (newly dubbed Bantu Commissioners) began aggressively implementing various agricultural "betterment" programs. These programs involved forced villagization, crop rotation and contour plowing, and compulsory cattle culling, none of which was popular among rural families. Typically, from a rural family's point of view, the costs—including labor—of these policies were high while the benefits were either nonexistent—especially in the short term—or very low.[77] Resistance to betterment schemes began in the 1940s, escalated in the 1950s, and reached its peak in 1960–62. Magistrates retaliated against small-scale acts of resistance, such as fence cutting or refusals to relocate homesteads, with sanctions against entire regions, punishing those who had complied with the laws along with those who refused.[78] Simultaneously, over a five-year period in the mid-1950s, a wave of livestock theft hit the Transkei. Police managed to capture only a few of the culprits, and that low arrest rate led many victims to believe that state officials, particularly those chiefs who tried court cases, were colluding with the thieves by restraining the police and by providing the thieves with magical medicines that enabled them to vanish.[79]

From the standpoint of African farmers, the state had become capricious and unpredictable in its exercise of power. Taxes went up, stock thieves stole at will, state officials coerced farmers in a seemingly arbitrary way to comply with costly and poorly conceived agricultural policies, and the state seemed more concerned with collecting taxes and protecting alleged stock thieves from vigilante groups than it was with stopping the thefts themselves.[80] People widely suspected chiefs and magistrates of shielding witches and stock thieves and of using witchcraft to consolidate their power and enrich themselves.

South African state officials responded quickly to the revolt. They arrested tax defaulters en masse in an attempt to reinstate this important ritual of rule. In 1961 magistrates repeatedly stressed in their reports to the chief magistrate the utility of arresting tax defaulters for defusing resistance and dispersing rebel organizations.[81] This seeming obsession with punishing tax defaulters was not just about the usually small amounts of money owed; it was also about reaffirming the dominance of the state and about making Africans once again acknowledge that dominance. In addition, the state brought in white police and "mobile police units" (paramilitary in nature) to combat the rebels.[82] These methods clearly demonstrated to many Africans the state's malevolence, and they may also have reinforced ideas about the state's ability to manipulate supernatural powers in its pursuit of continued authority.

Although the South African state reestablished control over the Transkei by the end of 1963, the whole system of taxation was in disarray, and Africans' relationship to state officials and various rituals of rule was permanently changed. The state had come to rely on overt domination and violence to maintain its rule. In the pursuit of grand apartheid, state officials continued to devolve authority to local chiefs and to the new puppet government of the Transkei "homeland," but that government proved routinely incapable of either creating a sense of its own legitimacy or, more weakly, persuading Africans to acknowledge its authority.

WHITE NARRATIVES OF TAXATION

Whites had their own beliefs about African taxes, and those beliefs also tended to change over time. Throughout the period under study, white officials frequently discussed taxes as simple tools for generating revenue. Taxes clearly did bring money in, but beyond that, taxes performed other functions for the state.

Magistrates used taxes in two nonmonetary ways. First, they used the yearly tax collection to develop personal contacts with the African population and to ritualize the subjection of Africans to the white-controlled state as personified by the magistrate. This use was perhaps best seen in more remote rural areas, where there were typically few whites or state officials. One long-time magistrate, George Mears, who went on to become briefly the Secretary of Native Affairs in the late 1940s, discussed his views of the relationship between the magistrate and the rural African population: "Humanism has characterised policy [in the Transkei] from its early inception. The 'vox humana' has been the dominant tone of the administration even under difficult circumstances." He elaborated: "Natives, like children, are most quick to sense the attitude of others toward them, and in a very short time a Native administrator is summed up. . . . The simple qualities of kindness, sympathetic handling, fairness are highly appreciated and strike a responsive chord; weakness is despised and firmness admired; punishment of offenders after a fair trial or enquiry is not resented, and, what is more even, expected." In establishing this relationship, this magistrate stressed the "value of personal contact" most commonly developed in the daily interactions, including tax collections, of the magistrates with the Africans of the district.[83]

Many magistrates shared his ideas. In fact, the relationship he describes is reminiscent of descriptions of the precolonial relationships that chiefs attempted to foster with their subjects. There is little evidence that people assumed that the district magistrate was identical with a precolonial chief, but it seems more likely that magistrates attempted to appropriate the precolonial ideology as a way of enhancing the legitimacy of their rule. The magistrate of Tsolo District testified to the Cape Native Laws and Customs Commission in 1881 that, especially in the light of the recent rebellion, magistrates should be cautious about instigating legal and cultural changes:

> I think we are in a country for the purpose of elevating the natives, civilizing them if possible, and gradually getting them to abandon their habits and adopt those of Europeans, and if you administer pure native law you are simply putting yourself in the position of a chief and only perpetuating the state of things you found among them. I think that caution is necessary, because it is a dangerous thing to bring in any laws, to which the natives are not accustomed and never heard of, at a day's notice. I think that any alteration made in their laws and customs should be done by degrees and modified gradually, that they may grow up as it were with it.[84]

People adapted their political attitudes to fit the new colonial situation, and the magistrates facilitated the adaptation and participated in it.

With the imposition of the East Coast fever restrictions in the 1910s and into the 1920s, fewer magistrates expressed ideas of this type, reflecting a generational change from the early magistrates, who had adhered to the paternalist ideology of the "civilizing mission," to later magistrates, who preferred a system of "scientific management" of Africans and African agriculture.[85] As their other administrative duties increased, magistrates themselves participated less frequently in tax collection, delegating that duty to their clerks. By the 1940s, as state policies advocating betterment schemes came into play, liberal paternalism had been almost completely replaced at the magisterial level and above with a condescending style of management that assumed both African inferiority and African patience with state policy. As the magistrate of Tsolo District commented in 1948,

> Meetings [with Africans] in the district are never held unless for a specific purpose, such as the installation of a new headman, and on these occasions one can not, on account of the volume of work awaiting one's

return to the office, spare any time for discussion of matters of general interest to the people, hear their difficulties or inform them of what is being done for them. It is therefore very difficult to express my opinion as to the attitude of the people; I should say they are patient as usual and "resigned to the ways of Government." They do not know what is going on and there is no time to tell them.[86]

Within a few years, with the outbreak of revolt in the 1950s, magistrates would better understand how impatient people had actually become during the time when they were too distracted by "routine work."

The magistrates' withdrawal from the process of tax collection may have diminished its importance as a ritual of rule. Yet there is evidence that people continued to esteem the tax receipt, not simply as a legal document proving its holder had paid taxes but also as an object that could protect them from the combined supernatural and legal powers of the state. For its part, this new generation of magistrates was less tolerant of beliefs in the supernatural, which they saw as evidence of a troublesome and stubborn African "backwardness." They derided some of the old rituals (and the old magistrates) as pandering to the African population, and they were determined to "modernize" Africans, by force if necessary.

Modernity, for the rising generation of administrators, was a streamlined administrative structure presiding over law-abiding, self-sufficient peasants who used the land to its fullest productive capacity while eschewing older, cultural practices that had previously governed the raising of livestock and land use.[87] Taxation's revenue-generating function rose to prominence for these magistrates, who, following the Native Taxation and Development Act of 1925, saw African taxes principally as the means for paying for the creation of an economically productive African population, one that would never be fully "civilized," that would never be citizens of "white" South Africa, and that would always be subordinate to a white-controlled state.[88] In some sense, this was the realization of South African industrialist and politician Cecil Rhodes's idea of the creation of a separate and subordinate form of governance for Africans who could not qualify for the franchise under the Cape Colonial (and later Cape Provincial) rules.[89] An addendum to the report of the 1930–32 Native Economic Commission suggested as much: "The investigation of the Commission has driven it to the conclusion that . . . the general economic welfare of the whole of the Union calls imperatively for wise and sympathetic assistance to enable the Natives to develop their Reserves, so as to make these sufficiently productive and attractive to stop the present compulsory migration to the towns. There would be little of that flow to the towns if the Natives could produce enough in the Reserves to meet their very modest needs."[90]

The commission's recommendations flew in the face of criticism by some of the older, experienced magistrates who felt that trying to make the reserves become agriculturally productive enough to support the entire African population that lived there was a hopeless task. The chief magistrate of the Transkei responded to the commission's report: "There is already a considerable landless population and it is difficult to reconcile the Commission's recommendation that individual Natives should be allowed to acquire additional arable land with its remarks in regard to the shortage of land which already exists. Any relaxation of the present system [of land allocation] would spell the increase of the landless population."[91] Many Africans testifying to the commission rightly suspected that the attempt to force "modern" agriculture on Africans in the rural areas was actually a scheme to pack additional Africans into the reserves and then blame their poverty on their own "backwardness." Dr. A. B. Xuma, then a prominent physician and political activist in Johannesburg but who was originally from the rural Engcobo District, commented, "It seems absurd to say all Natives must go back to the land and engage in agriculture, not only because there would not be enough land in which to place all of them, but because where all members of the community are producing the same thing and especially without market facilities as export, the produce is of little value or no *economic value* at all. . . . Besides, this idea of all Natives in agriculture is a mere platitude because it presumes and incorrectly that *all Natives* are fit for nothing else but agriculture."[92] The fact that the South African state insisted on pursuing goals of forced land management and livestock culling over at least the next thirty years, particularly after the end of World War II, became one of the central contradictions of its "Native policy." The enforcement of tax payments became especially complicated because, on the one hand, the official formula of "no tax, no land" was still in place; thus tax defaulters were technically liable to have their right to occupy land rescinded. On the other hand, to enforce the tax laws so aggressively would have meant an increase in the landless population, thus aggravating the problem of permanent African migration into the cities. Ultimately, by the early 1950s, the need to control the rural-to-urban migration of Africans trumped virtually all other policy considerations.[93] In this atmosphere tax payments became less significant as a revenue source and more vital as an indicator of the general disposition of the population toward the state.

This was the second nonmonetary way in which officials used the payment of taxes, especially in the 1880s in the Transkei, after 1906 in Natal and

Zululand, and from 1950 on: as a rough gauge of the level of unrest among the African population. Thus one official in 1961 noted, "The first indication that the attitude in any location was wrong [i.e., antistate] was a noticeable drop in the amount of taxes paid."[94] Similarly, when writing reports to their superiors, magistrates usually accompanied any rumor of unrest with a discussion of how well or poorly Africans were paying their taxes. Finally, when open revolt broke out in much of the Transkei from 1958 to 1963, magistrates and the police found that the easiest way of arresting the revolt was by arresting the tax defaulters.[95]

While magistrates in the 1940s and 1950s were aware that many rural Africans incorporated witchcraft beliefs into their daily lives, few whites ever saw a connection between those beliefs and their own rule. As unrest deepened into rebellion in the late 1950s, many magistrates expressed surprise at how Africans fused the idea of government with that of supernatural powers.[96] To the extent that white state officials became aware that they had been incorporated by Africans into a worldview that encompassed notions of witchcraft, it led them to conclude that Africans had not yet escaped their "backwardness"; in short, the official analysis of the rebellion legitimated the state's right to rule over "superstitious" and "irrational" Africans.[97] That conclusion, combined with the violent tactics adopted by some of the rebels, caused the state to suppress rebellion by particularly brutal means.

Once the rebellion had been crushed, by 1963, state officials deepened their resolve to pursue the grand apartheid scheme of dividing African rural areas into quasi-independent homeland states—often called Bantustans—and devolving authority on hand-picked African functionaries. The Bantustan policy was a final attempt to contain African political aspirations in the rural areas and to categorize Africans and their culture as so fundamentally different from whites as to be incapable of coexisting in a single country. Apartheid was also a monumentally self-serving political and economic strategy for whites, who had no intention of ending their reliance on Africans as wage laborers even as they alienated Africans from most legal rights. But political and economic expedients were not the sole supports of the ideology: many whites fervently believed that their differences with Africans were essential and inescapable; that belief was partly based on a vulgar and unscientific notion of the genetic basis of racial differences,[98] and partly on their dim understanding of African worldviews.

The differences in African and white narratives about taxation are indicative of the differences in these worldviews. For Africans, the material and spiritual realms were not distinct; thus the payment of taxes embodied a number of beliefs about the magical powers of the state. For whites, tax collection was a monetary transaction that was secondarily useful as a barometer of African political discontent but that also forged an intimate connection between rulers and ruled.[99] Africans saw tax payments as a quasi-magical ritual; whites, as a secular one.

It seems likely that for all states, even those outside a colonial context, taxes have an important ritual role.[100] They engage taxpayers in active participation with those who rule them: the more voluntary the compliance in paying taxes, the more engaged or "captured" the taxpayers are by the system of rule.[101] Conversely, when the state can enforce broad tax compliance only through the exercise of brute force and mobile police units, it must seriously question the basis of its own authority. Taxes are not the sole constituents of the relationship between ruler and ruled, but they are vital symbols of that relationship and they are frequently the only widespread and recurring contact that people have with the state.

In South Africa the ritual content of taxes extended into the territory of supernatural beliefs, and this helps to explain the patterns of political resistance and quiescence exhibited among rural Africans between 1880 and 1963. Taxes imbued the state with supernatural powers through the medium of the census and, at least in the early period, through the use of money itself; the tax receipt could be used to ward off the malevolent legal and supernatural powers of the state. With this kind of power lurking behind the state, it is less surprising that rural Africans so often complied with state demands for taxes. It also becomes more understandable why, during those times when tax defaults were common, both leaders and followers resorted to supernatural means to protect themselves from the state's magic. Thus taxation was not just a method for generating revenue, it was an important legal ritual that bound whites and Africans together in the context of a white-controlled state operating in an overwhelmingly African society. The ritual of tax collection informed the colonized consciousness of both African subjects and the state officials who attempted to control them.

CHAPTER 2

WAR AND REVENUE

*Taxation, Witchcraft, and Political Rituals in the
Consolidation of Colonial Rule in the Transkei, 1880–96*

> When I go to sleep I am a chief, when I rise in the morning,
> I am still a chief and a greater [one]. . . . You people say you
> have a Magistrate, I do not say so. What Pondomisi pointed
> out the spot for a Magistrate to build? Not one.
>
> —Mpondomise chief Mditshwa, August 1879

WAR

The resident magistrate of Qumbu District, Hamilton Hope, did not know he
had only a few days to live when he arranged a meeting with the Mpondomise
chief Mhlonthlo in late October 1880.[1] He was more than likely aware of the
danger of meeting the chief in a remote part of the district: there were numerous rumors that the Mpondomise were on the verge of revolt, and Africans
in the neighboring colony of Basutoland (now the independent country of
Lesotho) were already fighting British forces; Hope was the local representative
of an unpopular colonial state, but he lacked significant military or police
power with which to defend himself. In fact, he was meeting with Mhlonthlo
to persuade him to help Cape colonial forces put down the rebellion in
Basutoland.[2] In addition, Hope was in some ways responsible for the outbreak
of rebellion in Basutoland, where he had previously been a magistrate: he was
known for beating Africans—even chiefs—who disobeyed him. Since his arrival
as magistrate in Qumbu District in 1878, he had continued his imperious style of
rule, insulting Mhlonthlo's claims to authority and pressing people hard to pay
their taxes despite failures of recent harvests.[3]

Hope was apprehensive when he reached the meeting, but Mhlonthlo set him at ease with the words, "We are Government people in the true sense of the word. Govt is our rock and our shade."[4] Mhlonthlo promised that the Mpondomise would be more than willing to assist Cape forces, but that they required arms and ammunition. Hope, camping alongside Mhlonthlo and his army in a remote area, arranged for guns to be delivered to the Mpondomise. The next day, once the guns had been delivered, Mhlonthlo met again with Hope. During the course of this final meeting, the Mpondomise chief dramatically stepped away from Hope and two of the clerks; he grabbed a third white clerk and dragged him aside. Mhlonthlo then pointed to Hope and the two clerks still standing with him and shouted, "You Pondomise! There are your chiefs!" At this signal, as the surviving clerk, A. Davis, later reported,

> I saw nearly half of the crowd fall on Messrs Hope, Warren, and Henman. . . . Hope &c were killed, about two men rushed at me with their assegais and would have stabbed me but Mhlonhlo ordered them back saying no "no man was to touch me" that he had saved my life through my father being one of their old missionaries and my brother Rev Davis being their present missionary that he Mhlonhlo was fighting only against the Govt; and that all missionaries and their sons were to be saved as well as all shopkeepers.[5]

With the assassination of Hope and his two clerks, Mhlonthlo and his army started a rebellion against the white-controlled state.

Mhlonthlo's words revealed his motivation to rebel. While the chief tolerated the religious presence of missionaries and wished to retain his access to trade via the shopkeepers,[6] he wanted to get rid of government (the colonial state), reassert his own authority, and restore harmony to his community.

By killing the magistrate and his clerks, Mhlonthlo destroyed the local practitioners of government, but their corpses and disembodied spirits still posed a danger.[7] To keep government influence both physically and spiritually out of the land, Mhlonthlo refused permission to bury the bodies of the dead men: "The Rev S. Davis [brother of the white clerk saved by Mhlonthlo] has since been up to Mhlonhlo and asked him permission to be allowed to bury the bodies but the Pondomise one and all utterly refused saying it was not their custom and the birds of the air must eat their corpses."[8] Xhosa-speaking Africans usually buried their dead, except for the bodies of certain chiefs, which were thrown into a river or pool to ensure that rain would continue to fall.[9] The only situation in which, historically, Xhosa speakers left corpses unburied was during war, when the slain enemy were left in the open;[10] and this was the reason that Mhlonthlo himself gave to missionary Davis: "It is war, and the bodies of those who have died in war are not hidden under the earth."[11] Moreover, Mhlonthlo had his war doctor (a ritual specialist who created certain potions and medicines to assist a chief in the war) cut various pieces from Hope's body and use them in the preparation of war medicines.[12] Mhlonthlo was taking no chances when it came to engaging the colonial state in war—he needed all the supernatural assistance he could get.

The second major goal of the rebellion also had symbolic as well as strategic content: the destruction of the town of Umtata. The symbolism of this target was plain: Umtata was the local seat of the white-controlled state, and the abolition of white rule required the demolition of the white town. Magistrate Hope was killed on 24 October, an event that African rebels had calculated to coincide with a surprise attack on the town of Umtata. However, the attack force was not yet in place by the time the chief magistrate in Umtata, Maj. Henry Elliot, heard of Hope's death. Elliot reacted quickly to reinforce the town and later reported, "rumours [were] constantly reaching us that the Pondomisi had destroyed Government in their country and were coming to stamp it out in Umtata."[13]

With the surprise attack on Umtata thwarted, the rebellion began to stall. Independent Mpondo forces looted the outlying houses belonging to some of Umtata's white residents who had fled, but they balked at an outright attack on the central settlement. Without the military aid of the Mpondo, the Mpondomise decided to try to starve out the remaining settlers and officials instead of attempting a frontal assault. In Engcobo District, the Qwati, led by Dalasile, forced magistrate Walter Stanford to flee, then looted and burned his house and office. In Umtata District, most Thembu refrained from active participation in the rebellion, but white residents and shopkeepers fled their houses and abandoned their stores.[14]

Some of the chiefs' actions in supporting the revolt were less obviously symbolic and more clearly pragmatic in nature. In Tsolo District, the chief Mditshwa had in the months before the revolt quarreled with the district's magistrate over who had the right to try court cases and collect fines.[15] However, Mditshwa himself later alleged (while he was on trial for sedition, a fact that may obviously have tempered his testimony) that he had been reluctant to rebel and was forced to do so by his hot-headed sons.[16] These sons might have been thinking of their future claims to the title of chief and what would be left of the chief's authority. In fact, Mditshwa's actions during the rebellion did suggest less than wholehearted support for some of its aims: he spared the lives of several white officials, including his own resident magistrate—the man with whom he had quarreled—Alex Welsh.[17]

Yet, although Mditshwa's aspirations may have been worldly, he also invoked supernatural influences to achieve them. He was not blind to the superiority Cape forces had in the quality and quantity of arms at their disposal. He and other rebel leaders tried to counter this superiority through "doctoring" his weapons and men to make them impervious to bullets.[18] Through this doctoring the chiefs tried to mobilize their own supernatural resources to counter the malevolent powers of Cape officials.

But supernatural powers and symbolism were not enough to defeat the Cape forces. Within three or four days, Cape reinforcements arrived for the small settlement at Umtata, and they were able to break the African siege. Even with the immediate threat to the town removed, however, the fighting dragged on for several months, with many rebels holding out in remote areas.[19] The revolt eventually faltered, as the colonial military used its most reliable weapon against African rebels: a scorched-earth campaign, in which troops burned crops and houses of suspected rebels and slaughtered or drove off their livestock. From the bush, rebel chiefs faced the humiliating prospect of suing for unconditional surrender; most were eventually caught, tried for sedition, and at least temporarily deposed from their positions as chiefs.[20] By mid-1881 the only major rebel figures who remained free were Mhlonthlo and his sons and the rebel chief from Engcobo District, Dalasile: Mhlonthlo's sons had reportedly fled to independent Pondoland and Mhlonthlo to Basutoland, while Dalasile remained in hiding in the Transkei.[21]

Following the defeat of the revolt, white magistrates deposed rebellious chiefs and replaced them with loyalists. They also dispossessed rebels of their land and livestock, while deferring the collection of taxes in rebel areas until 1884–85 and allowing back taxes to accrue. There was a great deal of bitterness in the wake of both the rebellion and the reprisals taken by Cape forces, and administrators watched nervously for fresh signs of rebellion even as they rebuilt the homes and offices they had lost. Despite the bitterness and the fears, however, by 1890–92 Africans were not only paying their taxes again, the compliance rates typically hovered between 80 and 100 percent; rebels had been reassigned land, although their confiscated livestock was never returned; and some deposed chiefs or their heirs had been reinstated to their previous positions. By the mid-1890s, most Africans were politically quiet at least in their public roles as taxpayers and subjects. In this postrebellion period, the payment of taxes emerged as a significant ritual of state power. It is this symbolic and ritual content—at the level of meaning and understanding—that provides an explanation for the widespread political calm that overtook a region so soon after the defeat of a popular rebellion.[22]

The rebellion therefore offers an excellent vantage point from which to view how political symbols and beliefs in the supernatural affected the establishment and extension of colonial control. First, the colonial state had to combat armed resistance to colonial rule in general and to tax collection in particular. And then, once the rebellion was effectively quelled, state officials had to reconstruct an administration based in part on their own analyses of what had caused the rebellion. State officials were quite successful in exercising control in the aftermath of the war, but they never fully acknowledged their own engagement in the politics of the supernatural. Africans learned not only the futility of armed insurrection but also had their beliefs about the state's use of supernatural powers confirmed. This lesson informed the later actions undertaken by Africans as they struggled to come to some arrangement in which they, their families, and their aspirations could survive.

In these first two decades of colonial rule, taxes and taxpaying developed a rich political and symbolic content that both supported colonial administration and constituted its authority. Jean and John Comaroff have illuminated the issue of political symbols and their uses in both governance and resistance. Noting that the "colonizing process itself is rarely a simple dialectic between domination and resistance," they suggest that political symbols have been important for colonized peoples both as icons in struggles against the state and as clues with which to interpret the imperial presence and to gain "control over its 'magic.'"[23] Symbols were part of the process of gaining control and governing, part of the process of resisting, and part of the process of surviving under colonial rule. Taxes and the ritual associated with taxpaying were inscribed into both the public transcript of submission to colonial authority and the hidden transcript of attempting to divert—and occasionally subvert—colonial surveillance and power. As the Comaroffs argue, "the ripostes of the colonized hover in the space between the tacit and the articulate, the direct and the indirect. And far from being a mere reflection—or reflex expression—of historical consciousness, these acts are a practical means of *producing* it."[24] In short, during and after the 1880 revolt the historical narratives composed by participants constructed historical reality even as they described it.

REVENUE

The 1880 Mpondomise Rebellion, or Hope's War, attacked colonial control at its outset and attempted to reestablish African sovereignty. Yet the war was not only a military assault on colonial forces, it was also a political and cultural attack, as the rebels mobilized the precolonial symbols of African chiefs' authority to counteract the symbols and rituals, as well as the material effects, of colonial control. One of the pillars of colonial control was the collection of taxes.

The Cape Colony took effective control over much of the Transkei in the late 1870s, and consolidated that control in 1894. Until 1894, the northeast region of Pondoland was still an independent state under the Mpondo chiefs; the southeast region inhabited by the Gcaleka, Bomvana, and some Mfengu had been conquered by the Cape in the final Frontier War (of 1877–78); in 1878 the central and western regions, belonging to the Thembu, Emigrant Thembu, Qwati, Mpondomise, Hlubi, Bhaca, and Mfengu groups had "asked"—after considerable arm-twisting and bullying by delegates of the Cape—to be brought under Cape protection; the Griqua—in the districts of Matatiele, Mount Currie, and Umzimkulu—had been brought under Cape control in 1874, four years earlier than the rest of the region.[25]

The result of this governmental patchwork was that the various African chiefs initially—before the rebellion—had different relationships with the Cape regime. The independent Mpondo chiefs often acted as equals of the colonial state, an attitude that Cape officials found threatening and impudent even though it reflected political reality. The conquered Gcaleka chiefs, particularly Sarhili, fumed at their military defeat and political demotion even as they outwardly acknowledged the overlordship of the Cape. The Thembu, Mpondomise, and other chiefs who had "asked" to be brought into the Cape had written treaties with the colonial state that gave them certain rights and privileges as well as preserving some of their independence of action.[26] These different affiliations with the Cape directly affected how chiefs responded to various Cape demands, including taxation, but also including how much authority chiefs retained in the colonial hierarchy; chiefs who had signed treaties were supposed to retain greater authority than those who had been defeated militarily. Significantly, the chiefs who led the revolt in 1880 were among those who had submitted to the Cape under treaty, with a minor, supporting role played by the independent Mpondo.

Before the rebellion the colonial state's first two objectives with regard to its new African subjects were to control them and to tax them. To control the population, the Cape Native Affairs Department, which governed the Transkei, divided the region into districts and appointed a white magistrate for each. The magistrates were responsible for many administrative duties, including drawing up the hut tax registers. Magistrates also heard court cases, assigned land for use by African families, and commanded the small, local police forces (usually two or three men per district) charged with enforcing the laws. Magistrates expected chiefs and headmen to assist them in these tasks.

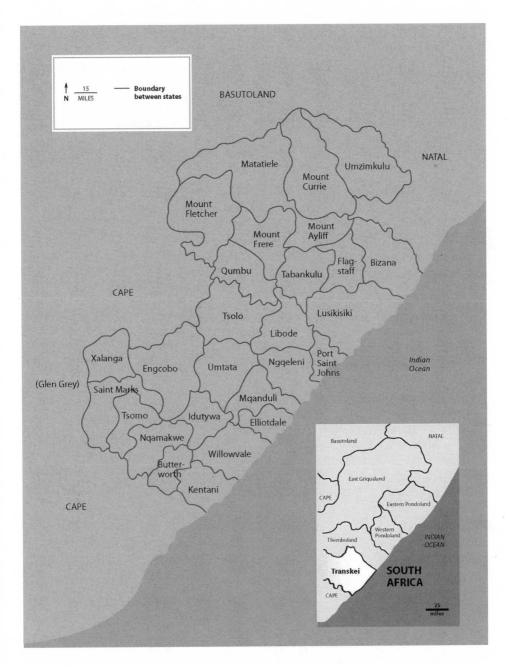

MAP 2.1. The Magisterial Districts of the Transkeian Territories post-1894.

The issue of taxation was central to the 1880 revolt and the peace that followed. With the coming of the white-controlled state to the Transkeian region, all married, adult African men had to pay yearly taxes on each dwelling hut. These hut taxes provided money for the Cape Colony, but they were not simply an instrument for raising revenue; they were also, from African and white perspectives, both a symbol and a constituent of state control.[27] The process of enrolling people on the hut tax registers, when combined with colonial officials' attempts to eradicate the naming and punishment of alleged witches or sorcerers, inspired in people a belief in the white-controlled state's spiritual malevolence that was partly responsible for sending them and their chiefs into revolt.

The hut tax was ten shillings per hut, payable in cash only.[28] Hut tax was a deceptively simple way of taxing the African population. In theory, the tax was levied on each inhabited hut;[29] in practice, however, the "hut" tax in the Transkei was really a tax on wives. The connection was that each wife usually had her own household hut, but there were significant economic connections as well. In this early period, each wife had her own plot of arable land, and women were primarily responsible for producing the staple crops of maize, sorghum, and cultivated vegetables. Men tended livestock—especially cattle—cleared arable land, and frequently did the plowing. Cape officials in imposing the hut tax made two assumptions about African society: that many men had more than one wife, and that the number of wives a man had was an indication of his wealth. Given those assumptions and the fact that women did much of the agricultural labor, officials saw the tax as a roughly proportional tax on income or wealth. In whites' view, the more wives a man had, the more income the wives could produce, and the more income a man had, the more he could afford to pay in taxes.[30] Following this logic, Cape officials initially thought that hut tax was both fair, in the sense that the wealthier paid more, and that it was a state-imposed fine on polygyny, a practice most white officials saw as immoral.[31] Cape officials expected that Africans would also find the tax equitable and just.[32]

RUMORS OF REVOLT

Some Africans, newly made colonial subjects, did pay their taxes more or less willingly. Others complained but paid, not seeing another option. But by mid-1880, there were persistent rumors of rebellion. These rumors emerged out of two other regional revolts and the increasing difficulties many Africans had in harvesting and marketing enough crops and livestock products (particularly wool) to pay their tax debt.

Two previous regional revolts inflamed dissent into plans for rebellion. The first was in Griqualand East in 1878 and resulted both from long-simmering land disputes and from the abrupt and aggressive manner in which Cape officials took over direct administration of the Griqua.[33] The second was in Basutoland in 1880, where a revolt had been sparked both by the high-handed methods of the magistrates (including Hamilton Hope) and by the paradoxically named Peace Preservation Act. This act proposed to disarm the Sotho population, and the Sotho responded with an armed revolt against colonial authority. The rebels in both cases lost their bids for independence, but they succeeded in fraying the nerves of colonial administrators, who feared new revolts as responses to colonial demands.

The rumors of rebellion were also related to the economic problems of African farmers. Their ability to pay taxes was conditional upon income from agriculture, and for many Transkeian districts 1879 and 1880 had been bad agricultural years. The success of the annual harvest depended on good rainfall and a lack of pests. Unfortunately this was a region that routinely experienced drought, that occasionally saw infestations of locusts, and whose livestock, particularly with increased trade and the movement of animals across regions, often succumbed to contagious diseases. Despite fluctuations in income, however, the tax was always ten shillings per wife per year. In a bad agricultural year, the outstanding tax debt continued to accrue.

The population of Tsolo District, which had been liable for hut tax since 1877, provided an example of the burden of back taxes. Many Africans had found it difficult to meet their tax obligations because of at least one bad agricultural year, low wool prices, and a lack of wage-paying jobs locally. By 1880 many Mpondomise in the district were heavily in arrears, with the average taxpayer owing a little over one pound in back taxes plus ten shillings for the current year.[34] Some Mfengu living in the district also owed back taxes, but others, possibly because of their rapid adoption of more productive technology, such as the ox-drawn plow, paid the taxes on time.[35] The poverty resulting from a poor harvest combined with fighting between whites and Africans in neighboring Basutoland to cause, in the words of the resident magistrate before the rebellion, "a strong *under current* of restlessness and doubt" among the Mpondomise.[36]

A more fundamental basis for the rumors of rebellion was the cross-cultural context. Magistrates misunderstood elements of African culture, causing them to take actions that many Africans found threatening. The misunderstandings arose from the fact that the magistrates, although many had grown up in the area and were fluent in the Xhosa language, dismissed the symbols and rituals of African political life—and especially the idea that supernatural powers and witchcraft underwrote political power—as "superstitious customs,"[37] important only for the trouble they caused individuals and families. Magistrates rarely acknowledged that the belief in witchcraft had larger social and political effects, nor did they discern any direct relationship between how they were governing and the belief in witchcraft. Yet many Africans did indeed see such a connection.

The census that preceded tax collection had deepened suspicions about the state. Resentment at the state's questions was not just evidence of a desire for privacy; it also reflected concern over what officials might do with such information. Would it be used to justify even heavier taxation, or as the basis for the outright expropriation of property, or for even more malevolent ends—witchcraft or sorcery on the part of either state officials or local enemies? Knowing how many wives or cattle a person had was essential to doing him harm, and knowing the names of family members made them easier to kill through witchcraft. The state's reasons for enumerating families and their possessions were highly suspect.[38] Tax collection and the census that went with it was not only symbolic of the state's authority but also enhanced the state's supernatural powers.

Beliefs in witchcraft and supernatural powers had not simply disappeared when whites intruded and made witchcraft accusations illegal. These beliefs have remained a part of everyday life for many Africans, both in South Africa and elsewhere, even when such beliefs can no longer be expressed openly.[39] In the precolonial period, witchcraft beliefs had been one part of the worldview that upheld the rule of the chiefs who, with the help of diviners, provided some protection against witches and sorcerers. The colonial state when it took over the region not only placed the chiefs below white magistrates in the administrative hierarchy, it also outlawed all accusations of witchcraft. Banning witchcraft accusations seemed logical to colonial officials, since they did not believe in witchcraft. But their lack of belief blinded them to a possible African interpretation of state actions: colonial officials, by outlawing accusations, were preventing people from protecting themselves against witches and sorcerers.[40] For those Africans who believed in witchcraft it was a short step to the suspicion that the state itself was in league with witches and sorcerers.

In 1879 in Tsolo District, the outcome of a court case regarding the disappearance of a woman may have led some to believe that the magistrate colluded with sorcerers. Magistrate Welsh reported:

On the 25th of August Mpahle—a headman . . . and formerly a noted
witch doctor in the tribe—reported to me that a woman of his location
had been missing since the reaping season. That lately the Bushmen . . .
had reported to him that they had discovered the dead body of a woman
and on proceeding to the spot the corpse was identified as that of the
missing woman. Mpahle therefore fined—ate up—Umgeleni son of
deceased woman's husband by another wife. I directed Mpahle to hand
over to me the whole of the fine. A portion only has as yet been handed
over.[41]

By fining the dead woman's stepson, the headman Mpahle had indicated
that the stepson was responsible for the woman's death, either through the
use of physical force or through witchcraft. By overriding the headman's ruling, the magistrate tried to usurp the authority of the headman. The magistrate also believed that he was neutralizing the supernatural claims to power
that the headman had as a noted "witchdoctor," or diviner. Some Africans,
however, may have understood his action differently, as an attempt to punish
the headman-diviner for ferreting out the wrongdoer, thus allowing the real
culprit—the stepson—to go free. This latter view of the magistrate as com-
plicit in the crime and its cover-up was supported by his unsatisfying resolu-
tion of the case: rather than accusing a murderer, he found that "deceased
committed suicide by throwing herself down a krantz [ravine]."[42]

There are some indications that the magistrate himself suspected that the
controversy caused by the woman's death and his handling of the case was one
current in a broader political stream. In the same letter in which he reported
the case, the magistrate went on to describe "an armed gathering Umditshwa
[the primary Mpondomise chief in Tsolo District] had at his Great Place
[headquarters]." Welsh continued: "It will greatly depend on the policy of
Government in certain matters whether this restlessness assumes a definite and
displayed form or not." Finally, he observed that the hut tax was being paid
very slowly. Yet, despite his perception that government policies might be
decisive in whether or not a revolt occurred, Welsh's new system of tax
enforcement seemed designed to provoke people even more: "I have now
adopted the plan of refusing to grant passes to persons who have not paid their
hut tax."[43] By not granting them passes, he prevented them from legally leaving his district, either to find wage labor elsewhere or to go on family or trade-
related errands.

A Tsolo-based missionary, Rev. Bransby Key, reached a similar conclusion
about Africans' views of the colonial state. He wrote in early 1880, before the

rebellion, "Now that the Government has become paramount in the Country the 'Umhlahlo' [divining ceremony] is forbidden and consulting the witch-doctor generally, so that the people in their ignorance believe that they have now no protection against the wicked practices of the 'Umtakati' [witches or sorcerers]." Africans had indeed stopped publicly accusing individuals of witchcraft and had mostly stopped consulting diviners (witchdoctors). Key continued:

> But in proportion as the practice of smelling out [divining witches] has apparently gone out I think the *belief* in witchcraft has increased; every illness with hardly any exception is attributed to some evilly dis-posed person, without going through the form even of consulting the witch doctor. Certain signs or symptoms such as sudden starting cry-ing screaming [sic] and delirium are assumed to be evidences of this magic influence on the patient, and some of these symptoms seem to be becoming a common form of hysteria among the girls of this neighbor-hood.[44]

Africans in the district were experiencing an epidemic of witchcraft,[45] and the colonial state was denying them the tools to deal with it. Moreover, the magistrate was actively preventing people who had not paid their taxes from leaving the district, thus preventing them from escaping. Both in a spiritual and in a physical sense, people's survival may have depended on the removal of a state that was prohibiting them from discovering and punishing all the witches.

Magistrates' actions threatened the African population as a whole in the context of widespread beliefs in witchcraft, while their supplanting of the chiefs' authority directly threatened the chiefs' status. By having to cooperate with the magistrates in collecting taxes, the chiefs found themselves playing the roles of subordinates and tributaries. Most objected to these roles.

Chiefs who had been brought under colonial control through treaties fre-quently asserted their rights to some autonomy. For example, the Qwati chief Dalasile in Engcobo District tried to delay the collection of hut taxes for as long as possible. His frustrated magistrate, Walter Stanford, noted in 1879 that "Dalasile's conduct can only be looked upon as contumnacious [sic], and will lead to considerable difficulty in getting a ready or full payment of the amounts." Stanford recommended "that a firm course be adopted in dealing with him," and that Dalasile be threatened "that should he or any of the men under him fail to obey this order [to pay their taxes], they will be punished."[46]

Stanford clearly desired a confrontation; whether Dalasile did or not is more obscure. Dalasile and most of his people paid their taxes within the next few months, but in so doing Dalasile stressed that he and others were paying because of his own decision, and not because he was coerced by Stanford.[47]

The chiefs Dalasile, Mhlonthlo, Mditshwa, and others became increasingly incensed as the white-controlled state encroached on their powers as chiefs. Ultimately, they decided to drive the white state out. The Tsolo District magistrate reported in August 1879 that Mditshwa had held several war meetings near his great place. An informant quoted Mditshwa mourning the loss of his power: "When I go to sleep I am a chief, when I rise in the morning, I am still a chief and a greater [one]. . . . You people say you have a Magistrate, I do not say so. What Pondomisi pointed out the spot for a Magistrate to build? Not one." Mditshwa then instructed his listeners to prepare for war, and to restore his authority: "My word is go home today, kill oxen, and make shields. . . . There is war in the land. I can see you won't plough this year. . . . You must bring all [court] cases to me not to the Magistrate."[48] The Engcobo District magistrate, Walter Stanford, noted that same month that he had "received information from reliable sources":

> Messengers from the Pondomisi chief Umditshwa arrived [from Tsolo District] last week at the kraal [rural homestead] of the chief Dalasile in this district [Engcobo] with the following message—
>
> "Umditshwa sends to inform Dalasile that messengers have arrived from Umqikela [a major chief in independent Pondoland] to him saying the white people are taking away all Native Chieftainship, and shall we submit without throwing an assegai? Let the word of the Chiefs be heard. Umditshwa wishes to know what Dalasile says."[49]

Magistrate Hope himself received warnings days before his fatal encounter with Mhlonthlo that Mhlonthlo was not being honest with him and was making preparations for war, warnings that Hope evidently discounted.[50]

As Mhlonthlo, Dalasile, and Mditshwa prepared to rebel, other chiefs wavered. The Thembu chief Ngangelizwe, living in Umtata District, was also displeased with white rule in 1880, but his plan was to wait: he kept messengers with those chiefs who organized the uprising, but once it became clear early on that they would not win, he threw himself behind the Cape state. The Gcaleka chiefs, who had so recently been defeated by the Cape, did not rebel, but neither did they actively support the Cape forces; while some headmen in otherwise rebellious districts split with their chiefs and took their own followings into support of the Cape. The chiefs who planned and led the revolt were among those who had quasi-voluntarily yielded to Cape rule.[51]

After the relatively quick defeat of the rebels, Africans and their chiefs found themselves in a different relationship with the Cape colonial officials. Beyond the loss of their autonomy, they had to face the idea either that their beliefs in supernatural powers were completely wrong, or that whites and their allies wielded both superior military and superior spiritual powers.

INTERPRETATIONS OF POWER

In victory, Cape officials began appropriating some of the symbols and methods of African chiefs to uphold their claims to rule. The colonial state confiscated the rebels' livestock and land, forcing many to leave the Transkei temporarily in search of wage labor.[52] The Cape Undersecretary for Native Affairs, James Rose Innes, recommended to the chief magistrate that those Africans who had rebelled should be relocated, "so that the impression may be removed that the act of rebellion has not caused any inconvenience [for them]."[53] Cape officials rewarded loyalist Africans, who were given paid positions as headmen and livestock confiscated from rebels. The colonial state, following African precedents, had "eaten up" the property of its enemies and distributed it to its friends.[54]

In appropriating these methods, Cape officials were executing policy based on their own analysis of the revolt, which characterized Africans as fundamentally primitive, childlike, and culturally conservative. For many whites, witchcraft beliefs were evidence both of primitiveness and childishness, while the fact that these beliefs persisted despite the availability of an alternative set of beliefs in the form of Christianity was indicative of cultural conservatism. In the official analysis, the rebellion was not an act of bravery but one of foolish gullibility on the part of commoners and treachery on the part of chiefs. The only blame that local white officials took upon themselves for causing the revolt was in trying to introduce too many innovations over too short a period.[55] The importance of this white analysis for state policy was clear: once the state succeeded in putting down the revolt and punishing those who had fought, it proceeded with caution, often cloaking its rule in an African idiom even as it tried to undermine the basis of African precolonial political institutions.

Writing one month after the outbreak of violence, Walter Stanford, magistrate of Engcobo District, analyzed the motivation behind the rebellion: "Childish as the idea [behind the revolt] may appear, it was this. 'If we kill all the Magistrates, no man of that class will venture among us again, but we shall want traders and missionaries.' . . . The war then is simply to regain independence, and it is as much a war of the people as it is a war of the chiefs."[56] Although Stanford characterized the motivation as childish, he recognized that a significant issue was at stake: did Africans have the right to select which state would rule them? It is unclear exactly what Stanford found childish. Was it the notion that Africans might presume that they had the right to choose their government? Was it perhaps that Africans might think they could rid themselves of the part of white culture they disliked (white officials) while retaining that which they found useful (traders and missionaries)? Was it the belief Africans might have had that they could defeat the colonial state in a war? Or did Stanford call it childish simply because he assumed all Africans were childish and could therefore act only in a childish, unreflective way? As Stanford over the years held increasingly influential posts in the Cape's Native Affairs Department, eventually becoming its head at the turn of the century, his use of the word *childish* is instructive of the attitudes and assumptions that would become the basis for the state's "Native" policies in the ensuing twenty years.

But Walter Stanford also recommended caution in dealing with the people he characterized as childish. Writing a year after the revolt, he noted, "Politically, the Tembus and other tribes are troubled by the ill success which has attuned [*sic*] the efforts made by those who took part in the outbreak but the native mind, as a whole, is far from a friendly feeling towards us. . . . Much delicacy of handling will be required to lessen the suspicion and general distrust felt by natives of our intentions regarding them."[57] In later comments Stanford suggested that where the chiefs led, the people would follow; thus to have a compliant population, the administration needed compliant chiefs. Stanford's personal dislike for the principal chief in Engcobo District, Dalasile, was apparent in the period preceding the revolt. Following the revolt, he made sure that Dalasile was deposed from his position as chief while he was in hiding; Stanford then simply governed through appointed headmen, most of whom had remained loyal during the rebellion. Eventually, Dalasile surrendered but he never regained his official standing; he died in 1895, and one of his sons was appointed headman in 1902.[58] In deposing the chief, the state reaffirmed its absolute control over his powers as well as its right to punish anyone who rebelled.

Yet the state also moderated some of its demands on the African population, particularly with regard to tax collection. Magistrates hesitated to do anything that might reignite the revolt, including collect taxes, even from those people who had remained loyal. The revolt had disrupted agriculture, as both sides had burned crops and killed or stolen livestock, depriving much of the population of the means to pay taxes; moreover, the state's expropriation of land and remaining livestock from surrendered rebels made it impossible for them to pay their taxes even had they wanted to do so.[59] Magistrate Welsh did not resume collections in Tsolo District until 1884, and in Umtata and Engcobo Districts magistrates did not collect hut tax until 1885.[60] In all districts, however, even though the magistrates did not collect them, the taxes were still technically due and they simply became arrears to be collected at a later date.

For white officials, the conclusion of the fighting in 1881 altered the conditions under which much of the Transkei came under the control of the Cape. The notion that any African chiefs had chosen or asked to come under the Cape's protection was no longer credible; instead, it seemed clear that only military force had kept them under Cape control.[61] Although Ngangelizwe and other chiefs who had remained loyal to the Cape continued to maintain that they had some kind of contract among equals, Cape officials, like Stanford, tended to see their own role as one of fathers supervising temperamental and destructive children. Of course, even if the rebellion had not occurred Cape officials might have arrived at this self-conception; but the conquest of Africans made it a certainty.

Africans constituted a much larger group than white officials and therefore had more varied responses to the defeat of the rebellion. The clearest splits within the African population were among loyalists, rebels, and those people we might call neutrals (who took no part in the fighting), and between chiefs and commoners. But these categories tell us little about how Africans might have explained the outcome of the revolt.

Some Africans saw the battle with the Cape not only in military terms but also in ideological or cultural ones. Thus, although the rebellion was quashed, disputes over the symbols of authority and the meaning of the military defeat continued. Some of the most revealing information about some African interpretations comes from Tsolo District in a dispute over the chieftainship.

The chief was not just the head of state in precolonial society, he was also the embodiment of a hereditary state authority. It was this authority that the colonial administrators hoped to assume. Following the revolt, in 1881, the Mpondomise chief Mditshwa surrendered and was tried for sedition. The all-white jury in King William's Town found him guilty, but recommended clemency in the light of Mditshwa's having spared most whites, including the magistrate, in his district. The court ultimately sentenced Mditshwa to three years' imprisonment.[62]

Mditshwa had his own interpretation of his punishment. In early 1885 he returned to Tsolo, received a lecture on good behavior from his new magistrate, Captain Hook, and also received the grant of a small farm at some distance from both his old Great Place and the homesteads of most of the district's Mpondomise population.[63] In physically relocating Mditshwa from his Great Place, state officials were making a deliberate point about his removal from the office of chief. (In fact, the previous magistrate had already parceled out Mditshwa's old land to loyalist Africans—another symbolic act). By March the magistrate was alarmed because Mditshwa had not occupied his new farm but was instead living with his wives near his old Great Place at the "Pondomise location." When the magistrate demanded that Mditshwa go to his farm, Mditshwa made a demand of his own: "I want the Magistrate to allow my sons and people to come back to the District because I have been to Cape Town [to serve his prison sentence] and served my time up thereby atoning for the guilt of my sons and people." As a chief he took the blame upon himself for the defeat. When reminded that he and his people had lost the war and therefore were in a weak position from which to make demands, Mditshwa reaffirmed his status: "I was born a chief and will die as such although the Government have deprived me of my authority. My nature is that of a chief and cannot be changed."[64] Mditshwa was asserting that a "chief is born and not made," and denying that the colonial authorities had the power to unmake him.[65]

This struggle over authority continued beyond Mditshwa's death a year later. By 1886 the Transkeian government was allowing Mditshwa's relatives and followers to return to farmland in the district, largely because there was nowhere else for them to go. The district magistrate deplored the policy of allowing rebels to return: "The Pondomise do not consider themselves either conquered, disgraced or punished by anything that has happened in connexion with the late Rebellion and this feeling is fostered and encouraged by their being allowed to return so easily and provided with land and every other consideration by Government, and is regarded by them only as a sign of weakness and indulgence on our part, without eliciting one single spark of gratitude or thanks on theirs." These returnees may have accepted Mditshwa's analysis that his imprisonment had atoned for the rebellion; or they may have hoped that by returning they could resurrect the authority of the chief, as the magistrate believed. In any case, they knew whom they wanted appointed regent during the minority of Mditshwa's heir, and they lobbied the magistrate heavily on their candidate's behalf. When the magistrate balked at appointing their choice, they, as the magistrate sourly reported, began to create "a good deal of mischief by dabbling with others of Umditshwa's family in witchcraft and consulting Witch doctors in Pondoland . . . evidently with the ultimate object of getting government to hasten the appointment of Ranuka as guardian to that family."[66] In short, they attempted to mobilize their own supernatural powers to choose their leaders and affect the magistrate's decisions. What's more, their strategy worked: the magistrate, on the instructions of the chief magistrate, appointed Ranuka as headman, and at Ranuka's death in 1904, Mditshwa's heir took over the position of chief.[67]

Clearly, the magistrate and his superiors had their own reasons for allowing the appointment of Ranuka as guardian and headman to go forward. The white-controlled administration, although strengthened by recent victory, was in a weak position over the long term. Continued military occupation was not feasible for two reasons. First, it would have been tremendously costly and there was no available source of revenue big enough to cover that cost. Second, white officials believed or wished to believe that once Africans saw the white-defined benefits of white rule and civilization, Africans would no longer want their chiefs and would no longer want to rebel. Whites felt that the benefits of their rule were obvious, but they needed Africans to believe in those benefits as well. In other words, they wanted Africans to agree to white rule, and if that agreement could in part be bought by compromising on political symbols, such as the headmen and rituals, then so be it.[68] A. H. Stanford, magistrate of Umtata District (and brother of Walter) noted in 1883 that the aims of compromising on selection of chiefs and headmen were to deny Africans a grievance and to substitute the authority of the white-controlled state for that of the chiefs, and these aims were, in his view, being achieved: "The power of the chiefs is very sensibly decreasing."[69]

In Qumbu District, the struggle over chiefs and their authority endured despite Mhlonthlo's escape to Basutoland. There were persistent rumors of Mhlonthlo returning to the Mpondomise and leading them in revolt. These rumors linked Mhlonthlo's ability to evade capture with his magical powers as a chief; the fact that he remained beyond the Cape's reach either as a prisoner or an employee made him a viable symbol of African discontent.[70] Many years later, in 1903–4, when Walter Stanford, by then Superintendent of Native Affairs, finally succeeded in capturing Mhlonthlo and putting him on trial for the 1880 murder of the magistrate Hamilton Hope, a jury in King William's Town acquitted him, further bolstering his reputation as a powerful chief. Following the trial, Stanford, in a move reminiscent of Mhlonthlo's refusal to allow Hope to be buried, denied the aging Mhlonthlo's request to return to Qumbu "in order that the Mpondomise might bury him."[71] Eventually, in

1906, Stanford relented and did allow Mhlonthlo to take up residence in Qumbu, although he was not officially employed as a chief. Mhlonthlo's lack of a state-sanctioned title harmed neither his reputation nor his power among Africans as a symbol, nor did it prevent him from acting like a chief and challenging official authority until his death in 1912.[72] Yet, the white-controlled state managed to outlast Mhlonthlo's challenges, as the oft-rumored revolts never transpired and Mhlonthlo and his people continued to pay taxes.

Not content with political peace, most magistrates were concerned that Africans accept the white definition of civilization; Africans, however, sometimes showed skepticism about the reputed benefits of "civilization." Tsolo District magistrate Hook lectured a gathering of seven hundred people in his district in 1885 about the need to become civilized. Hook linked the notion of being civilized with that of paying hut tax: Africans would become civilized under colonial rule, which would be paid for by hut tax revenues. One of the Mpondomise headmen questioned him at the meeting, "We are hungry. Be patient we all know the [hut] tax is due. In what way should we progress in 'civilization'? If we are told some of us may try and progress."[73] In responding, Hook warned that if people did not pay their hut tax, he would have to seize their property; he also advised that civilization consisted of good agricultural techniques, Christianity, education, and having the appropriate wardrobe, in that order. The headman responded, "I was anxious to hear your explanation of civilization. I have heard now." The irony in his reply is nearly unmistakable.

In the aftermath of the 1880 rebellion, hut tax had become more than an instrument for generating revenue; it was transformed into a lever with which to move the African population toward "civilization." When Africans refused or neglected to pay hut taxes, to whites it was just another indication of African backwardness.[74] This standpoint allowed white officials to deny that nonpayment of taxes—or almost any type of protest—was evidence of well-grounded discontent on the part of Africans about the way in which they were being governed.[75] It also enabled officials to see tax payments as positive evidence of childlike obedience and of progress toward "civilization," and thus as a barometer of African acceptance of the white-led state.

Just as tax compliance and default became incorporated into white stereotypes of Africans, they also became part of African interpretations of colonial rule. First, Africans understood the connection between paying taxes and being allowed to cultivate land by the magistrates, under the official formula of no tax, no land. Yet magistrates in this period had relatively few enforcement tools with which to compel payment: depending on the district, they could sue defaulters in civil court and seize livestock or try to charge them with criminal vagrancy.[76] The most commonly used tool was simple harassment: urging headmen to hound defaulters and delivering lectures about civic responsibilities. These methods allowed considerable latitude for evading tax payments, and yet once magistrates resumed tax collection after the rebellion, the overwhelming majority of Africans paid. Given the high levels of tax payments, Africans likely understood a connection between paying the hut tax and being allowed to farm in peace.

The level of tax payment depended on the farmers' sheer ability to pay. After an average or better harvest and a good year for sheep-raising, there was wool to sell and therefore money to pay taxes. Conversely, there was some correlation between bad harvests and delinquency in hut tax payments. Tsolo, Umtata, and Engcobo Districts were three of the principal districts involved in the rebellion and they were also three of the most populous districts. According to the magistrates of Tsolo, there were poor harvests in 1882, 1884, 1885, and 1889, and the rest of the years were average to excellent. Taxes were poorly paid (under 60 percent collected), however, only in 1882, 1885, and 1887; by 1890 over 99 percent of taxes were paid, a rate that varied by no more than four percentage points through the end of the century.[77] In Umtata District poor harvests occurred in 1881, 1883–85, and 1889.[78] Compliance among Umtata's taxpayers remained low (below 40 percent of taxes due were collected) through 1887, possibly because of continuing social unrest in the wake of the rebellion and also because of population movements in and out of neighboring Pondoland, which was still at this time independent. In 1888, however, tax compliance in Umtata District changed abruptly, and averaged above 80 percent through the end of the century. In the district of Engcobo, the bad harvest years were 1881 and 1882, yet the percentage of hut tax paid reportedly increased to over 99 percent in 1892, despite other poor agricultural years. Through the end of the century (with one dip, in 1894) Engcobo compliance rates averaged between 90 and 95 percent.[79]

The quality of the harvests clearly does not explain everything. High levels of tax delinquency in the early 1880s probably had more to do with the dislocation of the population in the wake of the 1880 rebellion than anything else. This dislocation made hut tax registration and collection difficult so that the magistrates' numbers are suspect; in other words, the magistrates may not have had a good idea themselves how much total hut tax was actually due in a given year. In fact, it is possible that magistrates may have covered up the true level of defaults so that their superiors would have no basis for criticism. In addition, some of the defaults may have resulted from extreme caution on the part of state officials. Unwilling to cause a fresh revolt, and equally unwilling to die while engaged in the noble task of collecting taxes, magistrates, police, and headmen may not have tried too hard to collect taxes from defaulters, preferring the threat of property seizure to the hazards of seizure itself.[80] Yet according to the magistrates' records, by the late 1880s Africans paid their taxes with great regularity.

Africans also understood that tax payments gave them access to the courts and to their magistrates. Africans used the courts considerably in this period, especially as parties to civil lawsuits concerning marriages, much to the dismay of the magistrates, who constantly complained of overwork.[81] Africans who were not up-to-date in their hut tax payments could not appear in court without the threat of having property seized to satisfy the tax debt. Since marriage was an extremely significant part of African family life, an inability to go to court was a powerful incentive for a tax defaulter to pay. At the same time, magistrates and their administrative superiors had come to personify state authority. Magistrates often noted how important tax collection was because it allowed them to meet people and hear their grievances.[82] Along the same lines, prominent headmen and chiefs often voiced the desire to meet their magistrates and to meet the Secretary for Native Affairs whenever he toured the Transkei.[83]

It is in this context of the symbols and day-to-day workings of state power that the payment of hut tax became a political ritual. The payment of tax was more than a repetitive exercise: every year a married man or his delegate had to travel to the magistrate's office, often wait in line for a full day, then come into the office, pay the tax in cash, and be issued a receipt. Receipt in hand, he could return home to farm his allotment of land undisturbed for another year. The payment of tax was a public acknowledgment of the power of the state, but at the same time it was a way of fending off that power.[84] In this way, tax payments re-created and reinforced bonds between ruler and ruled. It brought Africans into the magistrates' offices and into contact with the state, a ritual that signified the subordination of the subjects but that also deflected the state's power away from the subjects by allowing them to gain access to land and immunizing them against prosecution. The symbolic resonance of tax payment may be the deepest explanation for why the vast majority of Africans complied with the monetary demands made by an obviously unjust state.

For many Africans the ritual of tax payments became part of what James Scott calls the "public transcript." The benefits of a well-learned public transcript for those who rule are fairly obvious: "Every visible, outward use of power—each command, each act of deference, each list and ranking, each ceremonial order, each public punishment, each use of an honorific or a term of derogation—is a symbolic gesture of domination that serves to manifest and reinforce an hierarchical order."[85] The benefits for Africans, as those who were ruled, were more complex. The enactment of the public transcript in a reliable way—demonstrated by the high compliance with tax demands—may have enabled them to maintain not only some autonomy of action, but also autonomy of thought. Scott's notion of a public transcript is that of a performance, more or less cynically executed.[86] This would seem to contradict the Comaroffs' idea that actions over the long term do affect consciousness, so that rituals of subordination effectively create some kind of consciousness of subordination. The Comaroffs' discussion of colonized consciousness is actually more intricate, in that it suggests that Africans, and whites as well, may simultaneously hold and act on contradictory ideas of proper authority and deference. Thus it would be possible for Africans in the late 1880s and 1890s to fear and resent the colonial state but still respect its authority and power enough to esteem individual officials and to comply with their demands for taxes.

Africans did not enjoy paying hut tax. On the contrary, Africans frequently complained to the magistrates about taxation. Chief Magistrate Elliot described African indignation over taxation in his 1884 annual report: "No men . . . are fond of parting with money in payment of taxes. The Native view of hut tax is 'We agreed to pay it, and in doing so did a foolish thing, and we are justified in evading it, if we can. Government did not build our huts or provide the material, why should it tax us upon our own labour, and the natural products of our own land?'" Elliot was probably the most sympathetic, if paternalistic, of the Transkeian magistrates, and he believed that hut tax was grossly unfair: "The Native who has *nothing* but his hut or huts is taxed to the same extent as the one who possesses Horses, Cattle, Sheep, Goats, Ploughs, etc. etc." And he insisted that Africans shared his viewpoint: "Hut tax is intensely unpopular with the Natives, and I believe chiefly because it is inequitable."[87] Elliot might easily have been reading from the hidden transcript of many Africans, as they simultaneously paid and resented paying.[88]

If Africans did find the hut tax inequitable, then it is all the more remarkable that so many of them regularly paid it. As noted above, a set, yearly tax was a departure from chiefs' precolonial levies, so the high compliance rates did not result from force of habit. Nor, given the caution of the magistrates in seizing property, did compliance result from reasonable expectations of property loss if the taxes were not paid. Instead, the ritual of tax payment in the wake of the rebellion had become part of a complex system of meaning and monetary exchange. Africans did not like having to give money to the white-controlled state, but the demands for tax payments became part of what they expected from the state, in return for which they expected the right to farm land and to have access to magistrates and the courts.[89] Beyond the yearly demand for taxes, Africans expected the state to leave them alone. Over and beyond these pragmatic considerations were the lessons about supernatural power that some Africans learned from the military defeat of the rebellion in 1880. Whites had won partly because the supernatural power they wielded was stronger than that of the chiefs; it was wise to pay the taxes to avoid having that power turned against oneself. Beliefs in the supernatural potency of the state were further reinforced by the co-optation of some chiefs and headmen into the administration, since they were widely reputed to have supernatural powers in their own right.

White officials saw high tax compliance rates in a different light. High compliance was for them an indication not only that Africans were not about to rebel but, more strongly, that Africans actively agreed to colonial rule and deferred to white definitions of civilization and progress. Africans, on the other hand, may have agreed that their tax payments signified that they were not about to rebel, but beyond that the payments were not evidence of any active African consensus on the legitimacy of white rule. Additionally, whites saw defaulting on taxes as confirmation of African backwardness, while most Africans probably would not have agreed. The infrequent defaults derived from several factors, including economic hardship and personal disinclination, as well as occasionally from political discontent.

The 1880 rebellion was a foundational event of the colonial administration in this part of the eastern Cape. It was a lesson to colonial administrators about the potential costs of pressing Africans and their chiefs too hard to make tax payments and other concessions, and it was a lesson to Africans about the limits of their own powers—both military and supernatural—in contesting colonial authority. In the aftermath of the revolt, after dealing harshly with major rebels, white administrators moved more cautiously in implementing new laws and in enforcing those laws already on the books.[90] Africans also dealt more cautiously with the state, paying their taxes and expressing themselves in deferential terms when in the presence of administrators.

Given the caution of administrators and the population displacement caused by the revolt, the conditions of the late 1880s and early 1890s were perfect for people to resist the state covertly by defaulting on their taxes. The state had relatively little police power it could bring to bear on defaulters, and most officials were wary of using what power they had. Yet Africans paid. Many white officials naively saw these payments as a mandate for colonial rule, when it was clear that most Africans resented both taxation and the colonial state. But to understand why Africans paid their taxes and did not rebel again for several decades, it is necessary to look beyond brute force and acknowledgment of defeat.[91]

White officials began to borrow African political symbols and idioms for their own rule in the postrebellion period. There is evidence of this in the official confiscation of property of rebels that was comparable to the precolonial practice of a chief "eating up" a subject's possessions as punishment. There is also evidence in the overt attempt to usurp the authority of the chiefs, especially with regard to the land-granting and judicial functions they had previously exercised, and in the attempt to use chiefs and headmen as state employees. These borrowings allowed Africans to recognize some aspects of the white-controlled state as familiar and expected. Colonial officials also elaborated on other symbols and rituals, particularly tax collection, which caused Africans both to pay tribute to the state and to incorporate that payment into their own narratives of power and authority. In doing so, white officials revised the "public transcript" of African submission to authority so that the roles played by white officials were closer to those that had been played by precolonial chiefs.

A second element involved in the revision of the public transcript was the widespread belief in witchcraft and supernatural powers. For those Africans who believed in witchcraft, the defeat of their chiefs demonstrated the superior and malevolent supernatural power of the white-controlled state. If this power could overcome the powers of the chiefs, then what hope could the average commoner have to surmount it? In this analysis, state officials were actively collaborating with the witches and sorcerers whom they were protecting; and state officials were also using the information contained in the census and hut tax registers to gain supernatural control over the African population. Both these ideas contributed to the state's authority. Paradoxically, white officials did not comprehend how witchcraft beliefs assisted them in controlling the population, even as they aggressively tried to stamp out witchcraft accusations.[92]

Following the defeat of the rebels, tax collection became inextricably bound up with the colonial state's sovereignty. While it produced revenue to pay the salaries of state officials, it was far more important for its symbolic and ritual content. The payment of taxes symbolized the defeat of the chiefs, the supernatural powers of the colonial state, and a widespread desire among Africans to farm in relative peace. Compliance with tax laws reflected an acknowledgment of the historical reality of the loss of African independence, but it also helped create and maintain peace, or at least dampen resistance, in subsequent years as people's understanding of political reality derived partly from that compliance. The payment of taxes was not merely a reflection of African historical consciousness, it was also a constitutive element in the ongoing creation of African historical narratives.

Clifton Crais, in his discussion of the aftermath of Hope's War, suggests that it was the colonial state's imposition of boundaries, maps, laws, and categories on the African population that created a "rationality of rule." This mapping of the colonized population fundamentally denied or ignored African elements of African culture such as beliefs in witchcraft that whites labeled irrational. Moreover, from the white officials' point of view this bureaucratization of colonial rule was a compelling justification in and of itself for colonial rule.[93] But in his analysis Crais compresses what many administrators thought of as their "civilizing mission" in the 1880s and 1890s with the advent of a more pseudoscientific brand of administration that emerged in the 1910s and 1920s: "We also have argued for the modernity of the early colonial state. The ways in which the state came into being—the maps, censuses, regulations, and laws— locate early colonialism in the revolutionary changes of the Enlightenment, especially in the importance of information. The suggestion here is that the authoritarian possibilities that were already present in the early colonial state came to fruition in the twentieth century."[94]

However, there are important distinctions between the way in which the colonial state operated in the last two decades of the nineteenth century and the first two decades of the twentieth. As both Africans and state officials recuperated from the shock of Hope's War in the late 1800s, they allowed each other some space in which to maneuver. As shown in this chapter, after the war a large majority of Africans paid the hut taxes demanded of them as a way of gaining some autonomy of action. Similarly, many resident magistrates were not so aggressive in their imposition of various colonial laws, and the official credo was to go slow. This mutual disengagement explains much of the political quiescence of Africans during the last decades of the century. Most Africans and white officials met only during the ritual of tax collection. Africans continued to view individual white officials and the state in general as supernaturally powerful and potentially malevolent, but the power and the threat could be contained by proper attention to the ritual of taxpaying. From their perspective, whites continued to view Africans as childlike and backward, with a potential for violence when handled too roughly. But taxes would pay for government administration that would slowly erode the foundations of the precolonial social systems and that in a more immediate way insured that Africans assumed the proper deferential attitude toward the state. These different interpretations of taxpaying and colonial rule laid the foundations for future clashes in the 1920s and later, but in the 1880s and 1890s they were the foundation of widespread peace.

These narratives, however, depended on the ability of African families to carve out some independent existence for themselves in the rural areas. The colonial state's ability to rule was contingent on its contacts with the rural African population being kept to a minimum. Africans were wary of state officials and of state powers; but if the payment of hut tax satisfied the state and allowed Africans to continue to farm and raise their families more or less independently, most Africans were willing to make the payments. By the turn of the century, however, several serious problems arose for African farmers, all of which threatened both African rural life and the colonial state's claim to sovereignty.

CHAPTER 3

FROM RINDERPEST THROUGH INFLUENZA

Taxes and Politics, 1897–1920

We are the children of the Government and why are we called
another nation[?]
— Matatiele District resident Willem Nyakonoko
at a meeting with Cape officials, 1914

The period from 1897 to 1920 was important for Transkeian Africans, who witnessed a number of transitions that affected them both locally and across the broader region. First, the rinderpest virus killed approximately 90 percent of the region's cattle in 1897, threatening the rural economy. Then the South African War divided and eventually unified the country, at least politically and economically. Although no fighting occurred in the Transkei itself, the war, by disrupting the operation of the gold mines around Johannesburg, temporarily depressed the demand for migrant laborers, thereby preventing young African men from earning the money needed to replace the cattle lost to disease. Yet the war also created a huge market for agricultural and livestock produce, especially wool, meat, and horses, that tended to enrich those African farmers—usually older, wealthier men who had managed to maintain their herds despite rinderpest.

When the mines reopened at the end of the war, labor migration from the Transkei began again, slowly at first. Starting in 1906, the number of migrants going to the Rand steadily increased each year until 1916, when the number began to plateau for the next two decades. The expansion of labor migration from the Transkei was largely the result of the need of a young generation of African men to acquire cattle for bridewealth payments. On the national level, labor migration fueled the development of the South African economy; on the local level, it coincided with the imposition of the new poll tax, officially known as the General Rate, throughout many of the Transkeian districts. The poll tax entered each district separately and was originally linked to the imposition of the General Council, or Bunga, system devised by the Glen Grey Act of 1894. Originally set at ten shillings, the poll tax was due from all adult men, married or not, who were not already obligated to pay the hut tax.[1] By 1906 men in four districts were paying General Rate, and by 1908 men in fifteen districts (out of the total of twenty-nine) were so obligated.[2]

In 1914 the outbreak of World War I enlarged once again the market for agricultural products, and, by increasing the worldwide demand for manufactured goods and pulling white laborers into the military, it also expanded the wage labor market for Africans. However, other events hindered the ability of many Transkeian Africans to profit from these circumstances; in particular, farmers found themselves unable to get their produce to market because of a lack of transportation. Only one railway ran into the Transkei, and that only part of the way, and transport by ox-drawn wagons was limited by veterinary quarantines imposed to prevent the spread of a new cattle disease, East Coast fever. These quarantines extended well into the 1920s, artificially depressing the prices paid to Transkeian farmers for their agricultural produce and for cattle and other livestock because of the difficulty of getting them to market. The end of the war also caused an almost immediate slump in prices for various goods on the world market, cutting severely into the incomes of farmers.

Mining also expanded in the 1910s, drawing additional African men as laborers. As more African men worked in the mines and in new industries in the urban areas, they fell prey to several newly introduced diseases, including tuberculosis and influenza. Although over the long term tuberculosis has had broader social effects,[3] the worldwide influenza epidemic of 1918 dealt the African population a particularly hard blow. Influenza caused numerous deaths and short-term debilitation, sometimes lasting several months, to a broad population. Also, by occurring during the spring plowing and planting season, the mortality and morbidity caused by influenza reduced the year's harvest. The rural hunger and poverty induced by influenza presaged the deepening decline of the rural economy through the 1920s and later.

Despite the numerous political and economic transitions that took place in this period, change in the relationship of most Transkeian Africans to the Cape Colonial, and then Union (post-1910), state was remarkably slow. Rumors of political unrest abounded, some of them driven by the Bambatha Rebellion in nearby Natal and Zululand in 1906 (see chapter 4); but acts of political violence

FIGURE 3.1. "The First Furrow," Western Pondoland. Photograph by Mrs. Fred Clarke, n.d. (probably 1920s–1930s). The Campbell Collection of the University of Kwazulu-Natal.

in the Transkei in this period were few. What unrest did occur was focused largely on the harsh veterinary restrictions imposed by the state at the time of the East Coast fever outbreak and not on the newly imposed taxes, although grievances over taxation continued to stoke a more general sense of being preyed upon by the state. Africans for the most part had relatively little direct contact with the state except through the ritual of tax collection and, by the 1910s, through compliance with compulsory cattle-dipping regulations. African headmen, who lived in and policed their local areas, were the only state officials with whom most Africans interacted on a daily or weekly basis. Africans came into contact with white magistrates or their clerks on very few occasions: Africans paid their taxes at their magistrates' offices; a man planning on becoming a labor migrant had to visit a magistrate to get the proper pass for traveling; and any African brought up on a criminal charge or involved in civil litigation had to go to the magistrate's court. But overall, neither magistrates nor the "state," or "government," were yet a daily presence in people's lives in the early decades of the twentieth century.

Official control rested in part on the continuity of personnel, including magistrates, chiefs, and headmen, as well as on the continuity of the rituals of rule. Tax collection was one of the rituals, and it continued to have both secular and supernatural meanings. The interaction involved in tax collection did not just describe the power of the state over its subjects, it also helped to construct that power. In this time period, the state moved beyond controlling the rural homestead through the senior male in residence and the payment of hut tax to controlling all adult men as individuals through the poll tax. Many state officials, especially whites, understood the new poll tax to be an attempt to benefit from the wages of young men in particular, income that had not been directly taxed under the system of hut tax. Yet Africans saw the poll tax as part of a larger social context that included both the material realm of money and the spiritual realm of witchcraft and supernatural powers. The colonial regime's reputation for having supernatural powers, established in the 1880s and reinforced with the ritual of taxpaying, was enhanced by the various diseases and responses to those diseases that swept through the region in between 1897 and 1920.

THE "LIGHT HAND" OF GOVERNMENT:
RINDERPEST, WARFARE, AND TAXATION

Rinderpest was a devastating livestock disease that had worked its way down the east coast of Africa from Eritrea throughout the previous decades. By 1896 the disease had entered South Africa and was on its way to killing the cattle herds in the Transkei. It threatened the economic and social core of African rural life and had potentially strong implications for Africans' ability and willingness to pay taxes. It also, as many white officials were aware, had the potential to upset the state's control; how white state officials handled rinderpest was therefore of great importance to their continued ability to rule.[4]

In 1896 state officials attempted to keep rinderpest out of the Transkei altogether. Initially, they discussed creating a cattle-free buffer zone along the borders of the already infected regions of Natal and Basutoland, but magistrates in the districts that directly bordered those regions commented that the killing of all cattle in their districts would cause more unrest than the disease itself. The resident magistrate of Engcobo District wrote, "I venture to point out that the consequences of destroying native cattle [as a preventive measure], even if a certain amount [of money] is awarded as compensation, will probably be disastrous." The magistrate's reason for thinking such a policy would be disastrous was an indication of how deeply the notion that Africans were childlike—a notion that had emerged at the end of the 1880 Mpondomise Rebellion—was embedded into official doctrine: "Natives are utterly improvident, careless of the future, and suspicious and the killing of their healthy cattle by direction of the Government, can be very easily misunderstood by the Natives and would afford a splendid opportunity for any person who may

desire to induce them to rise in rebellion."[5] Officials finally settled on the imposition of strict cordons sanitaires along the frontiers to try to keep infected
cattle from crossing. This involved putting up wire fencing along much of the
passable border and posting guards along known roads to prevent the passage
of ox-wagons and grazing cattle.[6] These measures ultimately failed to prevent
the disease from entering the Transkei, however, as the first reported cases of
rinderpest occurred in June 1897 in Nqamakwe District, with widespread outbreaks in other districts immediately following.[7]

Having failed to keep rinderpest out of the Transkeian Territories, officials
tried to hinder its spread. Primarily, they relied on veterinary inspectors to
locate sick animals and quarantine them and all other cattle with which they
had come into contact. Secondarily, officials promoted the use of experimental vaccinations administered by state-employed inoculators. These were
significant measures, and how state officials implemented them contrasted
sharply with their implementation years later of quarantine regulations in the
face of the East Coast fever epidemic. In the case of rinderpest, obviously
infected cattle either got markedly better on their own or, much more commonly, died within a matter of days; the disease was also very contagious so
that if one cow had the disease, it was likely that most of the herd would show
symptoms within a short time. All these circumstances meant that for the
cattle owner the inconvenience of the quarantine was a small annoyance when
compared to the anguish of watching his livestock die. And cattle did die in
large numbers: overall, 90 to 95 percent of unvaccinated cattle died in the epidemic. White officials did not attempt to force people to vaccinate their cattle,
in part because the vaccines were experimental but also in part because public
opinion was so much against vaccination, particularly because it was sponsored by the state.

There were in fact two experimental vaccines. One was created from the
blood and the other from the bile of cattle that had survived on their own an
infection with rinderpest. In Umtata District, white and black farmers who
inoculated their cattle with bile vaccine lowered the mortality rate from the disease to about 50 percent, and in Engcobo District the mortality rate dropped to
25 percent among cattle vaccinated with the bile vaccine.[8] Vaccination was not
always successful nor even safe, however: inoculation with the bile vaccine
occasionally killed the cattle it was meant to protect; moreover, inoculation
with the blood vaccine almost always killed the cattle who received it, and
eventually the use of the blood vaccine was halted.[9] Unfortunately, these
results, both positive and negative, only became known as these vaccines were
used in the field.

Many Africans were suspicious of the inoculation process before it was even tried, and even many white farmers were suspicious enough not to use the vaccines initially. For Africans, the lethal results of the blood vaccine looked sinister because it was being provided by the state. In the early stages of providing the inoculations, Umtata's resident magistrate reported that Africans were "strongly adverse to inoculation which many of them allege to result as disastrously as the rinderpest itself."[10] He elaborated in a later report, "The outbreak of Rinderpest produced in the people a feeling strongly antagonistic to the Government, or to any measure introduced to prevent the spread of the disease and especially inoculation. It was firmly believed that Rinderpest had been purposely introduced, with the object of impoverishing the natives to such a degree as would compel them to go to work, and that inoculation was mere [sic] a device for its more rapid propagation."[11] A similar suspicion of vaccination was described by the resident magistrate of Bizana District: "The most absurd stories were circulated about it. At first it was only that the Government were attempting to kill the cattle by inoculation, but later on it grew to an attempt on the part of Government to kill the people themselves by poisoning the meat and then inducing people to eat it."[12]

The initial feeling against vaccination was so strong that government headmen often adamantly opposed it, siding with public opinion rather than with the state, which paid them. The headmen's opposition is highly suggestive of the amount of pressure they felt from the people in their administrative areas.[13] The fact that state officials did nothing to force the headmen into changing their positions is also suggestive of how cautious official policy was. This caution was likely adopted because of the aura of inevitability surrounding rinderpest: most officials were unsure that *any* measures would be successful in preventing its spread, and therefore they were unwilling to coerce people into implementing policies that might prove futile or perhaps even make the situation worse.[14]

Transkeian officials were also concerned about the political unrest in the East Griqualand districts of Matatiele, Umzimkulu, and Mount Currie. The self-styled leader of the local Griqua population, A. A. S. le Fleur, had been reviving discontent over grievances related to land tenure and ownership in the area.[15] This unrest preceded the local occurrence of rinderpest, but le Fleur's trial for treason coincided with the outbreak. When le Fleur was found not guilty in Umtata in October 1897, new rumors of impending revolt, involving not just the Griqua but also the neighboring Hlubi and other African groups, began to circulate among Africans and white settlers in East Griqualand. These rumors fused le Fleur's land issues with African anguish and bitterness as they watched their cattle die. Although a small number of white settlers demanded that the authorities send in troops to intimidate any would-be rebels, most of the magistrates derided the rumors. The chief magistrate of East Griqualand even suggested that "the [white] farmers in this neighbourhood seem to have fallen prey to panic and in order to justify themselves for getting into a funk they have grossly exaggerated every incident connected with Le Fleur's 'fizzle.'"[16] Despite the bravado of white officials, however, many may have avoided coercive measures against rinderpest to defuse a potentially explosive situation.

There were undoubtedly lingering suspicions among Africans about the origin of rinderpest and the state's possible complicity in introducing it. Rinderpest had followed in the wake of the British colonial invasion of eastern and southern Africa, a fact that gave the suspicions some credibility.[17] Suspicion often evolved into rumors about the supernatural powers being used by whites to spread the disease. The Mount Fletcher District magistrate reported that, after the initial diagnosis of rinderpest infection in a particular herd in that district, the herd's owner "firmly believes, as do all superstitious Natives, that he has been bewitched."[18] Moreover, throughout 1896 there had been persistent rumors among Africans that rinderpest was only one manifestation of the evil nature of the colonizing whites. The Umtata magistrate responded to the chief magistrate's query about rumors of a newborn child proclaiming doom that were circulating around the time of the local outbreak of rinderpest by stating, "ever since I have known the Kaffirs there have been repeated instances of these stories of children, monsters and others, giving oracular statements in a loud voice as soon as born."[19]

Suspicion of whites' complicity in the spread of rinderpest was passionate in Willowvale District. The magistrate reported that Africans were "strongly opposed to what they called 'the introduction of the disease amongst their cattle by means of inoculation.'" They refused to inoculate and

> when at last the dreaded plague reached their door, a bitter feeling sprung up against the "Umlungu" (white man, or scum of the sea) who, in order to reduce them to poverty with a view of enslaving them to the Western Province Farmers, and depriving them of their country, had struck at the root of their life by destroying their idolised cattle, and they most persistently objected to have anything to do with inoculation, feeling convinced that if they partook of the flesh of an inoculated beast, the white man's poison would be carried into their own systems, and to counteract this poison, on the principle I suppose, of like curing like,

took sea water and scum of the sea and dosed their cattle fore and aft, and not content with having the meat of cattle killed by the plague, hundreds of their best cattle were slaughtered and what little grain they had was converted into beer, and day and night they feasted and drowned their cares in drink, and in their drunken state brooded evil against the white man.

What changed this attitude of discontent bordering on rebellion was "the fact that many of the Fingoes . . . had actually prevented the spread of the disease to their kraals by means of inoculation, and it was only when almost too late that some of the Gcalekas, led by their headmen (the latter fearing loss of position) had some of their cattle inoculated, but not until the plague had carried off no less than 30,000 of their cattle" out of approximately forty thousand before the epidemic.[20]

Africans throughout the Transkei had initially feared that the vaccine was a device for spreading the disease, a fear given some substance by the lethal results of the blood-based vaccine. But, as the bile-based vaccine began to prove itself at least partially effective in saving cattle from the disease, Africans began to demand it. In late 1897, Mount Frere's magistrate stated, "The results of [bile] inoculation are now clear to all and the natives are convinced of its efficacy and [are] willing to pay for it."[21] Over time, this trend continued: when a much smaller outbreak of rinderpest occurred in Umtata District in 1902, the magistrate wrote, "The people are now as anxious for inoculations as they were opposed to it [sic] in 1897."[22] Belief in the supernatural origins of rinderpest did not necessarily prevent people from using a vaccine that was proven effective; in fact, such a vaccine might have enhanced the magical reputation of those who provided it.

Out of all the suspicion and death swirling around the rinderpest epidemic came a somewhat surprising result, and it was largely the product of the limited success of the bile vaccine. Africans, even those who had been strongly opposed to vaccinations at the beginning of the outbreak, began to accept that the bile vaccine worked. The fact that the state had been providing the vaccine for several months to those who would use it counted in the state's favor. In the aftermath of the epidemic, some Africans chided the Transkei's chief magistrate, Maj. Henry Elliot, for not promoting the vaccine more vigorously: "I have several times been told," he wrote, "by Natives that I am personally to blame for the heavy mortality amongst their cattle for that upon the appearance of the disease *I might have brought the Cape Mounted Riflemen into the Territories and compelled them to inoculate.*"[23] These Africans who admonished

TABLE 3.1 Percentage of Hut Tax Unpaid, Selected Districts, 1898–1908

Year	District			
	Bizana	Engcobo	Tsolo	Umtata
1898	—	9.20	—	11.03
1899	—	11.37	—	15.60
1900	16.70	—	1.30	—
1901	21.72	—	3.06	—
1902	5.76	2.61	1.00	6.83
1903	8.10	8.43	0.09	6.96
1904	3.93	—	0	0.06
1907	0.51	9.14	3.78	17.97
1908	0.53	15.13	6.15	32.33

Sources: Annual Reports from Resident Magistrates in these four districts. The data for the years 1905 and 1906 were unavailable for these districts.

Elliot had evidently come to believe that the state, by making the vaccine available, had made a serious effort to save their cattle. Although they proposed that the state should have compelled people to vaccinate their cattle, the fact that the state did not do so probably prevented rinderpest from becoming the focus for antistate *actions,* as distinct from rumors and general mistrust. Even in East Griqualand, with the acquittal of le Fleur, rinderpest ceased to be a significant source of political discontent only a few months after it had appeared.[24]

Lack of political unrest is difficult to prove, but there were some indicators that most people in the Transkei were not on the verge of revolt. One is the payment of hut tax immediately following rinderpest (see table 3.1 below). From 1897 to 1910, the rate of hut tax payments in Umtata District ranged from a low of 84.4 percent in 1899 to a high of 99.9 percent in 1904, with a rate of 86 percent in 1909.[25] For Engcobo District, compliance ranged between 88.63 percent in 1899 and 97.39 percent in 1902, and ended with 95 percent in 1909.[26] In Bizana District, the range was between a low of 78.28 percent in 1901 and a high of 99.5 percent in both 1907 and 1908; and in 1909 the rate was 98.6 percent.[27] All three districts were hard hit by rinderpest, with cattle losses averaging about 90 percent, yet the loss of cattle did not result in lower rates of tax payments. The magistrate of Bizana District expressed surprise at how well the taxes were paid in 1899: "I think the people have done very well [in paying their taxes]. Not only are they without any cattle which they can sell, but events in the North [the outbreak of the South African War], have shut them out from the Gold Fields, which was there [*sic*] great standby for earning money for Hut Tax."[28]

Although most people continued to pay their taxes, rinderpest was clearly an economic calamity for African farmers. The loss of cattle drastically reduced the availability of protein in the diet, both from milk and meat. Fewer cattle meant fewer draft animals to pull plows, thus decreasing crop yields on arable land.[29] Rinderpest also wiped out much of the social and economic wealth that was stored in cattle.[30] In addition, the disease, by killing so many cattle, threatened the institutions of bridewealth (*lobola*) and marriage.

Bridewealth was the formal payment made by the groom's family to the bride's family at the time of marriage. In the 1890s and well into the twentieth century, most Africans—including converts to Christianity—considered the bridewealth payment the defining element of the marriage. In the Transkei before rinderpest, the usual bridewealth payment in a marriage between non-royal families was six to twelve cattle. Before rinderpest, cattle were valued at approximately three pounds each; after rinderpest, each animal was valued at twelve pounds and more. Families trying to seal marriage contracts after the devastation of rinderpest did make adjustments by substituting other animals and sometimes cash for cattle in bridewealth payments, but the bridewealth was still reckoned in cattle, and some actual cows were usually considered a necessary part of the payment.[31]

Bridewealth payments, at least in theory, were more than a transfer of wealth from one family to another. They were an indication of the respect the groom's family had for the bride's family, and a visible sign of a much broader social compact. Historically, sons who wanted to marry had to depend on their fathers for the bridewealth payment, and that dependence gave fathers significant control over their sons' behavior as well as over the choice of brides. An unmarried woman could negotiate with her father over the choice of groom in an arranged marriage, but a high bridewealth payment was a source of prestige for both the bride and her family. Cattle were preferred in bridewealth payments because they had a cultural value that went beyond their monetary value. People equated ownership of cattle both with material wealth and with spiritual well-being and social maturity. Cattle were the favorite animal of the ancestors, and sacrifices of cattle were crucial to many rituals involving the ancestors and the family. In the wake of rinderpest, important ritual sacrifices had to be curtailed or other, less symbolically significant animals substituted. The disease had wiped out at least 90 percent of people's wealth, but beyond that the disease had undermined the family and its relations with the ancestors. Given that rinderpest was such a serious economic and social blow for most Africans, it is all the more remarkable that the rate of tax compliance remained so high.

The high rate of tax payment was linked to how Africans interpreted the state's connection with rinderpest. One possible interpretation was that

Africans ultimately did not blame the state for spreading the disease but instead believed that by providing the vaccine state officials had made a sincere effort to stop the disease. Africans who believed this may have continued to pay their taxes as well as they could because they bore no grudge against the state. The second possible interpretation is that some Africans may have feared that the state had killed their cattle through witchcraft and thus paid their taxes out of fear of the consequences nonpayment might bring. On a strictly pragmatic level, in the first few months after rinderpest hit, many African stock owners illegally sold their dead cattle's hides for five to ten shillings each (the hides were not supposed to be sold for fear that they might carry the disease but legally were to be buried); thus many did have some cash available to pay the tax.[32]

Rinderpest did not impoverish all Africans equally; instead, it sharpened rural economic stratification. Livestock owners who had large herds before the disease were more likely to have a few surviving cattle and thus continued to be relatively wealthy. Live cattle became more valuable in cash terms, and cattle could also be hired out to plow or lent to reinforce patron-client relationships.[33] Farmers who still had cattle after rinderpest thus could profit from their good fortune. In addition, those Africans who had previously invested more money in sheep to take advantage of the market in wool found that their sheep were largely untouched by rinderpest. The people who survived as livestock owners were in the best position to profit from the South African War, which broke out in 1899.

Great Britain went to war in 1899 with the help of its southern African colonies, the Cape Colony and Natal. The war was an effort to consolidate Britain's control in the region by conquering the two independent republics governed by descendants of earlier white settlers in southern Africa (Boers, or Afrikaners), who over the years had evaded British control by moving inland and establishing two independent republics. Both republics had been fairly poor agricultural backwaters until the mid-1880s, when gold was discovered in one of them. The gold discoveries came at a time when Britain was engaged with other European powers in a "scramble for Africa," and eventually these independent white-governed republics suffered the same fate as the independent African-governed polities elsewhere in southern Africa and across the continent. The war stretched out over three years, and the bulk of the fighting took place in the embattled republics and in border regions of Natal and the Cape. Massive numbers of British troops were brought in to beat the Boers into submission, and the military and colonial administration made strategic alliances with various African leaders to assist them in the war. These alliances were critical in several ways. Africans actively assisted the British by acting as scouts and support personnel, as well as occasionally fighting and denying safe havens to fleeing Boer fighters. Africans also continued to farm and became important suppliers to the war effort.

The South African War enabled some livestock owners in the Transkei and Natal to reestablish themselves as independent farmers after the devastation of rinderpest. The war enlarged the market for meat, wool, grain, and for cavalry and packhorses, mules, and oxen, and, since there were no battles in the Transkei, local Africans suffered no direct losses of life or property. In addition, when British forces captured enemy cattle and other livestock, whatever was not slaughtered or used by the military for draft purposes was sold at market, giving some African farmers the chance to restock.[34] However, those farmers who profited from the war were likely older men who controlled the labor of several people—including dependent children and wives—in their homesteads, and families who were already relatively well-off and well established in producing goods for the market.

The war also turned the attention of state officials away from Africans and focused it on Afrikaners. At the beginning of the war in particular, there were some rumors among rural Africans that the independent Afrikaner republics would win, and therefore Africans should side with them. However, these rumors were squelched by some influential chiefs, notably the Thembu chief Dalindyebo, who pledged support for British forces and organized scouting parties.[35] Even Africans in Engcobo, one of the districts most heavily engaged in the 1880 rebellion, volunteered for service with British forces, as the magistrate reported:

> Rumours were rife in this District to the effect that the Natives would probably take up arms against the British government. This wild talk can only be attributed to persons who are of a timid nature, for there were no grounds for alarm whatever. The feelings of the Natives of this District from the commencement [of the war] were, and are still, with the British Government. As a proof of this as soon as they heard that hostilities had commenced they came forward and offered their services, and on the arrival of Major Sir H. G. Elliot in this District in November last, for the purpose of forming a Native Force for the protection of the Territories, large numbers at once came forward to be enrolled and in a very short time the number required was obtained.[36]

This cooperation may have been solely strategic, done in the belief that Africans would be rewarded for their loyalty, or it may have represented a stronger commitment to British values on the parts of some Africans. The high level of tax compliance throughout this period, however, when combined with the absence of unrest and the enlarged opportunities for African farmers, suggests that most people did not see the colonial state as a threat to their way of life. Instead, twenty years after the initial takeover of the area by the Cape, Africans had incorporated the white-controlled state into their still predominantly rural lives; tax demands were not yet overwhelming; and many African families had successfully reestablished themselves—or had realistic hopes of doing so—as independent farmers. With the end of the war, in 1902, state officials began to turn their attention back to rural Africans, both as source of labor for industry and as farmers competing with white farmers in rural production for the market.

THE CONSPICUOUS STATE: GLEN GREY, POLL TAX, AND EAST COAST FEVER REGULATIONS

In the first two decades of the twentieth century, magistrates and the policies they implemented began to be more interventionist and less restrained. Other historians have placed this change at a later time, in the mid-1920s, with the passage of the 1923 Natives (Urban) Areas Act, the 1925 Native Taxation and Development Act, and the Native Administration Act of 1927.[37] Principally, the argument has been that these laws tended to centralize and systematize the Union's Native policy in such a way as to erode and demean the personal contacts between magistrates and Africans that had previously been the basis of Transkeian policy. These laws substituted a bureaucratized, "modernized" form of management that dictated policy from above rather than allowing policy to develop from the interactions between state officials and local populations, and this result was accomplished, according to this line of argument, very much against the wishes of Transkeian magistrates.[38]

But some of these changes began at an earlier time, and in the Transkei itself, as magistrates imposed restrictions in an attempt to halt the spread of East Coast fever (a tick-transmitted disease of cattle that has a high death rate; cattle usually die after a progressive illness lasting two to four weeks). In trying to avoid a replay of the high levels of mortality caused by rinderpest, magistrates recommended strict enforcement of measures to halt the spread of the disease, overruling African concerns and objections to these measures, especially to the regular dipping of cattle in chemical baths. Magistrates forced these measures because they felt they knew more about the science of disease than Africans did. Ironically, however, the quarantines, sales restrictions, and

FIGURE 3.2. "Headman and After-riders," Western Pondoland. Photograph by Mrs. Fred Clarke, n.d. (probably 1920s–1930s). The Campbell Collection of the University of Kwazulu-Natal.

coerced dipping did little to stop East Coast fever, and themselves did a great deal of damage to the health of African agriculture. At the same time, these policies set the tone for future interactions between state officials and Africans, the tone that was formally enacted into laws in the 1920s and later.

Policies on East Coast fever did not emerge from a vacuum, however; they were part of a whole web of measures dealing with African rural life. One of the more significant of these measures was the increase in taxes, and the connections between taxation and political representation as more districts came under the Glen Grey Act, passed by the Cape Colony's Parliament in 1894. With the Glen Grey Act came the General Rate (or poll tax) imposed on all adult men, as well as the surveying of rural land allotments and the issuing of quitrent titles. These measures laid the foundation for massive rural poverty in two ways: by increasing the overall tax burden at a time when agricultural incomes were threatened and by setting the stage for widespread landlessness in the upcoming generation. The chief magistrate of the Transkei, A. H. Stanford, noted in his Blue Book Report for 1907, "There are many indications that the state of the Native is one of growing impoverishment and, what is more serious, of growing indebtedness."[39] Thus with the increase in the state's demands for money came an increased necessity for Africans to find cash. After 1906 greater numbers of men sought wage labor at the gold mines around

Johannesburg; but in the short term they often had to satisfy tax demands with money borrowed from local white traders or from wealthier African neighbors, often at extraordinarily high rates of interest.[40] Taxation, the imposition and extension of the Glen Grey Act, cattle disease and compulsory cattle dipping, as well as increasing poverty and landlessness all came together to tighten the bonds between the state and rural Africans. Gradually through the 1920s, the bonds began to chafe many Africans in the Transkei.

The Glen Grey Act was in force in roughly half the districts of the Transkei by 1908.[41] This statute, with certain modifications since its original passage into law in 1894, had three basic intents. The first was to replace the old system of relatively free allocation of land to all adult men with a system of quitrent title for land (in other words, a specific parcel of land would be leased by the state to a specific individual) that was inheritable from father to firstborn son. The second intent was to create a form of local government known as the General Council, or Bunga. Previously, in the Cape Colony and then the Cape Province, an adult African man who owned (with a title deed) a fixed quantity of land or who earned seventy-five pounds or more per year could qualify for the franchise on the common voters' roll with whites and Coloureds. However, most land in the Transkei was legally designated as Crown land and not available for outright ownership; thus it could not qualify those who occupied it for the common voters' roll. However, having the quitrent right to a plot surveyed under the Glen Grey Act did qualify adult men to aid in selection of councillors for the Bunga, a quasi-parliamentary body that met in Umtata. The Bunga was supposed to advise the chief magistrate of the Transkei on policy matters, and much of the hut tax revenue still being collected went into the Bunga's coffers to pay for certain local expenditures.[42] Thus the Glen Grey statute set up an alternative and separate form of government for rural Africans—less representative than the Cape and Union franchise provisions were for registered voters and with decidedly less political and economic authority. In short, it was a second-class form of political participation for rural Africans.[43] In its original 1894 form, the act also proposed a Labour Tax, which taxed adult men at the rate of ten shillings per year in any calendar year in which they could not prove they had been employed for wages. Finally, another new tax—the General Rate, or poll tax, was added. The poll tax was an attempt to tax directly the incomes of unmarried men, many of whom worked as migrant laborers in the gold and diamond mines outside the Transkei.

The initial attempt to impose the Glen Grey Act in the mid-1890s had met with some resistance and, perhaps more important, with rumors of more widespread dissent. Rural dissent centered on two major issues: the surveying of land into a finite and fixed number of plots, thus rendering a large proportion of the next generation of Africans landless, and the imposition of new taxes.[44] (In fact, it was in response to provisions of the act that Chief Sigidi offered his "morsel of honey" in the form of advice to the Idutywa District magistrate; see chapter 1.) Some Africans, particularly those active in broader Cape Provincial politics, also objected strenuously to the separate and unequal political participation being mandated for rural Africans. Caution on the part of administrators, who did not want to provoke a new rebellion, led to a gradual implementation of the act. The Labour Tax was only ever collected in four districts of the Transkei, and magistrates in those districts believed the tax to be literally more trouble than it was worth. The Butterworth District magistrate noted in 1897 that he hoped that the Labour Tax would be abolished: "It is a most difficult and expensive tax to collect. . . . Its abolition would gain the greatest satisfaction to the natives throughout these four districts; and the object for which it was instituted—namely to make the young men go out to work[—]is quite sufficiently secured by the imposition of the general rate."[45] The magistrate of Idutywa District complained of similar problems with the Labour Tax in 1898:

> I find it difficult to get the Headmen to render active assistance in getting their people to come and register their periods of labour [to determine eligibility for the tax]. They say that they have warned their people to come and register and they cannot do more. The people are much opposed to the imposition of this tax and the elderly men who remain at home to look after their stock, ploughing, harvesting and family affairs seem to think that the tax is especially directed against them as since they cannot get away to the [Cape] Colony or the mining centres they alone have to pay. With few exceptions the young men in this District who have been circumcised [circumcision was a mark of adulthood for men] go out to work every year in other districts and some find work within this district, but they are very reluctant to come and register and when the police are sent out they are said to be away at work or absent from home for some reason or other.

This magistrate also contrasted problems with the Labour Tax with what he saw as the good effects of the General Rate: "Payment of General Rate causes a good deal of grumbling . . . [but] I think this tax influences the people to a great extent to go out to work."[46] The general caution of the magistrates and their conclusions that the Labour Tax was not worth collecting eventually led to its abolition.[47]

But the resistance to the Labour Tax and the General Rate also led administrators to characterize Africans as "backwards" and "conservative," and as irrationally unwilling to accept changes that, from the perspective of administrators, would advance the African political and economic position. The magistrate of Engcobo District in 1896 provided his view of the local population: "The natives as a whole are not making much progress towards higher civilization. The 'red' people are very conservative, and cling to the habits and customs of their forefathers."[48] The Bizana District magistrate in 1900 wrote in similar tones, "I fear there is very little progress to report amongst the Natives. Things in Pondoland move slowly."[49] The chief magistrate in 1907 noted the uniformity of official views: "There must be few officers engaged in administration in these parts who are not frequently admonishing the Native peasantry on its unproductiveness. . . . The Native is even slower than the European to adopt scientific methods."[50] This developing official view of the African peasant as a hidebound rustic suspicious of new ideas would deepen as everyone faced a unfamiliar cattle epidemic threatening the newly rebuilt cattle herds: East Coast fever.

Coming on the heels of the rinderpest epidemic (and rinderpest itself had come on the heels of several other cattle diseases in the nineteenth century), tick-borne East Coast fever encouraged the belief that whites controlled superior supernatural powers. Anthropologist Monica Wilson remarked in the 1930s that her informants believed that cattle sicknesses were sent by Europeans: "We always hear beforehand that they (the cattle diseases) are coming; that means that white people have sent them."[51]

East Coast fever was neither as quick nor as fatal as rinderpest, but in part because of those differences, the official view was that its spread could be stopped by aggressive measures. These measures included stringently enforced quarantines, both of individually owned infected herds and of whole districts in which the disease had been found, and compulsory, frequent dipping of cattle in tanks filled with chemical baths to eradicate the ticks.

In principle, at the beginning of the epidemic in 1908–9, few Africans were opposed to measures to stop the spread of the disease. In fact, many African livestock owners were keen to build dipping tanks and readily contributed the money needed; the Umtata newspaper *Territorial News* wrote:

> We challenge 'The Observer' [another Cape newspaper] or any other paper to state an area where the people have so wholeheartedly devoted

themselves to assist the Government in the campaign against East Coast Fever. The stock owners here are mostly natives, and raw natives at that, and yet they have voluntarily subscribed in the present year alone, by means of the General Council funds and the Tank Tax levied in Pondoland, Matatiele, and Cala, no less a sum than between £15,000 and £16,000 for the purpose of erecting tanks. The Government on the other hand, has contributed nothing for this purpose, although of course, it has paid for fencing one or two districts.[52]

In many districts, tanks that had previously been used for dipping sheep against scab were retrofitted for cattle dipping. White farmers scattered throughout the districts usually maintained dipping tanks for their own herds and sometimes rented them out for dipping African-owned cattle as well.[53]

State officials strongly promoted dipping as a preventive for the disease. For a short time, Africans were allowed to dip their cattle in a dip made from locally grown tobacco, which was mildly toxic for the ticks and relatively safe for the cattle.[54] However, state regulations soon required that cattle be dipped in a chemical dip that, when prepared correctly, was more effective against the ticks. However, even when prepared correctly the chemical dip could be lethal to mildly debilitated, underweight, or young cattle, and proportions when mixed with water had to be exact. Mixed too strong and the chemicals could badly burn animals, often resulting in death; mixed too weak or diluted by rain and the dip was largely ineffective (although possibly still more effective than the tobacco-based dip). The dipping tanks themselves had to be maintained in good repair to prevent leaks and to provide a safe ingress and egress for the animals. The chemical bath in the tanks had to be at the right depth so that it covered the animals' bodies but not so deep as to force the animals to swim and thus make accidental ingestion or inhalation of the toxic dip more likely. Such levels of precision were hard to maintain in the remote areas where many of the tanks were located.

State regulations mandated that all African-owned cattle be dipped once a week in the summer months (roughly November through mid-March) and once every two to four weeks during the rest of the year. This necessitated herding the livestock considerable distances (sometimes as much as five or six miles) regularly, often weakening the cattle and making them lose weight. Each livestock owner had a certificate that listed the number of cattle he owned and the dates dipped. This certificate was legal proof of compliance with the dipping regulations. It also became legal proof of ownership of these cattle and thus developed ancillary usefulness in court cases unrelated to dip-

ping in which one person might claim certain cattle as part of a lobola payment, for example. The certificate also served to prove to trading-store owners and other potential moneylenders that the person had cattle that could
serve as collateral for a requested loan, a fact that made the dipping regulations easier to enforce as farmers often needed loans. But foremost the
certificate was a form of registration of cattle with the state that gave the state
certain kinds of powers, both legal and potentially supernatural, over the
livestock owner.

The individual in charge of issuing the certificate and keeping it up to date
was the dipping inspector or stock inspector. These inspectors were whites,
and many had grown up locally as the children of white farmers; they often
lacked the formal education to become magistrates, assistant magistrates,
clerks, policemen, or missionaries, and they lacked the money and the opportunity to become trading-store owners or small businessmen. Many were
barely literate and some were habitually drunk. They were frequently rude and
imperious in dealing with the African livestock owners or their herd boys who
brought the cattle to be dipped. The archives are littered with complaints
about individual inspectors. In Mount Fletcher District in 1914, the assistant
chief magistrate of the Transkei felt that discontent over dipping was in reality
discontent over a particular dipping supervisor:

> It appears that one Supervisor had been instructed to fill two tanks with
> a 14 day strength of dip, and, after filling the tanks, to bring the dip in to
> be tested. He disobeyed these instructions, and instead of sending in the
> dip, dipped the cattle, with the result that they were badly scalded and 50
> head have died, others being still in a bad way. The matter is under inves-
> tigation, the Supervisor has been dismissed, and so soon as the cattle still
> suffering are either dead or recovered the Magistrate will send in a
> report. This is a most regrettable incident and it has given dipping in that
> district a bad set back.[55]

Similar discontent over a particular inspector came to light in the midst of
some of the dipping-related unrest in Qumbu District in 1916. The Qumbu
magistrate wired, "My messenger reports no cause [for] alarm this district."
But, the magistrate noted (alarmingly) in the same wire that the messenger
"also reports all feeling and discontent appears to be confined only to area
under supervision of dipping supervisor Pearce who is harsh in the execution
of his duties and that they [local people] intend to kill him." The assistant
chief magistrate elaborated on this message: "Complaint against Pearce may

or may not be well-grounded and Mr. Moffat [the chief magistrate] will doubtless enquire into it on spot but is only fair to Pearce to bear in mind that [Mpondomise chief] Mkwenkwe's people are like their surroundings a wild lot and need firm handling."[56] In many districts, these inspectors were also in charge of collecting the tank tax and issuing receipts.

A similar pattern of discontent over the particular circumstances surrounding the enforcement of dipping regulations, rather than discontent directed against the white-controlled state as a whole, emerged in Mount Frere District in 1916. A policeman investigating the causes of unrest reported to his superior:

> It is therefore not the actual "Dipping" but the surrounding circumstances that have caused the present trouble. . . . There is no doubt that to the native mind the variety of charges for the use of the dip is a distinctly debatable matter and the reasons for the necessity is [sic] not clearly understood by numbers of them, indeed many natives do not hesitate to say that the local authorities "pocket" the difference, absurd conclusion to come to, but we are dealing with stock owners who have only the mind of a child and it is therefore necessary to avoid anything but simplicity.

Moreover, he said, Africans felt that they were being asked to expose their cattle to all the risks of dipping while local white farmers were not: "Again many natives assert that the Dipping law is not evenly administered as regards white and black stock owners. White stock owners may dip without supervision, frequently evade without prosecution, and when prosecuted have not to pay such heavy fines as the natives."[57] Once again white officials interpreted legitimate African grievances—this time over cattle dipping—to be the product of "childlike" minds and "absurd" rumors.

The combination of potentially harmful chemical dips, poorly constructed and maintained tanks, possibly debilitated or underweight cattle, poorly educated dipping supervisors who were less than dedicated to their jobs, and hostility and suspicion on all sides, led to an awful lot of dead or chemically scalded cattle, relatively little prevention of the spread of East Coast fever, and general dissatisfaction and bitterness among the African population.

On top of the discontent generated by the practice of dipping were the restrictions placed on the movement of cattle. In the first few years of the epidemic, the Umtata district magistrate described the effect that these restrictions had on the trade in cattle and on agriculture in general:

The only remunerative industries carried on by Natives in this district are those of agriculture and stock-raising, the former is, however, at present almost entirely directed to the supply of local wants only. The difficulties of transport being too serious to permit of any extension of external trade being carried on. With regard to the latter I should say that wool brings into the district cash or store goods to the value of £18000 to £20000 annually; and the trade in cattle represents many thousands of pounds. East Coast Fever restrictions have, however, for the time being almost entirely paralysed this latter.[58]

In 1909 the rail line did not yet extend into the Transkei—that would happen in 1912. The transport of agricultural goods was almost entirely dependent on ox wagons, and the East Coast fever restrictions prevented oxen from crossing out of the Transkei into the rest of the Cape Province or into Natal. In addition, the restrictions severely depressed the market in live cattle, making them less valuable as sale animals in the local market.

The restrictions themselves extended well into the 1920s, and their effects extended even longer. The magistrate of Nqamakwe District detailed what he saw as the long-term impact in his report to the Native Economic Commission of 1932:

It is well known that, prior to rinderpest, large numbers of Transkeian cattle were exported to Ciskeian farms and there fattened for a few months for sale as primes. This trade revived somewhat after rinderpest, but ceased entirely when East Coast Fever broke out. Were such a market available now [in the 1930s], I would have no cattle fit to be fattened up as primes, their frames having deteriorated deplorably. In my opinion this is due to inbreeding enforced by the severe restrictions upon the movements of cattle, as well as to the lessened grazing. . . . The conclusion that the grazing has depreciated considerably, and at an increasing rate per annum, is inevitable.[59]

Thus the problem of too many scrubby cattle grazing too little land was caused more by the government restrictions surrounding the East Coast fever epidemic than it was by African cultural ideas about cattle.[60]

East Coast fever and the government restrictions undercut the rural economy just as it had been rebounding from rinderpest. Some government officials were not sorry that Africans were watching their wealth die on a daily basis, as this made it more likely that they would leave the rural areas in search of employment. The chief magistrate in 1911 commented wryly on such official heartlessness: "Nineteen of the twenty nine districts of the Transkeian Territories have now received what a recent Commission terms that 'blessing in disguise'—east coast fever. The disguise could scarcely have been improved upon." He went on to emphasize the degree of its economic impact: "For the whole system of transport in a thickly populated country . . . to be dislocated for a period of two years with every hampering restriction; for the currency of the people—as cattle are to the Native—to be disorganised, the passage of gold from hand to hand, the payment of every kind of debt to be subjected to meticulous investigation and 'the law of permits' . . . for crushing loss to follow upon all these: such has been the disguise. One theory after another has crumbled away and no preventive has prevented."

Still, he noted that despite the futility of government policies designed to halt the spread of the disease, including the killing of sick animals, as of 1911 Africans seemed to bear the state no ill will: "Long lines of fencing have been put in hand and the disease has crossed at the end first finished before the other [end] was approached. Zones supposed to be neutral [disease free] proved most partial; guards stopped everything but the tick and the bullet stopped nothing but the cow. The Natives bore the painful and useless surgery of the 'stamping out' process, which they never believed in, with a fortitude beyond praise, though some were so deeply moved that they declined the scanty compensation offered."[61]

The wave of destruction of dipping tanks that erupted in several districts from 1914 through 1916 should be discussed in this context of deepening economic crisis, continuing livestock losses, and heightened resentment against the ways in which dipping regulations and the culling of diseased animals were enforced. Dipping tanks were destroyed in Matatiele, Nqamakwe, and Tsomo Districts. In Matatiele telegraph lines and trading stores were looted as well in December 1915. Mount Frere trading stores had previously been looted in December 1914, and disturbances over dipping broke out in late 1916 with one white person killed. In addition, there was unrest and repeated rumors of impending revolt in Mount Fletcher District.[62] Looking specifically at some of the grievances expressed during this unrest will give us some indication of the complexity of its origins.

In Matatiele District in 1914 the chief magistrate and assistant chief magistrate of the Transkei (W. T. Brownlee and W. P. Leary, respectively) met with local headmen and residents and with Colonel Walter Stanford, the recent Secretary for Native Affairs. Africans attending did not all speak with one voice. Joseph Lupindo started the meeting with a slightly conciliatory note:

> We are glad to see you here today. Col. Stanford I was with you during the Boer War. Some of us have grievances re dipping. We are poor and have nothing and to dip requires money. There is famine amongst us as well and sickness and we live unhappy. The Government promised us assistance with the disease (E.C.F.) that was approaching. Our late Mr. Leary [W. P. Leary was their previous magistrate] gave us the assurance that before he left the District dipping was not compulsory. This dipping has now been forced on us.[63]

Lupindo's narrative followed the conventional public transcript of how African subjects should address colonial officials. He reminded the white officials that he had been loyal and had fought on the side of the colonial state during the Boer War, thus establishing that he was not against the state per se but was against the policy of dipping. He recalled his personal connections with Walter Stanford and W. P. Leary to ask current state officials to live up to their promises and to ease the dipping policy.

Lupindo's criticism of the policy may have been muted, but others voiced their grievances more directly. After thanking the chief magistrate for coming to hear their complaints, a man named Zondeki pointedly remarked, "People have their complaint against the General Rate. . . . We were not advised by our Headmen that Cattle Tanks were being built. We were told nothing. This dipping is unbearable. The sheep dipping is also a heavy burden. We can't get our cattle out to sell it. Our children are starving."[64] Zondeki's remarks are stark and unembellished by statements of loyalty or elaborate shows of submission. Not only was dipping a policy forced on them by an uncommunicative state, it was cutting into rural incomes and harming the welfare of children. His statement was the hidden transcript coming out into the open.

Another Matatiele resident, Willem Nyakanoko, summed up local sentiment and tied together many grievances over government policies. First, he criticized the Glen Grey Act and the way it was being forced on them despite local opposition:

> We were told that the Bunga [General Council] would be beneficial to us. But we considered this and we find that we cannot afford to pay for the Bunga. . . . A meeting was called here last year and our Magistrate told us that Government is requesting that General Rate be paid and our Magistrate told us that with seven [word illegible] we will have to pay. We obeyed and paid our rates [taxes]. We did not accept the Bunga. If it

was accepted it was [only] by the Chiefs. We are the children of the
Government and why are we called another nation[?]

With the latter remark, he seemed to be asking why Africans in rural areas were
being forced into a separate form of governmental representation. He sharply
criticized both dipping and the lack of official response to African objections:
"We told our Headman Ntebe that we refused to dip and that he must represent the matter to the Magistrate. There is no reply forthcoming. And we
expect a reply today." After this abrupt pronouncement, he explicitly compared government policy during the rinderpest epidemic with government
policy during East Coast fever: "During Rinderpest time Government made it
optional to our people as to whether we inoculate or not. These people who say
they welcome dipping are hypocrites. We all object to dipping. . . . This year
new regulations came saying . . . that we had to use Cooper's Dip. Why are the
Government killing us[?] Why can't we use our own dip[?]" He then brought
together the issue of dipping, quarantines and tax payments, and the bind that
government regulations had placed on African farmers: "Some of us have not
paid our General Rate and being in quarantine we cannot sell our cattle to pay
the Rate. We paid £550 to the Attorneys [to fight the dipping regulations]. . . .
In regard to the [looted] Shops we are sad about this. We don't know this dis-
turbance. In regard to dips [dipping tanks] that have been blown up some of
us know nothing about it. Our tank is still intact."[65]

The speaker was perhaps being disingenuous about not knowing who had
committed the looting and tank destruction, although many African farmers
relied on the shops to market their goods and probably deplored their destruction. However, the more interesting point is that the farmers hired attorneys,
at considerable expense, to fight the dipping regulations. This suggests that
they did not see the judicial system as implicated in the oppressive policies, and
they believed the law would actually vindicate them. More generally, it suggests
that Africans were not against the state per se; rather they opposed particular
policies and officials, even in the context of an agricultural crisis and sporadic
acts of unrest. The hidden transcript was full of criticisms of policy and of
official attitudes, but it was not yet scripting outright rebellion.

Walter Stanford, commenting on the meeting and the generalized unrest
over dipping in the district, warned administrators about the new trend in governing the Transkei. He too contrasted the policies surrounding East Coast
fever with those implemented in 1897: "When Rinderpest broke out in 1897,
Major Sir Henry Elliot then Chief Magistrate of Tembuland and the Transkei,
and I as Chief Magistrate of Griqualand East, successfully opposed the policy

of shooting the cattle; and later, when inoculation was introduced, we again resisted an endeavour to make inoculation compulsory." Stanford acknowledged that there were real inequities in the way that the East Coast fever restrictions were enforced, "I may here add that in the district of Matatiele European farmers with few exceptions are not dipping their cattle weekly or even fortnightly. This the Natives know." And Stanford concluded by suggesting both more lenient implementation of the regulations on dipping and cattle quarantines and by harking back to an earlier period of more personalized rule over Africans:

> In the Transkeian Territories we have a Native population of approximately a million souls. The large majority are still living under tribal conditions. . . . The personal influence and guidance of the Chief Magistrate and Magistrates are essential factors in their contentment. They regard these officers not merely as the judicial authority before whom their cases must be heard or the collectors of revenue to whom taxes must be paid, they are also representatives of that far away undefined power known to them as the Government, and the Magistrates are their channel of communication, and should be their friends and protectors. Yet more and more the territories are being administered as if they were European districts occupied by a highly civilized European race. The Magistrate's power for good is constantly undermined. Officers of various Departments abound, each responsible to some other officer stationed at Pretoria or elsewhere and unknown to the people.

He feared that the loss of the personal relationship between the magistrates and Africans would result in the erosion of state authority:

> These numerous [state] officers are in constant contact with Native life . . . but they do not all show consideration for the Natives in dealing with them. And yet if the Natives appeal to the Magistrate for assistance or sympathy, they find the man whom they regarded as their Chief unable to intervene. . . . Thus the Natives are bewildered. They have many masters—or many tyrants as possibly they may regard them—and no protector on the spot to given them aid. So they fall at times into the hands of bad advisers and mischief results.[66]

Stanford, veteran of the 1880 Mpondomise Rebellion, was trying to reinstate the lessons learned thirty-four years before—Africans were conservative,

TABLE 3.2 Percentage of Hut Tax Unpaid, Selected Districts, 1909–22

Year	Bizana	Engcobo	Matatiele	Mt. Fletcher	Tsolo	Umtata	Total Transkei*
1909	0	8.14	0.37	15.91	4.28	4.83	9.58
1911	0.41	5.27	0	10.19	5.41	4.95	6.58
1912	0.36	5.44	1.55	11.44	2.11	4.91	5.25
1913	1.38	5.06	3.44	10.57	1.86	4.06	5.45
1914	3.58	6.94	5.96	14.22	1.34	4.28	6.26
1915	7.58	4.08	13.82	17.53	4.06	10.39	9.59
1916	16.68	4.37	22.27	15.64	4.88	16.79	11.74
1918	36.70	5.88	24.43	21.62	11.88	9.86	18.73
1919	38.80	9.08	26.63	23.36	8.78	12.42	17.19
1920	40.30	12.33	29.10	17.52	8.97	16.98	18.63
1922	9.70	13.06	27.61	25.26	16.40	61.20**	20.04

Source: CMT 3/611, file 50.7, "Statement of Hut Tax and General Rate Collected and Outstanding," for all districts, all years 1909–22, with the exception of 1910, 1917, and 1921 figures, which were unavailable.

*Figures in the Total Transkei column are the mean for all twenty-nine districts, not just for those selected here.

**In 1921 the Glen Grey Act was extended to Umtata District, meaning that most homestead heads switched from paying hut tax to quitrent. The figure here includes only hut tax.

easily misled children who needed the guidance and protection of paternalistic state officials. However, he acknowledged the legitimacy of the grievances expressed by African cattle owners and concurred that new regulations and officials were overly harsh and unresponsive to local conditions.

Yet in spite of the horrible economic effects of East Coast fever, most Africans continued to pay their taxes, including the new taxes levied in several districts. As can be seen from table 3.2, there was no strict correlation between years in which there was active unrest and an increase in default rates on hut taxes. Matatiele District did show a dramatic increase in outstanding hut tax between 1914 and 1915 and again between 1915 and 1916, the same years in which dipping-related violence occurred. Mount Fletcher District, however, had already had a relatively high rate of defaults for a number of years, and no massive increases appeared from 1914 through 1916. In contrast, Bizana District did have a massive increase in the default rate, especially after 1916, but did not see any active unrest in this period. All the Transkeian districts taken together saw a fairly steady trend toward increases in the default rate on hut tax, but the overall percentage of hut tax unpaid remained relatively low in 1922 at about 20 percent, although the impact of the lost wages as a result of the temporary closing of the gold mines because of the 1922 Rand Revolt did accelerate the default rate.

The default rate on hut tax payments, however, did tend to go up as the absolute amount of taxes demanded by the state increased.[67] The imposition of the General Rate on all men over age eighteen who were not paying hut tax or quitrent, and the transition in some districts to the quitrent system under the Glen Grey Act, increased the total amount that families had to pay in taxes and related expenses. In the first year of the quitrent system, for example, the head of a family had to pay a substantial (one time only) survey fee. As the Umtata district magistrate noted in 1921, "In spite of the increase in outstanding [taxes owed] for hut tax and general rate the amount of taxation contributed by Natives has not decreased. The large amounts paid for Survey fees have no doubt reduced the capacity of Natives to pay their annual taxes as readily as in previous years."[68]

Overall, the amount of outstanding tax payments increased substantially between 1915 and 1918 in eleven districts of Pondoland and East Griqualand (including Bizana, Flagstaff, Libode, Lusikisiki, Matatiele, Mount Ayliff, Mount Fletcher, Mount Frere, Ngqeleni, Port St. Johns, and Tsolo), while it actually declined in other districts. The chief magistrate believed that the increase in tax defaults in Matatiele and Mount Fletcher might well be the result of "dissatisfaction with Government," but for the other districts, he thought it just as likely that shortages of staff, faulty tax rolls, and poor agricultural years accounted for the high number of defaults.[69]

The compulsory dipping of cattle and other East Coast fever regulations were the most urgent source of dissatisfaction. But there were also a number of rumors and disturbances surrounding Britain's and South Africa's involvement in the First World War. In 1914 an African reported to the magistrate of Harding District, which bordered the Transkei in Natal, that discontent over the imposition of the General Rate was simmering throughout the population:

> At Lusikisiki I was told by two Natives . . . that Marelane, the paramount chief in Pondoland, had called a large meeting of Natives and had discussed the Government's proposal of raising the hut tax from 10/- [ten shillings] to £1 for married men, [and] the levying of a tax of 10/- on unmarried men. He told the meeting that he had refused to allow this tax to be levied and that if Government enforced it blood would be spilt. . . . They also told me that the news was all round the country that a German impi [army regiment] would eat its Xmas dinner at Kokstad [in East Griqualand].[70]

But this incident never developed into any form of armed resistance, even though tax payments declined. When the Lusikisiki District magistrate questioned Chief Marelane about this rumor, Marelane essentially stated that it was ridiculous and that he would never try to engage in armed warfare against the government. He admitted that he was against the new taxes but noted that he had already expressed his people's feelings to various officials and that he was satisfied with their response.[71] In short, Chief Marelane was eager to keep the hidden transcript hidden and to reaffirm the public transcript of submission to colonial authority, at least while the authorities' eyes were on him.

The messenger of the court (who was technically in charge of notifying taxpayers of their arrears and of collecting arrears) in Lusikisiki District gave the district magistrate his own explanation for why hut taxes and General Rate were being poorly paid in that district in the between 1915 and 1920:

> I arrived here in September 1915 and found the natives of this district were in a very poverty-stricken condition. East Coast Fever had in 1912 wiped out practically all their cattle, following that came a starvation and in 1915 horse-sickness killed almost every horse in the District and the natives were solely dependent on what they could earn outside the District to pay for their taxes and food. During the 1917–1918 summer

they lost heavily in small stock, on account of too much rain. In 1918 came the influenza epidemic just at the ploughing season, and being unable to plough, they realised a very small crop, totally insufficient to allow them to sell any to raise the money for their taxes; and they were again faced with starvation during the 1919–1920 season on account of the drought, the first rains arriving only in January.[72]

The explanation he provided was very common throughout the Transkei. East Coast fever had killed a large number of cattle, and related quarantines had rendered the remainder virtually unmarketable. On top of that economic blow came repeated weather-related problems that were made worse by the influenza epidemic of 1918.

The so-called Spanish flu hit most rural districts of the Transkei as well as the rest of South Africa in October and November 1918. In Umtata District, with an overall population of forty-six thousand people, at least ten thousand were ill with the disease, and there were an estimated eleven to twelve hundred deaths.[73] Magistrates throughout the Transkei blamed the epidemic for the immediate economic decline in their districts and the accompanying drop in the ability of Africans to pay their taxes.[74] The timing of the epidemic prevented people from adequately plowing and tending their fields and so decreased the harvest of the following year. Over the next two years, moreover, there was a severe drought in the region, as well as a decline in world market prices for the wool and grain produced. At the same time, East Coast fever quarantines and restrictions were still in place, reducing the value of what cattle remained because of the impossibility of getting them to market.

Knowing that people had no money with which to pay their taxes, magistrates throughout the Transkei between 1918 and 1920 period tended to treat defaulters with leniency. This attitude was very much in keeping with administrative practices from 1880 through 1897. However, as the administration of all the Native Reserves throughout the Union was consolidated in the late 1910s and 1920s, upper-level officials of the Native Affairs Department became less patient with the methods of the Transkei administration's old hands.[75] They derided the Transkei system as too permissive and cited the relative ease with which people could evade taxes from year to year as proof of the lack of control magistrates had over their districts. The commissioner for inland revenue (in charge of all tax collection nationwide) began harassing individual magistrates to increase pressure on African farmers to pay their overdue taxes.[76]

This attitude confirmed the ascendance of "scientific management" and "efficiency" as it applied to governance in general, but particularly as it applied

to governing Africans.[77] It also presaged what was to become the central contradiction in the policy of the Native Affairs Department in succeeding gener-
ations: if magistrates began to bring tax defaulters to court, sometimes seizing
livestock and revoking quitrent titles, they would begin to drive people out of
the rural areas and into the cities. The people driven out would not just be
young African men looking for paid employment but would represent a broad
cross-section of African society, including women, children, and the very old.
Thus if magistrates and police enforced the tax laws strictly, they helped to
enlarge a more-or-less permanent urban African population living in the
major cities as well as in smaller towns; this urbanized population would
require both permanent housing and social services and would eventually (and
sooner rather than later) lose familial, cultural, and political ties to the rural
areas.[78] This potential outcome flew directly in the face of the desires of upper-
level administrators and white legislators, whose segregationist wishes were
best expressed in the passage of the 1923 Natives (Urban) Areas Act.[79] The act
deemed all municipal areas to be white; it officially designated Africans as temporary "sojourners"—nonresidents—in urban areas, there for the sole purpose of engaging in short-term wage labor for white employers before they
"returned home" to the rural areas.[80] For this contradiction, not even a state
thought to have magical powers could devise a lasting solution.

The period from 1897 to 1920 was one of repeated natural disasters whose
effects were often exacerbated by political events (the implementation of the
Glen Grey Act and the creation of the Union of South Africa), by aggressive
attempts to forestall disasters (East Coast fever restrictions), by the imposition
of higher taxes on Africans, and by broader social and economic trends (the
industrialization of South Africa and efforts to create systematic urban segregation). The rinderpest epidemic of 1897, the first in a line of natural disasters,
was not a deathblow to independent African agriculture, because Africans were
at least partially successful in rebuilding their herds after rinderpest. Instead, it
was the effects of East Coast fever and, even more important, the restrictions
imposed by the government to try to prevent its spread that combined with the
implementation of the Glen Grey Act and the imposition of new taxes to
impoverish people who had once had hopes of reestablishing themselves as
independent farmers and to render them landless as well as stockless and
increasingly defenseless against a state that they believed to be malevolent.

   The period beginning with the imposition of East Coast fever restrictions in
1909 was a break with the past. Officials of the Native Affairs Department
became more overtly and routinely intrusive in rural Africans' lives. Policies

designed from a public health template aimed to coerce Africans, ostensibly for their own good, to dip their cattle and not sell them into a broader market. The implementation of these official policies to halt the spread of East Coast fever ultimately failed. However, officials only rarely acknowledged the limitations of the policies themselves and more often blamed the failures on Africans as inferior farmers who did not understand modern farming methods and who were irrationally attached to their cattle.[81] The policies were extraordinarily successful, though, in souring African attitudes toward official attempts to "improve" agriculture, and in depriving African farmers of a market for their livestock and agricultural produce, thus impoverishing them further.[82]

Schemes to combat East Coast fever were not designed by white policymakers with the express purpose of crippling African agriculture. Instead, the imposition of these restrictions more clearly reflected the influence of public-health thinking—with all the coercion, pseudoscience, dictatorial paternalism, and elements of the "sanitation syndrome" that that entailed[83]—on agricultural policy. From their point of view, white policymakers destroyed African agriculture in order to save it. At the same time, they cemented the foundations of the migrant labor system by making it more likely that African men would leave the rural areas in search of wage-earning jobs to supplement declining incomes from their farms.[84]

Africans held onto their dwindling farms and deteriorating cattle not just because they valued rural life and had a culture that invested that life with rich meanings but also because they were hemmed in by regulations and ensnared by rituals of rule and beliefs in the malevolent powers of the state. Occasionally vocal in criticizing colonial policies, Africans in this period up to 1920 rarely threw the public transcript of deference to colonial authority out the window. The public transcript was declining in usefulness but it still had some meaning for both sides.

CHAPTER 4

GOVERNING THE ZULU BY KILLING THEM

Poll Tax and the Bambatha Rebellion in Natal and Zululand

In 1904 the former Secretary for Native Affairs for Natal Colony, J. W. Shepstone (the brother of the founder of the Natal system of African administration, Theophilus Shepstone) testified to the South African Native Affairs Commission. He told what he thought was a humorous story from many years before about the views of the precolonial Zulu king Mpande on ruling the Zulu:

> Old Umpande [*sic*] asked me one day when we were together, "What are you going to do with all the abatakati [witches] that go to you?" I said, "Of course we will let them live under us." He said, "you do not kill?" I said, "No, unless a man kills another man, and then he is killed." He replied—of course it was an Irishism—"You cannot govern a Zulu except by killing him; the only way to govern a Zulu is to kill him."[1]

Within two years of Shepstone's telling, events would have robbed the story of its humor: with the help of firepower undreamed of by Mpande, the colony of Natal found itself doing precisely what the king had suggested—"governing" the Zulu by killing them.

What became known as the Bambatha Rebellion is one of the best-known episodes of revolt against a colonial or settler state over taxes. The revolt resulted from the imposition and collection of a new tax in Natal Colony, the

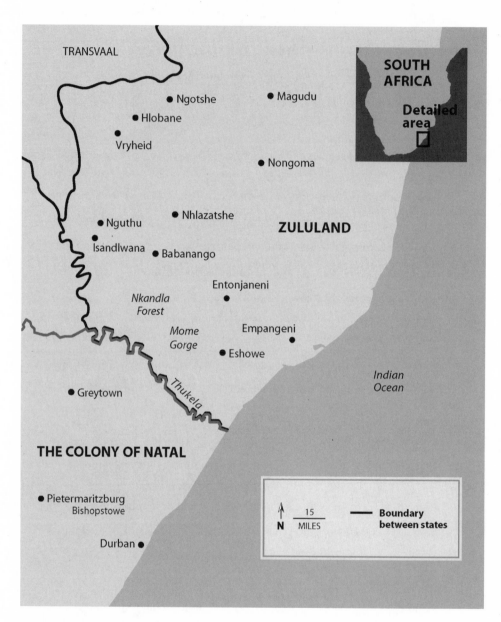

MAP 4.1. Natal and Zululand, ca. 1906.

poll tax (or head tax), similar to the General Rate that was at the same time being gradually imposed in the Transkei. While there were rumors of unrest and some dissent in the Transkei at the time of the imposition of the General Rate in a few districts in 1906–7, there was no active unrest and there was no organized boycott of tax payments. The revolt in Natal stands in contrast to events in the Transkei and thus deserves some analysis in any attempt to discuss taxation as an integral ritual of state control in South Africa.[2]

The immediate background to this violent outbreak began in late January 1906, when Natal's administrators began to collect the newly imposed poll tax from adult unmarried men. Many Zulu-speaking people and chiefs had verbally protested the new tax, to no effect.[3] For months there had been rumors among whites and Africans of an impending uprising. Many Africans began killing their white chickens and pigs, allegedly because of a belief that, if they did not do so, a coming thunder and lightning storm would destroy both people and property. White people saw this killing of white animals as a direct threat to themselves and fearfully—or in some cases belligerently—awaited events.[4]

On the first day of tax collection in Empangeni District, fifteen hundred African men, including four chiefs and six *induna*s (or headmen) were, in the words of a police sergeant, "exceedingly insolent and disrespectful to the Magistrate and when remonstrated with they shouted their war cry 'Usutu' twice in defiance of Magistrate and Court officials." Although most of the men present that day had with them sufficient money to pay the poll tax, none paid. When they left the magistrate's office, their leaders went to speak with Dinuzulu, the hereditary but officially unrecognized king of the Zulu, possibly to ask his advice.[5] At another collection site, in Mapumulo District, a group of a hundred or so men also refused to pay their taxes and threatened the magistrate.

On 8 February the magistrate of Umgeni District also met with resistance in collecting the poll tax. That evening, a small party of police (including two African constables) arrived at the homestead of the man accused of instigating the resistance in Umgeni District. When the leader of the police party, Hunt, tried to arrest one of the men, Mjongo, a brief but deadly fray ensued, resulting in the deaths of Hunt and another white officer as well as of at least one of the Africans who had refused to pay the tax. Mjongo, a member of a separatist (African-led) Christian church, later told administrator and historian James Stuart of the "miraculous" event he witnessed at the time of the attack: "The instant the firing [of guns] started, I saw a ball of fire fall from the sky to earth, near where the fighting was going on. It was so brilliant that a darkness arose after it. . . . In size, this ball was about 9 or 10 in. in diameter. . . . It was in no way connected with revolver or rifle fire. . . . The ball fell to earth and disappeared immediately."[6] The rebellion had begun.

In retribution for the two policemen's deaths, for almost two months Natal's (largely white) armed forces burned Africans' crops, razed their homesteads and stole their cattle. By late March, Natal officials were satisfied that they had crushed the rebellion, but, in actuality, it was only beginning. In Umvoti District, the minor chief Bambatha, whose name would later personify the revolt, had been having his own personal troubles with the law; he was also heavily in debt and a defendant in several civil cases. Earlier, at the time of the initial poll tax collection in his district, Bambatha had counseled against outright rebellion and had himself paid his taxes.[7] But because of Bambatha's legal difficulties, the white magistrate of his district fired him from his position as chief in early April, and Bambatha later retaliated by firing a weapon at him. In doing so, Bambatha reignited the rebellion and then went into hiding.[8]

Bambatha, on the run, also went to consult with Dinuzulu, trying to receive Dinuzulu's blessing for his rebellious acts. Dinuzulu was, by his own testimony, formally correct but personally cold to Bambatha, whom he had never before met. Dinuzulu was equally cold to Bambatha's suggestions that Dinuzulu use his authority as king to call the Zulu regiments into rebellion. However, Dinuzulu did allow part of Bambatha's family to remain as his guests for several months.[9] Both whites and Africans (for a time) saw this hospitality as evidence of Dinuzulu's tacit support for the rebellion.

With or without Dinuzulu's support, Bambatha proceeded to raise a small army of his own and then based the army in the forested Nkandla mountains, in the Zululand region. Significantly, Nkandla contained the grave of Dinuzulu's father, Cetshwayo, who was the last Zulu king to lead the regiments into battle during the Anglo-Zulu War (1879–82).[10] From this stronghold, Bambatha's army engaged in a number of skirmishes with Natal troops, with few African casualties. But on 10 June at Mome Gorge in the Nkandla forest, Bambatha, most of his fellow leaders, and many of the Zulu army were killed by Natal troops, and the disturbances again appeared to be over.[11]

A little over a week later, however, a new outbreak occurred in Mapumulo District in Natal—the site of the initial resistance to hut tax collection several months earlier—with ambushes of white traders and troop convoys.[12] Natal troops poured into the district and, using the most brutal methods available, suppressed the rebellion. By the end of 1907 the fighting was finally over, and the Colony was busy court-martialing rebels and confiscating their property.[13] Three to four thousand Africans and about thirty whites were dead. The widespread white belief that only Dinuzulu could have orchestrated a revolt on such a level resulted in his arrest and trial for high treason.[14] Dinuzulu was later acquitted of having encouraged or participated in the rebellion, although he was convicted of having sheltered the family of Bambatha during the rebellion, as well as of owning unregistered firearms.[15] Dinuzulu was imprisoned for four years and subsequently banished from Natal; he died in exile in 1913.

The Bambatha Revolt was directly sparked by the imposition of the poll tax on Africans, but scholars studying it have often come to disparate conclusions as to other causes, the revolt's timing, and the scattered participation of Africans in the revolt. The significant questions include: What was the connection between the revolt and the supernatural beliefs, prophecies, and visions that preceded and accompanied it? Why did the acts of rebellion occur in three distinct phases, beginning in February in Natal, then in April through mid-June in Zululand—the phase actually led by Bambatha—and ending in June and July in Natal? Finally, why, if widespread material grievances were the prime cause of the rebellion, did relatively few Africans take up arms?

Because historians have often neglected a discussion of beliefs in the supernatural, their explanations for the outbreak of revolt have depended heavily on an analysis of material grievances.[16] There is, however, an enormous difficulty in locating all the causes of the revolt in material grievances. Although most of Natal's and Zululand's Africans suffered deprivation at the hands of white settlers, only a very small proportion of the population actually revolted. Material grievances were undoubtedly an underlying cause, but they cannot have been the only cause.[17]

The earliest historian of the rebellion, James Stuart—a white official in Natal at the time of the rebellion—offered a broader explanation of causes. He described and then criticized the way in which most whites at the time viewed the rebellion: "Such conflict was, of course, between a race of savages on the one hand, and a number of Europeans or representatives of Western Civilization on the other."[18] Stuart, a fluent speaker of Zulu and an avid collector of African oral history, was sympathetic to some African grievances, which he carefully discussed. These included long-standing competition between Africans and white settlers over land and the rough treatment of all Africans, rebel or not, by Natal troops during the suppression of the rebellion.[19] Yet Stuart's principal conclusion was that the relatively small number of Zulu who took up arms against the state did so as a result of "the introduction and imposition on the aborigines [the Zulu] of a type of civilization radically different from their own."[20] This conclusion looks very similar to the conclusions reached by Walter Stanford and other Cape officials in the wake of the 1880

Mpondomise Rebellion in the Transkei—that Africans were culturally conservative and could be driven into revolt by rapid change. If anything, though, Stuart was even more culturally conservative than Stanford: in the category of influences that precipitated the revolt, Stuart included missionary activity and the systems of migrant labor and white land ownership, all of which tended to undermine precolonial social and economic structures. Moreover, Stuart was very suspicious of Christian Africans, especially members of separatist churches, and felt that they, like Mjongo who participated in the resistance in Umgeni District, were troublemakers. These Africans, for Stuart, represented an unhealthy hybridization of African and European culture that could only result in social unrest. He was also strongly critical of Natal's move away from the old paternalist policies of African administration, and he was an advocate of a strict form of segregation based on indirect rule through African chiefs; this strategy he hoped would avoid cultural hybridization and its political dangers.[21] In preferring these policies, Stuart explicitly disapproved of many administrative changes that were taking place at the turn of the century that made it more difficult for Africans to remain on the land as farmers and also made it difficult for them to remain in extended, patriarchal families. In addition to the broader social and cultural causes, Stuart also saw Dinuzulu as an active instigator of the rebellion, despite the findings of the colonial court that had acquitted him of such a charge. According to Stuart, Dinuzulu's motivation was to remedy the Zulus' degradation at the hands of the British imperial government after the Zulus' defeat in the Anglo-Zulu War.[22]

Stuart was an influential administrator, although he never held Natal's highest office, secretary for native affairs.[23] His analysis of the revolt, because it criticized many aspects of the administration, challenged the mainstream policies developed by white officials who set about to govern the Zulu—perhaps without killing them—after crushing the rebels and the Zulu king Dinuzulu. But Stuart was also significant because he collected a number of oral histories from Zulu-speaking Africans both before and after the rebellion. His archived interviews provide African voices, even if those voices were transcribed—and filtered—by himself as an employee of the colonial state.[24] The voices furnish a glimpse into the debates current within Zulu society before and after the revolt and show that some of the same divisions that existed within African society in the Transkei were also dividing Africans in Natal and Zululand.[25] In particular, African families in Natal and Zululand were under strain as rinderpest had killed the majority of cattle in the 1890s, thus undercutting (as in the Transkei) the social system as well as depriving people of their wealth. As in the Transkei, some African farmers had been able to restock with animals captured during the South African War, but areas of Natal and Zululand saw fighting in the war and had their farms disrupted and their livestock seized or killed. Young men were traveling to find jobs, and the money they earned allowed them to escape the control of their parents; at the same time they were facing an uncertain future as farmers. These circumstances threatened the African family over the long term and created a great deal of social anxiety as well as economic deprivation.

Other contemporary African voices are available from the records of magistrates in Natal and Zululand. These documents often demonstrate the same tensions between the public transcript of submission to colonial authority and the hidden transcript of dissent or rebellious thoughts that exist in similar documents from the Transkei. The topic of rebellious thoughts brings us back, as it did in the Transkei, to the widespread beliefs in the supernatural and the ways in which many Africans fused those beliefs with their interpretations of colonial power. The rumors leading up to the Bambatha Revolt of the need to slaughter white animals and to purify homesteads—and by extension to purify all of African society—strongly suggest that Africans were appealing to elements of their belief in supernatural powers to help them understand their colonization as well as to overturn it.

Taxation and economic and political grievances were inextricably bound up with these supernatural beliefs, which were not, therefore, only an attempt to restore a preindustrial or precolonial worldview. The beliefs in the supernatural and the rebels' aspirations were not evidence of backwardness, as James Stuart might have suggested, but rather as critical testimony about people's perspective concerning the rightness of rebelling and the chances for the rebellion's success.

What follows will not be an exhaustive study of Zulu or Natal history.[26] Instead it will be a targeted attempt to discuss some of the motives behind the Bambatha Rebellion, including a discussion of how reactions to taxes may have emerged from various African worldviews. It is the cultural and social meanings of people's interactions with the state that may help us understand why some Africans revolted following the imposition of poll tax and some did not. It may also help us understand why some Zulu speakers revolted when Transkeian Africans, under similar circumstances and with similar grievances, did not. Finally, it will give us greater insight into the ways in which supernatural powers and material circumstances were part of a developing narrative of colonial power in South Africa.

THE DECLINE OF PATERNALISM

Africans living in the area that became the province of Natal in the Union of South Africa had a long history with white settlers and white officials, dating back to the first sustained interactions with white traders in the 1820s and extending into the widespread intrusion of white settlers in the region from the 1830s onward. African interactions with whites were by no means always peaceful, but they were also by no means always dominated by whites. In fact, a good deal of the interactions between Zulu speakers and whites in the nineteenth century were at least partly derived from political rivalries within the Zulu state.[27] Whites also had their own political rivalries in which Africans played only minor roles, especially between British administrators and Afrikaner (Boer) settlers.[28] But it is significant that at the time that Great Britain took control over the small white settler area of Natal in 1847, the Zulu state, based in adjacent Zululand, was independent; only those Africans who lived in Natal proper were incorporated into colonial society and governed by the colonial state. Over the next fifty years, Natal's "native" administration, under its first self-styled supreme chief, Theophilus Shepstone, eroded the autonomy of the chiefs in both Natal and Zululand. Britain sapped that autonomy further in the course of the Anglo-Zulu War, when it manipulated King Cetshwayo into declaring war, then defeated the Zulu army and ended by fanning the flames of rivalry among the various chiefs into a civil war that engulfed the Zulu state, thus leaving Cetshwayo's controversial heir, Dinuzulu, with a gutted political inheritance.[29]

In Natal after 1847, the colonial administration pioneered an early version of "indirect rule" that was somewhat different than the administration of the Transkeian Territories after 1882.[30] As in the Transkei, chiefs who were willing to cooperate with the administration retained their title and some of their power in return for a small stipend, while the administration partly paid for itself by imposing a hut tax. In Natal, however, white administrators typically allowed chiefs and headmen (or indunas) to continue to exercise some of their precolonial powers, and there was a concerted attempt to discourage many influences that might undermine those powers.

As in the Transkei, the hut tax formed the basis for collecting revenue from Africans. In Natal the hut tax was payable by married African men at a rate of seven shillings per year per wife—again based on the common practice of each wife having her own hut—but in Natal all dwelling huts were taxable.[31] As a result, an adult man usually owed hut tax for each wife as well as a hut tax for any hut set aside for the use of adolescents. The hut tax met with little to no resistance from Africans when collections began in Natal in 1850.[32] Tax payments were tied to access to farm and grazing land, and people did not wish to lose that access. In addition, Zulu-speaking Africans had a comparable precolonial history of paying some tribute to their chiefs, and the tax payments to the colonial state replaced the tribute. A substantial historical difference from Africans in the Transkei was that Africans living in the white settler area of Natal often had moved there because they desired to live outside the control of the still independent Zulu state. They were refugees and the descendants of refugees from the wars that had initially established the Zulu state or from the conflicts that grew out of various succession crises. At the time of the original collection of hut tax, therefore, Africans residing in white-settler Natal most likely had a relatively benign view of paying the tax. This willingness to pay on the part of Natal-based Africans continued even after the government's unilateral decision to double the hut tax, to fourteen shillings, in 1875.[33] White settlers had pressured the government to increase the tax in the hopes of forcing more Africans into wage labor (at low wages) on white-owned farms; the administration had long resisted this pressure because of a fear that Africans would challenge a new tax and undermine Natal's social stability.[34]

Natal Africans paid additional taxes not paid by Transkeian Africans. They were liable for a dog tax (five shillings per dog), and young men could be compelled to work on roads (road-party work, or *isibhalo*) at a below-market wage, a duty that was widely considered by both Africans and whites as a form of taxation.[35] Until 1875, Africans had also had to pay a marriage tax of five pounds (which had been payable as a one-time fee upon marriage), but when the hut tax was increased the marriage tax was abolished to forestall any adverse African reaction. At that time Theophilus Shepstone—in his role as supreme chief—made a promise to Natal's Africans that taxes would never again be increased.[36]

When the Anglo-Zulu War ended and the British imperial government took control over Zululand in 1887, Africans there also began paying the hut tax and became liable for other taxes as well. Natal Colony subsequently annexed Zululand in 1897 and took responsibility for its administration. At the time of the first hut tax collection in Zululand, the colonial administration made no promises about future tax increases, but it did promise not to expropriate any more land from the Zulu.[37]

When Zululand Africans began paying taxes in 1887, they were in a different position than were Natal's Africans in 1850. Although Zululand had been politically independent, many of its inhabitants (particularly younger men) had already been migrating to urban centers in search of wage labor. Labor migration increased after the discovery of gold on the Witwatersrand in 1886. White traders were already established throughout Zululand, selling a wide range of goods, usually for hard cash. Few missionaries had ventured into Zululand because of the overt hostility of most Zulu chiefs to Christianity as an ideology;

chiefs also disliked the missionaries because of the mission stations' well-known tendency to attract people trying to avoid the discipline of either the chief or the head of the family. Small groups of Christian Africans, including adherents to separatist churches, did exist, however.[38] Moreover, Zululand's Africans had recently been defeated in a major war, and they were still engaged in an intense and violent civil conflict over which chiefs should retain title and which of the descendants of Shaka's house should be his heir. In short, although many Africans may have resented the hut tax and the overlordship of the colonial state, they were in a weak position to mount any unified resistance against that state.[39]

Although all Africans in the newly annexed Zululand (which included the home of Dinuzulu) may not have been content with being ruled by Natal, they did provide assistance to the British and colonial troops during the South African War (1899–1902). Natal officials encouraged Dinuzulu to use his officially unrecognized authority as king to raise a regiment used for scouting and raiding against Boers in the northern part of Zululand and the eastern part of the independent South African Republic.[40] Africans' willingness to scout out Boer guerrillas and raid white-owned farms emerged from a long and some-times bitter history of competition for land, and their assistance to the British army and their hostility to the Boer guerrillas were critical in the final defeat of the Boer forces. Whether or not any specific promises were made to Africans following the war, they did have a sense that they had performed a service for the victorious empire, for which the empire should be suitably grateful.

All these circumstances were part of the history shared among Zululand Africans, Natal Africans, colonial administrators, and white farmers. Tax pay-ments were a regular part of that history, and the only part that involved all parties on an annual basis. Senior African men living on the Natal and Zululand "reserves" (technically Crown land, assigned to individual home-steads) paid the hut tax and the dog tax; young men performed isibhalo labor. (Africans who lived on privately owned land—usually in Natal—were exempted from the hut tax because of the substantial rents they had to pay their white landlords). It was older, married men who were legally liable for the hut taxes, but it was their sons who often migrated to the cities, to the gold mines, or to large, white-owned commercial farms to earn cash with which to pay. The reciprocal relationship among family members and between African subjects and the colonial state was ongoing, and each side thought they under-stood the basic terms. As one informant told James Stuart in an interview in December 1906, "Hut tax is not a matter to which we object."[41]

One indication of the accepted nature of the relationship was the level of compliance in paying the hut tax. The default rate for the hut tax at the turn of the century through 1904 was quite low, an indication both that Africans found the tax within their means and that they were actively complying with the state's laws. In Natal in 1904, for example, a total of only 191 huts were in arrears; in Zululand the figure was 414.[42] But by 1905 the default rate was up sharply in both the Natal and Zululand regions. In Natal 2,328 huts were in default, in Zululand 1,283. What had changed in the course of one year?

The first big change, and the one that initiated many of the rumors of rebellion, was Natal's decision to take a census of Africans in 1904. The census was regarded with almost universal suspicion. Stuart described the suspicion as an "instinctive dread" when he reported that an African man had asked, at the time that the census had been announced, "'What guarantee have we that, in being enumerated in the fashion proposed, it is not in the mind of the Government, making use of the information gained, to do us an injury in the future?'"[43] As in the Transkei, people worried that the census recorded the kind of information that could be used to hurt an individual, his family, or his possessions. In fact, when the colony did later pass the poll tax law, the information from the census proved helpful in drawing up the tax rolls, a result that many Africans saw as doing them injury.

The imposition of the poll tax itself was also a substantial change in the relationship. First, many Natal Africans felt that the new tax reneged on the promise made by Theophilus Shepstone in 1875. The magistrate at Mtonjeneni reported that chiefs in his division had made that point explicitly. Some of them had met with the Prince of Wales when he toured southern Africa and "they were told that His Majesty would care for them as had Her Late Majesty, the Queen, but now they find they are to be taxed afresh. They consider this as a breach of the promise made to them on that occasion."[44] The new tax was more than a breach of contract, however: it marked a palpable change between two ideologies of white rule. White rule of Africans under the "Shepstone system" had been the epitome of paternalism: Africans were to submit to white colonial rule and offset the costs of that rule by paying taxes, and, in return, the government would ensure peace and stability and would allow individuals to have access to farm and grazing land. As Shepstone's son explained, under his father's system, "The Government is the father of the people, and it is bound, as their great Chief, to provide them [Africans] with sufficient land to live upon. That is the way they look upon it."[45]

The paternalism of white rule had depended on the paternalism of the African family.[46] An individual homestead might contain the huts of wives of the homestead head, as well as the huts for his married sons, and one or more *ilawu* huts, for the use of unmarried adolescents. Each of these huts qualified for the fourteen-shilling-per-year hut tax, but it was the homestead head who was legally liable for all of them. Thus he bore the responsibility of tax collector within his own extended family; sons who left the homestead to work for wages gave at least some of their wages to him to satisfy the tax bill either for their own wives' huts or, in the case of unmarried sons, for their mothers' huts.

This system had already begun to break down by the turn of the century. Increasing numbers of young men, as well as some young women, were migrating from rural to urban areas. The money they earned gave them economic and social independence that they were often unwilling to surrender by returning to their fathers' homes. Moreover, fathers were losing their ability to punish those children who did not abide by their rules. As in the Transkei, various cattle diseases had swept through Natal and Zululand in the last half of the nineteenth century and the early twentieth.[47] The loss of cattle meant that many fathers could no longer provide their sons with the cattle necessary to pay bridewealth nor could they withhold cattle as a punishment; instead, sons had to spend additional time as wage laborers to earn their own bridewealth.

Homestead heads, usually older men, regarded the proposed poll tax with suspicion. They feared that poll tax, payable mostly by young men not currently liable for hut tax, might further undermine their position by making it more likely that their sons would use their earnings to satisfy their own taxes rather than turning the money over to their fathers. The magistrate of Pinetown (just outside Durban) recorded fears expressed by several chiefs when he tried to explain the new poll tax. The chiefs commented that "the hut tax originally was 7/- per hut; we paid it and were content and so was the government. It was increased to 14/-, and again we paid the tax cheerfully. This hut tax has come to stay, and we have paid it annually ever since." The chiefs then took the magistrate to task for the new poll tax:

> Now comes this tax (*imali ya kanda*) and we know that it also has come to stay; all taxes imposed by the Government come to stay. We shall pay it if we can do so, but the King [of England] must not be surprised if some of us fail to do so, and find ourselves imprisoned on account of our inability, owing to poverty, to find the funds. The past dry and rainless years, coupled with the fact that all the arable land has been taken up by Europeans and Indians, who have forced us to use the poor, waste lands, soil that has now been thoroughly worked out, and for the use of which landlords still exact rent . . . has resulted in a yearly failure of our crops.

It was their sons' earnings, according to the chiefs, that had allowed their families to survive: "Famine threatened us, but we were saved by our sons. They became the wagons which carried us, the Gardens that fed us, and they assisted us by going out to work." But the poll tax threatened to undercut this strategy, as young men might keep their earnings to pay the poll tax and not give their fathers money to pay hut taxes and to maintain their households.[48]

Historian Ben Carton has suggested that the poll tax was driving a wedge further between older homestead heads and junior men. Many young men saw their fathers and uncles as overly deferential to colonial power and as colluding with the colonial state to maintain their own power. This entrenchment of the power of elder men within the family left younger men with few opportunities for acquiring their own adult status. These young men looked to the rumors of a revival of the Zulu state as an opportunity for them to reassert the power of youth.[49]

The Pinetown magistrate had another meeting with a different group of chiefs and indunas who made similar criticisms of the new poll tax law. The spokesmen "desired me [the magistrate] to convey to the Government that the imposition of this tax, in addition to those they have already to bear, was a hardship they have little merited by past conduct, and one they would find difficult if not impossible to comply with." Chief *Ndunge stated:

> By this tax you are really parting us from our good sons; those who actu-
> ally are our mainstay. . . . I am not quarreling with the Government, but I
> desire to ask you, What have we done to deserve this ill treatment? Why
> do not you tax those bad sons only who have deserted their kraals [rural
> homesteads], and are leading useless, vagabond lives in your towns and
> have ceased to look after, and support the families they belong to? . . . It is
> your towns and the women of bad fame in them that are ruining our sons.

Another chief, Mafingo, asked, "What have we done to our Government to merit this [tax]? We helped the Government to beat the Boers in Captain Smith's time [in the 1840s]. . . . The Boers oppressed us, and that is why we helped you. But instead of helping us you oppress us." He concluded by saying, "We have to pay, pay and always pay, that is all the interest in us that our Government shows." His portrait of what taxes and other changes had done to family life was stark: "Our own sons now, when we seek access to the izinkobe (mealies) in the pot, elbow us away from them, saying the izinkobe are theirs, whilst our wives deliberately stare at us, look on, and thereby back up our own sons to defy us."[50] Paternal power within the family had broken down. Deference was dead.

Embedded in the complaints of these African chiefs was an appeal to a long-standing public transcript of reciprocal obligations and expectations. The chiefs felt that they had fulfilled their obligations: they had assisted Natal's British settlers by paying their taxes and helping them against the Boers. The deferential tones in which they couched their complaints are evidence of real respect for the authority of the magistrates, but they were also an attempt to hold the colonial state to the original terms of the relationship. In this case, the public transcript was not just a set of roles to be played; on the contrary, in return for their deference, Zulu chiefs expected some assistance from the government or, at the very least, they expected not to be actively harmed. And they fully anticipated that the new tax would harm them, not only by taking more money away from them, but also by further alienating sons from their families and weakening the position of fathers. The poll tax, in their view, threatened to kill the authority of the father within the family and then the family itself.

The magistrate of Nkandhla held a similar meeting with African chiefs and headmen of his district and received comments that accentuated their feelings that, with the imposition of the poll tax, government officials were upsetting the complex system of social obligations that underlay the colonial political structures. Chief Tulwana stated, "we have never, nor do we intend ever to shew disloyalty to Government . . . but what I say is that Government must not anticipate that there will be no difficulty in collecting those taxes." He then reminded his magistrate that the structures of the state had, both literally and figuratively, been built by Africans:

> Government must remember that we pay our Hut Tax, last year we paid our Dog Tax. It is we also that with our own hands built these very Court buildings we are now in, and it is we who make the Government roads. It is a great burden on us to now be called upon to pay a new tax in addition to all the above, especially as the Government are now taxing our young men, who hitherto have been the means of providing us with the money to pay our Hut Tax. Government are separating us from our sons.[51]

Embedded in these complaints over the poll tax was another complaint that African men were rarely consulted about how they would be governed. Even colonial administrator James Stuart recognized this lack of consultation as a legitimate grievance in his testimony to the 1903–5 South African Native Affairs Commission:

> Take the one grievance that law after law is brought into operation without the Natives being consulted. That is a tremendous grievance. We

bring in law after law, year after year, and the Magistrate is directed by circular, or instructions from headquarters, to call up the Chiefs and to inform them that this is the fiat of the Government, and there is an end of it. They cannot express their feelings; they go away, they dare not show contempt or they would be punished; and they have to slink away to their homes and sit quiet. The same thing comes again and again, and it goes on day after day, and year after year, piling on what I call the agony on these people.[52]

At the imposition of the poll tax, many older African men condemned the magistrates for initially proclaiming the poll tax to the young men who lived in town, rather than to their fathers in the rural areas. One of Stuart's inform-ants, Msime, protested: "The men of the tribe said, 'What is the meaning of our children being addressed in this way in the towns?' By so doing *their chil-dren were being taken away from them.*"[53]

But, no matter how much older African men might have adhered to the older view of their relationship with the state, the current generation of white administrators no longer wished to live up to their old paternalist obligations. Instead, they saw colonial accounts that were out of balance, and they saw what they chose to characterize as an undertaxed portion of the African popu-lation, unmarried African men.[54] This change in the governing logic of the Natal administration corresponded to a similar, if more gradual, change in Transkeian administration that in the Transkei became more evident with the outbreak of East Coast fever. In Natal the crisis point was to be the poll tax. The administration needed money and the tax would provide it. The magis-trate of Entonjeneni described his own frustration at trying to explain the need for the tax: "It is difficult to explain to the uneducated native the causes which have made the new taxation necessary, as they have no idea of customs receipts etc. and seem to think that this hut tax is more than sufficient to carry on the government of the country."[55]

From the administrators' viewpoints, a final beneficial effect of this new tax would be to placate white settlers, who for years had been demanding that the state impose heftier taxes as a way of forcing more Africans into the labor market at the extremely low wages that white farm owners were willing to pay. Administrators were becoming more responsive to white settlers' demands even as they derided African objections as "uneducated." Beyond the imposi-tion of the new poll tax, the colonial state was altering the terms of its authority by taking some of the best farmland in Zululand for occupation by whites. A 1902 commission appointed by the Natal government set aside the land for sale to white owners of sugar plantations.[56] This sale of land directly violated the promises made to the Zulu leadership when the area was taken over, initially by the imperial government, in 1887. Africans living on the alienated lands obviously may have felt injured, and other Zululand residents may have seen the move as a harbinger of things to come.

There were other trends in Zululand and Natal having to do with veterinary restrictions on cattle that may also have played a significant role in altering the public transcript, just as oppressive veterinary restrictions did in the Transkei. Rinderpest had swept through the local cattle population with the same devastating results as elsewhere; East Coast fever was spreading, and authorities were taking strict measures—including some coerced killing of cattle in infected herds—that they thought might prevent it from becoming an epidemic.[57] The way in which these state veterinarians exercised their powers was inciting unrest, according to the *Greytown Gazette* which published this comment in January 1906:

> It is not the poll tax alone that is causing discontent. . . . The vast majority of vets carry out their duties with a sublime indifference to native opinion and sensibility; as if, in fact, no such things existed. As a matter of truth, however, when you come to handling native stock, you are dealing with an affair of the most vital interest to the Zulu, and on this point he is entitled to consideration and the exercise of the utmost tact on the part of all who have to see to the well-being of his stock. It appears that, through ignorance of this fact, the system in vogue strikes the Zulu as being one in which he is ridden over rough-shod, and it is causing a vast amount of dissatisfaction. Go where you will in Zululand and you will find opinions expressed as pointing to the one event which is described in terms as inevitable. It is that the policy of the Government generally will, sooner or later, evolve trouble.[58]

These remarks seem almost prophetic in retrospect, but trouble was clearly on the horizon.

RUMORS AND SUPERNATURAL POWERS

In late 1905 and early 1906 rumors had begun to circulate in Newcastle District and elsewhere that Dinuzulu had ordered all Africans to kill their pigs (often seen as a "European" animal), to stop living in European-style houses, to destroy all pottery and implements bought from trading stores, to wear African-style clothing instead of European-style, and to avoid settler-made roads. The rumor foretold, according to one African informant, that "there would be darkness over the land for three days and nights, and that all cattle were to be taken out of their kraals during the period to save them from dying for want of food while the darkness subsisted . . . and [everyone] was to prepare for war."[59] A second African witness at the trial of one of the men accused of spreading these rumors testified that the accused "said that the Poll Tax Law was the origin of these instructions from Dinuzulu, and that all natives had to revert to their primitive simplicity in readiness of what was to follow. They said Dinuzulu had two cannons to aid him, one an ordinary one, and the other an invisible aerial one."[60] At a later trial, the same witness recounted, "Dinuzulu said that the only Tax he would consent to was a poll tax of 6d. [sixpence] and a hut tax of 1/-."[61]

A trial in Bergville Division revealed similar evidence of rebellious rumors. One witness said that one of the men spreading the rumors claimed to be sent by both Dinuzulu and by Chief Lerothodi of Basutoland, who were planning to join forces to fight the whites. He testified, "Accused said 500 men had been sent out by Dinuzulu to tell all natives about [killing] the pigs, and also to say that European houses must no longer be inhabited by natives . . . that all 'Kolwa' [Christian] men were to put on 'Mutshas' [karosses] and women the ordinary skin petticoat; all girls and boys were to take off their bead works. . . . Our cattle were to be allowed to run in the open." In addition, there were penalties for people who ignored "these orders of Dinuzulu"—they "would be eaten up by Dinuzulu and his guns when he came to prosecute the war."[62] There were other rumors current among Africans before the rebellion that "fighting has already taken place between the English and the Basutos and that the English were exterminated by lightning," and that "a great war was imminent."[63]

The same *Greytown Gazette* article that complained about the conduct of veterinarians also stressed the significance of rumors. The article noted, "It is accepted as true throughout Zululand that, when the Civil Commissioner visited Dinizulu [*sic*] over the handing back of certain guns in the possession of the latter, Mr. Saunders was unable to lift any one of these, owing to the potency of the charm thrown over them by Dinizulu's witchdoctors." The article scoffed at the content of the rumor, "but behind it all remain these truths—the loss of prestige, the skilful appeal to magic, which in this instance has worsted the representative of the white Government in a face-to-face encounter, the implicit belief being that the incident is true."[64]

The immediate effects of these rumors were mixed. A witness in one of the trials stated that he knew that a number of people had killed their pigs or sold them for "absurd prices," and had destroyed their manufactured pots. However, other witnesses in this same trial testified that they thought that the men spreading these rumors were madmen.[65] One of the accused men denied at the trial that he had been spreading the rumors or had ever met Dinuzulu, and the other noted that his companion had spread the rumors, starting shortly after he had returned from a stint on the gold mines in Johannesburg, but verified that he had never met Dinuzulu.[66]

These rumors are evidence of talk current in the region about rebellion and about Dinuzulu and other chiefs planning rebellion with the aid of supernatural powers and the ancestors. There is no evidence, however, that Dinuzulu or any of the Sotho chiefs had anything to do with the men on trial for spreading the rumors, nor that the men themselves had any claims to leadership or had developed plans to revolt. Their rumors emerged out of real grievances that they and many other rural Africans had over taxation and cultural change, and they certainly seemed to hit a cultural nerve that made many Africans fear the consequences of not heeding the message.

Historian Luise White has discussed the historical significance of rumor in describing the stories that swirled around official policies of tsetse fly control in colonial central Africa. The reporting of rumors in the archives leavens the dry factuality of much official correspondence; and rumor, she writes, "opens a space in which historians can accurately see the failures of recording and the incomplete reterritorialization that was the practice of colonial rule."[67] Rumors may be evidence of wishful thinking or of resistant strains of thought that could potentially find expression in open dissent or even revolt. They may be part of a hidden transcript that never comes out into the open or the early attempts at working out a legitimate strategy for rebelling. In general, White notes, people pay attention to rumors only if the rumors "articulate and embody the concerns of the people spreading and hearing the rumor."[68] Coming from the mouths of well-traveled men, these rumors of Dinuzulu regenerating his power to engage a greedy, grasping colonial state encompassed a broader set of cultural and political aspirations.

The Natal colony put those Africans who spread the rumors on trial—an indication that whites were also paying attention to the message embodied in the rumors. Many Africans heard their own message as well. The injunction to kill white animals and pigs that preceded the revolt was a clear call to make sacrifices to the ancestors and to purify local African society. Among Zulu-speaking peoples in the precolonial and early colonial period, there was a belief that white—the color of sun-bleached bones—was the color of the ancestors.[69] Typically, diviners wore white animal skins, clothing, and beads as a symbol of their connection to the ancestors. The ancestors had a great deal of power over people's everyday lives and could protect their descendants from harm. But if they were ignored by their descendants, the ancestors could make them ill and cause them misfortune. In fact, common interpretations of unfortunate events involved the ancestors punishing their willful, stupid, or undutiful descendants.[70] To conciliate the ancestors, people had to make appropriate sacrifices, and white animals were the most pleasing. One of Stuart's informants, Mkando, explained to him in 1902 the power of the ancestors: "Illness is said to be due to *amadhlozi's [the ancestors'] having turned their backs on a person.* A *dhlozi* [ancestor] can cause the disease. . . . People will proceed to the diviner *(isanuse)* who will say the *idhlozi* has caused the illness and may direct not only a beast [a cow] but a particular beast be killed, and he (the *isanuse*) will describe the colour of the beast, for, the *isanuse* adds, the *amadhlozi* require that identical one."[71] In 1906 many Zulu speakers may have felt that the catastrophes they had suffered recently were strongly indicative of ancestral disapproval of their actions. They had lost most of their cattle to rinderpest; they had lost some of their best land to whites; in recent years, crops had been lost to locusts and various diseases. Elders had lost children to migrant labor and to life in the towns, and children had lost their sense of deference. Christianity had made inroads against the old beliefs and sometimes caused people to neglect the ancestors and the rituals associated with them. The colonial state, rather than protecting them and according with their worldviews, had taken a census, thus gaining the kind of information necessary to cause further harm, and had imposed fresh taxes, which state officials had previously promised never to do. One powerful interpretation of these events was that the ancestors were angry, that they had turned their backs on their descendants, and they urgently needed to be mollified.

Similarly, the notion that there was a coming thunderstorm that would destroy those who did not make the sacrifices was a part of the web of beliefs surrounding a being known as the Lord-of-the-Sky (*iNkosi yaphezulu*). The Lord-of-the-Sky features strongly in the creation narrative of the Zulu.[72] As anthropologist Axel-Ivar Berglund notes, the narrative "offers a divine origin of the Zulu clan" with the name Zulu deriving from the word meaning sky. Zulu speakers, as Berglund remarks, "visualize the Lord-of-the-Sky's anger in violent thunderstorms. . . . Informants seem to agree that the power reflected in the destructive ability of lightning emanates from the anger of the Lord-of-the-Sky and that, although sometimes legitimate, 'he (the Lord-of-the-Sky) should not act so harshly. It may be that we have sinned. . . . But he should give us some indications (i.e. warnings) so that people may repent before he strikes us.'" People went to great lengths to try to deflect lightning, including, "when thunderstorms are gathering, everything white must be either covered up or removed."[73] The widespread killing of white animals before the revolt was probably not intended as a direct threat against white people but rather as an attempt either to set things right with the ancestors or to divert the lightning soon to be sent by the Lord-of-the-Sky. Seen in the light of these beliefs, Mjongo's testimony about the ball of light he saw when the fighting commenced in Umgeni District may be interpreted as the beginning of the thunderstorm: people were about to witness the Lord-of-the-Sky's wrath.

Among those Africans who rebelled, there may also have been another change in their relationship to the colonial state and to society generally; and this was a change that found expression in these rumors of divine intervention. It is possible that the rebels felt that the issues that had previously divided Zulu speakers among themselves were no longer important, and that people, particularly the young, would respond to the symbols linked to the Zulu past. This would explain Bambatha's use of the Zulu war badge and the invocation of Dinuzulu's name as the heir to the kingdom.[74] A belief that supernatural powers could be rallied to help the rebels might also explain why Bambatha, whose own home was in Umvoti District in Natal, removed his family to Dinuzulu's home in Zululand (at least eighty miles away), and formed his army headquarters in the Nkandla forest in Zululand (a good forty miles from his home). Obviously, a forest is a favorable area in which to wage a guerrilla war, but the Nkandla forest had a particular significance. Historian Jeff Guy has described the Nkandla forest as being "throughout Zulu history . . . a place of mystery, the home of supernatural beings, and a formidable stronghold and place of retreat. The Chube [the local population] are the iron-workers [an occupation strongly linked to magic] associated with the Nkandla and they were never conquered by Shaka; it has always been the last retreat of the Zulu from Shaka's time to that of Bambatha in 1906."[75] The forest was also, as mentioned above, the gravesite of Cetshwayo—Dinuzulu's father and the last Zulu king to have led the army in war.

The grave itself of a dead king was not as important, according to one of Stuart's informants, Mtshapi, as the monument maintained for the king near the monuments of all the other kings. A monument usually consisted of a tree and a stone transplanted from the actual grave site to the monument site. According to Mtshapi, "The carrying of such stone and of the tree *constituted the bringing back of the ancestral spirit of the place*. . . . In the case of Cetshwayo, too, who was buried at Enkandhla, no *tetaing* [praising of the ancestors] is done there but in the Emakosini district where his (Cetshwayo's) *isitombe* [memorial] has been set up, i.e. tree and stone have been planted." Despite this informant's belief that the actual grave site of Cetshwayo was relatively unimportant, it does seem likely that, after having been discouraged from rebelling by Dinuzulu, Bambatha may have sought approval from Cetshwayo's spirit by going to the grave site. The approval of the past kings, as well as of the ancestors generally, was a necessity for waging a just and successful war, according to Mtshapi: *"The kings' spirits were teta'd* [praised] *when something important was about to happen, like war. The spirit would be consulted. It would be seen that the spirit agreed; it would be seen that the past kings agreed that the impi* [army] *should go out. The living king would dream that the past kings had agreed."*[76]

Bambatha may have felt he had the dead Cetshwayo's support, but the living Dinuzulu was clearly not cooperating. Ignoring Dinuzulu's wishes could have been a risky move for Bambatha to make at the outset of the revolt. However, two somewhat contradictory circumstances perhaps worked in his favor and lessened the risk. First, Dinuzulu's claim as the legitimate heir to Cetshwayo had always been insecure, thus making a direct appeal by Bambatha to Cetshwayo's spirit more acceptable. Dinuzulu's accession to the title of king had been controversial from the start, because his mother was not Cetshwayo's Great Wife (the wife chosen by both the king and the people to be the mother of the heir), and because, shortly after Cetshwayo's death, his Great Wife bore a male child who became a pawn for Dinuzulu's powerful rivals. Dinuzulu became king in 1884, partly because Cetshwayo himself had named him heir after having dreamed that the spirit of his paternal uncle, Dingane, had chosen Dinuzulu to rule,[77] and partly because Boers from the still independent South African Republic and, eventually, Natal's colonial administration supported his claim as heir and temporarily resolved the dispute with armed assistance.[78] In return for their assistance, the Boers demanded and received from Dinuzulu control over some of the best grazing land in Zululand, the area that also contained the monuments of Dinuzulu's kinsmen, the dead kings of the Zulu.[79] However, when in 1887–88 Dinuzulu tried to overpower his challengers (who resided within a British-controlled portion of Zululand), he and his allies were defeated by British troops and he was captured. Subsequently, British authorities tried and convicted him of high treason. Dinuzulu was exiled to St. Helena; when the British allowed him to return in 1898, they demoted him to the level of an ordinary chief. The government did not elevate any other chief to the office of king, but it had clearly put Dinuzulu on notice that it would not tolerate any attempt on his part to act like a king.[80] Dinuzulu's seeming acceptance of this humiliation undermined his support among Africans. In 1903–4, rumors circulated in Zululand that one of Dinuzulu's rivals would, in Stuart's words, "tak[e] the field against him on the ground of his being an usurper. A remark commonly made by Zulus is: 'The Zulu crown is won by force.'"[81] By 1906 it may well be that Dinuzulu's insistence that people pay the poll tax, as he himself did, and his discouraging attitude toward the rebellion further delegitimized his own claim to the Zulu crown.

A second circumstance that may have worked in Bambatha's favor was the presence of the enigmatic figure of Dinuzulu's messenger, Cakijana. Cakijana accompanied Bambatha as a guide to Dinuzulu's home immediately after Bambatha fired a gun at his local magistrate and, during the course of the rebellion, became Bambatha's closest ally. It is clear from the evidence that Dinuzulu had empowered Cakijana to do some kind of task for him after Cakijana left the royal home. What is not clear is what that task was. According to some versions of Cakijana's evidence (given after his surrender to Natal troops), he was merely sent by Dinuzulu to fetch an herbalist, because, as everyone acknowledged, Dinuzulu was physically unwell. Cakijana then simply got caught up in Bambatha's own scheme for rebellion, in which he used Cakijana's role as royal emissary to suggest that he (Bambatha) had royal approval for the rebellion. In other versions of the evidence, Cakijana received the word that Dinuzulu was covertly supporting Bambatha, and thus Cakijana felt compelled to assist Bambatha.[82] Whatever version of events one accepts, the very ambiguity of Cakijana's position allowed those who wanted to believe that Dinuzulu supported the rebellion to believe exactly that.[83]

Moreover, there was further popular support for the idea that Dinuzulu was directing events, supernaturally if not physically. According to Stuart, a common rumor among Africans in early 1906 was that Dinuzulu often visited Natal in disguise:

> He once visited Pietermaritzburg [the capital] and went to the top of the Town Hall tower, when he was observed at one moment to turn into a cow, at another into a dog; that, when in Pietermaritzburg, he was presented with a beast [a cow] by the Government. This was taken to the market square, where some white man fired at it twice without effect, owing to Dinuzulu having charmed it. On Dinuzulu firing, however, it fell dead. Here we have one of the origins of the rumour . . . that bullets fired at Natives by Europeans would not "enter" [the bodies of those protected by Dinuzulu].[84]

This rumor about Dinuzulu's powers being greater than those of whites or of colonial officials was still—in the prerebellion period—somewhat cautious: it was a cow that Dinuzulu allegedly killed and not a white person. But the rumored demonstration of his powers assigned him a real advantage over whites despite their superior firepower.

Most people who accepted Dinuzulu as the legitimate heir believed that he had the power both to call the regiments to war and to protect them from harm. Thus the fact that Dinuzulu himself appears not to have been an enthusiastic supporter of the rebellion does not necessary negate the notion that those who rebelled hoped to build a new, unified Zulu kingdom. Some who rebelled may have thought that Dinuzulu was covertly directing the resistance. Others may have believed that Dinuzulu was illegitimate and that Bambatha was acting on authority of the spirits of the dead Zulu kings.

BAMBATHA'S SPIRITUAL WAR

Bambatha himself tried to take advantage of whatever supernatural power might be available to him to make success in battle more likely. His army had some guns and ammunition, in addition to the old Zulu stabbing spears and shields, and by canvassing in his own district, Bambatha was able to pull together an army of young men willing to go to war in a short time. But, just as important, Bambatha had a war doctor apply medicines to his troops to protect them against the bullets of the enemy. And the medicine appeared to work: before the strategic retreat to the Nkandla forest, Bambatha led his compact army initially against a small party that included the Greytown magistrate and a few policemen. Although shots were exchanged, no one was injured, and the magistrate's party fell back. Within a day, the Umvoti Mounted Rifles, consisting of about a hundred and fifty men, mobilized in search of Bambatha's regiment. Bambatha ambushed them, killing four, wounding more, and stripping many of their weapons. Although several Africans were wounded, not one of Bambatha's men died, proof enough of the war doctor's efficacy. As Nsuze, one of Stuart's informants, noted in 1912, Bambatha's doctors had the reputation for using "*intelezi medicines for preventing bullets from entering,* which was proved by their success" in this engagement.[85] The body of one of the dead troopers, a Sergeant Brown, was then partially dismembered by the war doctor Malaza to provide the most powerful substance for war medicine.[86] Bambatha was meeting with success.[87]

FIGURE 4.1. "Bambatha's War-Doctor," 1906. The Campbell Collection of the University of Kwazulu-Natal.

After this success, Bambatha tried to consolidate his gains by moving his army to Mome Gorge, in the Nkandla forest. He recruited a number of new followers along the way, including much of Nkandla's local population. He and his thousand or so men made camp near Cetshwayo's grave, and additional war doctors arrived to minister to them. For about a month the Natal authorities were unable to take action against Bambatha, partly because of the inaccessibility of Mome Gorge and the hostility of the local people and partly because it took time to mobilize the troops necessary to engage the rebels. To the rebels, though, this inaction may have looked like weakness. In fact, the Natal troops' first attempt to capture Bambatha in late April failed and Bambatha escaped. Days later, in early May, the magistrate of nearby Mahlabatini District was shot and killed after he had spent the day collecting taxes.[88] The Natal authorities suspected Dinuzulu of having arranged the assassination, but it is not clear that the magistrate's death came at the hands of the rebels. Cakijana and other Africans believed he was killed by a white farmer whom he had fined on several occasions.[89] A few days later, when Natal troops tried their first open onslaught on the rebels camped around Cetshwayo's grave, transport problems caused the attack to fail, and once again most of the rebels were safe, although more than fifty-five had died in the attack. Bambatha was still successful, but he faced some questions about why his war medicines had not protected all the rebels.[90]

Bambatha's successes outweighed Dinuzulu's continuing opposition to the rebellion. At the request of Natal's secretary for native affairs, Sir Charles Saunders, Dinuzulu sent one of his closest advisers to meet Bambatha and his local ally, Sigananda, and dissuade them from further resistance. Sigananda himself carried some symbolic weight with popular Zulu opinion. A man in his nineties, he had taken part in the last of Shaka's wars, and he had provided Cetshwayo, wounded and pursued, a safe haven when he had lost the war with the British. More recently, Sigananda had strongly condemned both the poll tax and Dinuzulu's willingness to pay it. At the time of Sigananda's condemnation, Dinuzulu had scorned him by reportedly saying, "He is bodaring [talking nonsense] when he says I am afraid. Who can fight the white man? I have been sent over the seas by them. I do not want my children to suffer."[91] But Sigananda and Bambatha rejected Dinuzulu's advice and sent his emissary away without meeting him.[92]

Bambatha's war medicine, Cetshwayo's spirit, an inaccessible headquarters, and one thousand rebels were not able to hold out against a larger, better-armed, and better-provisioned Natal force for long, however. There were several skirmishes between Natal troops and the rebels over the month of May with casualties on both sides, but the rebels were steadily being drained of food and livestock and cut off from supporters outside Nkandla. On 10 June, Natal troops, using dumdum bullets (lead bullets with hollow or soft points that create horrendous wounds) and a Maxim machine gun, took the high ground around Mome Gorge and fired down on the rebels.[93] The fighting lasted for sixteen hours, and afterward at least six hundred of the original thousand rebels were dead. Bambatha himself was dead, although the Natal troops did not discover that until days later, when a surrendering rebel informed them. To forestall rumors of a miraculous escape by Bambatha, the leader of the Natal forces then found Bambatha's body, asked a doctor riding with the forces to cut off the head, and returned with it in his saddlebag.[94] The head was identified and then, as the official story goes, returned to be buried with the body.[95] (However, historian K. G. Gillings notes that there was a 1925 photograph that purportedly was of Bambatha's head, suggesting that white authorities had retained it.)[96] The episode with Bambatha's head was very similar to the episode with Sergeant Brown's body being dismembered by Bambatha's war doctor: although whites did not use the head to make war medicines, they did take it as a way of protecting themselves from rumors about Bambatha's powers. Sigananda surrendered and, over the course of the next few weeks, most of the Zululand rebels followed his lead. Eventually Cakijana also surrendered.

Among Africans, one interpretation of Bambatha's defeat at Mome Gorge was that Bambatha had simply been overpowered by British weaponry.[97] A second interpretation was that the Natal troops not only had more and better weapons, but they also had used supernatural powers to overwhelm the rebels. An informant named Mpantshana told Stuart, "At Mome, Bambata [*sic*] and company were subject to *umnyama*" powers imposed on them by the whites.[98] That Bambatha succumbed to the supernatural powers was shown by his failure "to put out scouts or even to listen to the boy who said the Europeans were coming."[99] Another oral account suggested that Bambatha had been misled by a traitor named Elijah into believing that the Natal troops had left the area, "not knowing that this man Elijah was sent by the European soldiers to lead us into a trap." As a result, Bambatha and his men were caught unaware.[100]

THE DEFEAT OF THE REBELS

After Mome Gorge, the last phase of the rebellion shifted back to Natal, to Mapumulo District, scene of the unrest on the first day of poll tax collection and of the strongest Natal reprisals. After the initial success of their surprise

FIGURE 4.2. "Chief Sigananda taken prisoner during 'Dinizulu [*sic*] Rebellion,'" n.d. (probably 1906). The Campbell Collection of the University of Kwazulu-Natal.

attacks on traders and troops on 18–19 June, the estimated five thousand rebels suffered defeat after defeat, and the majority had capitulated by mid-July. Some rebels managed to hold out for several months, but the intensity of the white troops' counterattacks forced most to surrender.

The reason behind the timing of this new outbreak of rebellion is obscure. The explanation of historian Shula Marks as to why a new group of Africans would have rebelled "after the rebellion was so clearly a hopeless and dying cause . . . especially after many of them had already paid their poll taxes and had suffered for their previous recalcitrance"[101] was that it was the very ferocity of the Natal reprisals in February that "finally prompt[ed] into action those Africans who had already watched their cattle confiscated and their kraals destroyed." Although Natal's harsh response was a provocation, it does not fully explain why Mapumulo's residents would have waited four months after the initial military engagement (and *after* the defeat at Mome Gorge) before reacting.[102] It may be that, as Marks suggests, many of those who rebelled felt that the colony's actions had backed them into a corner. She cites the testimony of one nonrebel, who stated that "the Natives felt themselves overburdened and considered that they might as well fight and be killed straight away."[103]

But this explanation may give too much agency to the colonial state for instigating the revolt; the people who rebelled were not just angry or desperate, and they were not just looking backward to the glory of the Zulu state under Shaka, especially since many of the Africans living in Natal and participating in this last stage of the revolt were the descendants of refugees from the precolonial Zulu state. A more compelling explanation is that they believed that a new Zulu state was emerging, at the direction of either Dinuzulu or his ancestors; that Bambatha had been merely an instrument of this new order; and that is was appropriate for others to take up the battle once Bambatha had fallen. Moreover, some Africans, despite colonial attempts to prevent it, thought that Bambatha and his rebels had survived: There was a rumor current in Mapumulo in 1906 that, contrary to official reports, the rebels had actually won at Mome Gorge and had killed all the Natal troops.[104] As late as 1912 stories circulated that Bambatha was still alive. An informant, Mjobo, told Stuart, "Bambata is said still to be living and to be . . . in Portuguese territory [Mozambique]. It is said that he comes down to various places in Natal, even here in Pietermaritzburg, when he assumes even another colour and even has wings like a bird."[105] Drawing perhaps on these rumors, Stuart wrote in 1913, "Bambata, as many Natives believe, in spite of every proof to the contrary, is still living. For them, his spirit, i.e., dissatisfaction with European rule, or, to put the same thing positively, a desire to control their own affairs . . . is certainly alive, though he may be dead."[106]

While the spirit of rebellion may have survived, acts of rebellion were washed away by the force of Natal's "mopping up operations."[107] By the next year, Mapumulo's magistrate was reporting positively on the prompt tax payments made by people in his district:

> When it is remembered that since the last [tax] collection, this Division has been the scene of the chief events of the recent rebellion, and that more than half of the natives here were implicated in that rebellion, and had all their property confiscated, and huts burnt, and that about 1500 natives were killed, and over 1300 imprisoned for terms of imprisonment of two years and upwards, the results of this year's collections, as reflected in the enclosed statement, cannot be regarded as unsatisfactory. Besides the ravages of the Rebellion this "most distruthful" Division has been afflicted with the East Coast Fever which has well nigh killed all the cattle that escaped confiscation during the rebellion, and a plague of locusts, that ate up at least one third of the grain crop. But notwithstanding all these troubles those natives who have paid up have done so cheerfully and willingly, and those who have not, are making every effort to find the money to pay their taxes.[108]

The outline of a renewed deference to colonial authority was emerging. While it is difficult to believe that Africans in Mapumulo District, so soon after the rebellion, were really "cheerful" about their circumstances, they were evidently paying their taxes. The magistrates of all the Natal and Zululand districts reported some problems with defaults on both hut and poll taxes in the years following the revolt, but they also reported a steady increase in tax payments.[109] People found the money to pay the new tax, although when combined with the previous levels of taxation and rent paying it was an onerous burden, and they also sometimes found legal loopholes that let them avoid the tax.[110]

The rebels had lost and Africans were coping with that defeat and the reinvigoration of colonial rule. If rebels and their supporters had believed that they were fighting a just war, endorsed by the ancestors and the spirits of the dead kings—if not the living Dinuzulu—what did they make of their defeat? Did Africans see the plagues of East Coast fever and locusts as evidence of the ancestors' disapproval? If so, what did the ancestors disapprove of, the rebels' actions or their defeat? Or did Africans see the plagues as emanating from the supernatural power of whites, proof that whites commanded not only the material resources to rule, but also the magical ones? Alternatively, did Africans see these disasters as random misfortune that undermined any further attempt to resist the colonial state? Stuart, as is evident in the above quotation, felt that Bambatha's spirit lived on, because the underlying cause of the rebellion—the clash of the different cultures of the colonists and the Zulu—continued.

For the colonial state, the reimposition of the poll tax after the rebellion was central to the reestablishment of the rituals of control. People paid the tax because they recognized the subordinate position in which their defeat had left them. Moreover, the incredible violence of Natal's suppression of the rebellion had illustrated and elevated to the level of policy the grim view implicit in King Mpande's injunction that "the only way to govern a Zulu is to kill him." But the colonial state, at the end of the rebellion, had something else in common with Mpande. Many Africans were wary of the supernatural power—as well as the military power—wielded by the state, just as their ancestors had feared the supernatural powers used by Shaka and his heirs. While whites insisted on tax collection as a gauge of their control over the Zulu, many Africans saw it as an extension of state control into the homestead, directing and disrupting the family at the material, social, and cosmological levels.

People did not relinquish their supernatural beliefs after the catastrophic defeat of the rebellion. The fact that many of Stuart's informants spoke to him about these beliefs in the decade after the rebellion strongly supports the notion that they persisted.[111] This is not to suggest that the beliefs in the supernatural continued unchanged, or that all Africans held precisely the same beliefs and acted identically because of them. As people's beliefs changed, they increasingly had to make agonizing choices about their loyalty to their ancestors as opposed to their loyalty to their children. One of Stuart's informants, Mqaikana, noted in 1916 the intense spiritual dilemma involved in these choices: "When we kill a beast [make a ritual sacrifice of a cow] nowadays we do not *praise the ancestors*. We simply remain silent, for if we *praise the ancestors* our own children who have *become Christians* will not partake of it [the meat of the slaughtered animal]. . . . This surprises me, for who but God told us of *the ancestral spirits?* But we are told not to *declaim their praises—for to do so is a thing of Satan.*"[112] But not praising the ancestors carried its own risks, and the ongoing problems endured by Africans might have been interpreted as the predictable result.

The vast majority of Zulu people did not actively participate in the rebellion, perhaps an indication that they lacked the conviction that a rebellion might succeed, even if many had listened to the rumors and slaughtered their white animals beforehand. Those who actively rebelled were mostly young men, although with a great deal of both tacit and overt support from elder men and women. They were trying to overthrow a state that was harming both their own families and their prospects for a prosperous future as farmers, and they were also trying to enlist the support of their ancestors. But after the defeat, beliefs in the supernatural persisted as a category, informing Africans' interpretations of the rebellion's outcome. It was not that the ancestors or the Lord-of-the-Sky no longer existed; they were simply not powerful enough to defeat the white-controlled colonial state.

After the rebellion, and particularly after Dinuzulu's death, in 1913, any possibility of large-scale, organized revolt against the white-controlled state was largely finished for several decades. The erosion of the power of the rural family continued, accelerated by increased labor migration, until in the 1920s even white state officials became alarmed and tried to help a newly emerging Zulu elite to rebuild patriarchal control.[113] This rebuilding went hand in hand with the creation of a new, ethnic Zulu identity that tended to gloss over the rivalries and divisions of the previous seventy-five years. At the same time, the new elite minimized the significance of violence in Zulu political history and downplayed any suggestion that violence would be necessary to achieve future political autonomy; instead, this new elite committed itself to work within state institutions.

There were significant material and political causes that precipitated the Bambatha Rebellion. These causes included the added costs of the new taxes;

the difficulty of finding wage labor that paid enough to cover those costs; the declining incomes of most African farmers and the loss of livestock in recent years; long-standing grievances between whites and Africans over control of some of the best farm and grazing land; newer grievances between older and younger Zulu men over control over wages and the lack of political power; generalized unrest created both by the aggressive administrative measures and military reprisals adopted by the Natal Native Affairs Department; and the intrusion of new social norms and religious teachings at the hands of the missionaries.[114] These were all real concerns for Africans in Natal and Zululand and predisposed at least some of them to act violently when the poll tax took effect.

There were additional causes linked to spiritual beliefs held by many Africans at the time of the rebellion. People resisted the poll tax partly because of fears about the state's having acquired additional supernatural power over Africans via the census that preceded the tax. Rumors that circulated before the rebellion suggested that many Africans believed that their misfortunes resulted from their ancestors' having turned their backs on them, and they fully expected the Lord-of-the-Sky to vent his anger at them in a coming storm. One way of rectifying these problems was through active participation in the rebellion against colonial rule. Moreover, rebels were not merely reacting to state actions; they were acting in accordance with their own belief system, which indicated that the ancestors and other supernatural actors strongly supported their resistance and would allow them to prevail.

That there was no single "African" or "Zulu" interpretation of events is demonstrated by divisions among Africans at the time of the revolt. As stated above, only a small proportion of the Zulu-speaking population revolted. One might attribute the unwillingness of the majority to take up arms to increasing doubts about the veracity of the precolonial belief system as well as to doubts about the ability of a lightly armed Zulu army to defeat an imperial force. Those who rebelled may have felt that they had received a signal from the ancestors to strike and that their ancestors and leaders would shield them from harm. Those who chose not to rebel may have had exactly the same material grievances as those who did rebel, but they probably were a good deal more skeptical of the supernatural interpretation of the signs around them.

This explanation also holds true for Transkeian Africans at the turn of the century. They too had suffered substantially at the hands of colonial officials and settlers. They had experienced similar social dislocations; in fact, the social dislocation in 1906 in the Transkei was probably greater in extent than that felt by Zululand's Africans, because of the heavier exodus of migrant laborers from the Transkei and the longer and more pronounced exposure to missionaries and their teachings. They had similarly witnessed the erosion of the authority of chiefs, although they lacked the historical experience of a strong, centralized state on the scale of the precolonial Zulu kingdom.

One important difference was that, unlike in Natal and Zululand, the poll tax had not been imposed all at once on the Transkei in 1906. Instead, the General Rate was only gradually extended, district by district. The Labour Tax in the Transkei had aroused substantial African opposition in the 1890s as well as provoking several rumors of revolt and of supernatural signs foretelling revolt.[115] Transkeian magistrates were reluctant to collect that tax as a result, and it was eventually abolished. The caution of Transkeian magistrates may have been a direct result of the memory of the 1880 rebellion (see chapter 2), and of the real—if limited—political power of at least some of the residents of the Transkei, particularly in the districts where the Glen Grey Act was first implemented and the Labour Tax was imposed.[116] This caution might have prevented a rebellion.[117] It was not until the passage of the Native Taxation and Development Act of 1925[118] that the General Rate was collected throughout all districts of the Transkei, by which time the administration was better able to quell any unrest and the percentage of African voters had diminished. Transkeian Africans had numerous grievances in 1906, but they lacked a single, lightning rod–type grievance that the poll tax provided for Natal's and Zululand's Africans. Nor did they have even a legendary basis for united military action along the lines of the historical Zulu kingdom: there had been multiple African polities in the region, and rivalries among various African groups were still fresh and ongoing. Also, and significantly, in 1906 Transkeian Africans lacked a sign that supernatural powers would help them against the superior firepower of the colonial state in a generalized rebellion. However, Transkeian Africans watched events in the colony to the north with interest and took the lesson of the Zulu defeat to heart.

The brutality of the Natal regime's suppression of the rebellion deserves some discussion as well, particularly given my contention in previous chapters that brute force, especially over the long term, was not a viable strategy for the colonial state. Observers in Britain and the Cape Colony, as well as some in Natal, were often critical of the amount of force and lack of restraint used by Natal troops in suppressing the revolt.[119] This use of force amounted to a frenzy of destruction, similar to that described by historian Helen Bradford in her discussion of British troops' violence during the scorched earth campaigns of the South African War against Boer families. For Bradford, the violence of British troops was largely a way of asserting a destructive male identity over pro-war Boer women and farmers absent on commando.[120] Troops tore apart the settled domesticity of Boer homesteads in a reprise, as Bradford notes, of tactics commonly used by the British military in its "pacification" campaigns against resistant "native" populations. These same tactics, used by Natal colonial troops against Zulu rebels, may have been an attempt to assert the essential and superior "maleness" of white men over the Zulu: by destroying the homesteads and livelihoods of the rural population, the troops tore at the foundation of adult male social status among the Zulu. But the tactics were also a dramatic display of authority and domination, designed to force rebels and their sympathizers into a compliant and subordinate demeanor, to reimpose the public transcript on a new generation of Zulu speakers.[121] The confiscation of livestock owned by rebels was a forceful expression of the colonial state "eating up" its enemies, in the long tradition of Shaka, Dingane, Mpande, and Cetshwayo. The swift return of high rates of compliance with tax demands showed the effectiveness of this brutal strategy, at least in the immediate aftermath of the revolt. Natal had succeeded at governing the Zulu by killing them.

CHAPTER 5

TAXATION AND FLAMING PIGS IN THE TRANSKEI, 1921–30

Wellington and le Fleur Challenge the Magic of the State

Butler Wellington (a.k.a. Wellington Buthelezi) and his followers were eloquent on the issue of taxation. According to a Tsolo District magistrate's report in 1927, two local followers of Wellington were promoting the idea that "America is coming to invade the Union and that when America takes over this country they [Africans] will pay no taxes and that the white men are to be driven out of the country. Also that natives that do not belong to their society will also be driven out of the country."[1] Wellington's adherents in Ngqeleni District were even more outspoken: "The Government were hard on us (meaning natives). The Government was [*sic*] making the natives pay taxes and causing sickness amongst their cattle."[2]

The Griqua leader A. A. S. le Fleur, although he was no friend of Wellington, equally condemned taxation. In 1926, in Matatiele District, he stated that "the whole of Africa belonged to him [le Fleur]. . . . As there are no more taxes to be paid you will live where you like, there will be no passes and permits for the removal of stock. . . . They [Africans] must refuse to pay the forthcoming taxes. Because the ground now belong [*sic*] to le Fleur, and in Adam Kok's time there were no taxes to be paid." According to the same Matatiele informant, le Fleur went on to suggest that "all the natives must unite with the Griquas, as they must believe him, what he is saying is true. Because to date not one of them has been arrested. . . . He said that the Americans are going to cause war against the whites in Africa, and the Natives and Coloured in Africa must do likewise."[3] The followers of both Wellington and le Fleur frequently linked the notion of ending tax payments to the state with an impending showdown between South African whites and Africans, with the Africans being possibly assisted by Griquas or Americans (or both). The vivid prophecies of the two leaders fore-saw an agrarian utopia in which there would be no taxes, no dipping of cattle, and no whites.

The strong words of Wellington and le Fleur elicited strong responses. Between them, Wellington and le Fleur commanded a considerable, if short-term, following among Africans in the Transkei. But equally large numbers of Africans either rejected their prophecies entirely or else maintained a skeptical distance. White South Africans, including officials and local farmers, found both Wellington and le Fleur bizarre, but whites divided on the issue of how dangerous they were. Some whites saw them as revolutionary agitators under-mining state control and others, as impostors defrauding Africans out of money they could not afford to lose.

Scholarly opinion has also divided over how these men and their move-ments should be interpreted. Historian Robert Edgar has suggested that both le Fleur and especially Wellington were part of a millenarian wave that swept through eastern South Africa in the wake of tremendous social, cultural, and economic changes.[4] Edgar's views find some support in William Beinart's work on Herschel District in the 1920s, although Beinart focused more on the eco-nomic basis for the movements and less on their spiritual implications.[5] None of these studies, however, did more than touch on the issue of taxation, an issue that was at the heart of both movements. Both Edgar and Beinart discuss the unwillingness to pay taxes only as the product of hard economic times and disaffection with the white-controlled state.

In contrast, historian Helen Bradford has written of the importance of taxa-tion as an issue for the Wellingtonites and for the Industrial and Commercial Workers' Union (ICU). She writes that the ICU's "focus was fitting: the rapid decline in political and economic fortunes associated with the imposition of this burden [taxation] was possibly the single most important factor facili-tating the emergence of a millenarian movement in Pondoland during this period."[6] However, Bradford too separates taxation, as an economic issue, from the "millennial fervour" embodied in the claims and predictions made by Wellington and his followers, and by some adherents to the ICU.

One of the talents of both Wellington and le Fleur was their ability to fuse economic issues with beliefs in supernatural powers and express this potent mixture in a powerful and charismatic rhetoric that appealed to a wide audience. Before discussing the nature of the movements initiated by Wellington and le Fleur, however, I shall examine some social and economic events that formed the backdrop to the movements.

RURAL LIFE IN THE 1920S

Rural Africans suffered through economic hardships in the 1920s. Economic distress actually had begun with the imposition of various restrictions and quarantines related to the cattle disease East Coast fever in 1908 (see chapter 3). These included cattle dipping and registration as well the quarantines that effectively shut off access for African livestock owners to livestock markets beyond the Transkei. Economic problems deepened in 1918 with two separate events, the end of World War I and the worldwide influenza epidemic. The war had provided a substantial market for African farmers' agricultural products, in particular for wool to make uniforms. In addition, with many white men away in the military, there had been a considerable demand for African labor in mining and manufacturing, thus making it relatively easy for African farming families to supplement agricultural incomes with wages. The end of the Great War saw the end of these economic benefits. The war had social effects as well: along with the influx of money into the Transkei came an influx of news about the role of the United States in the war. The idea of Americans as influential outsiders with a strong military clearly took hold among many Transkeians.

The 1918 influenza epidemic also had a direct impact on the rural economy by killing or disabling a large number of people. African farmers found that they could not recoup their losses in subsequent years, as the bad harvest of 1918–19 was followed by two seasons of drought.[7] Flagstaff District's resident magistrate in 1920 summarized that "the following are the reasons for the deterioration [in the collection of taxes]: Failure of crops and famine, war and profiteering [on the part of traders], Spanish influenza."[8] In addition to its economic effects, influenza was a frightening disease: the swiftness with which it spread and killed people initiated some rumors of witchcraft being used by the state (as well as by other Africans) against African farmers.[9]

Unfavorable world markets, bad harvests, deaths, and fears of witchcraft combined to create a crisis in tax collection throughout the Transkei in the early 1920s. Some of the crisis was a result of administrative procedure. It was the practice of the magistrates to revise the tax registers only every three years; as a result the names of men who had died in the epidemic often remained on

the registers for some time, artificially inflating the amount of unpaid tax. Some
of the crisis ensued from the continuing implementation of the Glen Grey system. As the land in individual districts was surveyed and people changed over
from paying hut tax to quitrent, there was some confusion among Africans as
to who still continued to owe hut tax. In addition, individual families had to pay
the costs of having their land surveyed under the Glen Grey Act or else lose their
quitrent titles, and, although this was a one-time payment, it took a substantial
amount of the cash on hand for many families. The imposition of the poll tax
on unmarried men and increases in stock rates to pay for compulsory cattle
dipping pushed the total tax bill so high that families frequently found themselves short of cash and unable to pay. Finally, the widespread labor unrest in
Johannesburg and the gold mines that culminated in the Rand Revolt of
1921–22 froze the hiring of African miners for several months; as a result, there
were fewer opportunities for Africans to find paying jobs. As the Bizana
District magistrate concluded in 1923, tax collections were being undertaken
"in the face of the two economic obstacles we most fear, namely, the complete
failure of native crops, and the total restriction of recruiting for the Mines for
some months, and partial restriction for several months of the year."[10] As a
result, a large proportion of taxes went unpaid in the early years of the decade.

The widespread defaults on taxes caused concern among upper-level officials, who from 1920 through 1924 constantly berated magistrates to increase
their collections and bring down the default rates. Magistrates responded by
issuing writs and court summonses against defaulters, by seizing property such
as livestock that belonged to defaulters, and rarely (and usually only in extreme
cases) by evicting defaulters from their land.

To avoid the worst consequences of not paying their taxes, families used
several strategies. One was to pay first the hut tax or quitrent on the land—
whichever applied in their particular districts—to protect their land allotments;
pay the stock rates second, to shield their livestock; and pay their unmarried
sons' general rates or poll taxes last, with whatever was left over. Since the sons
rarely either owned livestock or had their own land, this strategy sheltered the
families' assets.[11]

A second strategy for evading punishment was simply to hide the family's
movable property and livestock with relatives, making it difficult for the police
to find any property to seize. Magistrates were notably reluctant to throw families off their land, sometimes for humanitarian reasons but more often because
of the prevalence of the default problem. In Bizana District in 1921, for example,
46 percent of the hut tax owed was in arrears; it would have been impossible
for the magistrate to evict 46 percent of the population.[12] Instead, the magis-

trate sent the police out to issue arrest warrants to defaulters, but that tac-
tic had its limitations as well, as white policemen frequently could not speak
Xhosa, and African policemen and headmen often had a limited command of
English or Afrikaans, making their attempts to work together difficult.[13] In
Bizana District, with no more than three or four policemen for a population of
45,063 (including 7,095 hut taxpayers),[14] magistrates relied on headmen and
chiefs to perform many policing functions. However, headmen and chiefs,
alert to their need to retain some popularity, were unwilling to press people for
tax payments.[15] The limitations on enforcement techniques were common to
all Transkeian districts.

In the first two years of the decade, despite the high rates of default on taxes
and state officials' efforts to collect arrears, there was little general political unrest or dissatisfaction expressed against the state. Most Africans still
acknowledged their obligation to pay the taxes eventually, even if they could
not do so by the due date. Even as magistrates stepped up their criminal prosecutions of defaulters in 1923, they rarely reported resulting unrest in those
years. With good harvests in both 1923 and 1924, as well as the resumption of
labor migration to the mines, Africans had more cash on hand with which to
pay their taxes.

Hoping to maintain African respect for the state, the chief magistrate felt
that it would be foolish to press Africans too hard for tax payments. In a 1926
report discussing taxes generally, the chief magistrate referred to his and his
subordinates' reluctance to collect a newly imposed tax on African tobacco
production: "Had attempts been made to collect the [tobacco] tax from the
Natives the ease with which payment could have been evaded would have
tended inevitably to turn their minds to the possibility of evading the payment
of taxes generally and diminished their wholesome fear of the Government
power to enforce payment."[16] The chief magistrate did not specify what exactly
instilled this "wholesome fear." His comments suggest that he was aware that
much of the state's reputation for enforcement was based on a bluff and that if
the magistrates tried to collect yet another tax, Africans might very well call
that bluff. Given the serious limitations on the state's enforcement ability, the
wholesome fear was possibly related to the respect people had for the supernatural powers of the state. As the chief magistrate noted, tax evasion was actually fairly easy, even if not commonplace. Payment came less out of a justified
fear of the material consequences of defaulting (such as having one's livestock
seized) than as an acknowledgment of one's obligation to pay as part of the
ongoing ritual of state control. In essence, the chief magistrate, by deciding not
to squeeze Africans for payments when they could not pay, was reenacting the

role of the precolonial chief, who in lean times might have shown the same lenience to his subjects. This attitude toward defaulters may have served to defuse, at least temporarily, whatever political unrest that economic hardship and disease might otherwise have caused. Official caution also kept whatever African dissent existed over taxation from crystallizing into antistate actions. Scott notes: "Patterns of domination can, in fact, accommodate a reasonably high level of practical resistance so long as that resistance is not publicly and unambiguously acknowledged."[17] As long as white officials could convince themselves that the decline in tax payments was not really a form of active resistance against the state, but rather an indication of difficult economic times, they could tolerate nonpayment.

In fact, most of the open discontent expressed in the first half of the decade was aimed at the traders on whom people were dependent for a market for their crops. In Idutywa District in 1921, the magistrate reported, "A fairly general complaint in regard to the payment of taxes was the difficulty in obtaining markets for their stock and cash for produce from the traders, the majority of whom, it appears, give stock [dry goods from their stores] in exchange for the value of [live]stock and grain."[18] In short, people were complaining less about paying taxes and more about the traders from whom they received the cash with which to pay those taxes. This resentment against the traders found its greatest expression in 1922 in the women's boycotts of trading stores in Qumbu and Herschel Districts.

WOMEN'S BOYCOTTS OF TRADING STORES IN 1922

The frustration with low agricultural prices and high tax bills found an initial outlet in the women's boycotts of trading stores in various districts, especially in Qumbu and Herschel Districts. In these protests, groups of women accused the traders both of charging too much for the items they sold and of not paying enough for the agricultural produce they bought from Africans. These allegations led women not only to boycott trading stations but also to threaten those Africans who did not adhere to the boycott. Despite its militancy, the women's boycott was not a direct challenge to state authority; in fact, one of the women's complaints was that with the low prices they were being paid for produce, they did not have enough money to pay their taxes.[19]

The boycotts occurred in 1922. They were partly orchestrated by influential women (many were wives or mothers of headmen, one was the Mpondomise chief Mhlonthlo's daughter) of the Qumbu and Herschel Districts. The boycott consisted of picketing trading stores and actively interfering with customers: according to the Qumbu magistrate, the boycotters appointed their own "policewomen . . . to picket the stores with instructions to prevent all people from buying and to destroy all purchases."[20] The "policewomen" performed their tasks with zeal as they armed themselves with sticks and accosted those who entered the stores. One trader, seeing these armed women outside his store, sent an African boy to them "to ask if he could come and buy here [at the store]." The trader "heard what they replied. . . . They said 'you talk wonderful get away otherwise we will kill you.' They were lying down at the time but sat up and the boy ran away."[21]

The protest was apparently split along gender lines, and most men disavowed any knowledge of the women's plans. When the chief magistrate came to Qumbu to investigate the boycott, he convened a meeting with two hundred or so African men and expressed surprise that women would be in charge of such activities. Although the men at the meeting suggested that their female relatives were complaining of genuine economic grievances, the chief magistrate rejected this explanation and chided the men for not controlling their wives: "If the men were unable to restrain their women then perhaps it was time the Government appointed women headmen to replace a few of those who said they did not know what was going on." Seeking to reinstate what he saw as the proper gender hierarchy, the chief magistrate, when he very briefly met with a delegation of the boycotting Qumbu women, brushed them off, saying their "men would inform them of what he had said."[22]

Despite the chief magistrate's brusqueness, the women at the meeting made clear that their grievances were not with the state but with the traders. One spokeswoman listed their complaints: "We have to complain of hardships in the high prices we have to pay for things, and the low prices we get for our mealies. Widows are unable to pay their taxes because they get only bits of iron in exchange for their mealies. On discussing the matter we decided to come to our father [the chief magistrate]."[23] The women involved in the boycott were not trying to sever their connection to the state by defaulting on their taxes; on the contrary, they were concerned that their lack of money would force them to default and that they might either go to jail (although the chief magistrate explicitly denied this would happen) or else lose their access to land. In fact, the women actively looked to the chief magistrate to intervene with the traders on their behalf, but this he declined to do. Possibly because of the women's deferential attitude toward the chief magistrate and his advice, the boycott in Qumbu ended shortly after his visit.

The Herschel boycott followed a similar trajectory. Women organized and led the boycott, starting early in 1922, again with the aim of forcing traders to lower their prices and to pay more for local agricultural produce. In August

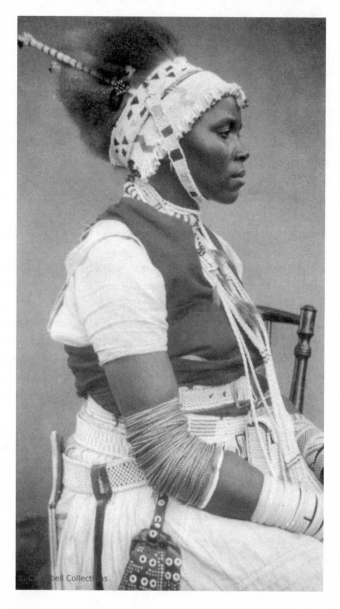

FIGURE 5.1. "The Doctor poses," Western Pondoland.
Diviners were often women, and typically dressed in white
when practicing as diviners. Photograph by Mrs. Fred Clarke,
n.d. (probably 1920s–1930s). The Campbell Collection of the
University of Kwazulu-Natal.

1922 the women also wrote to the Secretary of Native Affairs about their grievances and to ask that they be sent a "scrupulous" shopkeeper. Later that month
the district's magistrate met with about a hundred and fifty of the women and
attempted to explain the world commodities market to them to illuminate the
reasons for their receiving such low prices. He also, misleadingly, stated that
"trading is free and competitive," ignoring the fact that the state stipulated that
there could not be more than one trader within a five-mile radius, exclusive of
towns, thus giving each rural trader a virtual local monopoly. Finally, without
really addressing the women's grievances or suggesting any alternative actions,
the magistrate forcefully suggested that they were acting foolishly and should
end the boycott. As in Qumbu, the women deferred to the magistrate's advice:
"We hear how Magistrate has warned us. We will not go beyond his orders and
advice but we listen like children to their parents."[24] These protesters' words
show just how firmly the public transcript of deference to authority was in
place. The boycotting soon ceased.

There was also a postscript to the Herschel boycott that shows that the
women organizing these boycotts were not extensively rewriting the public
transcript. On 28 August 1922 the Herschel District magistrate reported to
the Secretary for Native Affairs that "at a meeting of women they were told,
presumably by their Committee of Management, a letter had been received in
which it was stated the Government supported them in their endeavours to
force the reduction of prices of shop goods, and that America was behind the
Government."[25] In 1922, therefore, Herschel women active in the boycotts saw
the state not so much as an enemy, but as a potential ally in bringing about better economic conditions. They also, apparently, already believed that America
was influencing the state's actions on behalf of African interests.

However, people living in these East Griqualand districts clearly suspected
that some form of disaster would soon overtake them. In 1922 a rumor about
a coming blizzard of red snow ran through the African population in the East
Griqualand districts of Mount Ayliff, Mount Fletcher, Mount Frere, Qumbu,
and Tsolo. Frank Brownlee, then magistrate of Mount Ayliff District, reported,
"there is an idea current among Natives that before Spring sets in there will be
a fall of snow which will be red and that it will destroy all life."[26] He thought
the rumor might have resulted from the harshness of the preceding winter,
combined with an old story of Shaka's Zulu regiments being destroyed on
Insizwa Mountain by a snowstorm in the 1820s. An African court clerk, J. Bam,
when asked to comment on the story, linked it to various evangelical Christian
sects that had been proselytizing in recent years: "Personally I attach no importance to the Red Snow Scare. It may probably have originated in the fertile

brain of some superstitious native who may have read Mrs. Johanna Brandt's works, e.g. 'The Millennium,' or the excitable emotions of my Mount Ayliff Countrymen may have been incensed by the broadcasting of the Hickson Faith Mission which is now effecting some cures in the Union."[27]

These dismissive attitudes of officials, however, became more muted in November 1922, when there was a severe hailstorm in the East Griqualand districts. According to Johannesburg-based newspaper the *Star:*

> Information reached Kokstad today concerning a terrific hailstorm which broke over the districts of Qumbu and Mount Frere, in East Griqualand. Many of the hailstones were jagged pieces of ice weighing half a pound, while the smallest were not less in size than a pigeon's egg. In the Qumbu district, on the Pondoland border, 14 natives are reported to have been killed by the heavy hailstones—eight women, three men and three children. Natives ploughing in the fields had to forsake their ploughs and oxen and seek the nearest shelter, not having time even to outspan [unyoke the oxen]. Some of the teams stampeded, with their ploughs following them, and went over the steeply inclined krantzes [ravines], the oxen and ploughs being dashed to pieces on the rocks below. Mount Frere village just missed the storm, but the roar of it towards Qumbu was terrifying, causing hundreds of natives to become panic-stricken. At the Osborn Wesleyan station, near Mount Frere, wheat and forage lands were simply wiped out within half an hour. The magnificent garden at the mission house was a mass of garbage. Never within the memory of the oldest inhabitant has a storm of such severity been experienced in any part of East Griqualand.[28]

The chief magistrate of the Transkeian Territories, W. T. Walsh, added a handwritten note to this newspaper clipping when he forwarded it to the Secretary for Native Affairs: "Yes, the severe hailstorm may possibly be connected by some of the natives with the 'Red Snow' scare." As there was in Zululand before the Bambatha Rebellion, there was a long-standing belief among people in this region that storms had a supernatural origin. Africans may not have displayed an active animosity for the state or most state officials, but this rumor and the storm that followed it reinforced a certain wariness.

Wariness of state officials' supernatural powers was compounded by its policy initiatives. The Glen Grey Act was immensely unpopular even as it was imposed on more districts throughout the Transkei by 1925. Enforced land registration and survey fees combined with the District Council—or Glen

Grey—system and additional taxes to radicalize public opinion and to cause women in Herschel District and elsewhere to spearhead a new politically based movement—the removal of their children from missionary-run and state-supported schools. Historian William Beinart writes, "What had started as a fight on specific issues had become a generalized resistance to state, progressive [African] and white domination. . . . Their [the women's and their allies'] adoption of an 'anti-white' ideology and their support for a political system based on a popular chieftaincy . . . reveal the direction of their political thinking."[29] This turn to a more separatist political ideology made the women protesters quite receptive to the preaching of Dr. Wellington when he turned up in Herschel District in 1926. In Qumbu District and other areas of East Griqualand, many Africans gravitated instead toward the fiery oratory of A. A. S. le Fleur.

TAX RECEIPTS AND FLAMING PIGS:
THE RHETORIC OF WELLINGTON AND LE FLEUR

The rhetoric of both Wellington and le Fleur was vivid and specific, if somewhat fantastic. They both promised the end of white domination; they both suggested that self-help and spiritual purification would combine with the intervention of external actors to end white rule; and they both insisted, at least in some forums, that their adherents cease paying taxes to the South African state. Although followers of le Fleur and Wellington often confused their distinct policies, the two men did operate independently of each other and need to be considered separately.

Wellington and the Wellingtonites
The self-styled Dr. Butler Hansford Wellington first appeared in the Transkei in the mid-1920s. Although he claimed to be Chicago born with an American medical degree, he had in fact been born in Natal of Zulu-speaking parents and had apparently received some training as an herbalist. Wellington's claim to be an American was not merely an attempt to seem exotic; rather, it lent credibility to his story that Americans were all black and that they would be coming to free black South Africans soon.[30]

Wellington was building on the message of Jamaican leader Marcus Garvey and Garvey's Universal Negro Improvement Association (UNIA) based in the United States. Garvey never visited South Africa, but he had numerous devotees who followed his writings published in the widely circulated UNIA newspaper the *Negro World*. Garvey's vision of black self-improvement and liberation excited a new level of political consciousness in the South African context. This transformation was captured by African historian W. D. Cingo: "The mad dreams and literature of Marcus Garvey, a black American Negro, were broadcast on the winds. Hopes for political and economical emancipation were revived and to-day the word American (*i Melika*) is a household word symbolic of nothing else but Bantu National Freedom and liberty."[31]

Operating in the Transkei, Wellington linked Garvey's message with that of the South African-based Industrial and Commercial Workers' Union (ICU) headed by Clements Kadalie, an organization that was also growing by leaps and bounds in the 1920s. At times, Wellington tried to pass himself off as an ICU organizer, probably to take advantage of the ICU's name recognition: Transkeians with experience of migrant labor often had had direct contact with the ICU, which had its largest chapters in Cape Town and Johannesburg, with a very active chapter in East London, all of which were common destinations for migrant laborers from the Transkei.[32] Kadalie, like Garvey, espoused black self-help and the potential benefits of creating a mass organization that could promote issues of importance to blacks in the political arena. The South African-based Kadalie was arguably more confrontational on economic issues than Garvey, and his movement did not initially endorse Garvey's brand of black separatism; but, like Garvey's UNIA, Kadalie's ICU became so big so fast that the amount of ideological control Kadalie actually wielded over his followers may have been quite small, particularly in the rural areas.[33] Thus, Garvey and Kadalie may have been more important to Wellington and his followers as familiar and symbolic names and generally as leaders who challenged the white-controlled state, rather than as people with specific ideological programs.

The Umtata journal *Umteteli wa Bantu* (The advocate of the people) announced Wellington's arrival in the Transkei in these terms: "There is a man here who calls himself Dr. Wellington . . . [who] said he has not come about Church matters but about politics; and that he has come to free the nations oppressed by the white people." The story also paraphrased Wellington as saying,

> You are not going to pay taxes nor dip your cattle. He said forces are coming, armies coming from America to drive away the white people from Africa, to go to their own country. He said people who did not register their names with him in his book will die together with the white people. People are coming forward for registration for fear of being

killed. This is how this registration is done—each individual, man and woman, registered for 2/- each; except young people who belong to the choir.[34]

Three elements of this report are noteworthy: first, that Wellington promised an end to tax payments and cattle dipping; second, that Wellington suggested there was an external force—the American armies—that would come and drive away all the whites and kill all blacks whose names were not registered; and third, that the registration fee was payable by both men and women directly to Wellington.

Taxes, never popular, had recently become even more unpopular with the passage of the 1925 Native Administration and Development Act. This act had systematized the number and amounts of taxes throughout South Africa; in the Transkei it had resulted in all unmarried adult men having to pay the General Rate—poll tax—of one pound (although men in some districts had been paying the tax since the 1890s). In addition, a recent increase in excise taxes on many goods commonly bought by Africans, such as cotton blankets, raised the cost of living substantially, particularly for rural Africans. The African Court Interpreter for Tsolo District noted the unpopularity of the new taxes with Africans and how it affected Wellington's renown: "The natives who to some extent resent the increased taxation, firmly believe this man's saying and look to a happy time of release from European rule which the [black] American Government will bring. . . . They believe he [Wellington] has great magic powers and that the white men fear him and they say that is why he is not arrested and sentenced to a long term of imprisonment."[35]

Resentment over cattle dipping was also perennial. The compulsory dipping of cattle initially arose out of the tick-borne East Coast fever epidemic between 1908 and 1922, although dipping was not a particularly effective preventive. Dipping was also immensely costly: stock owners had to pay stock rates (another form of taxes) to offset the costs of the equipment and the dip; cattle were frequently weakened by the weekly or fortnightly march to the tank; once at the tank infected cattle mingled with healthy cattle with predictable results; the chemicals in the dip itself commonly burned and occasionally killed the cattle it was supposed to help; and cattle and especially calves sometimes drowned or broke their legs in the poorly maintained tanks.

As in earlier years, in the 1920s both taxes and dipping had spiritual dimensions. The payment of taxes demonstrated, reinforced, and to some degree constituted the link between individual Africans and the South African state. That Wellington proposed to end taxes was part of his plan to sever that link.

At the same time, cattle embodied the connection between living Africans and their ancestors and were both the actual form of wealth and the currency in which bridewealth was paid at the time of marriage; the fact that the state taxed these animals and forced them to be dipped, which sometimes resulted in their death, represented a direct intrusion not only into the economic lives of Africans but also into their family lives and spiritual connections. Cattle dipping was a way for the state to maintain and deepen control over its African subjects. The cessation of dipping, like the cessation of tax payments, weakened the state's control. Open resistance began to coalesce around these two core issues articulated by Wellington.

Wellington's idea that black American armies would come to liberate black South Africans may have initially derived from the rhetoric of Marcus Garvey and his UNIA, but the way in which these armies were to arrive was unique to Wellington's movement. Rumors abounded, some of which built on older rumors dating back to the First World War. For example, there was a rumor circulating in southern Natal and eastern Pondoland in 1915 that local German Catholic mission stations were harboring German warplanes. According to this rumor, the German planes were supposed to help Africans against what Africans saw as an invasion (into the rural areas) by South African troops who would confiscate African-owned cattle. South African troops did enter the area (while patrolling the coast), but when they made no attempt to seize cattle, the rumor evaporated.[36] In the 1920s warplanes also figured significantly in rumors, but this time they were flown by black American pilots. Reports from the Harding District of Natal, which adjoined the Transkei, noted that the Wellingtonites believed that Americans would fly their planes overhead and drop burning coals. These burning coals would cause all pigs to burst into flame "and burn their owners and owners' property . . . and the fowls would catch fire and the fowls would fly about and set fire to the huts and grass." In some areas of the Transkei, people expected the Americans to use lightning to ignite pigs and to kill whites and unregistered Africans.[37] Wellington himself reportedly called on his followers to kill all pigs and white fowls.[38]

These rumors, which look very similar to the rumors that preceded the Bambatha Rebellion to the north, were part of the beliefs in witchcraft and the supernatural current in various regions of the Transkei at the time. Wellington himself, although he portrayed himself as an American who could not speak any African language, was actually a Zulu speaker from KwaZulu-Natal, and it is certainly possible that he was recycling the Bambatha rumors from twenty years before. The rumor about lightning being used as an offensive weapon was a clear reference to the magical qualities of lightning and the impundulu

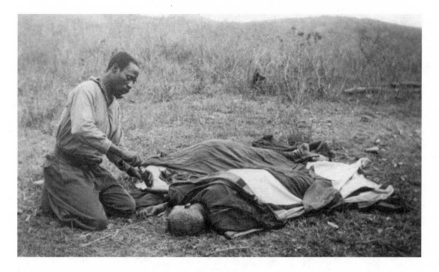

FIGURE 5.2. "Lightning Doctor at work treating victims of a lightning strike before burial," Western Pondoland. Any surviving members of a household that had been struck by lightning were supposed to hire a doctor to purify victims before they were buried and survivors before they had contact with other people. Photograph by Mrs. Fred Clarke, n.d. (probably 1920s–1930s). The Campbell Collection of the University of Kwazulu-Natal.

bird. Anthropologist Monica Wilson in the 1930s wrote that "lightning is said to be a bird *impundulu;* forked lightning is its droppings, and thunder the beating of its wings"; and the bird was surprisingly American in its coloration: "The *impundulu* has red legs and beak and a pure white body, but sometimes it appears blue."[39] In this context, the fact that Africans were beginning to refer to the poll tax as the impundulu shows that many equated the state's demands for taxes with the use of magical and malevolent beings. Africans hoped that the flying Americans would be using an impundulu of their own against a state with reputed supernatural powers.[40]

Not all Africans killed their pigs, but, as Bradford notes, for those who did, this appeal to pig slaughter had a strong mystical component. Pigs were symbolic of spiritual pollution and death, and "were natural vehicles for beliefs about degradation and decay."[41] Thus the killing of swine could be interpreted as a ritual purification to prepare Africans for the coming utopia. It could also be seen as a preventive against being struck by the lightning to be wielded by Americans: Wilson documented that in the 1930s in Pondoland the killing of a pig and the smearing of its fat, mixed with various herbs, on sticks or spears placed around a hut was the common protection against lightning strikes.[42]

The general idea of killing pigs may also have built on the killing of white animals and pigs in the preparation for what became the Bambatha rebellion in Natal and Zululand. While in the case of the Bambatha Revolt, the animal killings were probably either sacrifices to the ancestors or attempts to prevent lightning strikes, the pig killing associated with Wellington may also have been directed against the magical powers of the state: an East Griqualand magistrate in 1927 had ordered a census of pigs and Bradford suggests that "helped fuel a belief that Wellington was sending an enormous hog to threaten ordinary pigs and their owners."[43] But, as discussed in chapter 2 with regard to the cattle census, a swine census could have had two other meanings for African stock owners: first, that the state might have been preparing to tax livestock owners on their pigs; and second, that state officials wished to deepen their magical control over livestock owners through the medium of the census itself. The fact that pigs were considered European, because in some areas they had been introduced by whites, enhanced their appearance as magical animals, perhaps on a level with the impundulu itself.[44]

Finally, the payment of registration money to Wellington or his lieutenants, as well as to ICU organizers, duplicated the payment of taxes to the magistrate. Many Africans paid the two-shilling registration fee to enlist the aid of Wellington and his American armies against magistrates and other state officials. Those who registered also received membership cards that people assumed had the same protective powers as the old hut tax receipts. The protection provided was against imprisonment and also against the malevolent witchcraft of the state. Bradford observed, "When confronted by the magistrate and police, numerous [tax] defaulters in both Bizana and Lusikisiki confidently whipped out their red tickets [ICU membership cards]." From this attempt on the part of tax defaulters to ward off state demands with their red tickets, she concluded, "Consequently, refusing to pay tax was not necessarily a sign of the acquisition of political consciousness appropriate to resisting the white state."[45] But open defiance of the magistrate and his demands was a significant change from the compliance of previous decades and suggests that there was a broader population who was dissenting or grumbling less openly.[46]

The fact that Wellington collected his fees from both women and men hints at two other facets of his movement. First, the state's tax policies along with other social and economic trends had effectively reduced African women to the status of permanent legal minors, lower in status than even their own sons.[47] But women were still powerful domestic actors and Wellington was trying to use them to develop his own movement. Women's discontent had already been deepened by the magistrates' dismissive responses to the women-led boycotts of trading stores in Herschel and Qumbu districts in 1922 and other attempts by women to organize politically. By allowing women to pay fees and register in the organization personally—rather than in their husbands' or guardians' names—Wellington implicitly accepted them as adults of a status equal to men. Second, the substantial number of men who were away as migrant laborers left a large proportion of women in charge of rural homesteads. As a simple, pragmatic measure, therefore, Wellington may have decided to enroll women individually because so many women actually controlled rural finances.

Wellington as well as the ICU rechanneled the belief in the magical qualities of tax payments. Registration on membership rolls replaced or augmented registration on hut tax rolls, as the magic formerly wielded by whites and the white-controlled state would be turned back against them. As Wellington did this, he drew on an enormous well of grievance, based on material hardships, but also based on spiritual unease and a sense of loss.

Wellington was an excellent speaker and fund-raiser, but his weak spot was organization. In fact, only a skeletal organization stood behind Wellington. He made numerous promises everywhere he spoke, but he rarely had the means or the personnel to keep his promises. For instance, he and his followers advocated that people withdraw their children from state-subsidized, mission-operated schools and put them into new Wellingtonite schools that were supposedly to receive subsidies from his organization. The separatist schools, founded mostly in Tsolo, Qumbu, and Kentani Districts, typically lasted a few years and then folded for lack of funds. This was more or less the fate of all Wellington's initiatives.[48]

A crucial blow came in 1927, when both the ICU and the UNIA warned its adherents against Wellington, warnings that undoubtedly diminished his following.[49] Monica Wilson notes, "The Government, singularly lacking in imagination, sent a group of aeroplanes over the Transkei as a display of force," to discourage Wellington's followers further, "and of course Wellington pointed them out as his American allies. They were even painted in the colours that he had predicted!"[50] Later in 1927 the Qumbu District magistrate tried and convicted Wellington for fraud, and the chief magistrate subsequently banned him from the Transkei. Wellington could no longer appear as the omnipotent prophet allied with the powerful American state.

In the wake of the trial and banishment, there was a sudden but short-lived surge of support for Wellington, as a trader from Tsolo District reported: "It now appears that the natives are more confident than ever that the Europeans are dead scared of them and the Americans. . . . The general cry today is that before the end of the present week blood will be flowing as rivers. In response to advice I have given to one or two of the more sensible men I have received replies to the effect that 'even if we are killed it matters little as we may as well be dead as live under the present white mans rule with heavy taxation dipping Etc.'"[51] Despite the militant tone, the bloodbath never happened, possibly because Wellington himself discouraged it, and the prophesied intervention of American forces never took place.[52] Although some of his followers (including the prominent chief Lutshoto in Tsolo District) held out hopes that Wellington would return with American troops behind him, gradually people became discouraged, and by the early 1930s the movement had faded or, in some areas, merged with Kadalie's newly established Independent Industrial and Commercial Workers' Union (IICU).[53]

The IICU was Kadalie's attempt to reestablish an independent organization after he lost control over the original ICU to some of his lieutenants and white advisers.[54] Particularly after Kadalie coordinated a massive strike of African laborers in East London in 1930, the new IICU quickly spread into the Transkei.[55] The new union found its greatest support among ex-Wellingtonites, who had, since Wellington's departure, been in search of an organizational home. Bradford notes that one IICU branch in Nqamakwe District had a reputation for "all-night religious services infused with apocalyptic prophecies": "Thus one gathering was treated to a long exposition of a dream about the white man and his *impundulu,* which was threatening to 'eat up the Bantu,' while black mushrooms were singing 'Arise! O! Native and take your position!"[56] This dream is a story about taxation and its magical implications. Under this interpretation, the white man's impundulu was the poll tax, and the phrase "to eat up the Bantu" was a reference to the historical practice of "eating up" or seizing all of the property of one's enemies or of people accused of witchcraft. Thus there was the same fusion of economic and spiritual issues that had characterized Wellington's movement. Although the IICU kept elements of Wellington's message alive for a time, it did not have a long life itself: financial mismanagement and the scandal attached to it effectively crippled and killed the IICU by 1933.[57]

Le Fleur, Taxation, and the Griqua Utopia
A. A. S. le Fleur was in some ways an even more enigmatic figure than Wellington. Since the 1890s he had been involved in various schemes attempting to reinvigorate agrarian Griqua communities. The Griqua were largely Afrikaans-speaking Coloured (mixed-race) descendants of Adam Kok's original followers, many of whom had migrated to the area in the Transkei known as East Griqualand in

the 1840s and the 1860s. At the time of their migration, the Griqua had formed an independent state, and they remained independent of direct colonial control until the late 1870s when the Cape Colony finally swallowed them up and began administering them as part of the Transkeian Territories. The Griqua had a number of long-standing grievances with the colonial state, particularly surrounding land ownership and political rights. A. A. S. le Fleur had at the time of the rinderpest epidemic been tried by the colonial state for sedition because of his political agitation (see chapter 3). He was acquitted of that charge and he continued his sporadic political campaigning. By the 1920s le Fleur's rhetoric appealed to a broader population than just the Griqua.

Le Fleur is probably best known for his numerous attempts, dating back to the 1890s, to buy land and set up independent Griqua farming communities. These attempts usually involved his raising money from a few well-off Griqua backers, making a down payment on some land (that was always overpriced and underirrigated), encouraging other Griqua families to trek to the new farm, then failing to earn enough money to be able to continue making the payments on the mortgaged land, and finally being evicted, losing both the land and the down payment.[58] Despite le Fleur's failures, he almost always rebounded, finding new backers to finance his next plans. According to historians Robert Edgar and C. C. Saunders, le Fleur's settlement schemes and his promotion of (Griqua) ethnic consciousness and self-pride held out to his followers the promise of an escape from poverty, a means of preserving a cultural cohesiveness, and a way of distancing themselves from Africans, who were being relegated to the lowest strata of South African society.[59] Given le Fleur's efforts to distance the Griqua from Africans, it is all the more ironic that he developed a following among Africans in the 1920s.

Le Fleur's African following seemed to be attracted by two elements of his message. First, in 1926 he suggested that he had somehow managed to have all the land in South Africa ceded to him: an African man who attended a meeting addressed by le Fleur reported, "Chief Le Fleur then said I am here to inform you that the ground in Africa has been handed back to me by King George [of England] and General Hertzog [the South African Prime Minister]." Second, le Fleur promised to redress the many grievances felt by Africans, in particular cattle-dipping and taxes. The same African man quoted le Fleur as saying, "I have heard your grievances in regard to dipping of cattle . . . the dip has burnt the cow's udders and the cattle are also dying from the dip. . . . I will forward your grievances to the Government. But you must pay taxes as I am also paying same."[60] There was an obvious inconsistency in le Fleur's statement: if he had been handed back the land by the king and the prime minister, then why would they still constitute the effective government? Why could not le Fleur simply end dipping and taxes himself?

Le Fleur thrived on inconsistencies and his speeches often contradicted each other. In an earlier address in March 1926 (quoted at the beginning of this chapter), he explicitly stated that since the whole of Africa now belonged to him, there would be no more taxes and no further need for passes or permits for moving livestock. Like Wellington, he promised American assistance: "The American troops are coming over and take South Africa by force, and the Europeans will leave in blood. . . . The coloured and natives must simply walk into the Europeans, and stab and kill as far as they go."[61] Yet on other occasions during the same year le Fleur lectured that hard work and racial uplift were the cure for the ills suffered by Griquas and Africans and, repudiating violence, he denounced the apocalyptic rumors that swirled around the region.[62]

Le Fleur himself disparaged Wellington, calling his ideas "evil influences sown by the native who stiles [sic] himself as an American."[63] In 1927 he told an African audience that it was foolish to believe that bombs dropped from airplanes would kill white people only, and he compared Wellington's message to Nongqawuse's tragic cattle-killing prophecy of the 1850s, in which an adolescent African girl claimed to have spoken to the ancestors, who ordered her and all the Xhosa-speaking people to kill their cattle and destroy their crops in anticipation of a rebirth of all the people and cattle who had already died.[64] At the same 1927 meeting, le Fleur castigated both the ICU and the African National Congress. He criticized the ICU for not fulfilling its many promises to improve the lives of working men, and he lampooned the ANC for being too concerned with African voting rights, which he depicted as an exercise in futility, given that all the political parties were controlled by whites: "all your [ANC dues] money is spent for the Franchise, which means only signing a cross [on the ballot] in 5 years time, and then you have to wait 5 years before you select your enemies, the Labour Party."[65] In addition, le Fleur "repudiated any allegations that he was disloyal or at any time had preached or talked sedition . . . and . . . he was not responsible for the rumour that he preaching [sic] that the white men would be driven into the Sea, and land returned to natives, Griquas and Coloureds."[66]

In some speeches in 1926 and more consistently in 1927, le Fleur retreated from his aggressive stance against the white-controlled state and its policies, including cattle dipping and taxes, and toward a more accommodationist and, at times, even segregationist outlook.[67] Instead of confronting the state, he suggested complying with it; instead of riding the wave of belief in his (and Wellington's) supernatural powers, he deprecated such beliefs. The size of his African following shrank in direct proportion to the cooling tone of his rhetoric. From late 1927 until his death in 1941, le Fleur spent all his energy trying to establish new Griqua communities, first in Knysna and then at Krantzhoek, near Cape Town.[68]

By the late 1920s and early 1930s, the movements sparked by Wellington and le Fleur had ground to a halt. The movements' failures probably had more to do with the limitations of their leaders than with anything else. Africans were still upset over taxes and dipping regulations, although with several years of good harvests and strong labor migration, Africans were less starved of cash than they had been at the beginning of the decade. In the same report in 1929 in which the chief magistrate noted that support for Wellington, le Fleur, and the IICU was waning, he disclosed that collections of all taxes had risen, to 65 percent of all taxes due (including both current taxes and the substantial arrears that had accumulated).[69] As people began to suspect that the magic of Wellington, le Fleur, and the IICU was failing them, their "wholesome fear" of the enforcement powers of the state evidently returned.

Despite the apparent popularity of Wellington's and le Fleur's apocalyptic visions, their movements did not long survive without them or their fiery rhetoric. This was true even though many of the underlying economic, social, and political conditions that predisposed Africans to support them endured. Most Africans continued to resent the demands made on them by the white-controlled state, but by the early 1930s they had recommenced paying their taxes on a regular basis and ceased supporting seditious movements. The state had once again reestablished its control and had restored the ritual of tax payment and collection.

Historian Helen Bradford, in analyzing the causes and implications of the rumors of supernatural influences at work in the Wellington movement and in the ICU in the rural areas, has suggested that these beliefs in the supernatural were the products of a "traditionalist" ideology. According to Bradford, the rural followers of both Wellington and the Independent ICU, unlike the ICU membership in the urban areas, were not "modern nationalists," but "were attracted instead to militant Africanist programmes, which—if they were to gain a mass following—had to be couched in the idioms of popular culture and to offer support to those resisting proletarianization. . . . Powerless as they were, the black rural poor turned to airborne Americans, precolonial military heroes and magico-witchcraft beliefs."[70] Bradford thus classifies these beliefs as imperfect attempts on the parts of rural Africans to interpret and change political and economic reality.

Historians William Beinart and Colin Bundy, in their essay on the Independent ICU in East London and the Transkei, also place these supernatural beliefs into the category of traditionalist protest ideology.[71] And they seem to draw the same conclusion as Bradford, that these beliefs impeded both a true understanding of the white-controlled state and the adoption of methods that might have more effectively challenged the state.

The term *traditionalist* is limiting in that it does not connote the dynamism and adaptability displayed by the belief systems of many rural people. Neither does it indicate the degree to which the "modern" South African state itself depended on "traditionalist" beliefs for its authority: the fact that so many Africans believed that white administrators had access to magical powers conditioned Africans' responses to the state and tended to inform the protests Africans initiated. "Traditionalists" like Wellington and le Fleur manifested many "modern" attributes, while the "modern" state employed "tradition." It is difficult to know where tradition ended and modernity began.

Wellington and le Fleur were not simply mirroring the state or mimicking modernity as they built their rural movements. These were African movements that borrowed (sometimes heavily) from a "Western" culture that Africans had helped to build in South Africa. Clifton Crais analyzes Wellington's rhetoric as a kind of camera obscura that took a blurry photograph of the state's reality and of the reality of Western material culture and then attempted to convince people that the photograph was as powerful as the reality.[72] This analysis underestimates Wellington's movement, depicting it as a captured moment— a snapshot—in the history of African political consciousness. Yet, although Wellington himself was a political flash in the pan, both the material conditions and the beliefs that had engendered his movement continued developing and were more than a fragmentary memory. Wellington and his movement were not imperfect expressions of a rational modernity as Crais concludes; for many Africans they were compelling reinterpretations of their political prospects.

The strength of Wellington and le Fleur (and of the IICU in the rural areas as well) had been that, in addition to challenging the white state on economic grounds, they understood the fusion of economic issues and spiritual values and contested the state's control over the spiritual lives of Africans. Their popularity was based, as other historians have noted, in the downward economic spiral that found many Transkeians watching their agricultural incomes erode even as their taxes increased. Yet the appeal of Wellington and le Fleur also depended on common beliefs in the supernatural. The authority of the state relied on these supernatural beliefs; what Wellington, le Fleur, and their followers were able to do was to update these beliefs, infuse them with twentieth-century technology, and turn them back against the state. They also created certain quasi-governmental structures that seemed to offer viable alternatives to the governing structures of the South African state. In so doing, Wellington and le Fleur asked that Africans no longer pay taxes to the white-controlled state and instead pay fees to these new organizations. This demand for payments, like the state's demands for taxes, had punishments built in for defaulters: people who did not join Wellington's and le Fleur's movements would die in the massacre designed to kill whites.

The specter of Wellington's Americans in airplanes combined the latest in technology with older beliefs about witchcraft and magic. His followers expected that Wellington would be able to manipulate lightning and destroy his enemies in the same way and more effectively as the state had manipulated the impundulu, or lightning bird, through the medium of the poll tax. Members of Wellington's organization and of the ICU wielded their two-shilling membership cards and hoped to fend off the American fire just as the ten-shilling hut tax receipt had previously fended off the magic of the magistrates. Building on one of the results of widespread male migrant labor—the large number of women left in control of rural homesteads—Wellington offered women full membership in his organization, according them the adult status that the state denied them. The fact that Wellington set up schools and said he could rely on the help of the Americans—just as Great Britain had relied on the help of the Americans in defeating the Germans in World War I— gave him some credibility.

Le Fleur was responsible for several contradictory messages that may have brought him a more diverse but smaller group of African followers than Wellington. For a time, he too apparently proclaimed that American invaders would be arriving to assist Africans and Griquas in their battles. He also claimed to be on speaking terms with both King George and Prime Minister Hertzog and strongly hinted that they supported his plans. Le Fleur, like Wellington, fixed on the major economic grievances of taxation and cattle dipping, and he too seemed to understand that the spiritual dimensions of taxation and people's relationships to their cattle could not be divorced from the economic dimensions. Le Fleur's African following flourished when he was at his most militant, and it fed on the popularity of Wellington and the ICU.[73] As le Fleur retreated into a better-defined position of Griqua ethnic nationalism by 1927, however, his African following abandoned him, which suggests that it had been his confrontational language on taxes and dipping that had made him most appealing to an African constituency. Wellington and le Fleur had magical plans, but those magical plans were designed to overturn a state that acted in malevolent ways.

Beliefs in witchcraft and the supernatural continued as part of Africans' hidden transcript of resistance to the state, and, significantly, they were also a part of the public transcript: Africans deferred to state authority partly because of the belief that state officials had access to supernatural powers. If Africans had not believed in witchcraft and the supernatural, the state would not have been able to exercise the kind of control it did. Africans, by creating seditious supernatural beliefs, were attacking the state at a crucial base of support: at the level of the popular African political consciousness. They were acting on the principle that the state did not monopolize all supernatural powers and could be confronted and beaten in the realm of the supernatural and, by extension, in the material realm as well. At that level both Wellington and le Fleur pioneered the notion that it was critical for African political movements to destroy the foundation for the state's supernatural control over its African subjects: the collection of taxes.

CHAPTER 6

LEGAL MINORS AND SOCIAL CHILDREN
Rural African Women, Taxation, and Witchcraft Accusations

Taxes affected African women dramatically even though the South African state officially collected taxes only from African men. The effects on women between 1880 and 1963 deepened as poverty in the rural areas deepened and increasing numbers of men departed the countryside for longer stretches of time, leaving their wives in many cases to fulfill the role of homestead head. The first tax instituted, the hut tax—although it did little to change women's social, cultural and economic status by itself—did set a precedent for treating African women as perpetual legal minors, not even able to achieve the limited form of adult status afforded by state policies to African men. By the late 1920s and 1930s, taxes combined with the development of migrant labor and the declining availability of arable land in the Transkei to restructure women's roles dramatically. Taxes were by no means the only or the primary cause of this restructuring but they were an integral part of the foundation. The 1940s and 1950s found rural women often trying to farm plots that were too small and depending on husbands and other relatives to leave the rural areas to earn wages.

The effects of taxes on women, particularly rural women, are important for three reasons. First, what little secondary literature exists on the taxation of the African population concentrates on how taxes affected the supply of male migratory labor.[1] While this is a crucial question, it tends to link taxes to labor migration solely as cause and effect while ignoring the more complex social consequences of taxes. Some of these consequences stretched over the long term as they played themselves out in people's self-definitions, especially with regard to gender and social roles. Moreover, because taxes were incorporated into a set of beliefs about the supernatural and because women were often suspected of manipulating supernatural powers for antisocial purposes, the effect that taxes had on women's social status is a rich topic to investigate.

Second, a study of the effects of tax regulations and tax collection on rural African women can provide a mirror in which are reflected the attitudes, assumptions, and priorities of state officials dealing with what they termed the Native Problem, particularly as it emerged as a central issue in the 1930s and 1940s. The imposition of the hut tax in the early years of colonial rule revealed the dominant white view of how African societies were constructed and how white officials thought they ought to be altered. Similarly, the new taxes imposed in the years after the passage of the Glen Grey Act in 1894 demonstrated that white assumptions and priorities had changed, even as the taxes responded to the changes in African society. With the broader changes in South African society from 1926 to 1958, new attitudes toward African women and families were incorporated into official policy.

Third, the link between taxes and witchcraft becomes more apparent when discussing the impact of tax collection on women. Many rural Africans believed that wives, as strangers within their husbands' households, often brought with them their ancestors, who had the potential for harming their husbands' families. Common witchcraft beliefs also often targeted women—single, married, and widows—as the sinister *abathakati,* or witches, who made use of malicious supernatural beings to achieve selfish goals (although men could also be accused of being witches).[2] As the number of men who left the rural areas to become migrant laborers increased through mid-century, women often delivered the tax payments in their husbands' names to the magistrates. This direct transaction between two groups—women and state officials—routinely suspected of having access to supernatural powers, created greater suspicion within the family as well as generating dissent over appropriate gender roles, and these suspicions undermined marriages in the rural areas while placing women in even more vulnerable social and legal positions.[3]

THE EFFECTS OF TAXES ON WOMEN, 1878–94

The colonial Cape imposed hut tax at a rate of ten shillings per wife's dwelling hut per year.[4] When officials of the state initially imposed the hut tax in parts of the Transkei in the late 1870s, they did so based on a set of assumptions about African family structure. First, the tax law assumed that the family was patriarchal, since only married men were legally liable. Second, by taxing only married men the law assumed that women, particularly wives, were the economically productive members of society because women did much of the daily labor in the fields and the products of arable agriculture were a significant part of a family's livelihood. Under the hut tax regulations each man received an arable plot for each wife and each wife/plot/hut was taxed at ten shillings per year. Thus if a man had two wives he controlled two arable plots and he paid two hut taxes. Third, the tax assumed that women and unmarried adolescents were legal minors and dependents, a status that changed for men in their lifetimes—through adulthood and marriage—but not for women. Neither women nor unmarried men could work an arable plot in their own names except in rare circumstances.[5]

These assumptions stemmed from a variety of sources including state officials themselves, men who testified to various state commissions or participated in the drafting of regulations. As they saw it, the basis for their expertise on African societies was their background: some were sons of other government officials or missionaries and had grown up in the rural Cape or Transkei; others had participated in military campaigns in the region and later settled there; still others had had government experience in other parts of the British Empire where hut taxes had been imposed on local populations. Their assorted experiences made these men claim they had a unique understanding of African (or, more generally, Native) societies and the appropriate means for governing them.[6] The state officials usually grounded their own authority in their familiarity with Africans and their knowledge of "native customs" and the "native mind."[7]

A second source of information on African culture was Africans themselves. Africans who counseled white officials included chiefs, headmen, ministers, mission station residents, servants, and employees. Many of these informants were men, although officials stated that their own partiality for male testimony was based on an overwhelming African (male) belief in the untrustworthiness of women.[8]

Both officials and African informants emphasized the subordinate roles women played in African society. A few took an extreme view of African women as the chattel of men, exploited for their labor and exchanged, often unwillingly, against cattle (that formed the bridewealth payment) at the time of marriage.[9] In 1881 Thembu chief Ngangelizwe took this position in testifying to the Native Laws and Customs Commission of the Cape Parliament:

Ukulobola [bridewealth] amongst us is selling. You sell your children the same as you buy this jacket, and pay for a girl the same as you pay for this jacket. I will prove to you that a girl is sold. A woman will run away from her husband, and go home, and the man will either go to the chief or to the magistrate, and demand his cattle back. . . . In olden times the woman had no rights, and therefore the man got back his cattle, because women are naturally wicked and have no good ways with them. They are the same now, and therefore a woman has no rights.[10]

A white Lutheran minister and missionary at Stutterheim, in the Cape, Rev. Beste, reprised this view of women as chattel, although in a more critical tone: "Native women have to work for their husbands. They must build the huts, and perform all the necessary domestic and agricultural labours, &c., while their lord can eat and drink, bask in the sun, and talk and smoke the whole day."[11] These descriptions of women as chattel were provocative, but how accurate were they? There are few contemporary written records comparing the actual work hours of precolonial African men to women, nor is there much evidence about the power of women in making decisions, especially in nonroyal households. What we do have are highly generalized and unspecific accounts of gender relations given by men, both black and white, often Christian or mission educated, often from wealthy or prestigious backgrounds. For example, Chief Ngangelizwe, although he had not yet converted to Christianity in 1881, had spent several years being taught by Wesleyan missionaries at Clarkebury before becoming chief in 1863. In addition, he himself had had a problem with African women of high status: Ngangelizwe's Great Wife was Novili, daughter of the great Gcaleka chief Sarhili. A rumor that Ngangelizwe beat and otherwise abused Novili and one of her friends was one of the causes behind Sarhili attacking the Thembu in 1871, an episode that ultimately resulted in Ngangelizwe surrendering control over the Thembu to the Cape Colony.[12] For his part, Rev. Beste was a German missionary of seventeen years who held particularly strong, disapproving views about non-Christian practices.[13]

Compare the evidence of Chief Ngangelizwe and Rev. Beste above with that of Umgudhlwa, chief of the Jumba clan of the Thembu, and of Rev. Dr. Henry Callaway, Anglican bishop of St. Johns, in the Transkei. Umgudhlwa described to the commissioners a woman's position regarding the choice of a husband as being subordinate to her father's wishes but not without some say in the matter:

The woman is not purchased. The payment of "ukulobola" for a girl distinguishes a married woman (*umfazi*) from a mistress (*dikazi*). The cattle passing serves to form a link of friendship between the families.

Cases do occur where the *ikazi,* or cattle payment, is returned; as, for instance, when a woman says she dislikes her husband and goes home. Sometimes a father refuses to receive the daughter, and will talk to her and send her back to her husband, and if she does not go, the father may beat her. The husband is sometimes selected by the father, and sometimes by the daughter; but she has no choice if the father wills it. If the girl objects to her husband she can appeal to the chief, and it sometimes happens that the chief does not compel the girl to marry, and orders the cattle to be given back.[14]

Chief Umgudhlwa described a situation in which fathers clearly expected their daughters to do as they were told, but, just as clearly, daughters occasionally frustrated these expectations by exercising their own wills. In addition, he did not lump all females together in the same category of men's dependents or subordinates; instead, there were different social categories of married women, unmarried women, mistresses, daughters, sisters, and mothers, each of which had responsibilities and rights.[15]

Similarly, the Anglican bishop of St. Johns stated that the church did try to discourage both the payment of bridewealth and polygyny. Nevertheless he refused to condemn African customs completely and cautioned against a harsh judgment of the customs: the payment of bridewealth "confers rights and obligations . . . and he [the bride's father] has a right to interfere in her behalf should his daughter be ill-treated in any way. We are too apt, at times, to look at Kafir customs through our English mode of thought, and thus put wrong interpretations upon them."[16]

By 1883 even state officials recognized that the extreme view of women as chattel was just that: extreme. The report of the Native Laws and Customs Commission summarized that conclusion:

All the evidence, however, proves that a woman is not the slave of her husband. He has no property in her. He cannot, according to native law, kill, injure, or cruelly treat her with impunity. He cannot legally sell or prostitute her, and with the exception of paying cattle to her father, as dowry upon marriage, there is nothing to indicate that native law or custom treat the wife as a chattel. . . . The only native witness who boldly asserted that a woman was her father's and husband's chattel was the Chief Gangelizwe.[17]

Despite this conclusion, the commissioners—in over two years of taking testimony—did not interview a single woman, white or black. The commissioners themselves were not ready to credit women with an intelligence and analytic ability equal to that of men.

African women and men often had different social statuses. But divisions between elder and junior cut across gender divisions, so that an older married woman was junior to her husband but was also senior to her son and other men in the younger generation, particularly those not yet married. All younger family members, both male and female, were dependent on their parents, as young men themselves were often married by their parents' arrangements and needed their fathers to provide the cattle for bridewealth. Elder men who married an additional wife usually did so out of personal choice rather than familial obligation; but chiefs typically married at least some of their wives to seal political alliances and strengthen their spiritual claims to rule. Wives who were married for political reasons often had relatively high status and some autonomy. Insider status in the individual family also cut across gender divisions: a woman in her father's or brother's household usually had more rights and authority, regardless of age, than a woman in her in-laws' household.[18] Women could not accumulate and exchange wealth with the same ease as men, and they were usually economically dependent on elder men even though they were economically productive. But there was considerable difference of opinion among Africans as to the degree of women's subordination, both actual and theoretical, to men.

Certain sources indicate that at least a few African women did have some independence of action and some ability to accumulate and establish claims to wealth.[19] Those with the most established claims to autonomy and wealth were women herbalists and diviners and the wives and daughters of chiefs. Female herbalists and diviners used their medicinal and supernatural knowledge to promote their social station so that while they were exercising their profession, they had authority over both women and men.[20] They could also accumulate wealth in the form of cattle and other livestock. Typically, when a woman went into a marriage, she took a cow from her father's herd with her. This cow (the *ubulungu* cow) was both to provide milk for the woman, particularly during the first year of her marriage—when she was forbidden to drink the milk of her in-laws' cattle—and symbolic of a continuing link to her father's household and the protection of her ancestors.[21] For their part, female members of chiefs' families could use their status (albeit enforced by access to their fathers' or husbands' powers) as a way of protecting their own wealth.[22] Older women who were widowed or whose marriages collapsed frequently had some say in whether they remarried or not, although their choices about remarriage might be limited by their children, since children were ordinarily members of the father's family, and if the woman remarried she might have to leave them behind.[23] Women were not uniformly without choice in the matter of marriage, nor were they always exploited or entirely dependent on men.

Recognizing the difference of opinion as to the degree of women's economic and social subordination to men in the precolonial period is crucial to an understanding of administrators' motives in imposing and retaining the hut tax. If by 1883 Cape administrators knew that a man's control over his wives and daughters was not complete, while they simultaneously believed that women produced most family income through raising crops, then why continue to collect a tax that assumed that a married man controlled all the family's economic assets? If administrators were aware that they were not simply allowing the tax law to reflect the structure of African families, then what were they doing in continuing to collect the tax?

Part of the reason for the hut tax's longevity was probably plain bureaucratic inertia. By 1883 the hut tax had been collected in parts of the Transkei for five years. A revolt had been sparked by the tax, and any attempt to change it or link it more effectively to actual income was probably not even considered at the time.

A second, related reason for the persistence of the hut tax was its ease of administration. It was far simpler to make only one family member legally liable for taxes than it was to make all adults liable. Similarly, it was easier to calibrate a tax based on the number of wives in a family than one based on a family's actual income or wealth, especially given the problems of evaluating noncash income among a predominantly illiterate population.[24]

In addition to these largely pragmatic reasons for retaining the hut tax, there was a final reason that had to do with white ideas about gender relations and the proper division of labor within African families. There were features of African family structure that many whites deplored and hoped to change to make them more like the emerging ideal for white—specifically, British colonial—families in which women were the spiritual and domestic center of the family and men controlled the economic sphere. (I do not mean to suggest that this ideal was monolithic or uncontested, but it was gaining popularity in the social circles of colonial administrators).[25] First, most whites were against polygyny.[26] By placing a tax on each wife, the state essentially fined a man with multiple wives. Some white officials understood that there already was an economic cost to having many wives in the form of bridewealth. At ten shillings per year, the hut tax was pitifully small when compared to a bridewealth of up to ten to fifteen cattle—valued at anything between three and fourteen pounds apiece depending on market conditions.

Moreover, polygyny as a practice was never as widespread as many whites believed. Magistrates found this surprising fact out after initially compiling taxpayer rolls. In Tsolo District, for example, in 1882 there were 2,014 adult men and only 1,637 married women; there were also 423 unmarried women and 4,241 children.[27] While some of these adult men must have been unmarried or widowed, it still seems likely that only a few could have had more than one wife. The Umtata District magistrate in 1880 reported he had "discovered by the census returns that poligamy [sic] is not nearly so much practised by the natives as generally supposed, fully two thirds of the married men not having more than one wife."[28]

Commissioners taking testimony in 1881 at the Native Laws and Customs Commission found it difficult to believe that there were quite a few African men who did not want to have more than one wife. One of the commissioners asked a headman, Tshuka, "Why did you not marry two wives according to Native Custom?" He answered, "I don't want two wives." The commissioner persisted, insisting that all Africans liked large households, to which Tshuka responded that that was not always true. The commissioner continued to probe: "Do you think it better to have one wife?" Tshuka replied, "I find the trouble of marrying one wife to be quite sufficient for me." That reply prompted still more questions from the commissioner, and Tshuka retorted, "What do I want with a second wife?" With stunning persistence, the commissioner stated, "That is what we want to know, namely, why do Kafirs [a derogatory term for Bantu-speaking Africans] like more than one wife?" Tshuka patiently explained, "Well, people are not all alike; there are among the Kafirs some who like only one wife, and there are others who like more than one. It is according to their inclination."[29] That marriage practices might vary among individual Africans was almost beyond the commissioner's comprehension.

While some Africans had a personal preference for monogamy, others were Christians who, following Christian practice, had only one wife. Some of these Christians were relatively wealthy and for them wealth was not correlated with having multiple wives. In practice, therefore, the hut tax was a flat tax—often both the wealthiest and the poorest (if both were monogamous) had to pay the same amount per year to the state. Yet some whites thought hut tax an appropriate even if largely symbolic indication of their disapproval of polygyny. Despite all intentions, however, the state's available evidence indicated that the hut tax had no impact on the rate of polygyny, which remained low.[30]

Many whites also frowned on the division of labor within the family along gender lines. As they saw it, women and children did much of the work while the adult men idled or, worse, attended beer drinks.[31] (When women attended beer drinks, officials were even more scandalized.) Major Elliot, then chief magistrate of Tembuland, wrote in 1881 that he considered polygamy "an obstacle to the advance of civilisation. The practical evils attending it are that it enables men to live in idleness and compels women to work. . . . The only reasons I have ever heard natives advance in favour of polygamy are that it is convenient and pleasant, and I have never attempted to meet or refute this argument."[32] Whites associated men's idleness with heathenism, hedonism, and economic backwardness.[33] Conversely, they associated men working on a daily basis with spiritual enlightenment and economic prosperity. These associations were reinforced by the historical connection among mission stations, by men being drawn into agricultural labor through the use of plow and draft oxen, and by the production of marketable cash crops.[34] White officials hoped to strengthen this linkage by using the hut tax to force all Africans into the cash economy; a corollary to this reasoning was an assumption that only by African men taking on a greater share of the labor would families be able to produce enough to pay the hut tax. The man who had originally implemented the hut tax in Natal, Theophilus Shepstone, explained his intentions to the Native Laws and Customs Commission in 1881. He considered it "a good foundation for revenue," a "tax on polygamists," and an inducement to participate in local markets.[35] The Cape-based commissioners did not explain their motivations any more succinctly.

Hut tax did compel Africans to participate in a cash economy, even if only at a low level, because the tax could be paid only in cash. But the ten-shilling hut tax was a relatively small financial obligation that few had difficulty meeting in this early period. This was true even though the hut tax alone was a higher proportion of income than most whites had to pay in all their taxes combined.[36] A flock of fewer than ten sheep provided enough wool to sell to settle the yearly tax (assuming that each sheep produced a modest four pounds of wool, for which the going rate hovered around four pence per pound; at 12 pence per shilling and 20 shillings per pound, 10 sheep could produce 13 shillings and four pence per year of wool). On the basis of 1904 census averages, the average flock owned by Transkeian farmers had eighteen sheep.[37] In areas where sheep raising was impractical, tobacco and grain substituted as cash crops; in desperate circumstances, the hide of one cow was usually worth at least ten shillings, while a live cow was worth between three and twelve pounds.[38] In 1904 the "average" rural African family was paying approximately 6 percent of its gross income (one pound, ten shillings—this figure included one poll tax and one hut tax—out of twenty-six pounds' worth of produce and wool).[39] As a result, the hut tax by itself did not effectively force most African men to shoulder more agricultural labor or to become wage earners.[40]

In sum, before the implementation in some Transkeian districts of the Glen Grey Act in the mid-1890s, white officials hoped that the hut tax would not only produce revenue but that it would also assist in reshaping gender and social roles for African women and men. Specifically, they hoped, first, that polygyny would decline and eventually vanish and, second, that men would work harder. African women were to become more like the ideal for colonial Englishwomen: women who concentrated on domestic duties while leaving their men to do the monetarily productive labor; women who committed to monogamous marriages in which they were the junior, silent partners. Simultaneously, African women were to remain "Native" women who would not aspire to the same high social station as that held by white women.[41] Yet hut tax by itself did not impose a high enough price either to deter polygyny or to propel men into wage labor. What it did do was lay the legal groundwork for social, cultural, and economic changes in African women's roles, changes that would be catalyzed by additional taxation, the development of migrant labor, population growth, and the impact of legislation that severely restricted women's choices.

THE EFFECTS OF TAXES ON WOMEN, 1895–1925

Once again in this period, state policymakers imposed new taxes based on their own assumptions about African society, how it had changed, and how they as officials would like to see it develop. The primary intent of these taxes was to generate revenue for the state; but in choosing what new taxes to impose, officials made some revealing value judgments.

The new taxes included General Rate—poll tax—and the livestock rate (sometimes called dipping tax) in both the Transkei and the Cape.[42] Moreover, in the Transkei the state imposed the Glen Grey scheme on several districts from the 1890s onward. The Glen Grey Act of 1894 was not only a scheme for separate political representation—through the establishment of district councils and the General Council (Bunga) in Umtata; it also provided for the survey of individual landholdings and the assignment of quitrent title, and each year the titleholder of a surveyed plot had to pay rent to the state.[43] Although this might superficially appear to have been a system of land leasing rather than taxation, in fact in surveyed districts the quitrent replaced the hut tax for titleholders; those African men who were not lucky enough to be assigned surveyed lots usually did have access to much smaller garden plots and grazing land and had to continue to pay hut tax at the usual rate.

Once a district was surveyed the annual amount of money each African man owed to the state increased. In a surveyed district a married man with a plot paid quitrent, usually fifteen shillings per year but up to thirty and forty-five shillings in some places, depending on the plot's size, which ranged from ten to twenty-five acres in the various districts. (In the Glen Grey District of the Cape and in a few districts of the Transkei, the government also imposed a Labour Tax on each adult man who could not prove he had been a wage laborer in the previous year. Although the framer of the Glen Grey Act, Cecil Rhodes, initially intended for the Labour Tax to be collected throughout the Transkei, it proved unworkable and was collected only sporadically and eventually abolished.)[44] In addition, each man, married or not, had to pay a General Rate (poll tax) of ten shillings per year until that amount was doubled, with the 1925 Native Administration and Development Act, to one pound per year. All adult men in the Transkei had become taxpayers by the mid-1920s: an unmarried man owed at least one pound per year for General Rate; a married man without a surveyed plot owed at least thirty shillings per year for General Rate and hut tax; and a married man with surveyed land, at least forty-five shillings (two pounds, five shillings) per year for quitrent and General Rate. Along with these taxes there were stock rates imposed throughout the Transkei by 1911; these varied from sixpence to one shilling per cow.

The payment of General Rate was the responsibility of the individual man and was not a family responsibility in the way the hut tax had been. As a result, the poll tax implicitly recognized that all African men reached their majority at age eighteen regardless of marital status. It also presumed that migrant labor or other wage-earning opportunities had made unmarried men at least as economically productive as wives. The poll tax also, as we saw with its imposition in Natal and Zululand before the Bambatha Rebellion, had the potential to divide families over who had the right to control the money earned by migrant laborers. The replacement of hut tax with quitrent in surveyed districts also shifted the tax system's emphasis away from women as economic producers and instead focused on land as a productive resource and men as the tenants of the land. The notion behind quitrent was that long-term security of tenure (as represented by the quitrent title) made the land inherently more valuable and thus taxable or rentable (or both) at a higher rate. Both the General Rate and quitrent ignored women, however, and as a result, they further divorced African women from both an officially recognized adult status and any legal claim to the land. As we shall see below, although new taxes were a significant material burden, they recognized and created an enhanced legal status for men—at least those men who had access to surveyed plots—both as the most economically productive members of society and as the principal trustees of the land.

In contrast to those men who had devised the hut tax system of the 1870s and 1880s, policymakers in 1894 and later, like Cecil Rhodes, tended to be professional politicians, beholden to a largely white electorate whose primary interest in Africans, especially younger African men, was as a potential wage-labor force. Beyond Africans' usefulness as laborers, whites tended to discuss them as the Native Problem or the Native Question.[45] Before the 1890s the major problem that Africans had posed for whites was a military one, but with the final incorporation of most of the independent African polities into the various white-controlled states in South Africa in the 1890s, the "problem" for whites became social, economic, and political. As historian Saul Dubow has noted, the theory behind the British imperial mission in southern Africa was subtly changing. Rather than striving for the eventual assimilation of Africans into imperial culture, many whites, including those in the Native Affairs Department, were beginning to believe that Africans could not be assimilated culturally and could at best be taught to be useful as laborers within a white-controlled society.[46] These changes in outlook became embodied in the separate tax structure for Africans.

The policymakers who devised the new taxes did so with particular aims in mind. They hoped to tax the wages of young unmarried men, and also to force those young unmarried men who had previously avoided wage labor onto the labor market. They did this despite the fact that there was much evidence available that previous taxes attempting to force people into wage labor had no net effect.[47] Policymakers ignored women for two reasons. First, white officials in the early 1900s were less interested in promoting African agriculture (still dominated by female labor), and instead chose to promote (male) industrial labor. They wanted African men as wage-earning employees and not as independent farmers in competition with white farmers.[48] Second, as policymakers began to believe that African culture, including gender roles, could not easily or quickly be changed, they began to lose their interest in the long term (or even the short term) social effects on women of the taxes they proposed. Telling evidence of this neglect of women is provided by the *Second-Third Reports of the Select Committee on Native Affairs* of the South African Parliament in 1912. In the whole publication (277 pages of testimony taken over a two-month period in 1912), all of which is dedicated to the topic of African taxation, the only question explored with regard to women and taxation was what consequences hut tax had on the rate of polygyny. In fact, the rate of polygyny remained relatively low and unchanged in most districts of the Transkei (see table 6.1).

TABLE 6.1 Polygyny among Taxpayers in the Transkei, 1903

District	1 wife	Percentage	2 or more wives	Percentage	Total
Bizana	3,615	83.5	714	16.5	4,329
Engcobo	7,692	83.4	1,529	16.6	9,221
Mt. Frere	2,425	78.4	768	21.6	3,093
Tsolo	2,876	79.2	754	20.8	3,630
Umtata	4,572	79.5	1,181	20.5	5,753
Umzimkulu	3,859	81.0	887	19.0	4,746
6-district total	25,039	81.1	5,833	18.9	30,872
Total	95,232	77.9	27,019	22.1	122,251

Sources: Acting Resident Magistrate Umtata District to CMT, 23 March 1903, CMT 3/172, letter 280; Resident Magistrate Mt. Frere District to CMT, 27 February 1903, CMT 3/131; Resident Magistrate Engcobo District to CMT, 23 February 1903, CMT 3/92; Acting Resident Magistrate Bizana District to CMT, 4 March 1903, CMT 3/55; Acting Resident Magistrate Tsolo District to CMT, "Conjugal Condition of Natives in the Native Transkeian Territories, District Tsolo," 13 March 1903, CMT 3/161; Acting Resident Magistrate Umzimkulu District to CMT, 11 March 1903, CMT 3/174; evidence of E. E. Dower, Chief Clerk, Native Affairs Dept., Cape Colony, 2 October 1903, Records of the 1902–3 South African Native Affairs Commission, C17, vol. 3, Union Archives Depot, Pretoria.

In creating these new taxes, the framers had less of a social agenda for African women in mind than they had an economic agenda for African men. But simply because there was no agenda for African women did not mean that there was no effect on women. In fact, the General Rate and quitrent had two important effects on women. The first was on women's social and legal status, including status within the family, and the second and related effect was on women's economic prospects.

Registration as a taxpayer conferred higher status—the status of being an adult and, in the case of quitrent, a landholder. Many Africans were themselves aware of the status implications of being recognized by the state as taxpayers.[49] The magistrate of Mount Frere District in 1913 noted the relative ease of registering men for hut tax, as compared to the difficulty in registering men for the General Rate: "Few seek to avoid registration for hut tax as their occupation of land depends on this and to be a hut taxpayer gives a man a certain amount of status which a mere general rate payer does not acquire."[50] The colonial state allowed a few African men in the Cape to vote if they could pass a means and literacy test, but the Glen Grey Act had effectively foreclosed the possibility of widespread rural African enrollment on the common voters' roll. This exclusion from the broader society's political life was a serious departure from the precolonial African version of male adulthood that had accorded adult married men certain rights and that had recognized changes in a man's status and wealth over his lifetime: typically, as a man's wealth and numbers of dependents had increased, his status and influence had also increased.[51] State officials (as well as Christian missionaries) had also commonly disapproved of the circumcision ceremony through which African society had historically recognized the beginning of the transition to adult male status.[52] For most African men the requirement to pay tax and the tax receipt itself was the only recognition of their adult status that they ever received from the white state. From the perspective of the white-controlled state, taxpayers were the only adults in African society.

By imposing the General Rate on unmarried men, the state endowed them with some kind of legal adult status, even if it was less "prestigious" than the old status of hut taxpayer or the new status of quitrent payer. A young man had to register himself on the tax rolls when he reached the age of eighteen and afterward became liable for his own tax. By constituting a relationship between all men—married or not—and the state, taxes reinforced and added a new dimension to women's subordinate status. As discussed in previous chapters, the state's demand for taxes was partly a straight monetary demand, but it was also an engagement of the African population in a ritual of rule. While male taxpayers did play the role of subordinates to state officials in the payment of taxes, they also walked away with tax receipts that brought with them some of the power of the state. There was danger involved in allowing one's name to be inscribed on the tax rolls, but the danger was partly offset by the acquisition of adult status and the protections against prosecution and the witchcraft of the state that paying taxes conferred. Women in this early period, by not commonly participating in the ritual of tax payment, were kept away from the dangerous eye of state scrutiny, but they also lost status as adults.

The allocation of land with quitrent title in the districts surveyed under Glen Grey, as well as the ossification of the system of individual tenure and male inheritance of quitrent rights, tended to debase women's economic and social station as well, especially since it began to take effect as the African population continued to grow.[53] Glen Grey surveys and individual tenure put a finite limit on the number of plots, and with the concurrent increase in population it became common by the late 1920s for newly married couples to be unable to get large arable plots of land because there was none available.[54] (Most couples were able to acquire a small garden plot that was usually less than an acre, but this was not big enough to support a family.)[55]

With the decreasing availability of land, men's access to land became less dependent on marital status and more dependent on the luck of inheritance. A titleholder's eldest son (or if there were multiple wives, his eldest son by his Great Wife) legally inherited the title; in practice, however, the heir had either to be married already or marry within a year of his father's death to take over the land. In short, before 1895 marriage had been necessary and sufficient for a man to receive arable land; after 1895 marriage was still necessary but it was no longer sufficient. In addition, the administration of quitrent became more rigorous about women not being able to hold title in their own names.[56] With increasing competition for arable land, state officials were looking for ways to disqualify claimants, and being female was legally an obvious disqualification.[57] Thus women became even more dependent on their male relatives for access to land.[58]

In the surveyed districts of the Transkei those rural wives unlucky enough to be without access to large plots of arable land stood little chance of raising enough food to support their families. Yet their husbands were still required to pay hut tax (renamed local tax) for them. These wives, unless they had wage-earning jobs themselves, were no longer economic assets for their husbands, they were economic liabilities.

The fact that a decreasing proportion of adults could reasonably expect to have arable plots contributed to further social consequences. First, it caused some men to engage in migrant labor for longer periods. Second, it might have fueled an increase in the numbers of men deserting their rural wives or absconding to avoid marriage.[59] Third, it might have lessened the expectations among rural women of having stable marriages, which in turn may have provided greater impetus for women to become wage laborers themselves.[60]

After 1906, approximately thirty years after the hut tax was first imposed in the Transkei, an increasing number of men from the Cape did become migratory wage laborers.[61] Many were young unmarried men who sought wage labor as a way to buy cattle for bridewealth (lobola) in the wake of both the rinderpest epidemic and, after 1907, the East Coast fever epidemic, when so many livestock owners lost the majority of their cattle. It was not the hut tax that forced these men onto the labor market; it was rather a combination of environmental, cultural, and demographic factors.

As husbands and sons more commonly spent longer periods engaged in migrant labor, women had to take greater responsibility for the actual physical payment of taxes. This real responsibility contradicted one of the principles of the tax system: that women were legal minors unable to fulfill adult obligations. As early as 1907 women sometimes paid the tax, although magistrates usually allowed male migrant laborers extra time to return from the mines to pay taxes themselves if necessary.[62] As men spent less time in the rural areas, women had to suffer the brunt of the consequences of nonpayment even though they were not in any legal sense liable. The punishments for nonpayment of taxes could be severe: the man could be tried and stood virtually no chance of being acquitted.[63] After the trial, the police could seize the family's livestock and other movable property, they could imprison him, or they could confiscate his usufruct title to the land, evicting his whole family in the process, and assign the land to someone else.

In reality, however, the state rarely resorted to these punishments (although the times it did may have left vivid impressions on people's minds). In looking through the record books of court cases for some Transkeian magistrates, it becomes apparent that in most cases the court had only to serve a summons for the quitrent or tax to be paid.[64] In some of these cases, men came home or sent money when they heard of the impending crisis. But in others women procured the money themselves. Some women were successful commercial farmers, selling produce, eggs, or wool to earn sufficient cash for the taxes as well as for additional needs.[65] Others took advantage of the land shortage by earning wages while illegally renting out their plots to other African farmers or allowing them to farm on the halves (the local term for sharecropping).[66] Some got money by taking a lover who could be coaxed into providing the cash.[67] Others took out loans from white traders or wealthier (often male) relatives.[68] Still others became migrant laborers themselves while leaving their extended families to occupy the land.[69]

These strategies paid the quitrent and taxes, and they may also have elevated these women's positions, at least to the extent of making them more economically independent from their male relatives. But the fact that the state did not legally recognize them as adults with rights to the land or to most forms of property undermined their efforts.[70] The state effectively taxed women without according them the status of taxpayers or adults.[71] Women were still economically productive, but the tax regulations (as well as other laws) treated them as legal minors without defensible property rights.

THE EFFECT OF TAXES ON WOMEN, 1926–58

As the proverb says, *Umbango uvuth' emolotheni* (Strife blazes up in the [family] ash-heap). (Xhosa proverb quoted in Monica Wilson, *Reaction to Conquest*)

Bantu life is changing rapidly. The subjection of women is not now a universal practice; witchcraft is on the wane. . . . Tribalism has been shattered on the rock of individualism. . . . The quiet Arcadian existence is no more. (Testimony of journalist H. Dhlomo to the 1930–32 Native Economic Commission)

These two quotations reflect some of the tensions of African family life that were emerging in this period. The sardonic nostalgia that Dhlomo (who was born in KwaZulu-Natal) had for the "quiet Arcadian existence" of the past contrasts sharply with the Mpondo proverb that suggests that the family was and always had been a significant source of strife. The material circumstances for African families were changing for the worse even as women and junior men continued to gain some independence from parents and older men in the countryside. That independence, born of migrant labor and the changing cultural climate, came at a price, however. Many junior men found themselves without claims to land in the rural areas, and women often took on the burden of working the land, holding the family together, and taking the blame for problems and failures. Despite Dhlomo's assertion that the subjection of women and witchcraft were both fading from the scene, women were still legally subordinate to men and were socially more likely to face witchcraft accusations. Strife continued to blaze up within the family.

The implementation of the 1925 Native Administration and Development Act provides a convenient historical marker in the development of the tax structure and its effects on African gender relations. This act finally unified and systematized the various tax systems that had existed in the four provinces of South Africa (Cape, Natal, Orange Free State, and Transvaal). In addition, it altered the destination of tax revenues, so that some were earmarked specifically for African education and some for the development of local African councils administered by the Native Affairs Department. But the bulk of revenues still went to pay for the direct governance of the African population by white magistrates. A particular philosophy underpinned this tax system: the white-controlled state treated Africans as though they constituted a homogeneous group with few differences in background or aspirations, and as though they were immutably alien to white society. Africans needed to be allowed some local autonomy (in the form of councils), but beyond the local level they still needed a firm white hand directing them.[72] And, since Africans and their customs were deemed immutable, the tax legislation made no overt attempt to alter the status of women within that culture.

The systemization of the tax system came at the same time as women were assuming more responsibility for paying the taxes, and as life in the rural areas was becoming impoverished. By the 1930s and 1940s the financial situation for many African families in the rural areas had become desperate, and taxes simply added to that desperation. By the 1940s and 1950s tax and quitrent arrears in the Transkei hovered between 20 and 35 percent, much higher than any time previously.[73]

One analyst, a former chief magistrate of the Transkei, estimated that the total average tax liability per family in 1943 was forty-four shillings, a figure little changed from that of the late 1920s.[74] What had changed was the family's ability to pay those taxes. Taxes were part of an overall budgeted expenditure by the family (if it had three children and the husband worked on the Rand) of £57/12 (fifty-seven pounds, twelve shillings) per year. These expenses could not be offset by a total gross income of £44/10/08 (if the man held a surface job at the mines) or £48/07/02 (if he was an underground worker). The cash value of grain and other goods (including vegetables grown and eaten by the family and wool sold for cash to local trading stores) produced in the Transkei was only a little under £18 per family in 1943; in 1904 the value had been £26.[75] What these figures show is that the agricultural income for the average African family had declined substantially over the first four decades of the twentieth century, and that in 1943 that same average family was being taxed on a nonexistent or minute net income.

The figures assumed that the family had access to arable land and that it was able to produce a substantial quantity of grain, meat, and milk for its own consumption and that the bulk of the husband's wages reached the family in the rural areas.[76] Despite these optimistic premises, a family with one wage earner could not earn sufficient income to cover its expenses; the only alternatives were for a second family member to become a wage earner or for the family to go heavily into debt or both.[77] That second wage earner was frequently a woman.[78]

But women faced ever greater restrictions on their ability to find wage-earning jobs. The greatest restrictions resulted from legislation curtailing women's migration. Before the 1920s Transkeian officials allowed women freedom of movement into, out of, and within the rural areas. This contrasted with the situation in Natal and the Transvaal, where women were legally required to obtain their guardians' permission to leave their homesteads.[79] But with the findings of the Stallard Commission of the late 1910s and the consequent passage of the 1923 Natives (Urban) Areas Act, the state began to implement uniform statutes relating to segregation in cities and towns across the provinces. The act gave white municipal authorities the right to exclude African women from urban areas as a way to deny urban land rights—and future political rights—to Africans generally.[80] By gradually denying women legal migration to the urban areas, officials often succeeded in cutting many women off from the more lucrative jobs. Instead, women who went to towns did so illegally and often had to settle for illicit and sometimes degrading occupations, such as prostitution and beer brewing, or else they had to work as domestic servants, who earned little for long hours of work.[81]

Another more subtle restriction resulted from the cultural, social, and economic changes women's status had already undergone as the legal position of African women as minors gradually leached into women's social identities. Discussions of African family life in the 1930s and 1940s frequently depicted women as childlike in both good and bad ways. For example, many Africans (and whites) feared that the migrant-labor system and the long absences of adult men from the rural areas fostered a loss of control and discipline among African women that was leading to the breakdown of the African family.[82] As one male African writer to the *Bantu World* complained in 1938, "There is something wrong with our womenfolk to-day. They have lost their respect, discipline, and manners to the opposite sex." The crux of his argument was "the looseness of their [women's] lives, the illegal unions, unhappy marriages, and the easy love which Bantu daughters accept without thinking, only to be left with illegitimate children whose fathers could not be traced and be compelled to maintain them." The writer left little doubt as to where he felt the responsibility for this moral decay lay: "It is no use hiding the poisonous misdeeds of women, they must be told straightway [sic] of these wrongs, perhaps a small number of them might repent."[83] This commentator saw the root of the problem in women's childlike nature—childlike in the sense of being undisciplined and present-oriented. Women needed men to control them, and anything that forced men to leave women on their own for extended periods of time was bound to have unfortunate consequences.[84]

A concurrent strand of thought about African women still saw them as childlike but more benevolently, as the innocent victims of circumstances beyond their control. By the time the Native Economic Commission of 1930–32 met, many commentators—both African and white—remarked on the role taxation and other economic requirements played in forcing African women out of family life in the rural areas and often into illegal occupations in the towns. For example, Dr. A. B. Xuma, originally from Engcobo District of the Transkei, pointed out to the commission that rural women were often caught in financial crises:

> Almost all the Native people with income or without, with or without even this four morgen plot of land [about 3.5 hectares; available in Native Reserves] are saddled with a tax which is *proportionately* much

higher than what any European pays on the basis of income. . . . This is a heavy burden to so poor a community. The consequence is that both those who have these small plots of land and those who are landless must spend some time away from home in some industrial centre to get cash to meet these demands. . . . Women come to the industrial centres: For work usually as domestic servants; to join husbands usually after the husband has been in the city for some time; I have never known any women (Native) who came to town for immoral purposes.[85]

Xuma was clearly trying to acquit African women of the charge that they came to town with the express intention of becoming prostitutes or beer brewers and shebeen queens (women who illegally sold alcohol in towns). In trying to clear them of such charges, however, he implicitly conceded that they often *ended up* by earning a living through "immoral" activities.[86] Xuma carefully couched his defense of women both in terms of their inherent industriousness (they wished to work) and of their marital fidelity (they wished to be with their husbands). He was appealing to a particular ideal of women as respectable wives and helpmates, an ideal that might find favor with white officials and that he himself might have believed.

But to what degree did women themselves accept gender identities partly based on their childlike status? Women delegates of the Universal Negro Improvement Association, Engcobo branch, appealed poignantly to members of the Native Economic Commission by juxtaposing taxation, marital and filial desertion, and influx control measures:

> 1. As regards our grievances, we are complaining about the various taxes inflicted upon us, having no husbands and sons. We complain of having no eye to plead for us to the Government and our local traders have no mercy to pay cash for our agricultural produce.
>
> 2. Another grievance we have is the Pass Law. We are called upon to produce passes we being women when we visit large areas like towns— we are being searched, arrested and fined our monies.[87]

They professed that their husbands and sons were their legitimate protectors and mediators with the world outside the home; but, the women implied, their male relations could not be counted on and the government ought to step in and take their places. At the same time, in the second point, the women objected to being legally identified as criminals if they did go to the urban areas. Overall, the women presented themselves as passive and blameless, subordinate to men and the state and asking for mercy.

Legally, mercy was all women could ask for from the state, and officials did grant mercy to individuals, especially to deserted wives. For example, one women in Tsolo District in 1946 used a Cape Town–based male relative to plead her case with the magistrate when she had been threatened with eviction after her husband's desertion and default on taxes. The male relative complained, "Sir in this occasion the government is very unfair by assisting Henry in killing his family of six including the wife, because the quickest way of killing a native by starvation is stopping him from growing mealies."[88] The magistrate responded by telling the local headman to let the wife "carry on" cultivating her husband's land,[89] but he also cautioned the Cape Town kinsman, "You must remember that if you do not pay your taxes and owe two years or more the land may be taken away from you."[90] The wife in this case successfully mobilized her male relative on her behalf and retained the right to the land. But the male relative had taken the place of the husband as the responsible party, and the woman and her children still had only a derivative legal claim to use the land.

The legal restrictions imposed by the state magnified many of the social difficulties faced by women in the rural areas. Historian Keith Breckenridge in interviews with older, former migrant laborers from the Transkei noted that money (in particular the gold coins that were in circulation in the 1930s) was considered "the property of male homestead heads": "Informants insist that married women and daughters were not allowed to possess their own hoards of gold coins. . . . Women were expected only to keep small change or pocket money."[91] This expectation that women not control money was in direct opposition to the necessity for women to control a homestead's finances while the male head of the family was away. The difference between expectations and reality created the potential for conflict and blame when the man returned from his urban job. Tensions within a rural family could erupt into open hostility. A woman whose husband left to become a migrant laborer often felt isolated within her husband's family; and she was subject to the whims of her in-laws, particularly during the onerous first year of marriage. If the husband did not return when expected, she might be accused of being a witch who had driven him away.[92] In contrast, older women with grown children often had considerable power within their husbands' households, and that power was usually exercised over junior members of the household, including daughters-in-law. Widows frequently found themselves the targets of suspicions: anthropologist Philip Mayer quoted one widowed

African woman as saying, "'To be a widow in the country is to be made responsible for all the misfortunes of the neighbourhood. A widow is always being suspected.'"[93]

The suspicions surrounding women increased as they found themselves increasingly unable to rely on their husbands for support and access to land. In particular, long-held beliefs about women's access to supernatural powers intersected with beliefs about the supernatural powers available to state officials to enlarge the social problems faced by women.

WOMEN AND THE SUPERNATURAL STATE

Historically, African women living in the Transkei were often believed to have access to supernatural powers. These powers could derive from the force of their ancestors, who might harm others if they felt that their descendant would then benefit, or from the force of evil supernatural actors, such as the tikoloshe (a mythical, one-legged, sexually rapacious dwarf), the impundulu (lightning bird), the icanti (an evil snake), or through various medicines made for evil purposes.[94] Men were also accused of witchcraft, but women, particularly married women living in their in-laws' households and widows, were at the greatest risk for such accusations. Monica Wilson wrote in the 1930s, "The vast majority of accusations of witchcraft or sorcery are against women."[95]

One can explain this tendency to accuse women of witchcraft in structural-functionalist terms: young women were often literally strangers in their new husbands' households, and they brought with them into the marriage both material possessions and personalities that occasionally brought them into conflict with members of their new families. This conflict sometimes worsened to the point where, if something went wrong with the harvest or some family member became ill, the newest wife or daughter-in-law became the easiest target for blame, and even if no direct proof of guilt could be found, the woman was often accused of witchcraft.[96] This view tends to see women as victimized by witchcraft accusations because of their relative weakness within their husbands' families. But the people making the accusations did not see themselves as blaming someone who was weak; rather they believed that these women had real supernatural *power*.[97] Moreover, this supernatural power was enhanced by more mundane sorts of power—the power to have and raise children, the power to labor productively for the good of the household, and the power of having created through marriage a broader web of social relationships that could support the marital family if necessary.[98] Witchcraft accusations thus emerged from women's weaknesses and isolation within their in-laws' household, as well as from a common set of assumptions about women's strengths.[99]

Two specific court cases provide examples of the changes in women's roles, and the propensity for blaming women for domestic disasters. While neither of these cases directly relate to taxation, they do illustrate the ways in which women's social roles were changing and often made them more vulnerable to witchcraft accusations.[100] In particular, the consequences of men's prolonged absences as migrant laborers figure prominently in the following two cases.

The first case was from 1933 in Cofimvaba District. A widow was accused of witchcraft by a diviner who was hired by her brother-in-law to discover the reasons behind several recent illnesses and deaths in the rural household. The brother-in-law testified at the trial of the diviner that the diviner, who was also a woman, "said there was a witch bird [probably a lightning bird, or impundulu] at the kraal. I asked her to whom it belonged. She replied it belonged to the wife of my younger brother. She said the husband of that woman had died. She said that witch bird killed the man and the children of that wife. She did not name the woman by name. The person indicated was present. My brother referred to had only one wife—Noorange."[101] Noorange herself had her own version of events: "She [the diviner] indicated me as killing the people of the kraal. She said this woman who has no husband. She killed her husband and the children and the [live]stock at the kraal. She said it was a widow whose husband died at the Mines. I am the only one to whom this description applies."[102] As a widow, Noorange was immediately an object of suspicion when people began to fall ill; the fact that her husband had died while away working at the mines increased the suspicion that she had killed her husband from afar with supernatural agents or familiars.

Migrant labor caused a number of anxieties among African families. Working in the mines was above all dangerous, and deaths and serious injuries were common among miners. Accidental deaths might sometimes be attributed to the use of witchcraft. Young men also sometimes "absconded" to the mines—abandoning young wives or pregnant girlfriends or overbearing parents—and thus disrupted the socially accepted norms of family life. Having stated that "Xhosa witchcraft is predominately a women's affair," anthropologist Mayer noted that Africans believed that witches turned "migrants into absconders," reflecting some lingering tensions in parentally arranged marriages.[103] Even the majority of migrant laborers who did maintain ties with their rural families often could not perform social rituals needed to insure that the homestead both survived and flourished.[104] If something went wrong in the homestead, the neglect of rituals might seem an obvious cause. In addition, migrant labor disrupted gender roles as wives of migrant laborers had to take responsibility for the herds of livestock that represented the life savings of their families. Historically, Africans had believed that livestock were to be handled only by the men of the homestead.[105] This violation placed the cattle and the whole family at risk, according to many Africans' beliefs. Widows and other women who remained in the rural areas often bore the blame for deaths, social disruption, problems with the livestock, and other familial disasters.

A 1939 civil suit brought in Umtata District for the return of four head of bridewealth cattle (or their value, twelve pounds) illustrates a conflict over children caused partially by the husband's status as a migrant laborer. The husband claimed that his wife had abandoned him for no reason while he was away at the gold mines. The wife had a slightly different version of events, stating that after thirteen years of marriage she had been driven away by her husband because all three of their children had died. "I asked him to take me to the doctor," she said, meaning a Western-trained doctor.

> But he said he would not do so as I was killing my children myself. He was imputing witchcraft to me. He threw my belongings outside and told me to clear out as he did not want me. . . . After I was driven away I was given a necklace of a horse's tail by my husband's people. . . . The necklace was a reproach to me, i.e. that they were driving me away. . . . [Headman] Johnson sent for my husband who came and admitted that he had given me a horse tail necklace but refused to say anything more as the case was in the hands of the attorneys.

Her husband had been away at work for three years, and she denied that she had taken a lover or neglected his home or given him any reason to drive her away. "My husband said he could not live with a woman who could not rear children. . . . I wanted to be taken to a European doctor because my children were dying." The assistant magistrate trying the case found for the husband and ordered either that the wife return to her husband or that four bridewealth cattle be returned to the husband's family and the marriage would then be dissolved.[106]

If we accept the wife's testimony as accurate, then the marriage fractured over the deaths of the couple's children. Whether or not the husband had openly accused the woman of witchcraft as she claimed, as the person in charge of the homestead in his absence she was open to suspicion. That suspicion may have been enough for her husband to prefer the return of the cattle instead of the return of his estranged wife. His relationship with his wife, which might in a different era have had a stronger emotional and social content, came down to the issue of whether she had used malevolent supernatural powers to kill her own children during his absence at the mines.

As more men spent longer periods away from the rural areas at work, their wives became the primary agents for physically paying the taxes. People had to pay taxes to retain access to farmland. The ritual of tax payments, though, brought the taxpayer into direct contact with state officials, usually either the magistrate himself or one of his clerks, and the payer came away with a receipt that had legal powers and that also had the ability to deflect the power of the state. When African men participated in the ritual, they partook of some of that power and returned home with it in the form of the receipt. For men, the power they thus acquired was both legal and magical: the receipt acknowledged their adulthood and their social power as well as the discharge of their debt. When African women participated in the ritual, as they more frequently did from the 1920s onward, they too partook of state power, but this power could be either a benefit or a liability for the men of their families. As a benefit, it was an essential part of a family strategy of survival, with women simply doing what was necessary to hold the family together and retain access to land; as a liability, it elevated women's position visàvis the state at the expense of men's position. But the power that women acquired was not in the legal realm (since they were legal minors) but in the realm of the magical and symbolic. In short, the fact that women frequently paid the taxes due even though they were not, as individuals, legally liable for the taxes both heightened their power within the family and rendered that power even more potentially suspicious and disruptive.[107]

By the 1940s and 1950s women's economic and legal positions in the rural areas had become even more marginal. Before the 1895–1925 period, rural wives were extremely important to male labor migrants because a man could not legally be assigned an arable allotment unless he was married; in addition, until the 1910s or 1920s (depending on the district) a man could still receive an additional allotment for each additional wife, assuming that there was land available, but the wife and family had to be in continuous occupation of the land for him to retain it. If the man had any hope at all of establishing himself as a farmer independent of wage labor, he had to have a wife. Men who had land thus felt pressure to marry and to keep marriages together. By the 1940s and 1950s, though, the number of African families was greater than the number of available land allotments. A man who was still fortunate enough to have access to land was under even more pressure to have a wife and family to farm the plot in his absence. The absolute need for a wife and family to retain such a landholding gave some wives a new power within their families, and that power could very easily be attributed to the manipulation of supernatural powers. The fact that wives typically also were responsible for making the tax payments suggested a way in which they and the state jointly acted with supernatural powers.

For widows living on their deceased husbands' land, the routine suspicion that was often leveled at widows was magnified by their occupation of that very scarce resource—land. Magistrates sometimes stepped in to prevent headmen from reallocating land away from a widow to a new family. One case in Tsolo District in 1943 had a widow complaining to the magistrate that her headman had reallocated her land when she traveled to Cape Town to take care of her ailing son.

> I am a widow and taxpayer in the District of Tsolo. Some four years ago I received information that my son, who was in Cape Town was ill, and I went to Cape Town. I was away about three years. On my return last year I found that my land had been re-allotted by the Headman of the Location to Ntsompelwana Bobotyana. Ntsompelwana Bobotyana has taken a mean advantage of my absence on account of my son's illness. I left him in charge. I sent my money for my taxes to him. On one occasion he misappropriated the whole amount of £2/10/- [two pounds, ten shillings]. . . . I now appeal to this Office against this action of the Headman.[108]

The chief magistrate forced the headman to give her back her land. This apparent complicity between the state and a widow may have been merely annoying for the headman involved (although he was probably not pleased that his own dishonesty had come to light), or it may have had a more sinister aspect as he contemplated the power that this widow had apparently acquired through her taxpaying and appeal to state authority.

Women who were accused of witchcraft or who were treated badly by their relations could take their case to court to rectify the problem, even if they had few legal rights. However, the alliance between women and the state in these cases had the effect of magnifying the suspicions surrounding them both: the state seemed to collude with witches or otherwise immoral and selfish women against African families and male authority. The effect of taxes and of state regulations regarding land was like gasoline being poured on the conflict that had historically blazed within the family.

Taxes and the way they were collected severely eroded women's social position. Women became perpetual legal minors who had no defensible legal ownership of property and few rights, yet they often bore the burden of taxpaying and defending their husbands' rights to property. Women also took the blame, often in the form of witchcraft accusations, for much that went wrong in rural society, from an increase in the number of illegitimate children to the devastation of the rural economy. They were also increasingly responsible for maintaining their husbands' claims on the land, both by occupying it and by paying the taxes due. Taxes empowered the state and the state's culpability for the multiple failures of rural life became linked with those who paid taxes to the state. As we will see in the next chapter, dissent against state policies in the 1950s flared into open revolt, and women who continued to pay taxes often found themselves identified by rebels as collaborators with the white-controlled state and as witches.[109]

By the 1950s women, legally prevented from rural land-owning and most legal urban wage-earning, often had to default on making tax payments themselves because of the financial conditions in the Transkei. In defaulting on the taxes, women once again were faced by a dual threat: the state could legally evict them from the land and their husbands could blame them for the loss. Those women who still had sufficient money to pay taxes faced the question of whether to pay the money to the state and be denounced by rebels or pay the money to the rebels and risk eviction or jail. Women were caught in the midst of a developing battle over political rights, gender roles, and women's access to supernatural powers.

CHAPTER 7

GOVERNMENT WITCHCRAFT

Taxation, the Supernatural, and the Mpondo Revolt in the Transkei, 1953–63

> When I turn on my radio, when I hear that someone in the
> Pondoland forest was beaten and tortured, I say that we
> have been lied to: Hitler is not dead, when I turn on my
> radio, when I hear that someone in jail slipped off a piece of
> soap, fell and died I say that we have been lied to: Hitler is
> not dead, he is likely to be found in Pretoria.
>
> —STEVE BIKO, "I WRITE WHAT I LIKE"

At the time that Black Consciousness leader Steve Biko wrote the above words in the early 1970s, the South African state was far along in its plans to turn the former Native Reserves—including the Transkei—into so-called homelands. These homelands would, in the eyes of the apartheid planners, become independent states and would compensate Africans for the loss of all political rights within "white" South Africa. The far-reaching grand apartheid plan, enacted between 1948 and the mid-1980s, set aside approximately 13 percent of the total land area of South Africa for several African homelands, leaving the remaining 87 percent to be the property of white South Africans. Apartheid was a set of policies built on the framework laid down by the Glen Grey Act and subsequent Land Acts to confine African land use to restricted areas and to channel African political aspirations into political entities, like the General Council, or Bunga, in the Transkei, that were theoretically independent of—but were actually subordinate to—the central South African state controlled by whites.

As apartheid planning took shape in the 1950s and 1960s, Africans contested the political futures being mapped out for them. Biko's statement about beatings and torture in the Pondoland forest was a reference to the Mpondo

Revolt of the late 1950s and early 1960s, which shredded the old public transcript of African deference to authority and compelled the state once again to
resort to outright coercion and paramilitary force to reassert its control over
the region, as it had in 1880.[1] Biko tied the brutal suppression of the revolt to
later violent state actions that led to the death of political detainees (including,
ultimately, Biko himself) while in state custody. The need to use violence to
suppress dissent in the rural areas in the 1950s and 1960s was a foreshadowing
of the political future of the apartheid regime.

When a full-fledged revolt broke out in the Transkei in 1959, white South
African authorities were caught off balance. Magistrates and officially appointed
chiefs and headmen all over the Transkei—not just in Pondoland—were in the
process of implementing Bantu Authorities legislation that would eventually
bring apartheid-generated "self-rule" to the territory in 1963.[2] As part of the new
legislation, the General Rate was increased and Africans found themselves more
and more ruled by chiefs who had been handpicked by white magistrates and
were often tainted by a reputation for corruption and nepotism as well as for
using witchcraft to insure their positions and enrich themselves. Low-level
unrest had been simmering for several years, particularly in those locations
where "betterment" and "rehabilitation" schemes had already taken effect. Yet
white officials consistently acted as if this unrest were of little consequence and
could either be ignored or defused. The revolt proved them wrong.

Students of colonial history in Africa have often grappled with the issue of
why Africans did not rebel more frequently against imperial rule. Yet when analyzing the revolts that did occur, scholars sometimes find the causation unprob-
lematic: colonial states provoked the revolts by being discriminatory and
oppressive. While this was manifestly true, the question of why people revolted
at one historical moment may be linked to why they did not revolt previously,
so that the violence of the Mpondo Revolt may be linked in substantial ways
to the absence of armed rebellion in the Transkei since 1880. The interplay
between rebellion and years of quiescence is related to the interplay between the
public transcript and the hidden transcript described by political scientist James
Scott. The long periods of relative quiescence represent those times when dissenting members of the African rural population either kept their dissent to
themselves, or at least kept it out of earshot of state officials. But the long periods of quiescence may also represent times when many rural Africans retained
enough autonomy that open resistance or rebellion against the state was not a
favored or attractive option.[3] In this context, historian John Lonsdale's notion
of "civic virtue," developed out of his study of the causes behind the Kenyan
(Mau Mau) rebellion of the 1950s, raises some important issues.

Lonsdale notes that until the 1940s in most areas of colonized Kenya the cultural meanings of African rural life had altered only subtly. Many Kikuyu were still able to achieve the status of honorable adults (civic virtue, in Lonsdale's phrasing) as they grew older, by marrying, farming successfully, and acquiring dependents and wealth. As they achieved this merited virtue, they also, according to Kikuyu historical patterns, achieved a greater political voice within their community. But by the 1940s the colonial state and the expansion of settler agriculture had closed down many avenues for achieving this social adulthood for the vast majority of Kikuyu. Young men in the rising generation found themselves without any access to farmland or even to squatters' rights on white-owned farms; if they instead chose to go to the cities to work, they found it almost impossible to bring their families with them legally, while the wages themselves remained too low to start and maintain a rural household. Men were thus stuck in a kind of perpetual adolescence, unable to live out their visions of a proper and prosperous adulthood: "The despair of aging adolescents caused criminal abandon; hope of generation succession inspired insurgent discipline."[4] Moreover, women in the rising generation also found themselves bereft of an imagined future of prosperous adulthood. Yet if women journeyed to the city to earn money, they were doubly condemned: first, often by their own families who feared that they might tarnish their own reputations and that of their families by becoming prostitutes; second, by the colonial state, which usually regarded them as illegal inhabitants of the urban areas.[5] This inability of men and women to achieve social adulthood either in the rural or urban areas gradually pushed them toward resisting the state and white settlers openly, as well as blowing open several rifts within Kikuyu society between those few who had still managed to do well under the colonial system and the larger number who had not.[6]

What happened in the mid- to late 1950s in the Transkeian countryside was a similar breakdown of the old moral order, as younger men—as well as some older men in some districts—faced a future without land and without any meaningful prospect of achieving the kind of adulthood that their fathers and grandfathers had had. The complicated and internally contradictory system of rule that had developed over the previous seventy years in the Transkeian administration finally foundered. It foundered partly because of the material deprivations faced by the rural African population and partly because the various interventions (betterment schemes, cattle culling, etc.) engaged in by state officials were punitive and disruptive to rural life. But the breakdown of state control was also symptomatic of the interpretation that many Africans had of the causes of these problems as they analyzed them in the light of long-held beliefs about witchcraft and state officials' access to supernatural powers.

These beliefs about a supernatural basis for state power were essential to the "hidden transcript"; white officials themselves were largely oblivious to any possible connection they might have with a set of beliefs that they themselves tended to characterize as "backward" and "superstitious." In enacting their roles as representatives of the state, they followed the public transcript of either benevolent paternalist (the obverse of which was the stern father) or, in the more recent period, of scientific manager. But for Africans, the military power of the state and the rituals of rule—including tax collection—made plausible another explanation based on a web of natural and supernatural powers in which they were enmeshed.[7]

Beliefs in witchcraft are still common in both rural and urban areas of South Africa,[8] and they clearly had repercussions in the Transkeian region in this period. What Monica Wilson noted in the 1930s of Mpondo society held true in the 1950s: "Much space has here been devoted to witchcraft and magic, but it is commensurate with the part they play in Pondo life. The belief in them permeates the whole of life."[9] It is essential to explore how witchcraft beliefs and African ideas of the achievement of civic virtue permeated state administrative practices in the 1950s and early 1960s and affected the development of the revolt and its aftermath.

BACKGROUND TO THE REVOLT:
THE POLITICAL AND SUPERNATURAL CONTEXT

Various policies began to upset the state's control as early as the 1940s.[10] The increasing intervention of officials into the everyday lives of African farmers in the name of conservation, "betterment," and economic development caused many Africans to reevaluate their relationships with the state and state officials. Most seriously, that intervention usually involved coerced cattle culling as well as cattle dipping, fencing, and villagization in an attempt to reduce the pressure on grazing land and increase agricultural productivity. The South African state also began in the 1950s its extended effort to create a puppet state in the "homeland" of the Transkei. With the National Party in power, officials instituted grand apartheid schemes, building on the existing base of urban segregation and African rural reserves. The Transkei was to become a self-governing country, and to bring this about, the National Party enacted laws (collectively known as Bantu, or Tribal, Authorities) that transferred power (or its appearance) from the Native Affairs Department to so-called paramount chiefs and headmen.[11] Significantly, the South African state's plans for "self-government" did not allow chiefs to abandon the hated rehabilitation schemes, so that chiefs increasingly found themselves being directly blamed for the schemes' continuation. Moreover, with the transfer of responsibility to the chiefs also came an increase in their salaries, and it was widely suspected that the chiefs were enriching themselves at the expense of common people through the Bantu Authorities schemes and the higher taxation that accompanied them. The transfer of power to the chiefs deepened the rift between state-recognized chiefs and commoners and, between 1951 and 1963, accelerated the expanding unrest throughout the Transkei.

Yet the unrest that began in the 1950s resulted not just from the economic costs of various state agricultural schemes, nor was it exclusively the result of resentment over the reenergized intrusion of the state in the rural areas; it was also a result of the social and cultural lens through which Africans saw state actions. The fact that the state was forcing cattle culling, fencing, and villagization led to renewed suspicions that the state was colluding with witches or other malevolent people (including chiefs, who were themselves state officials) against the interests of African farmers. Evidence for this suspicion can be seen in a number of areas. First, resistance to rehabilitation became strongly linked to Bantu Authorities schemes and discontent over tax increases, which in turn led to a decline in tax payments. Second, there is some evidence that those people who attempted to rally resistance to state policies used, at least in some forums, the language of punishing witches to promote their cause. Finally, a widespread increase in the number of livestock thefts, and the state's inability to capture and punish the culprits, led some to believe that state officials themselves were implicated in both the thefts and the witchcraft used to accomplish the thefts and shelter the thieves.

Rehabilitation and betterment schemes were unpopular with African farmers. From the viewpoint of stock owners, cattle culling was their worst nightmare come true: the state was no longer satisfied merely to tax the cattle and dip them, it now proposed to kill them outright or force their sale at depressed prices. In many districts of the Transkei in the 1950s, up to 35 or 40 percent of the people had no access to land to cultivate, but they did have access to grazing land. For their agricultural income they were entirely dependent on their livestock, and as livestock populations increased the grasslands became overgrazed. The state's rationale for culling cattle and other livestock populations was to reverse the worst effects of overgrazing, but for many Africans cattle culling was a direct attack on their livelihoods.

But cattle culling also had significant social consequences: cattle were essential to bridewealth, which still in the 1950s was the only way of sealing a marriage in a socially acceptable way. Many of the cattle grazing in the Transkei in the 1950s had either been part of someone's bridewealth or else were intended to be someone's bridewealth or both.[12] With fewer cattle available, either young men had to postpone marriage or else fathers had to be willing to accept much lower bridewealths for their daughters. In either case, the threat to African marriage and family life was unmistakable. The concern over bridewealth also involved the family's relationship with the ancestors: after death, a person's veneration as an ancestor depended on the existence of recognized descendants, and many of the sacrifices required by local beliefs could properly be completed only with the sacrifice of a cow. A thriving cattle herd was a significant marker of a prosperous farmer with a flourishing (and moral) homestead.

Sheep and other livestock, including the extremely hardy goats and donkeys, were also threatened by the culling campaign. Sheep and wool had for many years been the most reliable exports for African farmers; goats and sheep could also be used for some kinds of sacrifices and the meat for entertaining important guests; and donkeys provided transport. Officials were always keen to eradicate donkeys altogether, and they were intolerant of stock owners' protests. Officials thought that Africans were "irrationally" attached to their animals, and they were determined to force Africans to streamline and modernize their animal husbandry practices, even if it meant killing every last animal a stock owner had.[13]

At the same time, fencing restricted the very old practice of free-range grazing while limiting the total available grazing land, thus directly curbing the number of livestock that could survive and the number of people who could survive as livestock owners.[14] Fencing also cost money, usually paid for by African farmers themselves through higher stock taxes. Even for people who were only partly dependent on livestock for their livelihood—along with income from arable farming and wages—these were serious economic costs.

A third component of rehabilitation, villagization was intended in theory to rationalize the allocation of crop, grazing, and residential land to maximize productivity. However, villagization had unsettling social effects. Families were forced to move their homesteads closer together, which may have fostered both the transmission of diseases and the development of disputes among neighbors—two common causes, historically, of witchcraft allegations. Second, relocation may have weakened people's familial defenses against witchcraft and other misfortunes by removing them from the vicinity of their ancestors' graves and outside their ancestors' protection. Finally, the relocation often meant that there was less land available for small garden plots, further undercutting women's already diminished economic roles. Thus the state's rehabilitation programs were both economically and socially destabilizing and were often seen by Africans as reckless exercises of state power and as evidence of increasing use of malevolent witchcraft on the part of state officials.

The rehabilitation schemes became even more unpopular because state officials frequently used force to implement them. Often, whole villages were punished with fines when anonymous individuals protested rehabilitation policies—for example, by cutting fences. Families who resisted villagization caused magistrates to refuse to allocate new homestead sites in entire administrative areas. Those who balked at cattle culling found themselves unable to get government permits to move livestock between districts.[15] People who owed back taxes found that when they took their cattle to be dipped, the dipping inspectors seized the cattle to satisfy the tax debt.[16] Agricultural officers tried to bully people into complying with soil stabilization measures, such as contour plowing and ridging, and alienated people to the point where some residents of Xalanga District told their magistrate in 1961 that they "wanted nothing that comes from Government."[17] The fact that officials tended to impose collective responsibility, punishing all—including the innocent—for the crimes of the few, revealed state officials as capricious, vindictive, and dangerous.[18] It may also have had the effect of building a greater sense of community in opposition to the state.

One indication of the rise in African unrest was the decline in tax payments in the 1950s. By 1956 the chief magistrate complained, "The last returns of native taxes show that outstandings in respect of local tax [hut tax], quitrent, stock rate and General Council levy [poll tax] are considerable."[19] As an extreme case, in 1959 in Bizana District only about 4 percent of the poll tax and 17 percent of the hut tax was paid.[20]

Widespread defaults on taxes resulted from a number of linked events. Tax payments no longer exempted people from the penalties of rehabilitation measures; in other words, the receipts ceased to perform as protection against the power of the state. In fact, several people interviewed in the rural Transkei stated that they had no idea what the taxes were used for. In the words of one informant, "We paid because the government wanted the tax. If you didn't pay they took what you had in the kraal."[21] Another man commented, "you were taxed for your existence, for your presence in the world."[22] In addition, many Africans linked tax increases in the 1950s with the establishment of Bantu Authorities and the empowerment of the chiefs. According to an investigating committee composed of Bantu Affairs Department officials, "The average Bantu finds the [new] system complicated and looks upon the Authority as a means of imposing further taxes. He is ignorant of any rights or advantages he may have under the system, and generally considers that it is not in accordance with his own laws and customs. The result is an ever-widening rift between the masses and those in control."[23] In eastern Pondoland, the dislike of the pro-government paramount chief, Botha Sigcau, was so great that it by itself drove many Africans to reject rehabilitation schemes. Sigcau's unpopularity predated tax increases and Bantu Authorities, but it reached its zenith in 1957, when, at a meeting in Bizana, people's vocal protests drowned out the prepared remarks of both Sigcau and the magistrate.[24]

Botha Sigcau was not the only unpopular chief. As the South African state gave chiefs additional judicial and administrative powers, they seemed more threatening to the African population at large. "The greatest objection to the system (Bantu Authorities) I encountered," reported the Transkei's chief magistrate in 1960, "was the granting of jurisdiction and considerable authority to the Chiefs. The expression was continually voiced that . . . the Chiefs living amongst the people could not be impartial."[25]

Fears that the chiefs might be regaining and using supernatural powers were advancing as well. A pamphlet produced by the African National Congress and sent to another pro-government chief, Kaiser Matanzima, in 1957 decried the malevolent powers used by chiefs who supported the state. Matanzima was a supporter of Bantu Authorities laws and rehabilitation policies; the ANC, for its part, was trying to raise its profile in the rural areas by allying itself with opponents of Bantu Authorities and rehabilitation. The pamphlet, entitled "Where There Is Neither Back Nor Front There Is No Truth," declared that the South African state was using chiefs as tools: "The Government has failed in the matter of the limitation of our livestock now it is giving that work over to be carried by the chiefs themselves. . . . Under this plan the chiefs will compel the people to pay more taxes than they are able to bear; they will compel the people to go out to work in the mines and on the farms. . . . they are going to force people to limit their stock so that they become perpetual slaves." The pamphlet castigated those chiefs who involved themselves in Bantu Authorities plans and attacked the white leadership of the South African state, who had created the apartheid policies. The policies, in the words of the pamphlet, meant "that it should be the chiefs themselves who should plant their knee on the chest of their own people while [South African prime minister and the architect of apartheid policies] Verwoerd and his colleagues will suck in oppression the warm blood of the Natives who have been made the sacrificial lamb to feed the families of the Europeans." The pamphlet went on to threaten those chiefs who collaborated with the state:

LET THEM [the chiefs] REFUSE TO CO-OPERATE AND LEAVE IT
TO VERWOERD TO APPOINT HIS RASCALS, BUT THE PEOPLE
WILL REFUSE TO SUPPORT THOSE RASCALS. SUCH PEOPLE
WILL BE LIKE WIZARDS AND THE PEOPLE KNOW HOW TO DEAL
WITH WIZARDS WHEN THEY CAUSE TROUBLE AMONG THEM.
On the other hand, let the chiefs know that whenever they allow them-
selves to be used as tools for collecting ripe loquats for which the
Europeans are craving, their end will be the same as that of the wizards
themselves.[26]

In short, the pamphlet linked taxation, migrant labor, and cattle culling
with chiefs who acted "like wizards," and declared that "the people" would discover and punish as witches and wizards (these terms were used interchangeably) those chiefs who cooperated with the state. Verwoerd and other white
officials were labeled as vampires, much like the *izulu,* a human incarnation of
the lightning bird (impundulu) The izulu was described by Wilson in the 1930s
as a "very beautiful young man, who becomes [a woman's] lover. Some
[Mpondo informants] say he is always in European dress. One informant
described him: 'He is a very beautiful man with a stiff collar, and dressed as if
he came from the goldfields. He has whiskers [probably sideburns] and a very
red mouth.'"[27] Although from this single pamphlet it is impossible to know
how widely accepted the analogy between chiefs and wizards was, it is suggestive of prevailing attitudes. The Xhosa name for the General Rate was *irhafu
yempundulu,* or impundulu tax, a very evocative name for a blood-sucking
tax.[28] Belief in the witchcraft of the state may have been accepted as a metaphor
by some and as literal truth by others, but in either case it implied that methods that had historically been used to punish witches were appropriate for
dealing with collaborators. Many took the analogy to heart.

A final factor that began to erode the state's authority in the 1950s was the
increase in livestock thefts in many districts. These thefts were rooted in the
decaying economic conditions in the Transkei. Many residents had no access
to arable land[29] and no prospect of finding wage labor locally, while state-
imposed influx controls hindered them from legally migrating elsewhere.[30]
Even those people who did plow land or own livestock were victims of deteriorating agricultural conditions: throughout the Transkei the maize crop of
1955–56 was only 20 percent of average, and in 1957 the market price for wool—
one of the most important sources of cash income—plummeted.[31] At the same
time, there were substantial numbers of live cattle, sheep, horses, and goats in
the Transkei, and the geography of the area, particularly in the more moun-
tainous districts, made their theft relatively easy.[32]

Thefts were also rooted, as Clifton Crais notes, in a rural gang culture of young men who had slipped the control of their elders and acted in a variety of antisocial ways. They stole livestock; they impregnated young women and then did not pay "damages" that local custom demanded to legitimize the children; they defied and often openly despised their parents; and they used their networks to evade capture and punishment. They terrorized those people who betrayed them to headmen or police, and they began burning their huts as well.[33] Older Africans, particularly those victimized by stock thefts, saw these thieves as evil and indicative of a frightening moral decay that had gripped rural society. The thieves often called themselves Nephews, and the name resonated with the cultural license often taken by nephews, particularly in their aunts' households.[34] (The name may also have resonated with the social and supernatural danger posed by wives and widows as strangers within their marital households.) The Nephews were young men who were more not yet rebels but who were disrupting the social order and revealing how fragile rural life had become.

The increase in stock thefts coincided with the implementation of Bantu Authorities legislation. As chiefs took over judicial powers, stock thefts increased. In Tsolo District, for example, reported stock theft cases rose from 105 in 1950 (involving the theft of 34 horses, 86 cattle, one pig, 387 sheep, 192 goats, and 45 fowls) to a high of 289 cases in 1955 (involving 114 horses, 319 cattle, only 66 sheep, 45 goats, and 18 fowls). Magistrates in other districts noted similar increases.[35] Many Africans were under the impression that the chiefs themselves were implicated in the crimes, either directly, by controlling the thieves and then protecting them from prosecution, or indirectly, by receiving bribes to look the other way. Stock theft victims showed their distrust of the chiefs' courts by bypassing them and continuing to take their cases to the magistrates' courts.[36] While it may seem surprising that Africans trusted their court cases with white magistrates and not with African chiefs, there were several factors at work. Most Africans living in the Transkei in the 1950s would have had little or no experience with taking cases to the chiefs' courts, except as a clandestine method of avoiding the law; the magistrates' courts, however, were well integrated into African life. In addition, the magistrates' courts allowed litigants and defendants to use lawyers to present their cases; typically cases in chiefs' courts had to be presented without lawyers. Although the Xhosa word for lawyer, *igqwetha*, can be loosely translated as "perverter of truth," there was a strong faith in the importance of hiring a lawyer to insure the best outcome of a case.[37] Witnesses who testified in trials in magistrates' courts could also be reimbursed for their expenses, which was not done if they testified in trials in chiefs' courts.[38] Africans viewed the chiefs' courts in the same way that they viewed the General Council that had been created with the Glen Grey Act—as a second-class form of governance designed to cheat people of their rights. When the Mpondo Revolt became more widespread in the late 1950s and 1960s, one thing that rebels usually insisted on was that people stop taking their court cases to either the chiefs or the magistrates and instead bring them to a rebel-constituted court.[39]

Stock thefts galvanized distrust of the state and collaborating chiefs. Allegations of witchcraft began to surface against individuals widely believed to be stock thieves, the rationale being that the thieves used medicines to spirit the livestock away quietly and disappear.[40] According to a headman in Tsolo District, a man was battered to death in 1959 who had "for many years been an active associate of stock thieves and, although not himself actively engaged in stealing, functioned as a go-between and witchdoctor, providing stock thieves with medicines and potions to render them immune from detection and prosecution."[41] People's suspicions about connections between chiefs and livestock thefts were fueled by the aggrandizement of the chiefs under Bantu Authorities: chiefs were becoming richer and more powerful, and they were suspected of doing this via taxation and witchcraft at the expense of the common people.

Victims of stock thefts looked to the magistrates' courts to apprehend and convict the thieves and to return at least some of the stock. But overworked magistrates and the nature of stock theft—particularly the edibility of the evidence—combined to make the prosecution of stock thieves haphazard. Again in Tsolo District, of the 105 reported cases in 1950, only 27 ever came to trial and only 17 cases (or 16.2 percent of the total number of reported cases) resulted in convictions. By 1955, with 289 reported cases, 62 cases resulted in trials, with only 23 (or 8 percent) ending in convictions.[42] Apparently, thieves stole many head of livestock without facing much real risk of apprehension and conviction, a judicial failure that began to make the magistrates as well as the chiefs look as though they might be implicated in the thefts. That state-sponsored cattle culling also made animals disappear, and that chiefs and magistrates openly promoted culling as part of their agricultural betterment schemes, was an obvious parallel to stock theft that deepened the suspicion that chiefs and magistrates were using witchcraft to empower and enrich themselves while they impoverished the majority of Africans.

The unrest that developed in the 1950s emerged out of the discontent caused by the agricultural and political policies of the South African state. But rural discontent with material conditions was not distinct from popular beliefs in the supernatural and the suspicion that state officials used supernatural powers to enrich themselves. This suspicion had always been a part of the hidden transcript of African political life since the 1880s, and it deepened as material conditions worsened, prompting some Africans to look to older methods of ridding society of witches for a cure for their social and material ills.

ORGANIZATIONS AND METHODS: THE REVOLT BEGINS

Witchcraft beliefs, the decline in tax payments, increasing stock theft, and punitive rehabilitation schemes combined to set the stage for the development of new rural organizations that gradually began to claim some of the state's powers. These organizations used methods that historically had been used to punish witches, with hut burning being one of the most often used tactics. In addition, the rebel organizations imposed their own fees and insisted that Africans cease paying taxes to the state. During the revolt, often for several months at a time, rebels succeeded in taking effective control over many areas, partly through local support for their general aims, partly through their willingness to use coercion, and partly through their manipulation of the symbols of supernatural and political authority. When state forces did finally intervene to crush the revolt, they too used hut burning and coercive tax collection to challenge the authority of the rebels.[43]

The earliest of the new organizations to challenge the state was Makhulu Span (Big Span).[44] Makhulu Span existed in many districts, but it was initially strong in Tsolo, Qumbu, Mount Ayliff, and Umtata Districts. According to accounts from both magistrates and African observers, it began sometime in 1955 as a vigilante organization to impose rough justice on stock thieves: "An organisation known as the 'Makulu span' was brought into being to combat stock thieves. The kraals of known or suspected stock thieves were razed by fire."[45]

A letter sent in 1955 by the Tsolo District chapter of Makhulu Span to one of the local chiefs made clear the organization's intention to stamp out theft. "Honourable Chief!" the letter began, "We are writing this letter to you so that you should summon a general meeting of all your location residents with a view that in the course of that meeting you should read out the contents of this letter and the list of names contained herein. You must tell them to return things belonging to other people before September 25. Those are thieves. We, 'Mkulu [sic] Span,' will get to know when you have done this thing." Although the letter writers addressed the recipient respectfully as chief, they also suspected him of participating in the thefts:

You are also labelled as a suspect, although there is no certainty in your case. You are being given a hint to make you wise so that you do not run the risk of being killed and burnt. . . .

Thieves must return things which do not belong to them to the rightful owners. We hope that you will act accordingly. May we remain, Chief, We are, Makulu Span (Above described).

The time for the thieves is past. We kill them and burn them.[46]

As the letter's last sentence promised, Makhulu Span's justice consisted of burning down the huts of suspected thieves, usually at night while the suspects slept within. Hut burning was intended either to force the alleged thieves to relocate or else to kill them, just as burning the huts of witches had historically served to expel them from the community.[47] The forms and methods of the revolt that later emerged throughout the Transkei after 1959 replicated Makhulu Span's earlier treatment of stock thieves.

A dramatic increase in hut burnings occurred in 1955–56 in response to stock theft. In 1956 in three districts (Qumbu, Tsolo, and Mount Fletcher), approximately five hundred huts belonging to eighty-six homesteads were burned, resulting in the deaths of twenty-one people. Faced with this violence, the same magistrates and chiefs who were having difficulty prosecuting stock thieves vigorously pursued the arsonists. The chief magistrate lamented in his report, "A difficulty encountered by the forces of order [the police] was the reluctance of victims of incendiarism to give information to the police."[48] Makhulu Span was able to enforce silence on witnesses to the arsons, while the state's attempt to prosecute them reinforced the notion that magistrates and chiefs were protecting and colluding with stock thieves. The chairman of a Cape Town–based group called the Pondomise Public Safety Committee wrote to the magistrate of Tsolo District in 1958, "Concerning the situation of the devastation of thieves . . . a meeting of about 230 people, all Pondomises met and discussed. The conclusion was that Let the thieves be burnt. . . . They did [commit the thefts] and they must do and die."[49]

Although some magistrates initially felt that Makhulu Span did a better job of eradicating stock theft than did ordinary criminal prosecution, state officials did not let Makhulu Span's bid for authority go unchallenged.[50] Under pressure from the state, Makhulu Span became more organized and more overtly rebellious. To safeguard its members, the organization began demanding money from every homestead to pay attorneys' fees and fines. People had either to pay the demanded money or else face death threats.[51] Some widows in

Tsolo District complained (anonymously) to the magistrate about Makhulu Span's demands for money: "Makhulu Span is demanding this money by night. . . . They demand £1–2–6 [one pound, two shillings, sixpence] each kraal [homestead]. . . . A person who does not intend to issue this money is killed and burn the huts. No one has not issued this money because we are afraid of being killed."[52] The fears of these women were born out by the high number of hut burnings that occurred in that district alone in 1958, when 191 huts were destroyed. These women were clearly not collaborators with the state in any ordinary sense, and in a letter they expressed their own criticisms of the Tribal Authorities laws: "Please sir take it to your hands this matter, we are in a bad stage, and the Tribal Authority had raised up bad thing to Africa's [probably Africans]."[53] They did not fear reprisals from the rebels because they were stock thieves or collaborators, but because they had defaulted on the payments demanded by Makhulu Span.[54] The organization had begun to act like a state in its demands for taxes. And the amounts that it demanded increased over time: in Qumbu District in 1961 they were demanding twenty rand from each homestead and threatening those who did not pay.[55]

Makhulu Span's targeting of widows reflected a broader problem of land-lessness in the Transkei. These widows continued to farm their deceased husbands' land, and that prevented other landless men from farming the land and establishing their families. It also reflected a deeper suspicion of widows as a category of people who were spiritually contaminated by the deaths of their husbands. Ordinarily, there were rituals that could be performed that would cleanse the widows of the contamination, but if those rituals were not done or if there were lingering suspicions that witchcraft might have caused the husband's death, a widow could find herself socially ostracized. At the same time, their claims to their husbands' land were legally shaky: if the couple had a son, he became the titleholder (if he was eighteen or older) and he also became his mother's legal guardian; if there was no son, the widow only farmed the land at the magistrate's pleasure. Widows still had to pay the taxes and quitrents due on the land if they wished to continue farming. Makhulu Span's demands for payment thus struck at a very vulnerable spot for widows as they battled to retain access to land but also shied away from the label of collaborator or witch.

In fact, many households did make payments to Makhulu Span that began to replace tax payments to the state. One possible explanation of this shift was one of strict practicality: homestead heads had only enough money to pay either Makhulu Span or the state, but not both, and since Makhulu Span was more of an immediate threat than the state, they paid Makhulu Span.[56] A second explanation might be that Makhulu Span had usurped the state's place by punishing stock thieves, and therefore people, especially victims of stock thieves, had transferred their allegiance as well as their payments. By the late 1950s and early 1960s, it was clear that both magistrates and Makhulu Span leaders equated their respective abilities to extract revenue from rural Africans with signs of their own power. One magistrate was explicit on this point: "The first indication that the attitude in any location was wrong [i.e., antigovernment] was a noticeable drop in the amount of taxes paid."[57] The actual money involved was important to both the state and to Makhulu Span, but beyond the money itself was the greater importance of the taxpaying ritual, which both acknowledged and constituted the power of the collector.

Unrest expanded during the late 1950s and early 1960s throughout the Transkei. New chapters of Makhulu Span emerged in other districts, notably Engcobo District, and pursued stock thieves as well as holding nighttime meetings to talk politics. In the words of one Engcobo man, "Taxes formed part of the discussion. The meetings were only lit by paraffin [kerosene] light so people wouldn't be able to see each other clearly. . . . Stock thieves were seen as collaborators with the government, and others collaborated by paying taxes. It was dangerous even to go to the magistrate's office," for fear of reprisals by Makhulu Span.[58] They attacked and killed several stock thieves and burned the huts of any chiefs and headmen suspected of assisting the thieves.[59] They also in 1961 attempted to firebomb the magistrate's office: "A person had entered the office [at night] and dropped or broken open a plastic jerry can containing petrol, spilling the contents over the floor . . . the jerry can had a type of detonator in it which burst the can but did not ignite its contents."[60] In areas of Engcobo where Makhulu Span was strong, they charged each person a five-rand fee in 1962 to help pay court fees at upcoming trials.[61]

The causes of violent unrest were similar throughout the Transkei: unpopular Bantu Authorities policies and personnel, stock theft, and the breakdown of the state's judicial machinery. Insurgents took many of the same measures: threatening chiefs and alleged collaborators, burning huts, and making monetary demands of the local population. By 1960, however, the resistance in Pondoland had become more consciously engaged in opposing the state by providing a local alternative that not only collected taxes and punished stock thieves but also effectively governed.

In Bizana District, in eastern Pondoland, an assault on three African members of the local Tribal Authority—the local administration set up by the South African state—started the disturbances in March 1960. The assault culminated in the burning of one of the local administrator's huts, the slaughtering of his pigs and chickens, and his own death.[62] Shortly after these assaults a list of grievances began to circulate in the district. The list had been drawn up by the rebel movement, called Congo or iKongo, in mid-1960, and it was inclusive: Bantu Authorities, taxation, installation of chiefs, allocation of land, court cases, reference books (passes), rehabilitation policies, and influx control were all listed as complaints.[63]

Magistrates usually stated that Congo was a short form of Congress, or the African National Congress, and an ANC leader who wrote a history of the revolt, Govan Mbeki, agrees.[64] (Congo may also have been a reference to the newly independent central African nation, formerly the Belgian Congo, that was much in the news in 1960 as it sank almost immediately into the five-year "Congo crisis"—including disastrous international intervention and neocolonial civil war.) Although there were ANC members involved in the Congo movement in the Transkei, it would be a stretch to state that it was an operation planned and directed by the ANC.[65] The list of grievances revealed the rebels as less concerned about the more mainstream issues that were staples of ANC rhetoric at the time—the right to vote, equal treatment under the law, and an end to racial discrimination—and more directly worried about access to rural farmland, taxes, immorality, and the power of chiefs.

The Pondoland rebels were directly challenging the control of the state, but they did so principally by attacking Africans who were either identified as collaborators with the state, or who otherwise continued to submit to the state. They "drew up lists" of people who "were summoned to appear before the Rebel's 'Court' and warned that their kraals would be burnt." Although these rebels had concrete political aspirations, the magistrate noted that they had spiritual motives as well: "The Rebel movement has a religious slant. Three of the ringleaders are Evangelists. When they start their meetings all the rebels prostrate themselves on the ground with their foreheads touching the ground. They refer to the Rebel court at their National Headquarters at Ndlovu Hill [in Bizana District] as a 'Holy Court.'" The magistrate concluded that the religious beliefs of the rebels influenced their conduct: "It would almost seem as if the Rebels are under the impression that they are conducting a Holy War and that what they are doing has the approval of the Deity. . . . This religious slant may perhaps explain why the rebels cannot understand that they have broken the law by burning kraals." The rebels saw themselves as engaged in moral work as they rid their society of antisocial elements, including witches and collaborators. The magistrate quoted an unnamed rebel informant who had claimed, "We found a list under a stone containing the names of the Tribal Authority Councillors and this list was placed there by the Deity."[66] Since the rebels were targeting these councillors as collaborators, God's assistance was real for the rebels.

While the obviously Christian beliefs of some of the rebel leaders might superficially seem at odds with beliefs in witchcraft, it is important to remember that many South African Christians maintained some witchcraft beliefs; they disapproved of and feared witchcraft but they still believed it to be a real force in the world.[67] Most Africans did not see a necessary contradiction between beliefs in Christianity and beliefs in the reality of witchcraft, just as they did not separate spiritual beliefs from the exercise of political power. Moreover, Congo's religious beliefs reflected the rebels' concern that the moral order in rural society had been seriously upset.

Spiritual beliefs infused the movement's political symbolism. A man from Lusikisiki District, in the criminal trial of an alleged leader of the Congo movement, identified the three types of people whom Congo punished with hut burning: people suspected of being traitors (including informers and people who had not paid their fees), men who had seduced and impregnated young women and who had not paid damage fees to the women's fathers, and people accused of witchcraft.[68] Another Congo meeting in Lusikisiki District revealed the same constellation of moral and political issues. The meeting had been opened "with Methodist Hymn No. 9 and prayers":[69] "Ready the Spirit of His love / Just now the stony to remove, / To apply, and witness with the blood, / And wash and seal the sons of God."[70]

Points taken from a "Constitution of the Congo," which circulated in eastern Pondoland in late 1960, illuminated people's concerns about the moral order and the way in which these concerns were fused with the organization's political aims. Point 1 insisted, "[court] cases must not be taken to the sub-chiefs," followed by point 2: "cases are dealt with by Congo." In point 5 Congo also reserved the authority, previously held by headmen and magistrates, to assign plots of arable land. In points 7 through 9, Congo levied taxes (in the form of admission fees) on chiefs and others considered to be too closely associated with the state, and stipulated, "When he does not pay it [the money] we must see to him." Levying these fees or tax substitutes was not only a way for the rebel movement to raise money, it also was a way of forcing people to choose sides.[71] Points 13 through 16 of Congo's constitution prohibited the drinking of distilled liquor and attendance at dances and parties and mandated that "Congo meetings will be opened by prayer and closed by prayer."[72] The politics of morality and the politics of land were one and the same for the rebels.

A witness at the Lusikisiki trial of participants in a rebel meeting quoted one organizer as saying, "We don't want Bantu Authorities and we don't want to pay taxes. We don't want our cattle to be dipped. We want to be ruled by the Russians and each man must pay 3/6 [three shillings, sixpence] to buy firearms from the Russians and to hire lawyers." The money "was to be used to buy guns from the Russians and to employ an attorney from America. . . . The Russians would abolish [cattle] dipping and that they did not want to be ruled by the white people but by the Russians and that they did not want Bantu Authorities. . . . It was said that no cases would be brought to court but would be tried by the Congo and lands and kraal sites would be issued by the Congo and hospital admissions would be sanctioned by the Congo."[73] The rumor about the roles that "the Russians" would play in the revolt is reminiscent of the rumors about the coming role of American bombers in the Wellington movement of the 1920s (see chapter 5). It is also reminiscent of a part of the 1857 Xhosa cattle-killing prophecy that suggested that the Russians were coming to assist Africans in their fight against the expansion of white settlement.[74] It seems likely that in 1960 the Russians featured in the rumor because they were prominently in the news and because the South African state was promoting itself as an enemy of the Soviet bloc. (The name Russians [Marashea[75]] was also used by an urban-based African gang that had some presence in the rural Transkei.) Rebels were not positioning themselves as Russian allies in the Cold War, however, as Americans were also going to provide assistance: they were lawyers who would assist the rebels in the courts. In the 1960 version of the rumor, the Russians and the Americans were very much against the dipping of cattle and the various policies initiated by the white-controlled South African apartheid state. Grievances over taxation, cattle dipping, court cases, witchcraft beliefs, and prayer were fused with rebellion, and the rebellion would be assisted by Russians and Americans.

Although Bizana District witnessed some of the most violent unrest, all Transkeian districts had similar outbreaks between 1960 and 1963.[76] The Engcobo District magistrate reported in 1961 that the hut of the chairman of District Authority (in charge of implementing Bantu Authorities locally) was burned down and later he and another man were "brutally murdered." Twenty-four persons were allegedly implicated in those murders, while a total of 270 people in Engcobo District were arrested for failure to pay taxes, for not having their passbook on them, for being in possession of dangerous weapons, or for a combination of these charges. The magistrate stressed the connection between support for government policies and the murder: "The deceased headman was a loyal supporter of government policy and it was gleaned from the evidence that the motive for the murder might have been the deceased's share in the establishment of Bantu Authorities in this district."[77] The magistrate of Umtata District reported that there was considerable opposition to headmen who carried out government policies, to land improvement schemes, and to fencing.

He stated that in one area of the district "Headman Mqekela Dadeni . . . was, during 1960, burnt to death together with a woman in a hut. The late headman was a strong supporter of the government policy and his location is a better-ment area."[78] That magistrate also noted that a virtual war among neighbors had broken out in various locations of the district, and some had fled into neighboring districts to escape the fighting.

In Butterworth District in 1960 a policeman reported that one headman was organizing a boycott of a particular trader's store and was also holding meet-ings attended by an attorney and "a stranger, a so-called herbalist." The attor-ney was collecting a fee of three pounds per person, "the receipts being marked 'rehabilitations.'" Another dissident was intimidating any African farmers who went along with soil reclamation measures and who built huts in state-planned villagization sites.[79] In 1961 an elderly pro-government headman asked for pro-tection from rebels who were threatening to burn down his huts and destroy his crops as well as threatening to kill him. His antagonists had held a meeting and then "went from hut to hut demanding money. They wanted each person to pay 10/- [ten shillings]. . . . The money was for the purpose of engaging an attorney. Then we asked was what the attorney was for and were told the attor-ney was 'to destroy fencing.'" This particular informant refused to pay. "I have heard that the headman's crops are to be cut down. I also heard that the new kraal next to mine has so far escaped being burnt down on account of my dogs. My kraal site happened to be in the planned residential area [a villagization site]. There is a rumour that any new kraal in the new residential areas will be burnt down."[80]

In Ngqeleni District in 1961, Chief Douglas Ndamase received three threat-ening letters, two sent from Umtata and one from Port Elizabeth, outside the Transkei. They opened by addressing him as Quisling Douglas Ndamase. The letters had a broader analytic framework than just local opposition to better-ment schemes: "In 1652 there came a plague in the form of white imperialism, oppression and economic exploitation. . . . In 1936 Hertzog with his power, struck another blow, viz. the Lands Acts, Native Rep Bills [sic]. Thereafter came the World War I which your father joined where he met a doggish death." The writer went on to vilify the current chief for his self-enrichment:

> Verwoerd, your "father" came with his colleagues and puppies. In his Bantu authorities you have been one of the chief protagonists. . . . This is shown by your fleecing the people in buying your cars, from the Willy's jeep van you had, to the two-tone car, to the two-tone Buick you are using now. Your masters have given your [sic] three farms

which have to be tilled by the poor voiceless peasants in those locations over which you are the chief police-chief. Poor widows at Mtyu,
Mamponomiseni, etc. are suffering under your burdensome yoke. I
will say nothing about white oppression. Only I wish to point out your
hand in the oppression of Africans.

The letter writer demanded that Ndamase resign from his position as chief
and denounce Bantu Authorities: "Stop prospering at our expense." The letter
was signed "Oppressed."[81]

In many of these districts, rebel movements—whether called Makhulu Span
or Congo—showed comparable concerns. The Tsolo District magistrate
reported to the chief magistrate in 1961 that Makhulu Span had "openly
declared war on all alleged stock thieves, witches and informers" and that "the
members of Makulu Span maintain that thieves, witches and informers must be
exterminated to the last man or woman."[82] Some rebels turned to diviners to
assist them against the supernatural powers of state officials, as "they believed
the witchdoctors could treat them so that they would be immune from arrest
and prosecution."[83]

The unrest was so generalized throughout the Transkei that in mid-1960 the
state appointed a Committee of Enquiry to research the background of the
revolt, particularly in eastern Pondoland. Committee members, all Bantu
Administration and Development Department (the new name for the Native
Affairs Department) personnel, heard from eighty-three African and twenty-
five white witnesses. The report comprehensively listed grievances against the
state, including hatred of increased taxation and rehabilitation schemes and
distrust of the Bantu Authorities system and of Chief Botha Sigcau. But the
report concluded that many of these grievances were "imaginary," and that
they "were carefully nursed and kept alive, presumably by subversive elements," by which the committee meant the ANC or its newer rival, the Pan-
Africanist Congress. As to Botha Sigcau's unpopularity, the committee decided
that it was "a direct outcome of his loyalty to the Government, his progressive
outlook on matters such as rehabilitation etc., and his untiring efforts to further the cause of Bantu self-Government."[84] Not surprisingly, when the report
became public in early October 1960, many Africans rejected this dismissive
version of their problems. According to Govan Mbeki, Pondoland rebel leaders met on 25 October and "formally announced their rejection of the report,
and expressed their determination to continue the struggle against Bantu
Authorities. They decided to stop paying taxes."[85] The rebels proposed to end
an essential material and ritual foundation of the state.

The rebels went beyond not paying their taxes to assassinating pro-government chiefs and headmen. As noted above, they killed one chief and four of his councillors in Bizana in December 1960, as well as burning the huts of two headmen and attacking their families.[86] A Bizana agricultural demonstrator was also killed for his participation in betterment schemes and his association with the state, and teachers were "told not to go to schools."[87] In February 1961 the chairman of an Engcobo District Tribal Authority was murdered, and in March, an Umtata headman, and there were persistent rumors that Makhulu Span planned to kill two chiefs in Qumbu District and several headmen in Tsolo District.[88]

In November 1960, the South African officials had declared a state of emergency in the Transkei; after officials learned of the killings and attempted assassinations, they became even more aggressive in their pursuit of rebels.[89] The Engcobo District magistrate arrested numerous people, many of them for not paying their taxes.[90] Known members of Makhulu Span in Qumbu District were arrested in early 1961 along with tax defaulters.[91] The state also began issuing revolvers to any chiefs who had received threats, and it supplied some with bodyguards.[92]

Escalating the official response, the state sent in special, paramilitary mobile police units to sweep the countryside. They were there to suppress rebellion, and one of their primary methods was to arrest tax defaulters. In 1961 magistrates repeatedly stressed in their reports to the chief magistrate the utility of arresting tax defaulters for defusing resistance and dispersing rebel organizations. The Idutywa District Bantu Affairs commissioner (the new name for the old office of magistrate) expressed his views on how nonpayment of taxes may have led to rebellion:

> [A headman] asked for his location to be combed by the [mobile] Unit. His view was that there were many of the residents in his ward who had not paid taxes for some years and were now openly saying in effect that they are above the law. Without wishing to digress into a tirade on tax prosecutions I have always and still hold the view that a total relaxation on tax enforcements such as we have witnessed in recent years is a retrogressive step—administratively even more so than financially.[93]

Tax arrests occurred all over the Transkei. The Qumbu District magistrate reported in mid-1961 that the mobile unit had arrested 116 people, most of whom were charged and convicted of defaulting on their taxes. He was satisfied that "the visit of the mobile unit has had a salutary effect on the payment of tax. . . . One of the significant aspects of the arrear tax payments was that many of the 'die-hards' with whom the Messenger of the Court has been struggling for settlement of taxes for a long time, came and paid tax voluntarily."[94] In Kentani District, over the course of one month, 681 people were arrested and charged, 90 percent with failure to pay taxes, and only 10 percent with failure to produce a passbook, illegal possession of firearms or dangerous weapons, or holding illegal meetings. The sentences that the magistrate imposed on tax defaulters included substantial fines or "7 days of imprisonment in respect of each year of default," and he ordered all tax arrears were to be paid immediately "and in default of payment [people] were sentenced to further period of imprisonment ranging from 14 to 30 days for each year of default." The magistrate concluded that although the punishments "appear rather severe, the effect on the adverse elements in the district has been most satisfactory."[95] In Bizana District in 1960–61, the magistrate tried 33 cases of arson (in which 177 were accused), 38 cases of murder or culpable homicide, 9 cases of holding an illegal meeting, 250 cases of pass-law violations, and 76 cases of possession of dangerous weapons; but by far the most significant percentage (80 percent) of the cases was for failure to pay taxes—1,633 cases.[96]

In addition to arresting tax defaulters, the state "suppressed the revolt by bringing in the military to assist the police, by using sten guns, Saracen armoured cars, and jets."[97] The mobile units frequently used brutal tactics, including beating, looting, and, it was alleged, rape.[98] The police also burned huts and killed livestock to punish those who supported the rebels. Some pro-government chiefs and headmen carried out their own punishments in the wake of the mobile units' visits. These punishments included a number of hut burnings and punitive reassignments of land, as well as the imposition of fines.[99] Both the police and the chiefs were "eating up" their enemies and using methods against rebels and rebel sympathizers that Africans had used to punish witches. Some chiefs and headmen used the revolt as a convenient cover to get rid of political enemies (even those who had not sided with the rebels) and provide benefits, like access to land, to their own supporters. In one case people in Umtata District complained that various headmen had been not informing quitrent titleholders when they had defaulted on their taxes: "The Headmen then, instead of so delivering the notices [of default], withhold them and the lands become forfeited without the knowledge of the owners. The Headmen can thereupon arrange for the sale of such lands to persons of their own choice who are prepared to pay a 'fee' (usually a beast [a cow]) to the Headman concerned."[100] The rebellion had developed into a civil conflict in many areas.

Sporadic rebel attacks on chiefs and headmen continued through 1962 into 1963. They targeted chiefs for their participation in betterment schemes or because they were suspected of participation in stock theft, or both.[101] Rebels continued to attack agricultural demonstrators and other government employees either by physically assaulting them or by burning their huts.[102]

State forces also engaged in widespread intimidation and violence through 1963. A report from the Bantu Affairs commissioner (the magistrate) of Engcobo District was typical. He began by suggesting, "There has been considerable police activity against subversive elements and a number of Bantu have been detained." But it was not just the regular police force that was engaged in these arrests: "A section of the Mobile Police has been stationed here and has been carrying out patrols. Helicopters have also been employed in rounding up suspects. On the surface everything is quiet in the district, but the situation requires to be carefully watched." He closed by noting that the local head of the Tribal Authority had fled the district for fear of his life.[103] In a later report, the Bantu Affairs commissioner conceded, "Police activities against subversive elements continue, and it now appears that the Bantu are more involved [in rebel politics] in this District than was at first suspected. Hardly any locations are not involved."[104] The hidden transcript was finally completely out in the open, and the state was battling to suppress it.

GOVERNMENT WITCHCRAFT AND THE IMPETUS FOR REVOLT

By the end of 1963 most of the disturbances in Pondoland and elsewhere in the Transkei had been crushed. The state had arrested over five thousand people during the previous three years, and of those over two thousand were eventually tried for various offenses related to the revolt.[105] In 1963 the state went ahead with its plans to grant the Transkei self-governing status,[106] and Chief Kaiser Matanzima emerged as the leader of the Transkei government. Much of the Bantu Authorities legislation was implemented, although rehabilitation schemes—particularly those involving cattle culling—lapsed in many areas of the Transkei. The Transkei received "independence" in 1976, a status that was recognized by only the South African government and the governments of other, similar "homelands," until the postapartheid South African state officially reabsorbed the homelands in 1994.

While the South African state had in 1963 survived a prolonged challenge to its authority, it is not clear that white officials were any the wiser about why the challenge had occurred. For the most part they concluded that the revolt was the result of nefarious "subversive elements" who whipped up "imaginary" grievances and hindered the "progressive" work they were trying to accomplish. To the extent that state officials understood that Bantu Authorities policies, rehabilitation programs, increased taxation, and stock thefts had deeply threatened African rural society, they saw rural society as being at fault for being backward or "red"—a reference to the red ocher that culturally conservative Africans used as a cosmetic. Evidence of African beliefs in witchcraft merely bolstered these official views, which were part of the state's own version of the public transcript.[107]

From the perspective of African farmers, however, there had been strong material grounds for the revolt: they were concerned about their extremely poor economic conditions and understood that they largely resulted from state policies and official actions. An integral part of African explanations for their material deprivation was spiritual beliefs, and these beliefs strongly shaped both the substance and timing of the revolt. People's beliefs that the state manipulated supernatural powers through its taxation and law enforcement policies had helped the state maintain its control over Africans; these beliefs had historically made it possible for a small number of whites—and the Africans they employed—to rule a vastly larger number of African subjects. In the late 1950s and early 1960s, witchcraft beliefs played a role in the attempt to overturn that rule. The malevolent nature of state witchcraft became increasingly obvious to many Africans during the 1950s as increases in stock theft, taxation, cattle culling, and other rehabilitation measures resulted in broad social destabilization that undercut the state's control.

Fears of the state's supernatural powers combined with poor economic conditions to provoke a crisis in the Transkei, a crisis that could be met only by punishing the witches and collaborators who had caused it. State witchcraft depended on local witches or wizards, and it was these people on whom rebels focused their attacks as they burned their huts and threatened their lives. People stopped paying taxes to the state, in part to sever their connections to the state, and instead paid them to rebel committees. Some did this willingly, others did so only under threat of punishment for collaboration, stock theft, or witchcraft.

Beliefs in the supernatural were important because they were part of people's everyday lives.[108] They were present in attitudes about the state and African chiefs; they carried over into agricultural practices and influenced livestock ownership; and they provided a partial explanation for the misfortunes suffered by African farmers while also suggesting a possible remedy. In the 1950s and 1960s they influenced the decision to revolt.

People revolted using the tools they had available to them. This meant that they burned huts down and clubbed people with iron-studded knobkerries, and it also meant that they targeted people and legitimized the violence with the cultural language they had grown up with. For some rebels the language was one of smelling out witches, for others it was the language of Christianity and holy justice. Govan Mbeki called the Mpondo Revolt a peasants' revolt, with the insurgents not motivated by their spiritual assumptions but instead goaded into action by an incipient class consciousness of their material exploitation at the hands of the apartheid state. This explanation, though, tended to depict the African rural population as split only between "rebels" on the one hand and "collaborators" on the other, without leaving much room for meaningful differences in status and opinions. Rural society had many rifts within it, as is evidenced by the degree of coercion that rebels often had to use to force people to stand behind them.

The rebels were angry, and they, as anthropologist Philip Mayer stated about so-called red Africans, held whites "responsible for the evil days that had befallen the people."[109] It was not their culture that made them angry, and their anger was not madness: the rebels were not people who had been maddened by modernity; they were not atavistic traditionalists fighting the white-controlled government because it was advocating modern bureaucratic management techniques.[110] They used spiritual beliefs to justify the rebellion because spiritual beliefs had for so long been a part of the system of rule by the white-controlled state.

To show that people enlisted their spiritual beliefs in the rebellion does not deny the significance of their material grievances. Supernatural beliefs and their connections to state power were one element of the old precolonial culture that continued through the mid-twentieth century, as demonstrated by one of the ANC's pamphlets that analogized collaborating chiefs with wizards and by the participation of Christian evangelists in the revolt's leadership. Spiritual beliefs were the way in which people interpreted the world and so they had to be a part of any rebellion against the current political order.

The revolt from 1955 to 1963 was a gradual and violent emergence of various hidden transcripts out into the open. The old public transcript of deference to state authority was shredded as state officials themselves were smelled out as witches who profited from the lightning-bird tax—the poll tax—that sucked the blood of the rural African population. The vivid imagery of the witch's familiar—"the most potent and sadistic of all mythical creatures"—had embodied the magnitude of the state's supernatural powers, but it also suggested that the power was profoundly illegitimate.[111] Yet the public transcript was not easily shredded, since it was based on a seventy-five-year history of interaction between rulers and the ruled. The ritual of tax payment had reinforced the subordination of Africans over the same period and as much as people disliked, distrusted, and feared the state and paying taxes, they also feared the consequences of not paying taxes and of more openly revolting. In the Transkei the lack of any sustained, violent attack on the South African state between 1880 and 1955, a quiescence that many historians have noted, suggests that the rituals of rule (including tax collection) and beliefs in the state's access to supernatural powers had dampened attempts at violent resistance. Although quiescence and high rates of tax compliance were not indications of whole-hearted support for the South African state, they were acknowledgments of both the material and supernatural powers of state officials.

What impelled people to revolt in the 1950s was that the South African state began to delegate more power to appointed chiefs, and simultaneously the supernatural powers of the state seemed to take a more destructive turn.[112] Taxes went up, stock thieves stole at will, and the state was more concerned with collecting taxes and protecting alleged stock thieves than it was with stopping the theft. People widely suspected chiefs and magistrates of shielding witches and of using witchcraft to consolidate their power, enrich themselves, and disrupt the social order. Chiefs acted "like wizards" as they executed state policies. Malevolent state witchcraft called for sometimes brutal methods of punishing and disempowering the witches and their collaborators. A belief in the supernatural powers of the state between 1955 and 1963 shaped and informed violent resistance to its rule.

CHAPTER 8

CONCLUSION

State Control, Rebellions, and Supernatural Beliefs

The genesis of this book was my impression, based on my research in the South African archives and interviews in the Transkei, that for long periods people paid their taxes even though state officials were in a relatively weak position to compel them to do so. As I set out to do the research for this project, my goals were to find out if my impression held broadly true and, if so, why people paid those taxes. My questions resulted from research—both my own and that of other scholars—that demonstrated that rural Africans found a white-controlled state illegitimate and that rural Africans were, for the most part, poor and found the taxes a significant economic burden.

In doing the research for this project, I found that the whole question of why people did or did not pay taxes required much more historical depth and context than I had initially thought. Tax demands by the state and tax payments made by rural Africans were not simply monetary transactions. They entailed a wealth of attitudes, history, and understandings that changed dynamically over time. Moreover, the transaction between the agent of the state receiving the payment and the subject of the state making the payment simultaneously redrew and smudged the line between colonizer and colonized. This observation does not deny the rapacity of the colonial and apartheid states, nor their capacity for brute force. Colonialism was a "confrontation of different regimes of value," as the Comaroffs state,[1] so that the cash that the state required to pay the tax could never fully capture or embody the essence and value of rural life to those Africans who paid it. White officials invested the tax payments they received with one set of meanings, while Africans tended to invest the payments with another. But the common moment of paying the tax and getting the receipt linked the two groups together in a system that was unequal and authoritarian, but not entirely one-sided.

Throughout the previous chapters, I have often used Scott's notions of public and hidden transcripts to discuss the different meanings that officials and African subjects had for these interactions. The idea of the hidden transcript is useful in understanding why a more or less dominated population might have seemed subservient in one context—when following the public transcript of deference to authority—and defiant or even rebellious in another—when circumstances seemed right (for a variety of reasons) for the expression of the subject's "true" feelings.[2] (This is reminiscent of Steve Biko's famous comment that "powerlessness breeds a race of beggars who smile at the enemy and swear at him in the sanctity of their toilets; who shout 'Baas' willingly during the day and call the white man a dog in their buses as they go home.")[3]

The largest problem with using hidden and public transcripts as a framework for analyzing African responses to the state in general and to taxation in particular is that it imposes an artificial dichotomy. It suggests that the public transcript is a performance, a pragmatic form of make-believe, while the hidden transcript represents the real thoughts of the subject. There may be, as is evident in the discussion over people's attitudes toward their magistrates and other officials, a good deal more interplay between the public and the hidden transcripts; they may not in fact be all that distinct, as the deference (or, in Biko's analysis, fear) on which the public transcript is predicated leaches into the private beliefs that help to write the hidden transcript. Moreover, to discuss the public and hidden transcripts suggests that there were two and only two ways of interpreting the colonial situation. While polarization of opinion is a common trait once rebellion has broken out, in the long quiet spaces between armed outbreaks there were often multiple hidden transcripts, and more than one public transcript as well.[4] This multiplicity of voices is to be expected given the variety of African experiences of colonial rule, the stratification of African society, and changes in cultural meanings and values over the course of the period from 1880 to 1963.[5]

This book began by asking why Africans did not rebel more often and why those rebellions that did take place happened when they did. The answers change depending on the time period under discussion; broadly speaking, over time open confrontation between rural Africans and state officials became more likely as the early compromises made by officials and Africans in the 1880s became less and less workable.

From 1874 to 1894 the white-controlled colonial state established sovereignty over what became known as the Transkeian Territories. It established sovereignty through conquest, coercion, persuasion, a certain amount of deceit, and by playing on the existing divisions within African societies. Africans widely viewed the power of the state as coming in part from military force but also in part from the abilities of officials to manipulate supernatural powers. White officials may or may not have understood that Africans credited them with these powers, although they clearly understood that Africans were suspicious of policies such as the census because of the connections between knowing families' names and possibly doing harm via supernatural means. The imposition of taxes was predicated on a census, and the payment of taxes could only be made in money. The exchange of money for a tax receipt was not just a confrontation between "different regimes of value," it was the interface between deferential subjects hoping to be left alone and an overbearing and dangerously powerful state. As the twentieth century passed, rural Africans made more direct connections between the evils that befell them as farmers and householders and the policies of the state. The colonial and then apartheid state had achieved sovereignty over the region, but it never achieved legitimacy.

People decided to pay their taxes based on their own views of the state and its power to enforce its demands either through outright coercion (like the Cape Mounted Rifles used in Hope's War or the special mobile units used in the Mpondo Revolt), or through the potential use of supernatural powers. They diverted the power of the state by paying taxes and gaining a tax receipt. This strategy enabled them to coexist with agents of the state—including not only white magistrates but also chiefs and headmen—and while profitable farming was still possible, to maintain some autonomy. The strategy recognized adult men as household heads, and it recognized their wives as legitimate. Several Mfengu headmen from Butterworth District noted these advantages to the hut tax in 1881: "The hut-tax register shows how many wives we have. . . . If a wife is not paid for in hut tax, she is not considered as a wife at all."[6] When the poll tax (General Rate) was introduced, it demoted fathers and wives and promoted young men; this effectively sharpened the existing conflicts between elders and juniors among both Zulu speakers in KwaZulu-Natal and Xhosa speakers in the Transkei, and it led to a rebellion in KwaZulu-Natal and slowly disintegrating social networks among Africans in the Transkei.

This desire for autonomy that underwrote many decisions to pay tax was in opposition to the desires of state officials in imposing the taxes. Sir Theophilus

Shepstone, when testifying to the 1883 Native Laws and Customs Commission, replied that in his view the hut tax was neither an income tax nor a system of payments for renting land: "It is the native himself who by his practices makes the tax fall heavier or lighter upon him than upon his neighbour." When asked by Commissioner Barry, "But then revenue is a secondary consideration, the great object being to get the natives under our control, and to govern them justly?" Shepstone replied, "Yes, perhaps so."[7] The emphasis on control as a rationale for taxation is evidence of the importance placed by state officials on the ritual elements of taxpaying: Africans demonstrated their subordination by coming to the magistrates' offices on a yearly basis. When just the hut tax was collected, fathers were acting on behalf of their families by paying tax. By later imposing the poll tax on young, unmarried men, state policies attempted to control them directly and exact from each man an individual expression of compliance with state authority. Taxes were not the only means the state had of controlling people, nor did the payment of taxes preclude rebellious thoughts. But taxes were an important symbol of state control, and they were often effective as barometers of public opinion.

The sovereignty that the white-controlled state wielded was thus based on a complicated mixture of beliefs and material reality. Broader challenges to that sovereignty came only when Africans pulled together a similarly complicated mixture of alternative beliefs and material grievances. Typically, all the rebellions discussed—and even more localized outbreaks of unrest such as destruction of dipping tanks—began with a demand on the part of rebels that people stop paying their taxes, that they stop engaging in this intimate exchange with the state. Those who continued to pay taxes, thus demonstrating their continuing loyalty to the colonial state, might be derided as traitors to their chiefs (in 1880) or traitors to the Zulu state (in 1906); they might be condemned to die in the course of a violent thunderstorm sent by the Lord-of-the-Sky (in 1906) or via bombs dropped by Americans and pigs set on fire (in the 1920s); or they might be named as witches and burned out of their huts (in the 1950s and 1960s). Rebellion had to be based not only on material grievances, such as veterinary quarantines during East Coast fever or betterment schemes in the 1950s, but also on a challenge to the supernatural aspects of the state's control. The impundulu, variously the lightning bird or the poll tax, could be fought only by naming and punishing—through death if necessary—witches, many of whom were Africans employed by the state.

Even in periods of open rebellion—in 1880 and 1955–63 in the Transkei and in the 1906 Bambatha Rebellion in KwaZulu-Natal—Africans did not speak with one voice. Rebels—those people who were openly committed to fighting the state—were always in the minority, even though a wider cross-section of the population tacitly approved of the rebellions. The violence and threats that rebels often used to force people to end their connection to the state was indicative both of the "wholesome fear" (to use the 1926 chief magistrate's phrase)[8] Africans had for the power of the state and of real differences of opinion among rural Africans about appropriate or possible ways of opposing state policies. Many Africans (including Africans who held no office in the state) resented and feared being named as a traitor or a witch simply because they paid taxes. Elders, both men and women, often particularly questioned the motivations of younger men in instigating these rebellions and felt that the "traditional" gerontocratic hierarchy was under attack. Women felt doubly threatened both as legal minors in the law's eyes and as suspected witches in the eyes of rebels and in-laws. If the rebellions were attempts on the parts of rebels to re-create or reinvent a moral state, there were other Africans who disagreed with the rebels' definitions of morality. Thus the rebellions were not only insurrections against state authority, they were also civil conflicts that pitted Africans against one another.

In other accounts of these various rebellions in rural South Africa, the internecine aspects have often been subordinated to the dominant narrative of Africans against the colonial and apartheid states and their collaborators. While there is a compelling simplicity to the dominant narrative (and it is the narrative that rebels often told themselves), it loses the nuance and meaning of much of African rural life. Just as narratives that focus too much on material grievances to explain rebellions risk missing the broader cultural causes, so too a narrative of rebellion that focuses only on the polarized period surrounding the rebellion itself risks missing the discussions and disagreements (and occasional violence) within rural African society. These disagreements have come into increasing prominence with the dismantling of the apartheid state. Issues of morality and witchcraft emerged as comrades in the 1980s and 1990s challenged the state and necklaced (killed with a burning car tire) people named as collaborators and witches.[9] Fights between older, Zulu-speaking migrant laborers who belonged to Inkatha and younger ANC-leaning comrades broke out in the Vaal region and elsewhere, and these fights were partly about politics, partly about ethnicity, partly a reenactment of elder-junior conflicts, partly a clash between rural and urban constructions of morality and culture.[10] Violence within families erupted as juniors defied elders, women defied men, boys victimized girls, and as supernatural forces, bad luck, and government policies all seemingly conspired in "the destruction of wealth and health" (to use a Mau Mau combatant's phrase) of African families.[11] While the policies enacted by the colonial and the apartheid state played upon, exacerbated, and to some extent created the disagreements among Africans (or created the conditions that led to disagreements), the disagreements have developed a life of their own and have not disappeared following the demise of the apartheid state.

In the current state of these disagreements in twenty-first-century South Africa, taxation has played a minimal role. But that does not negate the historical significance of taxation and the ritual of taxpaying in establishing the sovereignty of the colonial state and in effectively setting precedents for other colonial polices that treated Africans as subjects who must show proper deference. The complex knot of beliefs in the supernatural and their connections to state power was tied with the rope of tax policies.

NOTES

Abbreviations

1/BIZ	Archives of the Resident Magistrate, Bizana District, Transkei, Cape Archives Depot, Cape Town
1/BUT	Records of the Resident Magistrate Butterworth District, Cape Archives Depot, Cape Town
1/ECO	Records of the Resident Magistrate, Engcobo District, Transkei, Cape Archives, Cape Town
1/LSK	Records of the Resident Magistrate of Lusikisiki District, Cape Province Archives Depot, Cape Town
1/TSO	Records of the Resident Magistrate, Tsolo District Cape Archives, Cape Town
1/UTA	Records of the Magistrate of Umtata District, Cape Province Archives Depot, Cape Town
BAC	Bantu Affairs Commissioner
CBAC	Chief Bantu Affairs Commissioner
CMK	Chief Magistrate of East Griqualand; Records of the Chief Magistrate of East Griqualand, Cape Province Archives Depot, Cape Town
CMT	Chief Magistrate of the Transkeian Territories; Records of the Chief Magistrate of the Transkeian Territories, Cape Archives Depot, Cape Town
CNC	Records of the Chief Native Commissioner, KwaZulu-Natal Archives Depot, Pietermaritzburg
NEC	Native Economic Commission
NTS	Records of the Union Native Affairs Department, Union Archives, Pretoria
RM	Resident Magistrate
SAP	South African Police
SNA	Secretary for Native Affairs; Records of the Secretary for Native Affairs, Natal-Zululand
USNA	Undersecretary for Native Affairs

Chapter 1: Sorcery and the State

1. Minutes of meeting held at Idutywa on 24 October 1894 for the purpose of explaining the provisions of Proclamation No. 352 of 1894, enclosed in RM to CMT, 25 October 1894, Records of the Chief Magistrate of the Transkeian Territories, Cape Archives Depot, Cape Town (hereafter CMT), 3/99. The chief quoted is Sigidi, an important chief of the Gcaleka Xhosa.

2. K. D. Matanzima to CMT (A. M. Badenhorst), 9 November 1957, with enclosure: "Where There is Neither Back Nor Front There is No Truth," CMT 3/1471, file 42/C.

3. James Scott, *Weapons of the Weak* (New Haven: Yale University Press, 1985); William Beinart and Colin Bundy, *Hidden Struggles in Rural South Africa* (Berkeley: University of

California Press, 1987); Peter Delius, "Migrant Organisation, the Communist Party, the ANC and the Sekhukhuneland Revolt, 1940–1958," in *Apartheid's Genesis, 1935–1962*, ed. Philip Bonner, Peter Delius, and Deborah Posel (Johannesburg: Ravan Press, 1993), 126–59; Shula Marks, *Reluctant Rebellion: The 1906–8 Disturbances in Natal* (Oxford: Oxford University Press, 1970).

4. J. B. Peires, *The Dead Will Arise* (Berkeley: University of California Press, 1989), 61–62; Peires, *The House of Phalo* (Berkeley: University of California Press, 1982), 27–44; Monica Hunter Wilson, *Reaction to Conquest: Effects of Contact with Europeans on Pondo* (London: Oxford University Press/International Institute of African Languages and Cultures, 1936; London: Oxford University Press, 1961), 311–19, 402–10, 413–20.

5. Rev. Shrewsbury to "Rev. Sir," London, 21 December 1826, Wesleyan Methodist Mission Archives, Wesleyville, Kaffirland, microfiche 55. According to Shrewsbury, Africans referred to missionaries as the "dogs of Jesus Christ."

6. Wilson, *Reaction to Conquest*, 392.

7. The Engcobo chief Dalasile noted, "It was an ancient custom amongst them to hold meetings in time of drought at the graves of their ancestors and 'cry' for rain, and . . . he and his people had met for this purpose at the grave of his late father." RM Engcobo District to CMT, 13 February 1878, CMT 1/27.

8. Wilson, *Reaction to Conquest*, 389.

9. Rev. Henry Callaway, *The Religious System of the Amazulu*, part 1, *Unkulunkulu* (Springvale, Natal: J. A. Blair, 1868), 417.

10. Historians have documented a number of different reactions among various African groups to the initial colonial conquest. A detailed discussion of various Transkeian responses is in C. C. Saunders, *The Annexation of the Transkeian Territories*, Archives Yearbook for South African History (Pretoria: Government Printer, 1978). Discussions of other regions in Africa include Terence O. Ranger, "Connexions between 'Primary Resistance' Movements and Modern Mass Nationalism in East and Central Africa," *Journal of African History* 9 (1968): 437–53; Ronald Robinson, "Non-European Foundations of European Imperialism: A Sketch for a Theory of Collaboration," in *Studies in the Theory of Imperialism*, ed. Roger Owen and Bob Sutcliffe (London: Longman, 1976), 117–42; Allen Isaacman and Barbara Isaacman, "Resistance and Collaboration in Southern and Central Africa," *International Journal of African Historical Studies* 10 (1977): 31–62.

11. James Scott, *Domination and the Arts of Resistance: Hidden Transcripts* (New Haven: Yale University Press, 1990), xii–xiii, 1–16.

12. Ibid., 45–107.

13. John Comaroff and Jean Comaroff, *Ethnography and the Historical Imagination* (Boulder: Westview Press, 1992), 235.

14. Jean Comaroff and John Comaroff, *Christianity, Colonialism, and Consciousness in South Africa*, vol. 1 of *Of Revelation and Revolution* (Chicago: University of Chicago Press, 1991).

15. Richard Elphick, "Africans and the Christian Campaign in South Africa," in *The Frontier in History: North America and Southern Africa Compared*, ed. Howard Lamar and Leonard Thompson (New Haven: Yale University Press, 1981), 270–307.

16. Bruce Berman and John Lonsdale have deeply investigated the infusion of Christian beliefs into the Land and Freedom Army (a.k.a. Mau Mau) in 1950s Kenya. See Berman and Lonsdale, *Unhappy Valley: Conflict in Kenya and Africa*, Eastern African Studies (Athens: University of Ohio Press, 1992), 440–47. Paul Landau discusses similar issues of conversion and social change in *The Realm of the Word: Language, Gender, and Christianity in a Southern African Kingdom* (Portsmouth, NH: Heinemann, 1995). See also Michael Mahoney's discussion of Christians' participation in the Bambatha rebellion in Mapumulo district: "The

Millennium Comes to Mapumulo: Popular Christianity in Rural Natal, 1866–1906," *Journal of Southern African Studies* 25 (1999): 391.

17. This created a crisis comparable to that discussed by Berman and Lonsdale in their study of the Kikuyu reserves in Kenya: young Kikuyu had historically achieved adult status through the acquisition and farming of their own land, which allowed them to marry, have children, and accumulate wealth. With the land restrictions that existed in the Kenya of the 1930s and 1940s, a rising generation of Kikuyu faced a collective identity crisis that was rooted partially in their inability to obtain farmland and that prevented them from attaining "civic virtue," comprising notions of personal autonomy, wealth, social respect, and a political voice. In Kenya, many young Kikuyu tried to resolve that crisis by initiating the Land and Freedom Army (the Mau Mau) to recapture land through which farmland, adulthood, and civic virtue could be attained. See Berman and Lonsdale, *Unhappy Valley*, 338–41, 432–37.

18. Anne Mager discusses the "thwarted masculinity" of stick-fighting boys in the rural areas in "Youth Organisations and the Construction of Masculine Identities in the Ciskei and Transkei, 1945–60," *Journal of Southern African Studies* 24 (1998): 654.

19. Ivan Evans, *Bureaucracy and Race: Native Administration in South Africa* (Berkeley: University of California Press, 1997), 199–207.

20. Muriel Horrell, *The African Reserves of South Africa* (Johannesburg: South African Institute of Race Relations, 1969), 32–39.

21. Sorcery is usually defined as the manipulation of various substances, magical medicines, or charms to create some effect that is harmful to one's enemies and beneficial to oneself, such as causing illness or death to a rival or destroying an enemy's crops. Witchcraft is a more comprehensive category that includes both sorcery (the manipulation of substances) as well as innate supernatural powers and the use of familiars, such as baboons, the lightning bird (*impundulu*), snakes (*icanti*), and the *tikoloshe*, a mythical quasihuman creature. The distinction between witchcraft and sorcery is useful for analytical purposes, but, as Monica Wilson noted in the 1930s, "Witchcraft and sorcery are not always distinguished by the Pondo. Often both are believed to have been used at once" (*Reaction to Conquest*, 309).

22. Mary Douglas, ed., *Witchcraft Confessions and Accusations* (London: Tavistock, 1970); W. D. Hammond-Tooke, "The Cape Nguni Witch Familiar as a Mediatory Construct," *Man* 9 (1974): 128–36; Audrey Richards, "A Modern Movement of Witchfinders," *Africa* 8 (1935): 439–51.

23. Officials did not outlaw witchcraft per se because, from their point of view, witchcraft did not exist, and therefore there was nothing to outlaw. Instead, they outlawed accusations of witchcraft (sometimes called the imputation of nonnatural means). This is a significant distinction and is discussed in chapter 2.

24. Wilson, *Reaction to Conquest*.

25. Harold Wolpe, "Capitalism and Cheap Labour-Power in South Africa: From Segregation to Apartheid," *Economy and Society* 1 (1972): 425–56; Charles Simkins, "Agricultural Production in the African Reserves, 1918–1969," *Journal of Southern African Studies* 7 (1981): 256–83.

26. For example, Norman Etherington, "Postmodernism and South African History," *New Contree* 40 (1996): 39.

27. Sociologist Karen Fields has discussed the intersection of colonial rule and supernatural beliefs with regard to British-controlled central Africa, a region that provides some useful comparisons with South African history. Fields notes that the British did not maintain colonial control through the constant use of military force; instead, British officials often found themselves portraying their regimes in precolonial African terms. In particular, Fields suggests, despite the overt hostility of colonial regimes to African witchcraft beliefs, state officials found themselves unable to rule without deferring to and tacitly participating in

them: "witches' and witchdoctors' power inhabited the quotidian and the humdrum [for African populations]. Led by their interest in command, British officials came repeatedly to the edge of this political *terra incognita;* seeking to annex political power they repeatedly crossed over into it." British colonial officials found that witchcraft beliefs—within certain limits—were often less disruptive of the colonial order than were beliefs in Christianity. Fields, "Political Contingencies of Witchcraft in Colonial Central Africa: Culture and State in Marxist Theory," *Canadian Journal of African Studies* 16 (1982): 574–75, 584.

28. Adam Ashforth, "On Living in a World with Witches: Everyday Epistemology and Spiritual Insecurity in a Modern African City (Soweto)," in Moore and Sanders, *Magical Interpretations,* 206–25; Benedict Carton, *Blood from Your Children: The Colonial Origins of Generational Conflict in South Africa* (Charlottesville: University of Virginia Press, 2000), 94–96, 105–9; Clifton Crais, *The Politics of Evil: Magic, State Power, and the Political Imagination in South Africa* (New York: Cambridge University Press, 2002); Isak Niehaus, "Witchcraft in the New South Africa: From Colonial Superstition to Postcolonial Reality?" in *Magical Interpretations, Material Realities: Modernity, Witchcraft, and the Occult in Postcolonial Africa,* Henrietta L. Moore and Todd Sanders (New York: Routledge, 2001), 184–205; Niehaus, "Witch-Hunting and Political Legitimacy: Continuity and Change in Green Valley, Lebowa, 1930–91," *Africa* 63 (1993): 498–50.

29. Carolyn Hamilton, *Terrific Majesty: The Powers of Shaka Zulu and the Limits of Historical Invention* (Cambridge, MA: Harvard University Press, 1998), 74–82; Crais, *Politics of Evil,* 97–103.

30. Achille Mbembe, "Provisional Notes on the Postcolony," *Africa* 62, no. 1 (1992): 1–37.

31. Wilson, *Reaction to Conquest,* 316–17.

32. David Hammond-Tooke, *The Roots of Black South Africa* (Johannesburg: Jonathan Ball, 1993); Niehaus, "Witch-Hunting and Political Legitimacy," 498–530; Isak Niehaus, "Witches of the Transvaal Lowveld and Their Familiars," *Cahiers d'études africaines* 25 (1995): 513–40.

33. Elphick, "Africans and the Christian Campaign," 270–307; John Comaroff and Jean Comaroff, *The Dialectics of Modernity on a South African Frontier,* vol. 2 of *Of Revelation and Revolution* (Chicago: University of Chicago Press, 1997), 78–165.

34. Landau, *Realm of the Word,* 124–9; Comaroff and Comaroff, *Dialectics of Modernity,* 323–64.

35. Early missionary William Shaw noted that converts were usually politically loyal to Cape forces. Shaw is quoted in Philip Mayer, *Townsmen or Tribesmen: Conservation and the Process of Urbanization in a South African City,* (Cape Town: Oxford University Press, 1961), 31.

36. Cape of Good Hope, *Report of the Government Commission on Native Laws and Customs, 1883,* facsimile repr., 2 vols. (Cape Town: C. Struik, 1968), 2:85–87, 435–36.

37. The classic discussion of separatist churches and the way they drew upon local African culture in South Africa is B. G. M. Sundkler, *Bantu Prophets in South Africa,* 2nd ed. (London: Oxford University Press, 1961), 23–25, 253–94. An early historical example of a separatist church in the Transkei is discussed in C. C. Saunders, "Tile and the Thembu Church: Politics and Independency on the Cape Eastern Frontier in the Late Nineteenth Century," *Journal of African History* 11 (1970): 553–70.

38. Church of England, *Report of a Committee Appointed at the Request of the Diocesan Missionary Conference to Enquire Into the Question of Witchcraft* (owned by the Strange [Africana] Library, Johannesburg) (Umtata: Thompson's Printing Works, 1936), 3, 5.

39. Wilson, *Reaction to Conquest,* 493.

40. Mayer, *Townsmen or Tribesman?* 161–62.

41. Whether or not people's behavior was actually becoming more immoral is a separate issue, as noted by both Philip Mayer and Anne Mager. Mayer, *Townsmen or Tribesman?*

150–60, 275–77; Mager, *Gender and the Making of a South African Bantustan: A Social History of the Ciskei, 1945–1959* (Portsmouth, NH: Heinemann, 1999), 173–88.

42. If a person was killed, the magistrates typically opened a Preparatory Examination after the district surgeon had determined if the death was a murder. This examination could lead to charges of murder or manslaughter; similarly, if a hut was burned down, a charge of arson could be brought against the perpetrator if there was sufficient evidence. The taint of witchcraft, though, did sometimes prevent people from coming forward to testify. RM Bizana District to Secretary, NEC, 20 February 1931, Records of the Native Economic Commission, Union Archives Depot, Pretoria (hereafter NEC), K26, file 68D; see also the reasons for judgment given by the presiding magistrate in R. v. Nokwenzini Miyeza, criminal case 1/43, 15 January 1943, Records of the Magistrate Umbulumbulo, Umlazi, KwaZulu-Natal Archives Depot, Pietermaritzburg, 1/1/1/1. See two particular cases of witchcraft-related arson: R. v. Mmoshi Joubert and six others, case 1039/51, 8 August 1951, Records of the Magistrate of Umtata District, Cape Province Archives Depot, Cape Town (hereafter 1/UTA), 1/1/1/78; R. v. Mketwa Mnganda and Kaizer Mtunywa, case 669/51, 5 September 1951, Records of the Resident Magistrate of Lusikisiki District, Cape Province Archives Depot, Cape Town (hereafter 1/LSK), 1/1/15.

43. Margaret Levi, *Of Rule and Revenue*, California Series on Social Choice and Political Economy (Berkeley: University of California Press, 1988), 10–40.

44. Comaroff and Comaroff, *Ethnography*, 260.

45. By calling the payment of tax a ritual, I am following a definition proposed by David Kertzer: "ritual [is] symbolic behavior that . . . follows highly structured, standardized sequences and is often enacted at certain places and times that are themselves endowed with special symbolic meaning." Kertzer, *Ritual, Politics, and Power* (New Haven: Yale University Press, 1988), 9.

46. In the Cape Colony (later the Cape Province) a very small number of Africans had the vote until 1936 and so were represented in Parliament. The Department of Native Affairs changed its name to the Department of Bantu Affairs in the 1950s.

47. In addition, in eastern Pondoland there was an education rate collected to support schools. NEC K26, vol. 27, file 95, Annexures B, E. See also the testimony of Sir Walter Stanford in South Africa, Select Committee on Native Affairs, *Second-Third Reports of the Select Committee on Native Affairs* (Cape Town: Government Printers, 1912), 117, pars. 1009–10.

48. W. D. Hammond-Tooke, *Command or Consensus: The Development of Transkeian Local Government* (Cape Town: David Philip, 1975); Colin Bundy, "Mr. Rhodes and the Poisoned Goods: Popular Opposition to the Glen Grey Council System, 1894–1906," in *Hidden Struggles in Rural South Africa*, William Beinart and Colin Bundy (Berkeley: University of California Press, 1987), 138–65.

49. All the taxes listed above were only the direct taxes that Africans paid. Africans also paid indirect taxes, such as excise taxes included in the prices of various goods bought at trading stores. Unfortunately, the amounts of money involved are difficult to calculate and the payment of excise taxes, import duties, and license fees included in the retail prices of goods did not bring Africans into immediate contact with the state in the same way that the direct taxes did. Thus indirect taxes cannot give us the same kind of information about the relationship between the colonial state and its African subjects. In the time period covered by this book, the Cape Colony and then South Africa used the British pound as their currency. One pound equaled twenty shillings; one shilling equaled twelve pence.

50. Michael Taussig, *The Magic of the State* (New York: Routledge, 1997), 129–46; Keith Breckenridge, "'Money with Dignity': Migrants, Minelords and the Cultural Politics of the South African Gold Standard Crisis, 1920–1933," *Journal of African History* 36 (1995): 291–92.

51. Breckenridge, "'Money with Dignity,'" 271–304; Koletso Atkins, *The Moon Is Dead! Give Us Our Money! The Cultural Origins of an African Work Ethic, Natal, South Africa, 1843–1900* (Portsmouth, NH: Heinemann, 1993), 94–97.

52. Sean Redding, "Sorcery and Sovereignty: Taxation, Witchcraft, and Political Symbols in the 1880 Transkeian Rebellion," *Journal of Southern African Studies* 22 (1996): 249–70; C. C. Saunders, "The Transkeian Rebellion of 1880–81: A Case Study of Transkeian Resistance to White Control," *South African Historical Journal* 8 (1976): 32–39.

53. For examples, see RM Umtata to CMT Tembuland, Umtata, 12 April 1883, CMT 1/36, no. 268/83; Minutes of a meeting with Major Elliot CME, Chief Magistrate of Tembuland and the Residents of the Engcobo district, dated 4 August 1885, 1/CMT 1/30.

54. Cape of Good Hope, *Commission on Native Laws*, 1:395.

55. Alan R. Booth, "'European Courts Protect Women and Witches': Colonial Law Courts as Redistributors of Power in Swaziland, 1920–50," *Journal of Southern African Studies* 18 (1992): 253–75.

56. RM Tsolo District to CMK, 2 April 1880, enclosing letter 27 March 1880, Rev. Bransby Key to Resident Magistrate Tsolo District, Records of the Chief Magistrate of East Griqualand, Cape Province Archives Depot, Cape Town (hereafter CMK), 1/97.

57. For evidence of fear and suspicion regarding census taking in Engcobo and Umtata districts, see RM Engcobo District to CMT, 2 September, 11 September 1879, CMT 1/27; RM Umtata District to CMT, 12 August 1879, CMT 1/35, no. 148/2. See also Wilson, *Reaction to Conquest*, 316–17; Hammond-Tooke, *Roots of Black South Africa*, 172–73.

58. William Beinart, "Chieftaincy and the Concept of Articulation: South Africa circa 1900–50," in *Segregation and Apartheid in Twentieth-Century South Africa*, ed. William Beinart and Saul Dubow (New York: Routledge, 1995), 176–88.

59. Colin Bundy, *The Rise and Fall of the South African Peasantry* (Berkeley: University of California Press, 1979).

60. In 1910, when South Africa became unified, the Act of Union entrenched the preexisting rights of qualified African landowners in the Cape Province to register on the common voters' roll along with qualified white and Coloured voters. This right was subsequently altered in 1936 with the Representation of Natives Act, which put Cape African voters on a separate roll and allocated them three representatives in Parliament. In 1956, as part of the grand apartheid policies, Africans were denied all political rights within "white" South Africa and promised political rights in "independent homelands" or "Bantustans."

61. Ralph A. Austen, "The Moral Economy of Witchcraft: An Essay in Comparative History," in *Modernity and Its Malcontents: Ritual and Power in Postcolonial Africa*, ed. Jean Comaroff and John Comaroff (Chicago: University of Chicago Press, 1993), 92–97.

62. RM Engcobo District to CMT, 6 July 1887, CMT 1/31.

63. RM Engcobo District to CMT, 30 March 1891, CMT 1/31.

64. Rex v. Mdopa, son of Ngoza, transcript dated Weenen, 23 January 1906, SNA 1/1/335, file 352/1906.

65. Robert Edgar, "Garveyism in Africa: Dr. Wellington and the American Movement in the Transkei," *Ufahamu* 6, no. 3 (1976): 31–57.

66. "An extract from Umteteli [*wa Bantu*, a Xhosa-language newspaper published in Umtata] dated 15 January 1927 (translation)," Records of the Resident Magistrate, Tsolo District Cape Archives, Cape Town (hereafter 1/TSO), 5/1/19, file 3/16/6. See also Post Commander, SA Police, Ngqeleni District, to District Commandant, SAP Umtata District, 10 December 1927, Records of the Chief Native Commissioner, KwaZulu-Natal Archives Depot, Pietermaritzburg (hereafter CNC), 348, file 271/19.

67. "Statement of Mgqushwa Lubelo ka Mabunu," Magistrate's Office, Harding District (Natal), 15 December 1927, CNC 348, file 271/19.

68. An extremely interesting chapter on the witchcraft beliefs associated with the ICU and Wellington in the Transkei appears in Helen Bradford, *A Taste of Freedom: The ICU in Rural South Africa, 1924–1930* (New Haven: Yale University Press, 1987), 213–45.

69. Statement taken in RM Tsolo's office, 12 March 1927, file 3/16/6, 1/TSO 5/1/19.

70. CMT to SNA, 8 April 1930, enclosing annual report for 1929, Records of the Union Native Affairs Department, Union Archives, Pretoria (hereafter NTS), 1771, file 64/276/4.

71. T. R. H. Davenport, "The Triumph of Colonel Stallard: The Transformation of the Natives (Urban) Areas Act Between 1923 and 1937," *South African Historical Journal* 2 (1970): 77–96.

72. T. Dunbar Moodie and Vivienne Ndatshe, *Going for Gold: Men, Mines, and Migration* (Berkeley: University of California Press, 1994), 11–43.

73. Belinda Bozzoli, *Women of Phokeng* (Johannesburg: Ravan Press, 1992); Ellen Hellmann, *Rooiyard: A Sociological Survey of an Urban Native Slum Yard*, Rhodes-Livingston Papers, no. 13 (Cape Town: Oxford University Press, 1948); Mamphela Ramphele, *A Bed Called Home: Life in the Migrant Labour Hostels of Cape Town* (Athens: Ohio University Press, 1993).

74. Duncan Innes and Dan O'Meara, "Class Formation and Ideology: The Transkei Region," *Review of African Political Economy* 7 (1976): 69–86; Martin Legassick, "South Africa: Capital Accumulation and Violence," *Economy and Society* 3 (1974): 251–91; Gwendolen Carter, Thomas Karis, and Newell Stultz, *South Africa's Transkei: The Politics of Domestic Colonialism* (Evanston: Northwestern University Press, 1967), 11–29.

75. RM Nqamakwe District, Transkei, to SNA, 24 October 1932, NTS 1771, file 64/276/5.

76. William Beinart, "Soil Erosion, Conservationism and Ideas about Development: A South African Exploration," *Journal of Southern African Studies* 11 (1984): 52–83.

77. Ibid.

78. RM Tsolo District to CMT, 23 March 1949, 1/TSO 5/1/108, file N1/1/2; 30 December 1949, Records of the Resident Magistrate, Engcobo District, Transkei, Cape Archives, Cape Town (hereafter 1/ECO), 6/1/48, file N2/11/2; replies to circulars sent to Chief BAC by BAC, Willowvale District, 20 February 1961, "Confidential," CMT 3/1471, file 42/1; BAC Nqamakwe District, 23 February 1961; BAC Cala District, 1 March 1961; BAC Umtata District, 2 March 1961; BAC Qumbu District, 4 March 1961; BAC Tabankulu District, 6 March 1961; BAC Kentani District, 9 March 1961; BAC Cofimvaba District, 22 February 1961; BAC Mount Fletcher District, 9 March 1961; BAC Engcobo District, 18 February 1961; BAC Port St. Johns District, 25 March 1961; BAC Idutywa District, 12 April 1961; BAC Libode District, 5 April 1961; BAC Lusikisiki District, 29 March 1961.

79. Sean Redding, "Government Witchcraft: Taxation, the Supernatural, and the Mpondo Revolt in the Transkei, South Africa, 1955–63," *African Affairs* 95 (1996): 555–79.

80. Ibid.; J. B. Peires, "Unsocial Bandits: The Stock Thieves of Qumbu and Their Enemies," University of the Witwatersrand, History Workshop (1994).

81. Kentani District BAC to CMT, 9 March 1961, "Confidential," CMT 3/1471, file 42/1. See also CMT to Secretary for Bantu Administration and Development, 25 January 1961 and 4 February 1961, CMT 3/1472, file 42/Q (vol. 1).

82. Govan Mbeki, *South Africa: The Peasants' Revolt* (Harmondsworth: Penguin, 1963), 117.

83. W. J. G. Mears, "A Study in Native Administration: The Transkeian Territories, 1894–1943" (DLitt diss., University of South Africa, 1947), 411, 417, 419.

84. Cape of Good Hope, *Report of the Government Commission on Native Laws and Customs, 1883*, 1:453–54.

85. Evans, *Bureaucracy and Race*, 284–85; Saul Dubow, "Race, Civilisation and Culture: The Elaboration of the Segregationist Discourse in the Inter-War Years," in *The Politics of Race, Class, and Nationalism in Twentieth-Century South Africa*, ed. Shula Marks and Stanley

Trapido (London: Longman, 1987), 71–83; Dubow, "Holding 'a Just Balance between White and Black': The Native Affairs Department in South Africa c. 1920–33," *Journal of Southern African Studies* 12 (1986): 228–37.

86. "Report on Native Affairs for the year 1947–1948," by RM Tsolo District, dated 15 July 1948, 1/TSO 5/1/136, file 2/9/2.

87. For an example of this line of thought, see S. E. Humphreys, Location Superintendent, Herschel, to "My dear Mr. Barrett," SNA, 23 May 1919, NTS 2486, file 41/293 (1). See also James Scott, *Seeing like a State* (New Haven: Yale University Press, 1998), 223–61; William Beinart, "Agrarian Historiography and Agrarian Reconstruction," in *South Africa in Question*, ed. John Lonsdale (Portsmouth, NH: Heinemann, 1988), 134–53.

88. Mahmood Mamdani, *Citizen and Subject* (Princeton: Princeton University Press, 1994), 16–23; Howard Pim, *Introduction to Bantu Economics* (Fort Hare: Lovedale Press, 1930), 12–15.

89. R. Parry, "'In a Sense Citizens, but Not Altogether Citizens . . .': Rhodes, Race and the Ideology of Segregation at the Cape in the Late Nineteenth Century," *Canadian Journal of African Studies* 17 (1983): 384–91.

90. Addendum by Mr. F. A. W. Lucas, Commissioner, in Union of South Africa, *Report of the Native Economic Commission, 1930–1932* (Pretoria: Government Printer, 1932), 183. See also the recommendations of the commission as a whole: ibid., 47–48.

91. CMT (W. T. Welsh) to SNA, 23 August 1932, NTS 1772, file 64/276/6. A number of magistrates expressed similar views; for example, see RM Nqamakwe District to SNA, 24 October 1932, NTS 1771, file 64/276/5.

92. Evidence to the Native Economic Commission by Dr. A. B. Xuma, NEC K26 15, no file number; emphasis in original.

93. Evans, *Bureaucracy and Race*, 112–15.

94. Reply to CMT's circulars by the Kentani District magistrate, 9 March 1961, "Confidential," CMT 3/1471, file 42/1; see also reply by the Idutywa District magistrate, 12 April 1961, and reply by the Qumbu District magistrate, 10 August 1961.

95. RM Idutywa to CMT, 12 April 1961, "Confidential," CMT 3/1471, file 42/1.

96. BAC Bizana to CMT, 11 July 1960, memorandum, Archives of the Resident Magistrate, Bizana District, Transkei, Cape Archives Depot, Cape Town (hereafter 1/BIZ), 6/47, file C9/6/C; State v. Themba Njolweni, Sotolase Mpangati, Sibodwana Ntlokonkulu, Mqingelwa Fahla, Siboniwe Fulalela, Joko Qasayi, Tshobeni Mzanza, and Mahlaza Qasayi, case 700 of 1961, 12 June 1961, 1/LSK 1/1/16.

97. "Report of the Departmental Committee of Enquiry into Unrest in Eastern Pondoland," 9 August 1960, CMT 3/1472, file 42/Q.

98. Saul Dubow, *Scientific Racism in Modern South Africa* (New York: Cambridge University Press, 1995), 128–41.

99. On intimate connections between the postcolonial state and the ruled in Cameroon, see Achille Mbembe, "Prosaics of Servitude and Authoritarian Civilities," *Public Culture* 5, no. 1 (1992): 123–45.

100. Dubow, *Scientific Racism*, 89–95.

101. Goren Hyden, *Beyond Ujamaa in Tanzania* (Berkeley: University of California Press, 1981), 182–208.

Chapter 2: War and Revenue

1. The Mpondomise were one of several Xhosa-speaking groups who had lived in independent states in the precolonial Transkei. Mditshwa and Mhlonthlo were chiefs of relatively equal stature who ruled over separate sections of the Mpondomise people, Mhlonthlo in Qumbu District and Mditshwa in Tsolo District.

2. W. T. Brownlee, *Reminiscences of a Transkeian* (Pietermaritzburg: Shuter and Shooter, 1975), 81.

3. RM Qumbu District (Hamilton Hope) to CMK, 13 March 1880, CMK 1/94. See also Clifton Crais, *The Politics of Evil: Magic, State Power, and the Political Imagination in South Africa* (New York: Cambridge University Press, 2002), 57–65.

4. A. Davis, "Clerk to R.M. Qumbu (deceased)," to Chief Magistrate East Griqualand, 14 October 1880 (typescript copy of original), CMK 1/152.

5. The chief was quoted by an African policeman named Matanga who accompanied Hope to the meeting but managed to escape; the policeman's and the clerk's accounts appear in Brownlee, *Reminiscences*, 84–86.

6. Evidently not all Africans who rebelled were of Mhlonthlo's opinion on this matter. In Engcobo District rebels burned down at least one mission station—All Saints'—and missionaries were threatened in other districts. Also, in all the districts that rebelled, trading stores were looted. Cape of Good Hope, *Report of the Government Commission on Native Laws and Customs, 1883*, 2 vols., facsimile repr. (Cape Town: C. Struik, 1968), 1:388; C. C. Saunders, *The Annexation of the Transkeian Territories*, Archives Yearbook for South African History (Pretoria: Government Printer, 1978), 94–95.

7. T. O. Ranger, "Taking Hold of the Land: Holy Places and Pilgrimages in Twentieth Century Zimbabwe," *Past and Present* 117 (1987): 159–94.

8. A. Davis to Chief Magistrate East Griqualand, 14 October 1880 (typescript), CMK 1/152.

9. Cape of Good Hope, *Government Commission on Native Laws*, vol. 2, app. 1: "A Brief History of the Pondomise Tribe, . . . as related by Mabasa, late Regent of Umditshwa's Section . . . and Nomlala, an old Councillor, and written by E. S. Bam, Interpreter to the Resident Magistrate, Tsolo"; see also William Beinart, "Conflict in Qumbu: Rural Consciousness, Ethnicity and Violence in the Colonial Transkei," in *Hidden Struggles in Rural South Africa*, William Beinart and Colin Bundy (Berkeley: University of California Press, 1987), 135n57.

10. J. B. Peires, *The Dead Will Arise* (Berkeley: University of California Press, 1989), 30–32.

11. The quotation is given by policeman Matanga in Brownlee, *Reminiscences*, 87.

12. Crais, *Politics of Evil*, 65.

13. CMT to USNA, "Annual Report for 1880," letter 64/80, CMT 1/80.

14. Ibid.

15. RM Tsolo District to CMK, 2 September 1880, CMK 1/97.

16. CMT to RM Tsolo District, 28 July 1931, "Confidential," enclosing copy of extract from the *Kaffrarian Watchman*, dated 26 September 1881, containing report on Mditshwa's trial, 1/TSO 5/1/21, file 41.

17. Ibid.

18. Ibid. See also Cape of Good Hope, *Government Commission on Native Laws*, vol. 2, app. 1; J. B. Peires, *The House of Phalo* (Berkeley: University of California Press, 1982), 66–67.

19. CMT to SNA , letter 64/80, "Annual Report for 1880," CMT 1/80;RM Engcobo District to CMT, 18 August 1882, CMT 1/28; RM Engcobo District to CMT, 9 June 1881, CMT 1/27; RM Tsolo District to CMK, 2 April 1883, CMK 1/98; RM Tsolo District to CMK, 14 May 1883, CMK 1/98.

20. "Statement made in the Court of the Resident Magistrate, Engcobo, Tembuland," 9 December 1881, CMT 1/27; W. E. Stanford, "Report on Native Affairs, district of Engcobo, Tembuland 1881," 5 January 1882, CMT 1/28; RM Tsolo District to SNA, 13 April 1881, CMK 1/97; RM Umtata District to CMT, 10 February 1881, letter 142, "Annual Report for 1880," 1/UTA 5/1/1/3; CMT to RM Tsolo District, 28 July 1931, "Confidential," enclosing copy of extract from the *Kaffrarian Watchman*, 26 September 1881, 1/TSO 5/1/21, file 41.

21. Beinart and Bundy, "Conflict in Qumbu," 113–14.

22. James Scott, *Domination and the Arts of Resistance: Hidden Transcripts* (New Haven:

Yale University Press, 1990), 45–69; David Kertzer, *Ritual, Politics, and Power* (New Haven: Yale University Press, 1988), 9.

23. Jean Comaroff and John Comaroff, *Christianity, Colonialism, and Consciousness in South Africa*, vol. 1 of *Of Revelation and Revolution* (Chicago: University of Chicago Press, 1991), 31–32.

24. Comaroff and Comaroff, *Christianity, Colonialism*, 31; emphasis in the original.

25. Cape of Good Hope, *Report of a Commission Appointed to Inquire into the Causes of the Recent Outbreak in Griqualand East* (Cape Town: Solomon, 1879).

26. Cape of Good Hope, *Commission on Native Laws*, 1:425–31.

27. Helen Bradford, *A Taste of Freedom: The ICU in Rural South Africa, 1924–1930* (New Haven: Yale University Press, 1987), 215–35; Colin Bundy, "The Emergence and Decline of a South African Peasantry," *African Affairs* 71 (1972): 369–88; Bundy, "Mr. Rhodes and the Poisoned Goods: Popular Opposition to the Glen Grey Council System, 1894–1906," in *Hidden Struggles in Rural South Africa*, ed. William Beinart and Colin Bundy (Berkeley: University of California Press, 1987), 138–65; Shula Marks, *Reluctant Rebellion: The 1906–8 Disturbances in Natal* (Oxford: Oxford University Press, 1970), passim; Narissa Ramdhani, "Taxation without Representation: The Hut Tax System in Colonial Natal," *Journal of Natal and Zulu History* 11 (1986): 12–25.

28. Hercules Robinson to Lord Kimberley, 21 February 1882, enclosure: proclamation, Dispatch 62, Records of the British Colonial Office 48/503, Public Record Office, Kew Gardens.

29. Storage huts were not assessed for the hut tax. In Natal and Zululand the hut tax not only taxed the huts of wives but also the ilawu huts constructed for unmarried adolescents. This was not the case, however in the Cape.

30. In implementing hut tax, Cape officials drew upon the experience of Natal, where the hut tax had been in force since 1857. The man who had imposed hut tax there, Sir Theophilus Shepstone, told the 1881–83 Cape Native Laws and Customs Commission: "I think the hut-tax is a good foundation for a revenue; in Natal it produces £60,000 a year; it is besides a tax on polygamists, because if a man has 20 wives he has 20 huts, and pays a tax on each." Cape of Good Hope, *Commission on Native Laws*, 1:63.

31. Sean Redding, "Legal Minors and Social Children: African Women and Taxation in the Transkei, 1880–1950," *African Studies Review* 36 (1993): 49–74; Cape of Good Hope, *Commission on Native Laws*, 1:65.

32. See Answers by Chief Magistrate Elliot to Native Laws Commission, 27 September 1881, CMT 1/146.

33. Cape of Good Hope, *Recent Outbreak in Griqualand East*, 30–31, 71–72.

34. Cape of Good Hope, *Blue Book on Native Affairs, 1879* (Cape Town: Government Printers, 1879), 48.

35. RM Tsolo District to CMK, enclosing "Approximate Statement of Hut Tax Outstanding in the District of Tsolo," 7 May 1880, CMK 1/97. See also RM Tsolo District to CMK, 2 September 1880, CMK 1/97.

36. RM Tsolo District to CMK, 2 September 1880, CMK 1/97; emphasis in original.

37. RM Umtata District to CMT, 6 January 1880, 1/UTA 5/1/1/2, 280.

38. For evidence of fear and suspicion regarding census taking in Engcobo and Umtata districts, see RM Engcobo District to CMT, 2 September, 11 September 1879, CMT 1/27; RM Umtata District to CMT, 12 August 1879, CMT 1/35, 148/2.

39. Karen Fields, "Political Contingencies of Witchcraft in Colonial Central Africa: Culture and State in Marxist Theory," *Canadian Journal of African Studies* 16 (1982): 567–93; Cyprian Fisiy and Peter Geschiere, "Sorcery, Witchcraft and Accumulation: Regional Variations in South and West Cameroon," *Critique of Anthropology* 11, no. 3 (1991): 251–78;

Peter Geschiere, *The Modernity of Witchcraft: Politics and the Occult in Postcolonial Africa* (Charlottesville: University of Virginia Press, 1997), 15–25; David Lan, *Guns and Rain: Guerrillas and Spirit Mediums in Zimbabwe* (Berkeley: University of California Press, 1985); Henrietta Moore and Todd Sanders, "Magical Interpretations and Material Realities: An Introduction," in *Magical Interpretations, Material Realities: Modernity, Witchcraft, and the Occult in Postcolonial Africa*, ed. Henrietta Moore and Todd Sanders (New York: Routledge, 2001), 10–20; Randall M. Packard, "Social Change and the History of Misfortune Among the Bashu of Eastern Zaïre," in *Explorations in African Systems of Thought*, ed. Ivan Karp and Charles Bird (Bloomington: Indiana University Press, 1980), 237–67.

40. Alan R. Booth, "'European Courts Protect Women and Witches': Colonial Law Courts as Redistributors of Power in Swaziland, 1920–50," *Journal of Southern African Studies* 18 (1992): 253–75. See also the historical discussion of witchcraft in Luise White, *Speaking with Vampires: Rumor and History in Colonial Africa* (Berkeley: University of California Press, 2000), 3–51.

41. RM Tsolo District to CMK, 5 September 1879, CMK 1/97.

42. Ibid. Crais cites a similar case involving the supernatural claims to power on the part of chiefs in Qumbu District at more or less the same time. Crais, *Politics of Evil*, 59–60.

43. RM Tsolo District to CMK, 5 September 1879, CMK 1/97.

44. RM Tsolo District to CMK, enclosing letter, 27 March 1880, Rev. Bransby Key to RM Tsolo District, 2 April 1880, CMK 1/97.

45. The phrase "epidemic of witchcraft" is taken from Adam Ashforth, "An Epidemic of Witchcraft? The Implications of AIDS for the Post-Apartheid State," *African Studies* 61 (2002): 121–43.

46. RM Engcobo District to CMT, 3 November 1879, CMT 1/27.

47. RM Engcobo District CMT, 2 September 1879, 1 December 1879, CMT 1/27.

48. RM Tsolo District to CMK, quoting an informant named only as "Nombaduza's son," 29 August 1879, CMK 1/197.

49. RM Engcobo District to CMT, 27 August 1879, CMT 1/27.

50. RM Tsolo District to CMK, Letter 22 October 1880, CMK 1/197.

51. Saunders, *Annexation of Transkeian Territories*, 96.

52. RM Umtata District to CMT, 30 December 1878, "Annual Report for 1878," 1/UTA 5/1/1/2; RM Umtata District to CMT, 30 November 1880, 1/UTA 5/1/1/3, letter 82; RM Umtata District to CMT, 10 February 1881, "Annual Report for 1880," 1/UTA 5/1/1/3, letter 142; RM Umtata District to CMT, 25 October 1881, 1/UTA 5/1/1/3, letter 462; RM Umtata District to CMT, 3 April 1881, CMT 1/36; USI¹A to CMT, 15 September 1881, CMT 1/5, letter 2/484.

53. Rose Innes to CMT, 15 September 1881, CMT 1/5, 2/487. See also RM Umtata District to CMT, 5 April 1881: "Weekly Report re: Relocation of Rebels," CMT 1/36.

54. Chief Magistrate Elliot was asked by one of the commissioners on the 1883 Native Laws and Customs Commission, "In confiscating a man's property, do you carry out the Kafir custom?" Elliot replied affirmatively and later elaborated: "In native law, the term used by them is 'eating a man up,' which means, depriving him of all he possesses, in the hope that he will leave the district, and trouble it no more." Cape of Good Hope, *Commission on Native Laws*, 1:417.

55. Saunders, *Annexation of the Transkeian Territories*, 93–94.

56. RM Engcobo District to CMT, 23 November 1880, CMT 1/27.

57. RM Engcobo District to CMT, 5 January 1882, "Report on Native Affairs, District of Engcobo, Tembuland, 1881," CMT 1/28.

58. "Statement Made in the Court of the Resident Magistrate, Tembuland," 9 December 1881, CMT 1/27; RM Engcobo District to CMT, 21 January 1881, CMT 1/28; RM Engcobo District to CMT, 2 February 1882, CMT 1/28; RM Engcobo District to CMT, 22 February 1882, CMT 1/28.

59. RM Tsolo District to CMK, 14 May 1883, CMK 1/98.

60. (USNA) Rose Innes to CMT, 13 May 1891, CMT 1/13, 24/10H.

61. Cape of Good Hope, *Commission on Native Laws*, 1:458.

62. CMT to RM Tsolo District, 28 July 1931, "Confidential," with enclosure: typed extract from the *Kaffrarian Watchman*, 26 September 1881, 1/TSO 5/1/21, file 41.

63. Minutes of meeting held at Tsolo, 26 January 1885, CMK 1/98.

64. RM Tsolo District to CMK, 4 March 1885, CMK 1/98.

65. Monica Hunter Wilson discussed the proverb "a chief is born and not made" in the context of the Mpondo political system. Wilson, *Reaction to Conquest: Effects of Contact with Europeans on the Pondo of South Africa* (London: International Institute of African Languages and Cultures, 1936 London: Oxford University Press, 1961), 384.

66. RM Tsolo District to CMK, 18 October 1886, CMK 1/100.

67. RM Tsolo District to CMT, 5 August 1904, CMT 3/162.

68. See answers by CMT Major Henry Elliot to Native Laws Commission, dated 27 September 1881, CMT 1/146; Cape of Good Hope, *Commission on Native Laws*, vol. 2, app. C, p. 49, replies by Captain M. Blyth, CMK; RM Engcobo District to CMT, 10 January 1884, "Report on the District of Engcobo Tembuland for the year 1883," 1/ECO.

69. Cape of Good Hope, *Commission on Native Laws*, 1:447; W. J. G. Mears, "A Study in Native Administration: The Transkeian Territories, 1894–1943" (DLitt diss., University of South Africa, 1947), 34–41.

70. Beinart and Bundy, "Conflict in Qumbu," 112–14.

71. Statement made by Charles Mhlonthlo (the chief's son), quoted in Beinart and Bundy, "Conflict in Qumbu,"119.

72. Ibid., 120–25.

73. RM Tsolo District to CMK, 2 January 1886, "Native Affairs Blue Book for 1886," CMK 1/99.

74. For examples of this thinking, see RM Tsolo District to CMK, 11 January 1887, CMK 1/139; RM Tsolo District to CMK, 14 January 1888, "Report for Blue Book on Native Affairs for 1887," CMK 1/139.

75. There was one notable exception to this conclusion in the person of Maj. Henry Elliot, who for many years was chief magistrate of the Transkei. He did on several occasions suggest that Africans had legitimate grievances and that nonpayment of taxes might be linked to their feeling of being governed "like a flock of sheep." See CMT to USNA Rose Innes, 6 January 1885, "Annual Report 1884," CMT 1/82.

76. Again because of the different circumstances under which the various chiefs came under colonial rule, enforcement varied from district to district. In East Griqualand, Fingoland, and Gcalekaland districts, magistrates could imprison defaulters under vagrancy laws; in Thembuland districts they could not. RM Engcobo District to CMT, 27 June 1892, CMT 3/86.

77. RM Tsolo District to CMK, 14 May 1883, CMK 1/98; RM Tsolo District to CMK, annual report dated 2 January 1886, CMK 1/99; Assistant RM Tsolo District to CMK, 3 September 1886, CMK 1/100; RM Tsolo District to CMK, enclosing "Annual Report for Blue Book," 10 January 1887, 11 January 1887, CMK 1/139; RM Tsolo District to CMK, 7 January 1890, "Report for Annual Blue Book on Native Affairs," CMK 1/139; Cape of Good Hope, Native Affairs Department, Blue Book on Native Affairs, 1891 (Cape Town, 1891), p. 46; Cape of Good Hope, Native Affairs Department, *Blue Book on Native Affairs, 1892* (Cape Town: Government Printer, 1892), 46; RM Tsolo District to CMK, 10 January 1899, "Annual Blue Book Report," CMK 1/139; RM Tsolo District to CMK, 18 January 1901, "Blue Book Report," CMK 1/139; Assistant RM Tsolo District to CMK, 23 February 1902, "Blue Book on Native Affairs 1902, District of Tsolo," CMK 1/139; Cape of Good Hope, Native Affairs Department,

Blue Book on Native Affairs, 1903 (Cape Town: Government Printer, 1904), 80; Cape of Good Hope, Native Affairs Department, *Blue Book on Native Affairs, 1904* (Cape Town: Government Printer, 1905), 89.

78. RM Umtata District to CMT, 4 January 1882, letter 5/82, "Annual Report for 1881," 1/UTA 5/1/1/3; RM Umtata District to CMT, 11 December 1886, 422/86, CMT 1/37; RM Umtata District to CMT, 19 January 1888, 20/88, CMT 1/37; CMT to USNA, 14 January 1890, "Annual Report for 1889," CMT 1/84; Acting RM Umtata District to CMT, 7 January 1897, CMT 3/170, 12; RM Umtata District to CMT, 5 January 1898, CMT 3/170, 1; Acting RM Umtata District to CMT, 9 December 1898, CMT 3/170, 1153; RM Umtata District to CMT, 12 February 1900, CMT 3/171, 88; RM Umtata District to CMT, 4 February 1901, 86, CMT 3/171, 86;RM Umtata District to CMT, 30 January 1902, letter 128; RM Umtata District to CMT, 21 January 1903, CMT 3/172; RM Umtata District to CMT, 6 January 1904, 67, CMT 3/173.

79. RM Engcobo District to CMT, 5 January 1882, "Report on Native Affairs, district of Engcobo Tembuland 1881," CMT 1/28; RM Engcobo District to CMT, 1 July 1882, CMT 1/28; RM Engcobo District, December 1882, "Annual Report," 1/ECO 5/1/1/1; RM Engcobo District to CMT, 23 January 1885, CMT 1/30; RM Engcobo Districtto CMT, 8 October 1886, CMT 1/31; RM Engcobo District to CMT, 11 December 1886, CMT 1/31; RM Engcobo District to CMT, 14 December 1891, CMT 3/86; RM Engcobo District to CMT, 10 December 1894, CMT 3/87; RM Engcobo District to CMT, 7 January 1901, "Annual Report for 1900," CMT 3/91.

80. See remarks by Tsolo District Magistrate Welsh to CMK, 10 September 1883, CMK 1/98.

81. Sean Redding, "African Women and Migration in Umtata, Transkei, 1880–1935," in *Courtyards, Markets, City Streets: Urban Women in Africa,* ed. Kathleen Sheldon (Boulder: Westview Press, 1996), 31–46; Cape of Good Hope, *Commission on Native Laws,* 1:411–12.

82. As then chief magistrate A. H. Stanford wrote in 1910, "The question of 'personal contact' is one which weighs somewhat heavily upon me." Quoted in Mears, "Native Administration," 418.

83. In a meeting in Tsolo in 1885, one headman told the magistrate, "Since the war no SNA has visited us. Three times the SNA has passed us but not called. Our hearts are sore. We receive no answers to our complaints of losses during the war." RM Tsolo District to CMK, 2 January 1886, "Native Affairs Blue Book for 1886," CMK 1/99. See also Cape of Good Hope, *Commission on Native Laws,* 1:382, testimony of W. G. Cumming, RM Xalanga District; "Minutes of Meeting Held at Engcobo on the 19th February 1884, of the Native Chiefs, Headmen, and Their Councillors," CMT 1/30; "Minutes of a Meeting with Major Elliot CMT and the Residents of the Engcobo District," 4 August 1885, CMT 1/30; USNA (Rose Innes) to CMT, 22 June 1885, 2, CMT 1/9; CMT (Elliot) to USNA (Rose Innes), 6 January 1885, Annual Report 1884, CMT 1/82.

84. Kertzer, *Ritual, Politics,* 54. See also Achille Mbembe's discussion of fetishes used by people in postcolonial Cameroon to ward off the power of the state in Achille Mbembe, "Provisional Notes on the Postcolony," *Africa* 62, no. 1 (1992): 1–37.

85. Scott, *Domination,* 45.

86. Ibid., 66–69.

87. CMT to USNA, 6 January 1885, "Annual Report 1884," CMT 1/82; emphasis in original.

88. Scott, *Domination,* 44–69.

89. On what magistrates thought that Africans expected, see RM Umtata District to CMT, 21 May 1891, 92, CMT 1/37.

90. C. C. Saunders suggests that the most important effect of the revolt was to make the white-controlled administration move more cautiously, particularly in the matter of alienating land for white settlers. Saunders, "The Transkeian Rebellion of 1880–81: A Case Study of Transkeian Resistance to White Control," *South African Historical Journal* 8 (1976): 32–39.

91. The historical analysis constructed by William Beinart, in contrast, focuses on the local enmities that worsened after the defeat and concluded that it was these enmities that prevented another African revolt. While local enmities certainly existed, as in the aftermath of the revolt rebels and loyalists regarded each other with suspicion and scorn, they account neither for the complete lack of overt resistance directed at the state nor for the high level of compliance with state demands for taxes. Beinart himself speculates on an uninterrupted existence of covert or peasant resistance. Beinart, "Conflict in Qumbu," 106–37.

92. Fields, "Political Contingencies of Witchcraft." See also Crais, *Politics of Evil*, 35–95.

93. Crais, *Politics of Evil*, 68–112.

94. Ibid., 98.

Chapter 3: From Rinderpest through Influenza

1. South Africa, Select Committee on Native Affairs, *Second-Third Reports of the Select Committee on Native Affairs* (Cape Town: Government Printer, 1912), app. A, p. v. Most married men at this time would have been liable for hut tax; however, if their land had already been allocated under the Glen Grey Act, they would have been paying quitrent on the land rather than hut tax for their wives' huts and so would have been liable for the poll tax as well.

2. Blue Book Report on Native Affairs for 1908, CMT 3/678, file 175. The twenty-nine districts include two that were subsequently excised from the Transkei, Elliot and Mount Currie. Three districts in Thembuland still did not impose General Rate in 1908 (Elliot, St. Marks, and Xalanga), four in East Griqualand (Maclear, Matatiele, Mount Currie, and Mount Frere), and all seven in Pondoland (Bizana, Lusikisiki, Libode, Flagstaff, Port St. Johns, Ngqeleni, and Tabankulu). Those districts that did not pay General Rate usually had a tank tax to pay for local expenditures on dipping tanks, while all districts had a stock rate to pay the costs of stock inspectors, dip, and so on. All districts became liable for the General Rate after the enactment of the 1925 Native Taxation and Development Act, which also raised the rate to one pound per year per adult male, except in eastern Pondoland districts, where the rate remained ten shillings for many years. NEC K26, file 95, Statistics from the Native Affairs Department, "Survey of Native Taxation in the Union, Annexure C: Cape Province Taxation."

3. Randall Packard, "Industrialization, Rural Poverty, and Tuberculosis in South Africa, 1850–1950," in *The Social Basis of Health and Healing in Africa*, ed. Steven Feierman and John Janzen (Berkeley: University of California Press, 1992), 104–30.

4. Pule Phoofolo, "Epidemics and Revolutions: The Rinderpest Epidemic in Late Nineteenth Century Southern Africa," *Past and Present* 138 (1993): 112–43; Charles Ballard, "The Repercussions of Rinderpest: Cattle Plague and Peasant Decline in Colonial Natal," *International Journal of African Historical Studies* 19, no. 3 (1986): 421–50.

5. RM Engcobo District to CMT, 2 June 1896, CMT 3/88.

6. W. E. Stanford to RM Cala District, 24 June 1897, telegram, CMK 5/23; RM Tsolo District to Rinderpest Commission, based in Maclear, 1 July 1897, CMK 5/24; Acting CMT to Secretary to the Prime Minister, Cape Town, 8 September 1897, CMT 3/279. See also William Beinart, *The Political Economy of Pondoland, 1860–1930* (Johannesburg: Ravan Press, 1982), 47–48.

7. RM Nqamakwe District to CMT, 24 December 1897, CMT 3/148.

8. RM Engcobo District to CMT, enclosing report, 4 January 1898, CMT 3/89.

9. Statement by D. Hutchson, Colonial Veterinary Surgeon, "Mortality at Qumbu after Blood Inoculation; Report by Colonial Veterinary Surgeon in Evidence Taken at Inquiry," 22 October 1897, CMK 5/25.

10. RM Umtata District to CMT, 30 August 1897, CMT 3/170, no. 610.

11. Annual report for 1897 for Umtata District, sent to CMT, 5 January 1898, CMT 3/170, no. 1.

12. RM Bizana District to CMT, 30 December 1897, Blue Book Report for 1897, 1/BIZ 5/1/4/1.

13. CMT to SNA, Cape Town, 24 December 1897, CMT 3/279; RM Umzimkulu District to CMK, 6 September 1897, CMK 5/24; RM Umzimkulu District to CMK, 11 September 1897, CMK 5/24; RM Engcobo District to CMT, 22 October 1897, CMT 3/89.

14. Of course, not all officials were so cautious. Some police and veterinary inspectors did recommend coercion to enforce either quarantines, inoculation, or both. However, magistrates usually ignored their recommendations. For an example, see H. Raw, Inspector, to CMK, 2 August 1897, CMK 5/24.

15. Robert Edgar and Christopher Saunders, "A. A. S. le Fleur and the Griqua Trek of 1917: Segregation, Self-Help, and Ethnic Identity," *International Journal of African Historical Studies* 15, no. 2 (1982): 201–20; William Beinart, "The Anatomy of a Rural Scare: East Griqualand in the 1890s," in *Hidden Struggles in Rural South Africa,* William Beinart and Colin Bundy (Berkeley: University of California Press, 1987), 46–78.

16. CMT (Cumming) to Walter Stanford, quoted in Beinart, "Anatomy of a Rural Scare," 16 January 1898, BC 293 B52.219, Stanford Papers, 67.

17. Helge Kjekshus, *Ecology Control and Economic Development in East African History: The Case of Tanganyika, 1850–1950* (Berkeley: University of California Press, 1977), 126–32.

18. Acting RM Mount Fletcher District to CMK, 25 July 1897, CMK 5/23. See also RM Umtata District to CMT, 17 April 1896, CMT 3/170, no. 221.

19. RM Umtata District to CMT, replying to CMT circular letter no. G.17 of 15 April, 17 April 1896, 221, CMT 3/170. See also Charles van Onselen, "Reactions to Rinderpest in Southern Africa, 1896–97," *Journal of African History* 13 (1972): 473–88.

20. RM Willowvale District to CMT, dated 31 December 1897, Native Affairs Blue Book, 1898, CMT 3/180. The magistrate noted that these remarks "apply more especially to the Gcaleka tribe."

21. RM Mount Frere District to CMK, 11 November 1897, CMK 5/25.

22. RM Umtata District to CMT, 2 September 1902, CMT 3/172, no. 662.

23. CMT Elliot to Secretary to the Prime Minister, 22 July 1898, CMT 3/280; emphasis added.

24. Beinart, "Anatomy of a Rural Scare," 59–61.

25. Returns from all districts regarding taxation, Blue Book Report for 1910, CMT 3/679.

26. RM Engcobo District to CMT, 20 January 1899, Blue Book Report for 1899, CMT 3/90; Returns from all districts regarding taxation, Blue Book Report for 1910, CMT 3/679.

27. RM Bizana District to CMT, 30 December 1897, Blue Book Report for 1897, 1/BIZ 5/1/4/1; Acting RM to CMT, 21 January 1901, "Annual Blue Book Report for 1900, District of Bizana," CMT 3/54; Returns from all districts regarding taxation, Blue Book Report for 1910, CMT 3/679.

28. RM Bizana District to CMT, 31 January 1900, "Annual Blue Book Report for 1899, District of Bizana," CMT 3/54.

29. Cape of Good Hope, *Blue Book for Native Affairs, 1898* (Cape Town: Government Printers, 1898), report of the Chief Magistrate.

30. RM Umtata District to CMT, 5 January 1898, CMT 3/170, no. 1.

31. For examples of court cases that arose over issues of bridewealth and its payment both before and after the rinderpest period, see Sihaha v. Ncanda, case 311, 5 December 1901, 1/UTA 2/1/1/47, and Klaas Gqirana v. Mfazweni Joko, case 186/13, 23 July 1913, 1/COF 2/1/1/55.

32. Acting RM Mount Fletcher District to CMK, 25 July 1897, CMK 5/23.

33. RM Umtata District to CMT, 16 December 1897, CMT 3/170, no. 952.

34. RM Umtata District to CMT, 30 January 1902, CMT 3/171, no. 128.

35. Alfred Milner to J. Chamberlain, 11 July 1900, with enclosure of report written by Major Sir Henry Elliot on "Defence of Transkeian Territories in the War," Dispatch 122, Records of the Colonial Office 48/547, Public Record Office, Kew Gardens, London.

36. Acting RM Engcobo District to CMT, 3 February 1900, Blue Book Report on Native Affairs, Engcobo District, CMT 3/91.

37. Ivan Evans, *Bureaucracy and Race: Native Administration in South Africa* (Berkeley: University of California Press, 1997), 167–70.

38. Saul Dubow, "Holding 'a Just Balance between White and Black': The Native Affairs Department in South Africa c. 1920–33," *Journal of Southern African Studies* 12 (1986): 228–37.

39. Blue Book Report for 1907, CMT 3/681, file 175.

40. Civil cases heard by the magistrates often involved one African suing another for some form of debt repayment. Examples from this period include Xala v. Sileyi, case 19, 21 June 190, 1/UTA 2/1/1/55; Mariti v. Siliwana, case 493, 24 October 1907, 1/UTA 2/1/1/65. When white traders were involved sometimes the case became a criminal case of theft; see for example R. v. Sesekile, case 6/11, 7 January 1911, Records of the Resident Magistrate Tabankulu District 1/1/14, Cape Archives Depot, Cape Town.

41. A. H. Stanford, Blue Book Report for 1907, CMT 3/681, file 175. The fifteen districts were Butterworth, Elliotdale, Engcobo, Idutywa, Kentani, Mount Ayliff, Mount Fletcher, Mqanduli, Nqamakwe, Qumbu, Tsolo, Tsomo, Umtata, Umzimkulu, and Willowvale.

42. W. J. G. Mears, "A Study in Native Administration: The Transkeian Territories, 1894–1943" (DLitt diss., University of South Africa, 1947), 117–41; W. D. Hammond-Tooke, "The Transkeian Council System, 1895–1955: An Appraisal," *Journal of African History* 9 (1968): 455–77.

43. Colin Bundy, "Mr. Rhodes and the Poisoned Goods: Popular Opposition to the Glen Grey Council System, 1894–1906," in *Hidden Struggles in Rural South Africa*, William Beinart and Colin Bundy (Berkeley: University of California Press, 1987), 138–41.

44. RM Engcobo District to CMT, 1 March 1895, "Confidential Report," CMT 3/87; RM Engcobo District to CMT, 13 May 1899, CMT 3/90; RM Nqamakwe District to CMT, 20 March 1897, CMT 3/148, no. 300/97; RM Engcobo District to CMT, 3 June 1899, CMT 3/90; RM Umtata District to CMT, 16 June 1899, CMT 3/171, no. 390.

45. RM Butterworth District to CMT, report dated 1 January 1897, CMT 3/59.

46. RM Idutywa District to CMT, 15 March 1898, Accounting Dept. folder, CMT 3/100.

47. Bundy, "Mr. Rhodes," 141–62.

48. RM Engcobo District to CMT, enclosing report, 4 January 1897, CMT 3/89. The terms *red* and *raw* were frequently used by whites to characterize Africans who had not converted to Christianity and who maintained many of the cultural practices of their parents and grandparents. *Red* referred to the red ocher that many Africans used as a combination cosmetic and body lotion; *raw* referred to Africans who had little experience with white culture or white people.

49. RM Bizana, 31 January 1900, "Annual Blue Book Report for 1899 District of Bizana," CMT 3/54.

50. CMT (A. H. Stanford), Blue Book Report for 1907, CMT 3/681, file 175.

51. Monica Hunter Wilson, *Reaction to Conquest: Effects of Contact with Europeans on the Pondo of South Africa* (London: International Institute of African Languages and Cultures, 1936; London: Oxford University Press, 1961), 317.

52. *Territorial News*, 10 December 1910. See also, RMs of all districts to CMT, returns labeled "Stock," for Blue Book Report for 1909, CMT 3/679; E. G. Whikson, Assistant Surveyor, Office of Transkeian Territories General Council (Bunga) Surveyor, to Chairman of Umtata District Council, 24 February 1908, 1/UTA C1/1/3.

53. Blue Book Report for 1911, prepared by CMT, CMT 3/680, file 175.

54. CMT to USNA, "Annual Report for 1887," CMT 1/83.

55. Acting CMT to SNA, 14 April 1915, CMT 3/936, file 783 (3).

56. Telegram enclosed in letter from W. Carmichael for CMT to SNA, Pretoria, 9 December 1916, CMT 3/937.

57. Inspector SAP to Deputy Commissioner SAP, 17 December 1916, CMT 3/937, file 783.

58. Returns labeled "Stock," quoted in Chief Magistrate's draft for Blue Book Report for 1909, CMT 3/679, file 175.

59. RM Nqamakwe District to SNA, 24 October 1932, NTS 1771, file 64/276/5.

60. Howard Pim, *Introduction to Bantu Economics* (Fort Hare: Lovedale Press, 1930), 8–9.

61. Blue Book Report for 1911, prepared by CMT, CMT 3/680, file 175.

62. RM Nqamakwe District to CMT, enclosing transcript of inquiry into destruction of the shed at the Ezolo Dipping Tank, 7 January 1914, CMT 3/935, file 783 (1); RM Tsomo District to CMT, 31 December 1914, CMT 3/935, file 783 (1); Acting RM Matatiele District to CMT, 11 December 1915, CMT 3/935, file 783 (1); "Proceedings at an Inquiry held by me, E. L. Harries, RM for the District of Mount Frere, . . . 19th December 1914," CMT 3/935, file 783 (1); CMT to RM Mount Fletcher District, 25 January 1915, CMT 3/935, file 783 (1); CMT to SNA, Pretoria, file 783, 11 December 1916, CMT 3/937, file 783; Inspector Swinson, SAP, to Deputy Commissioner, SAP, 17 December 1916, CMT 3/937, file 783. For a comprehensive discussion and analysis of dipping-related unrest, see Colin Bundy, "'We Don't Want Your Rain, We Won't Dip': Popular Opposition, Collaboration and Social Control in the Anti-Dipping Movement, c. 1908–16," in *Hidden Struggles in Rural South Africa*, William Beinart and Colin Bundy (Berkeley: University of California Press, 1987), 191–221.

63. "Minutes of a Meeting held by the Chief Magistrate (W. T. Brownlee Esq.) with the Headmen and the natives of the Matatiele District this 25th day of November 1914 at Matatiele," CMT 3/936, file 33 Travelling (2).

64. Ibid.

65. Ibid.

66. W. E. Stanford to Secretary for Native Affairs, Pretoria, 8 December 1914, CMT 3/937, file 783 (4) Native Disturbances.

67. RM Umtata District to CMT, 16 August 1921, CMT 3/612, file 50/11.

68. Ibid.

69. CMT to all RMs, August 1918, draft for circular, CMT 3/612, file 50/11.

70. Acting Magistrate Harding District, Natal to RM Lusikisiki District, enclosing statement by Nikalasi, 6 October 1914, "Confidential," CMT 3/937, file 33 (8).

71. E. Tshongwana, Secretary to Paramount Chief Marelane, to RM Lusikisiki District, 26 November 1914, "Confidential," CMT 3/937, file 33 (8).

72. RM Lusikisiki District to CMT, enclosing note from Lusikisiki Messenger of the Court, 5 August 1920, 20 August 1920, CMT 3/612, file 50/11.

73. Acting RM Umtata District to "Health" Pretoria, 26 November 1918, telegram, 1/UTA 6/1/218, file 28; the total population figure for the District is taken from 1921 Census Returns—Raw Data (form), dated 26 May 1921, 1/UTA 6/1/41.

74. RM Nqamakwe District to CMT, 17 July 1920, CMT 3/612, file 50/11; RM Butterworth District to CMT, 24 July 1920, CMT 3/612, file 50/11; RM Cala District to CMT, 9 August 1920, CMT 3/612, file 50/11; RM Lusikisiki District to CMT, 20 August 1920, CMT 3/612, file 50/11; RM Flagstaff District to CMT, 30 September 1920, telegram, CMT 3/612, file 50/11; RM Umtata District to CMT, 16 August 1921, CMT 3/612, file 50/11; RM Idutywa District to CMT, 16 September 1921, NTS 2491, file 59/293; "RM Xalanga reports on the 5th December 1921," NTS 2542, file 251/293.

75. S. E. Humphreys, Location Superintendent, Herschel, to SNA, 23 May 1919, NTS 2486, file 41/293 (1); SNA to Magistrate, Herschel District, 7 June 1919, NTS 2486, file 41/293 (1). See also, Dubow, "Just Balance,'" 217–39, Evans, *Bureaucracy and Race,* 166–85; Mears, "Native Administration," 411–23.

76. See, for example, RM Bizana District to Commissioner for Inland Revenue, Pretoria, 12 October 1921, 1/BIZ 6/14, file 46; RM Idutywa District to Commissioner for Inland Revenue, Pretoria, 7 December 1921, NTS 2491, file 59/293.

77. Dubow, "Just Balance,'" 228–30.

78. See the remarks made by Sol Plaatje on this topic to the Native Economic Commission of 1930–32 in Sol Plaatje, "Influx of Natives into Urban Areas, Some Remarks on General Economic Conditions," Orange Free State Records, 16, K26, the NEC's records, held in the Pretoria Archives Depot.

79. T. R. H. Davenport, "The Triumph of Colonel Stallard: The Transformation of the Natives (Urban) Areas Act between 1923 and 1937," *South African Historical Journal* 2 (1970): 77–96; Evans, *Bureaucracy and Race,* 168–72.

80. Martin Legassick, "South Africa: Capital Accumulation and Violence," *Economy and Society* 3 (1974): 266–67.

81. Official attitudes in South Africa toward the abilities of Africans as farmers were similar to official attitudes elsewhere on the continent. Luise White has documented how official disregard for African farming techniques actually facilitated the spread of tsetse flies and trypanosomiasis. White, "Tsetse Visions: Narratives of Blood and Bugs in Colonial Northern Rhodesia, 1931–39," *Journal of African History* 36 (1995): 230–35. In South Africa the stereotype of Africans being irrationally attached to cattle became pervasive among whites. D. Hobart Houghton wrote in the third edition of his influential book *The South African Economy:* "African peasants have failed to adapt their farming practice to modern requirements. General conservatism, the system of land tenure, and certain social customs, like *ukulobola* [bridewealth], combine to perpetuate obsolete methods of farming." Houghton, *The South African Economy,* 3rd ed. (Cape Town: Oxford University Press, 1973), 73.

82. In making this argument, I am not attempting to revive the corpse (or rather the picked-clean skeleton) of underdevelopment theory.

83. Maynard Swanson, "The Sanitation Syndrome: Bubonic Plague and Urban Native Policy in the Cape Colony, 1900–1909," *Journal of African History* 18 (1977): 387–410.

84. Roger Southall, *South Africa's Transkei: The Political Economy of an "Independent" Bantustan* (New York: Monthly Review Press, 1983), 72–75.

Chapter 4: Governing the Zulu by Killing Them

1. Evidence and Proceedings of the South African Native Affairs Commission (hereafter SANAC), vol. 4, testimony by J. W. Shepstone, Pietermaritzburg, 12 April 1904, Union Archives Depot, Pretoria. By labeling Mpande's remark an "Irishism," Shepstone was explicitly equating the perceived irrationality and unconscious humor of two sets of colonial subjects—Irish and Zulu.

2. The Zulu name for the revolt was *impi yamakhanda,* the war of the head tax. There are several spellings of the name of the chief who has come to personify the revolt in scholarly accounts in English. Contemporary white commentators usually spelled it Bambata; many current scholars now use either Bhambhatha or Bambatha; a recent South African scholar follows an alternative spelling that he feels best reflects usage by Zulu speakers—Bhambada. See Moses M. Hadebe, "A Contextualization and Examination of the Impi Yamakhanda (1906 Uprising) as Reported by J. L. Dube in Ilanga Lase Natal with Special Focus on Dube's Attitude to Dinuzulu as Indicated in His Reportage on the Treason Trial of Dinuzulu" (mas-

ter's diss., Program of Historical Studies, University of Natal, Durban, 2002), 12n2. I have chosen to use Bambatha because the majority of the scholarly literature uses that spelling. On the Zulu name for the revolt, see also Benedict Carton, *Blood from Your Children: The Colonial Origins of Generational Conflict in South Africa* (Charlottesville: University of Virginia Press, 2000), 3.

3. See, for example, Report of meeting between Magistrate Pinetown and several chiefs, 2 November 1905, SNA 1/1/328, file 2678/1905.

4. C. T. Binns, *Dinuzulu: The Death of the House of Shaka* (London: Longmans, 1968), 181–82.

5. Sgt. C. Matthews to Inspector George, Natal Police, 25 January 1906, SNA 1/1/335, file 459/1906. "Usutu' was the war-cry used by the Zulu military in the precolonial period; the army was officially disbanded after the Zulu defeat by the British in 1881, and the war-cry was also forbidden.

6. James Stuart, *A History of the Zulu Rebellion, 1906, and of Dinuzulu's Arrest, Trial, and Expatriation* (London: Macmillan, 1913), 119–26.

7. Binns, *Dinuzulu*, 188–91.

8. Shula Marks, "The Zulu Disturbances in Natal," in *Protest and Power in Black Africa*, ed. Robert I. Rotberg and Ali A. Mazrui (New York: Oxford University Press, 1970), 216–17.

9. Natal Colony, *Further Correspondence Relating to the Trial of Dinuzulu and Other Natives in Natal* (London: His Majesty's Stationery Office, 1909), 18–20.

10. James Stuart, *James Stuart Archive of Recorded Oral Evidence Relating to the History of the Zulu and Neighbouring Peoples*, ed. and trans. Colin Webb and John Wright, 5 vols. (Pietermaritzburg: University of Natal Press, 1986), 4:75–76.

11. Marks, "Zulu Disturbances," 217.

12. Binns, *Dinuzulu*, 222–28.

13. Shula Marks, "Class, Ideology and the Bambatha Rebellion," in *Banditry, Rebellion and Social Protest in Africa*, ed. Donald Crummey (London: James Currey, 1986), 352.

14. Marks, "Zulu Disturbances," 217.

15. Natal Colony, *Trial of Dinuzulu*, 29–30.

16. The best known of all scholarly discussions of the Bambatha revolt has been Shula Marks, *Reluctant Rebellion: The 1906–8 Disturbances in Natal* (Oxford: Oxford University Press, 1970), as well as several articles that reprised certain aspects of the longer work. The kernel of her conclusions is contained in her title: that Africans were not eager to rebel, but the history of colonialism, which culminated in the imposition of the poll tax, combined with the heavy-handed actions on the part of Natal officials in stamping out the early phases of the revolt to force many Africans into revolt as a defensive measure. Land shortages, resulting from white expropriation, and the increasingly widespread system of labor migration were undermining social and economic structures within the rural areas: the revolt "was the last armed resistance to proletarianisation by Africans, and a crucial moment in the consolidation and restructuring of colonial domination and settler accumulation in twentieth-century South Africa." Marks, "Class, Ideology," 351.

17. More recent scholarship on the rebellion, such as the study by John Lambert, has tended to play down its importance, even as it still emphasizes the importance of material grievances in igniting the rebellion. See Lambert, "From Independence to Rebellion: African Society in Crisis, c. 1880–1910," in *Natal and Zululand from Earliest Times to 1910: A New History*, ed. Andrew Duminy and Bill Guest (Pietermaritzburg: Shuter and Shooter, 1989), 373–97.

18. Stuart, *Zulu Rebellion*, 1.

19. Ibid., 514–17.

20. Ibid., 517.

21. Carolyn Hamilton, *Terrific Majesty: The Powers of Shaka Zulu and the Limits of Historical Invention* (Cambridge: Harvard University Press, 1998), 157–59.

22. Stuart, *Zulu Rebellion*, 510.

23. Carolyn Hamilton has discussed Stuart and his career in great detail, as well as Stuart's particular concerns in the Bambatha Rebellion. Hamilton, *Terrific Majesty*, 156–59.

24. Stuart's interviews have been collected, transcribed, translated (when necessary), and annotated in five volumes. Stuart, *Stuart Archive*. Historian Julian Cobbing criticizes both Stuart and the material compiled in his archived interviews in "A Tainted Well: The Objectives, Historical Fantasies, and Working Methods of James Stuart, with Counter-Argument," *Journal of Natal and Zulu History* 11 (1988): 115–54. Hamilton has disputed Cobbing's blanket rejection of the Stuart material. Hamilton, *Terrific Majesty*, 156–59; Hamilton, "'The Character and Objects of Chaka': A Reconsideration of the Making of Shaka as Mfecane Motor," in *The Mfecane Aftermath*, ed. Carolyn Hamilton (Johannesburg: Witwatersrand University Press, 1995), 207–10.

25. Benedict Carton has used the interviews in the Stuart archives to suggest that the rebellion emerged out of generational conflict between Zulu elders and their sons, who increasingly had provided significant economic support for their fathers' rural homesteads through their wages from working on the mines and on white-owned farms. The grievances of the young men who rebelled, in Carton's view, were as much aimed at older Zulu homestead heads as they were at the state. Carton, *Blood from Your Children*, 91–94, 114–21.

26. There is a real problem in writing about "the Zulu" as though they were a unified group at the time of the revolt. They were, as Shula Marks points out, only Zulu in terms of the language they spoke. Politically and culturally, there were deep rifts among various groups of Zulu speakers, and those rifts had strong historical roots. See Marks, "Zulu Disturbances," 214–15n1.

27. Jeff Guy, *The View Across the River: Harriette Colenso and the Zulu Struggle against Imperialism* (Charlottesville: University of Virginia Press, 2001), 3–11; Peter Colenbrander, "The Zulu Kingdom, 1828–79," in *Natal and Zululand from Earliest Times to 1910: A New History*, ed. Andrew Duminy and Bill Guest (Pietermaritzburg: Shuter and Shooter, 1989), 83–115.

28. Bill Guest, "Colonists, Confederation and Constitutional Change," in *Natal and Zululand from Earliest Times to 1910: A New History*, ed. Andrew Duminy and Bill Guest (Pietermaritzburg: Shuter and Shooter, 1989), 146–69.

29. Norman Etherington, "The 'Shepstone System' in the Colony of Natal and beyond the Borders," in *Natal and Zululand from Earliest Times to 1910: A New History*, ed. Andrew Duminy and Bill Guest (Pietermaritzburg: Shuter and Shooter, 1989), 170–92; Jeff Guy, *The Destruction of the Zulu Kingdom* (London: Longman, 1979).

30. Ivan Evans, *Bureaucracy and Race: Native Administration in South Africa* (Berkeley: University of California Press, 1997), 164–76.

31. Cape of Good Hope, *Report of the Government Commission on Native Laws and Customs*, facsimile repr., 2 vols. (Cape Town: C. Struik, 1968), 1:63–67.

32. Narissa Ramdhani, "Taxation without Representation: The Hut Tax System in Colonial Natal," *Journal of Natal and Zulu History* 11 (1986): 16.

33. Ibid., 19.

34. Etherington, "'Shepstone System,'" 174–76.

35. See, for example, Magistrate Umlazi division, Pinetown, to USNA, Natal, November 2, 1905, SNA 1/1/328, file 2678/1905.

36. Testimony of Mr. H. C. Shepstone, former SNA, Natal, and son of Theophilus Shepstone, 12 April 1904, SANAC, vol. 3.

37. Testimony of Mr. C. J. R. Saunders, Chief Magistrate and Civil Commissioner of Zululand, 25 May 1904, SANAC, vol. 4.

38. Norman Etherington, "Christianity and African Society in Nineteenth Century Natal," in *Natal and Zululand from Earliest Times to 1910: A New History*, ed. Andrew Duminy and Bill Guest (Pietermaritzburg: Shuter and Shooter, 1989), 278–80.

39. John Laband and Paul Thompson, "The Reduction of Zululand, 1878–1904," in *Natal and Zululand from Earliest Times to 1910*, ed. Andrew Duminy and Bill Guest (Pietermaritzburg: Shuter and Shooter, 1989), 212–20.

40. Lambert, "Independence to Rebellion," 388.

41. Stuart, *Stuart Archive*, 4:55.

42. "Statement showing the amount of Hut Tax in Arrear on the 30th September 1905," SNA 1/1/331, file 3350/1905. In 1910 there were 200,792 taxable huts in Natal and 75,313 in Zululand, figures that give a sense of how low the default rate was in 1904. See testimony of A. J. Shepstone, Chief Native Commissioner of Natal in South Africa, Select Committee on Native Affairs, *Second-Third Reports of the Select Committee on Native Affairs* (Cape Town: Government Printer, 1912), 53.

43. Stuart, *Zulu Rebellion*, 101.

44. "Report notifying the natives of the District of the Poll Tax," from A. J. Maritz to SNA, Natal, 7 October 1905, SNA 1/1/238, file 2675/05.

45. Testimony of H. C. Shepstone, 12 April 1904, SANAC, vol. 4.

46. Magistrate Dundee to Chief Native Commissioner, Natal and Zululand, 6 November 1916, NTS 2490, file 55/293.

47. Charles Ballard, "The Repercussions of Rinderpest: Cattle Plague and Peasant Decline in Colonial Natal," *International Journal of African Historical Studies* 19, no. 3 (1986): 421–50.

48. Magistrate Pinetown to USNA S. O. Samuelson, 2 November 1905, SNA 1/1/328, file 2678/1905.

49. Carton, *Blood from Your Children*, 91–94, 114–21.

50. Minutes of meeting at Isipingo, 26 October 1905, SNA 1/1/328, file 2678/1905.

51. "Notes taken by Magistrate Nkandhla, by request of Native Chiefs in Nkandhla Division, for the purpose of submitting same to Government in regard to the official intimation received by them of the enforcement of the Poll Tax (Act 38, 1905)," SNA 1/1/328, file 2825/1905; meeting held 17 October 1905.

52. Testimony of James Stuart, 31 May 1904, SANAC, vol. 4.

53. Stuart, *Stuart Archive*, 4:53; italics in original (denoting phrase transcribed by Stuart in Zulu and translated by the archive's editors).

54. Stuart, *Zulu Rebellion*, 99.

55. A. J. Maritz to SNA, "Report notifying the natives of the District of the Poll Tax," 7 October 1905, SNA 1/1/238, file 2675/05.

56. D. H. Reader, *Zulu Tribe in Transition: The Makhanya of Southern Natal* (Manchester: Manchester University Press, 1966), 19.

57. K. G. Gillings, "The Bambata Rebellion of 1906: Nkandla Operations and the Battle of Mome Gorge, 10 June 1906," *South African Military History Journal* 8, no. 1 (1989): 1.

58. Extract from the *Greytown Gazette*, Saturday, 13 January 1906, SNA 1/1/334, file 245/1906.

59. Testimony of Cwalinyoni, "Rex v. Mdopa, son of Ngoza kraal of Ndabu Chief Mkankanyeki, Newcastle Division, age 30 Years," copy of trial transcript, SNA 1/1/335, file 352/1906.

60. Testimony of Johannes Gwamanda, Ibid.

61. Testimony of Johannes Gwamanda, Rex v. Makabakaba, January 12, 1906, copy of transcript of trial 1/06, SNA 1/1/335, file 352/1906.

62. "Extract from the Notes of Evidence in the Case of Rex vs. Mevana alias Frank Sikisana, son of Mpande Chief Tapane, Bergville Division, age 35 years," evidence of Mankini, SNA 1/1/335, file 352/1906.

63. The quotation is cited in Marks, "Class, Ideology," 356. Magema Fuze also discusses the rumors leading up to the revolt. Fuze, *The Black People and Whence They Came: A Zulu View* (Pietermaritzburg: University of Natal Press, 1979), 138–40.

64. Extract from the *Greytown Gazette*, Saturday, 13 January 1906, SNA 1/1/334, file 245/1906.

65. Rex v. Makabakaba, January 12, 1906, testimony of Mabizela, copy of transcript of trial 1/06, SNA 1/1/335, file 352/1906.

66. Ibid., testimony of Makabakaba (the accused), and of Mdopa, his companion. Other rumors of Dinuzulu's involvement in planning the rebellion are discussed in Hadebe, "Impi Yamakanda," 85–87.

67. Luise White, *Speaking with Vampires: Rumor and History in Colonial Africa* (Berkeley: University of California Press, 2000), 210. See also the discussion of rumor in Marks, "Class, Ideology," 355–57.

68. White, *Speaking with Vampires*, 205.

69. Axel-Ivar Berglund, *Zulu Thought-Patterns and Symbolism* (Bloomington: Indiana University Press, 1989), 371.

70. Harriet Ngubane, *Body and Mind in Zulu Medicine* (New York: Academic Press, 1977), 88–89, 113–34.

71. Stuart, *Stuart Archive*, 3:174; italics in original, denoting material in Zulu in the archives and translated into English by the editors.

72. See also Henry Callaway's description, dating from 1870, of the beliefs in the Lord-of-the-Sky and its control over lightning in Irving Hexham, *Texts on Zulu Religion* (Lewiston, NY: Edwin Mellen Press, 1987), 260–63.

73. Berglund, *Zulu Thought-Patterns*, 32–35, 250, 52.

74. Marks, *Reluctant Rebellion*, xv. Although James Stuart concluded from Bambatha's use of these symbols that Dinuzulu was actually involved in planning the uprising, there was no evidence of Dinuzulu's complicity at his trial following the rebellion. Historian C. T. Binns, by contrast, suggests that Bambatha cleverly manipulated several malcontents living at Dinuzulu's home to orchestrate the semblance of Dinuzulu's support. Binns, *Dinuzulu*, 198–200.

75. Guy, *Destruction of the Zulu Kingdom*, 206.

76. Stuart, *Stuart Archive*, 4:75–76, 77; italics in original, denoting material in Zulu in the archives and translated into English by the editors.

77. Ibid., 3:200–201. See also the account of Cetshwayo's naming of Dinuzulu as heir in Fuze, *Black People*, 119–21.

78. Laband and Thompson, "Reduction of Zululand," 212–13; Guy, *View across the River*, 99–101, 107, 139–42.

79. John Laband, *The Rise and Fall of the Zulu Nation* (London: Arms and Armour Press, 1997), 368–77.

80. Laband and Thompson, "Reduction of Zululand," 218–21.

81. Stuart, *Zulu Rebellion*, 111.

82. Marks, "Zulu Disturbances," 235–42.

83. Shula Marks speculates from the confusing evidence that Cakijana may himself have been the real force behind the rebellion. He was from an area that had been fought over by whites and Africans for years and he nursed a grievance; he saw an opportunity to use his own position as Dinuzulu's messenger and to use Bambatha's openly defiant stance as a way to create a wider rebellion. See Marks, "Class, Ideology," 358–64.

84. Stuart, *Zulu Rebellion*, 114.

85. Stuart, *Stuart Archive*, 3:323 italics in original, denoting material in Zulu in the archives and translated into English by the editors.

86. Gillings, "Bambata Rebellion," 4.

87. Binns, *Dinuzulu,* 201–6.

88. Ibid., 207–14.

89. Cakijana, who died in 1963, was interviewed by C. T. Binns. See Binns, *Dinuzulu,* 214, footnote. K. G. Gillings asserts, "It is generally accepted that Magistrate Steinbank was shot by Cakijana," without citing a source. Gillings, "Bambata Rebellion," 6.

90. Gillings, "Bambata Rebellion," 6.

91. Evidence of Maliba Sijulana at Dinuzulu's preliminary examination, 2 June 1908, *Natal Mercury.* Quoted in Marks, "Zulu Disturbances," 241.

92. Marks, "Zulu Disturbances," 240–43.

93. Gillings, "Bambata Rebellion," 11–12.

94. The website for Greytown features a letter from a woman who claims that her grandfather, H. S. Flook, was the person who cut the head from the body of Bambatha. A letter from another woman suggested that it was her grandfather, Maj. William Knott, who helped Flook with the head and then took a picture, "which my brother has since donated to the Pietermaritzburg Museum." See http://www.greytown.co.za/bambathastment.htm, letters from Diana Pretorius and Patricia Frykberg (accessed March 19, 2004).

95. Binns, *Dinuzulu,* 216–22.

96. Gillings, "Bambata Rebellion," 12.

97. Stuart, *Stuart Archive,* 3:234–35.

98. Ibid., 324. Umnyama was a power that "brings darkness onto them [the enemy] whilst it is light on the side of their assailants." Darkness might be literally lack of light, but it might also mean "paralysis of action inspired by fear, oversleeping . . . , futility or stupidity of plan when engaging their assailants, being overtaken by a mist whilst it is clear for their foes, etc. *Umnyama* is caused by a [war] doctor."

99. Ibid.

100. Greytown homepage: www.greytown.co.za/bambathastment.htm. Oral history of Mishack Mthalane, collected in October 1968, by attorneys Nel and Stevens, interpreted by Gilbert Maphanga (accessed March 19, 2004).

101. Marks, "Zulu Disturbances," 254.

102. In contrast, Stuart saw the hand of a desperate Dinuzulu behind the new outbreak, although Dinuzulu was acquitted of this charge at his trial. See Stuart, *Zulu Rebellion,* 347–48.

103. Testimony of Dhlozi at the Natal Native Affairs Commission, 1906–7, which was convened to inquire into the causes of the rebellion. Quoted in Marks, "Zulu Disturbances," 220.

104. Marks, "Zulu Disturbances," 254.

105. Stuart, *Stuart Archive,* 3:142.

106. Stuart, *Zulu Rebellion,* 536.

107. Natal Governor to Prime Minister, cited in Marks, "Zulu Disturbances," 255.

108. Acting Magistrate Mapumulo to USNA, 28 June 1907, SNA 1/1/371, file 1862/1907.

109. "Hut Tax Arrears, 1906, Natal and Zululand" and "Digest of Replies to SNA Circular 2/1907, on the subject of arrears of Hut Tax," SNA 1/1/360, file 93/1907; "Digest of Replies to SNA Circular No. 14/1907, on the subject of the collection of Taxes," SNA 1/1/371, file 1868/1907; "Summary of Replies to DNC Circular No. 52, 1909" regarding the collection of taxes, SNA 1/1/434, file 1807/1909.

110. For example, in the year after the rebellion the administration ruled that anyone who paid a hut tax (fourteen shillings) for a dwelling hut used by adolescents (an ilawu hut) was not liable for the poll tax (one pound, or in other words, six shillings more than the hut tax). A large number of ilawu huts were registered in the next year, and there were corresponding decreases in the amount of poll tax due. "Hut Tax Arrears, 1906, Natal and Zululand" and "Digest of Replies to SNA Circular 2/1907, on the subject of arrears of Hut Tax," SNA 1/1/360.

file 93/1907; "Digest of Replies to SNA Circular No. 14/1907, on the subject of the collection of Taxes," SNA 1/1/371, file 1868/1907.

111. The longevity of the beliefs is further supported by the collection of evidence by Binns (who interviewed a number of Zulu people in the 1950s in preparation of his book), and by anthropologists Berglund and Harriet Ngubane, who did their fieldwork for their books from 1959 through 1970.

112. Stuart, *Stuart Archive,* 4:15; italics in original, denoting material in Zulu in the archives and translated into English by the editors.

113. Shula Marks, "Patriotism, Patriarchy and Purity: Natal and the Politics of Zulu Ethnic Consciousness," in *The Creation of Tribalism in Southern Africa,* ed. Leroy Vail (Berkeley: University of California Press, 1989).

114. Marks, *Reluctant Rebellion,* 105; Stuart, *Zulu Rebellion,* 92–99.

115. Colin Bundy, "Mr. Rhodes and the Poisoned Goods: Popular Opposition to the Glen Grey Council System, 1894–1906," in *Hidden Struggles in Rural South Africa,* William Beinart and Colin Bundy (Berkeley: University of California Press, 1987), 138–65.

116. Ibid., 141.

117. For examples of magistrates' pulse taking on the issue of the labor tax see RM Engcobo District to CMT, 1 March 1895, "Confidential Report," CMT 3/87; RM Nqamakwe District to CMT, 20 March 1897, CMT 3/148, 300/97; RM Umtata District to CMT, 16 June 1899, CMT 3/171, 390.

118. Blue Book Report on Native Affairs for 1908, CMT 3/678, file 175.

119. Carton, *Blood from Your Children,* 122–24.

120. Helen Bradford, "Gentlemen and Boers: Afrikaner Nationalism, Gender, and Colonial Warfare in the South African War," in *Writing a Wider War: Rethinking Gender, Race, and Identity in the South African War, 1899–1902,* ed. Greg Cuthbertson, Albert Grundlingh, and Mary-Lynn Suttie (Athens: Ohio University Press, 2002), 40–51.

121. James Scott, *Domination and the Arts of Resistance: Hidden Transcripts* (New Haven: Yale University Press, 1990), 65–67.

Chapter 5: Taxation and Flaming Pigs in the Transkei, 1921–30

1. RM Qumbu District to RM Tsolo District, enclosing report by Constable Waldeck, December 1926, 1/TSO, file 3/16/6.

2. South African Police Ngqeleni District to District Commandant, SAP, Umtata, 10 December 1927, CNC 348, file 271/19.

3. Statement of Skova Mngeni, 4 April 1926, CMT 3/951.

4. Robert Edgar, "Garveyism in Africa: Dr. Wellington and the American Movement in the Transkei," *Ufahamu* 6, no. 3 (1976): 31–57; Robert Edgar and Christopher Saunders, "A. A. S. Le Fleur and the Griqua Trek of 1917: Segregation, Self-Help, and Ethnic Identity," *International Journal of African Historical Studies* 15, no. 2 (1982): 201–20.

5. William Beinart, "Amafelandawonye (the Die-Hards): Popular Protest and Women's Movements in Herschel District in the 1920s," in *Hidden Struggles in Rural South Africa,* ed. William Beinart and Colin Bundy (Berkeley: University of California Press, 1987), 222–69.

6. Helen Bradford, *A Taste of Freedom: The ICU in Rural South Africa, 1924–1930* (New Haven: Yale University Press, 1987), 231.

7. RM Umtata District to CMT, 16 August 1921, CMT 3/612, file 50/11; RM Lusikisiki District to CMT, enclosing note from Lusikisiki Messenger of the Court, J. S. Warner, 5 August 1920, 20 August 1920, CMT 3/612, file 50/11; RM Cala District to CMT, 9 August 1920, CMT 3/612, file 50/11; RM Butterworth District to CMT, 24 July 1920, CMT 3/612, file 50/11; RM Nqamakwe District to CMT, 17 July 1920, CMT 3/612, file 50/11; RM Bizana District to

Treasurer of the Eastern Pondoland Trust Account, Umtata, 14 November 1921, 1/BIZ 6/14, file 46; RM Idutywa District to CMT, 16 September 1921 NTS 2491, file 59/293.

8. RM Flagstaff District to CMT, 30 September 1920, telegram, CMT 3/612, file 50/11.

9. Abner Mdikane (Agricultural Demonstrator) to RM Umtata District, 30 August 1919, 1/UTA C3/3; Acting RM Umtata District to Medical Officer of Health, Pretoria, 3 March 1919, 1/UTA 6/1/219, file 28.

10. RM Bizana District to Commissioner for Inland Revenue, 7 August 1923, file 126/293, NTS 2525. See also RM Engcobo District to SNA, 7 March 1922, NTS 2542, file 250/293.

11. RM Umtata District to CMT, 16 August 1921, CMT 3/612, file 50/11.

12. Commissioner for Inland Revenue to the Receiver of Revenue, Bizana, 8 October 1921, 1/BIZ 6/14, file 46.

13. RM Bizana District to Commissioner for Inland Revenue, Pretoria, 12 October 1921, 1/BIZ 6/14, file 46.

14. RM Bizana District to Treasurer of the Eastern Pondoland Trust Account, Umtata, 14 November 1921, 1/BIZ 6/14, file 46; Hut Tax Return, 22 February 1922, signed by RM.

15. RM Bizana District to Treasurer of the Eastern Pondoland Trust Account, Umtata, 14 November 1921, 1/BIZ 6/14, file 46.

16. CMT to SNA, 3 September 1926, CMT 3/612, file 50/11.

17. James Scott, *Domination and the Arts of Resistance: Hidden Transcripts* (New Haven: Yale University Press, 1990), 57.

18. RM Idutywa District to CMT, 16 September 1921, file 59/293, NTS 2491. See also comments by Chief Magistrate in CMT to SNA, 3 September 1926, CMT 3/612, file 50/11.

19. Beinart, "Amafelandawonye."

20. Acting RM Qumbu District to CMT, 19 July 1922, CMT 3/951.

21. Sworn statement of Gordon Donald Brauns, taken at Sulankama, Qumbu District, 19 July 1922, CMT 3/951.

22. "Report of Meeting at Qumbu on Monday the 24th July 1922," CMT 3/951.

23. Ibid.

24. From four African women to the SNA, 18 August 1992, CMT 3/951; the quote is from minutes of meeting between RM and women at Herschel on 25 August 1922, CMT 3/951.

25. RM Herschel District to SNA, 28 August 1922, CMT 3/951.

26. RM Mount Ayliff District to CMT, 26 August 1922, NTS 9465, file 2/394.

27. Handwritten note, 5 September 1922, signed J. Bam, NTS 9465, file 2/394. Johanna Brandt was an Afrikaner woman who published a widely read book, *The Millennium*, in 1918, which purportedly suggested that the world was nearing its end. Jehovah's Witnesses, who were actively proselytizing in South Africa at the time, also preached that the world was nearing its end at roughly the same time.

28. Cutting from "Star" dated 14 November 1922, NTS 9465, file 2/394.

29. Beinart, "Amafelandawonye," 251.

30. Monica Hunter Wilson, *Reaction to Conquest: Effects of Contact with Europeans on the Pondo of South Africa* (London: International Institute of African Languages and Cultures, 1936; London: Oxford University Press, 1961), 571.

31. W. D. Cingo, "Native Unrest," *Kokstad Advertiser,* 30 September 1927, quoted in Robert Hill and Gregory A. Pirio, "'Africa for the Africans': The Garvey Movement in South Africa, 1920–40," in *The Politics of Race, Class, and Nationalism in Twentieth-Century South Africa,* ed. Shula Marks and Stanley Trapido (London: Longman, 1987), 211.

32. William Beinart and Colin Bundy, "The Union, the Nation, and the Talking Crow: The Ideology and Tactics of the Independent ICU in East London," in *Hidden Struggles in Rural South Africa,* William Beinart and Colin Bundy (Berkeley: University of California Press, 1987), 270–320.

33. Bradford, *Taste of Freedom;* Sheridan Johns, "Trade Union, Political Pressure Group, or Mass Movement? The Industrial and Commercial Workers' Union of Africa," in *Protest and Power in Black Africa,* ed. Robert Rotberg and Ali Mazrui (New York: Oxford University Press, 1970).

34. "An extract from Umteteli dated 15 January 1927 (translation)," 1/TSO 5/1/19, file 3/16/6.

35. Statements taken 12 March 1927 at office of RM Tsolo District, 1/TSO 5/1/19, file 3/16/6.

36. See R. H. Arnold, SAP of Estcourt, to Commanding Officer, 15 April 1915, report on unrest in Ixopo and Port Shepstone districts, CNC 192, file 81/1915.

37. "Statement of Mgqushwa Lubelo ka Mabuni," at the Magistrate's office, Harding, 15 December 1927, CNC 348, file 271/19.

38. Wilson, *Reaction to Conquest,* 571.

39. Ibid., 302.

40. "Statement of Mgqushwa Lubelo ka Mabuni," CNC 348, file 271/19.

41. Bradford, *Taste of Freedom,* 225.

42. Wilson, *Reaction to Conquest,* 298.

43. Bradford, *Taste of Freedom,* 226.

44. Bradford discusses the witchcraft beliefs associated with the ICU and Wellington in the Transkei in Bradford, *Taste of Freedom,* 213–45.

45. Ibid., 235.

46. Scott, *Domination,* 154–56.

47. Sean Redding, "Legal Minors and Social Children: African Women and Taxation in the Transkei, 1880–1950," *African Studies Review* 36 (1993): 49–74.

48. RM Tsolo to CMT, 2 June 1927, 1/TSO 5/1/19, file 2/16/4.

49. Edgar, "Garveyism in Africa," 49.

50. Wilson, *Reaction to Conquest,* 571.

51. Lionel E. Harris, General Trader, Tsolo, to RM Tsolo District, 11 March 1927, 1/TSO 5/1/19, file 2/16/4.

52. Edgar, "Garveyism in Africa," 47.

53. Ibid., 47–50. For Tsolo District, see RM Tsolo to CMT, 15 March 1927, 1/TSO 51/19, file 2/16/4. For discussion of the IICU see Bradford, *Taste of Freedom,* 240–45; Beinart and Bundy, "Union, Nation."

54. Bradford, *Taste of Freedom,* 174.

55. Ibid., 242; Beinart and Bundy, "Union, Nation," 308–13.

56. Bradford, *Taste of Freedom,* 244.

57. Beinart and Bundy, "Union, Nation," 312–14.

58. Edgar and Saunders, "le Fleur and the Griqua Trek."

59. Ibid., 220.

60. Statement by Moyo Lingani, 3 April 1926, CMT 3/951.

61. Statement of Skova Mngeni, 4 April 1926, CMT 3/951.

62. Report, SAP Kokstad to District Commandant, 24 March 1926, CMT 3/951.

63. Report from Criminal Investigation Department, Kokstad, 4 April 1927, CMT 3/951.

64. For a full discussion of the cattle-killing movement see J. B. Peires, *The Dead Will Arise* (Berkeley: University of California Press, 1989).

65. Report from Criminal Investigation Department, Kokstad, 4 April 1927, CMT 3/951. The Labour Party was the white-dominated official opposition political party. The Labour Party was somewhat more liberal than was the ruling party in its policies toward Africans and Coloureds, but, as le Fleur insinuated by describing the party as "your enemies," many Africans believed that the Labour Party was just sneakier in its racial policies and manipulated African and Coloured voters for the benefit of the white electorate.

66. Det. Sgt. SAP, Kokstad, to District Commandant Kokstad, 29 March 1926, CMT 3/951.

67. Edgar and Saunders, "Le Fleur and the Griqua Trek."

68. Ibid., 219–20.

69. CMT to SNA, 8 April 1930, enclosing annual report for 1929, NTS 1771, file 64/276/4.

70. Bradford, *Taste of Freedom*, 244–45.

71. Beinart and Bundy, "Union, Nation," 313.

72. Clifton Crais, *The Politics of Evil: Magic, State Power, and the Political Imagination in South Africa* (New York: Cambridge University Press, 2002), 140.

73. Robert R. Edgar, "The Fifth Seal: Enoch Mgijima, the Israelites, and the Bulhoek Massacre, 1921" (PhD diss., University of California, Los Angeles, 1977), final chapter.

Chapter 6: Legal Minors and Social Children

1. Narissa Ramdhani, "Taxation without Representation: The Hut Tax System in Colonial Natal," *Journal of Natal and Zulu History* 11 (1986): 132–33.

2. Monica Hunter Wilson, *Reaction to Conquest: Effects of Contact with Europeans on the Pondo of South Africa* (London: International Institute of African Languages and Cultures, 1936; London: Oxford University Press, 1961), 32–45.

3. Sean Redding, "Witchcraft, Women, and Taxes in the Transkei, South Africa, 1930–63," in *Stepping Forward: Black Women in Africa and the Americas,* ed. Catherine Higgs, Barbara Moss, and Earline Rae Ferguson (Athens: Ohio University Press, 2002), 87–99.

4. The South African Republic and the Orange Free State did not impose *hut* taxes—except for a few years in the case of the SAR—but relied instead on poll and labor taxes. Colonial Natal had been the first state in southern Africa to collect hut taxes, beginning in 1850.

5. South Africa, Union Native Affairs Department, *Report of the South African Native Affairs Commission (SANAC)* (Cape Town: Government Printers, 1903–5), vol. 4, para. 20512–21.

6. The most noted of these men were John Maclean (compiler of *A Compendium of Kafir Laws and Customs,* first published at Mount Coke in 1858), Theophilus Shepstone (who instituted the hut tax in Natal and later advised Cape officials), Walter Stanford (chief magistrate of East Griqualand for several years and later superintendent of the Native Affairs Department during the Anglo-Boer War), Maj. Henry Elliot (a member of the British marines who first served in the Crimea and later in the Eastern Cape; for a number of years he was chief magistrate of Tembuland and then of the whole Transkei), and Charles Brownlee (an influential magistrate on the eastern Frontier and later Secretary for Native Affairs). See SNA to Maj. Henry Elliot, 3 April 1877, "Private and Confidential," CMT 1/2, 5A/293.

7. Martin Chanock, *Law, Custom, and Social Order* (Cambridge: Cambridge University Press, 1985); Marcia Wright, "Justice, Women and the Social Order in Abercorn, Northeastern Rhodesia, 1897–1903," in *African Women and the Law: Historical Perspectives,* ed. Margaret Jean Hay and Marcia Wright (Boston: Boston University, African Studies Center, 1982), 33–50.

8. "Little weight is given to the evidence of wives or women [in judicial inquiries by chiefs] as they are supposed to be influenced almost entirely by their husbands or relations. Great weight is attached to the evidence of children if it is procured before they have been tampered with." Answers by CMT Elliot to Native Laws Commission, 27 September 1881, CMT 1/146.

9. An early observer of African society in this region, J. C. Warner, who was a colonial government agent, stated in 1856, "Marriage among the Kafir has degenerated into slavery,

and is simply the purchase of as many women by one man as he desires, or can afford to pay for." Yet he later notes, "Although in theory, perhaps, the power of the husband over the wife is considered absolute in every thing but taking her life; yet in reality there are many checks to his power." In John Maclean, *A Compendium of Kafir Laws and Customs* (Mount Coke: Wesleyan Mission Press, 1858), 70, 72.

10. Cape of Good Hope, *Report of the Government Commission on Native Laws and Customs, 1883,* facsimile repr., 2 vols. (Cape Town: C. Struik, 1968), 1:439.

11. Ibid., 2:148.

12. W. T. Brownlee, *Reminiscences of a Transkeian* (Pietermaritzburg: Shuter and Shooter, 1975), 20.

13. Cape of Good Hope, *Commission on Native Laws,* 2:143. Several historians, notably Jeff Guy and Margaret Kinsman, have developed the view of African women as exploited members of precolonial societies. This view owes much to missionaries' disapproving observations of women as the principal farmers of the soil, and of young women as sometimes unwilling partners in arranged marriages. See Guy, "Analysing Pre-Capitalist Societies in Southern Africa," *Journal of Southern African Studies* 14 (1987): 18–37; Guy, "Gender Oppression in Southern Africa's Precapitalist Societies," in *Women and Gender in Southern Africa to 1945,* ed. Cherryl Walker (Cape Town: David Philip, 1990), 33–47; Kinsman, "Beasts of Burden: The Subordination of Southern Tswana Women, ca. 1800–1840," *Journal of Southern African Studies* 10 (1983): 17–39.

14. Cape of Good Hope, *Commission on Native Laws,* 1:394.

15. Wilson, *Reaction to Conquest,* 180–213.

16. Cape of Good Hope, *Commission on Native Laws,* 1:404.

17. Ibid., 1:30.

18. Wilson, *Reaction to Conquest,* 33–43.

19. Cape of Good Hope, *Commission on Native Laws,* 2:63.

20. Compare this with the situation described by Iris Berger in Berger, "Rebels or Status-Seekers? Women as Spirit Mediums in East Africa," in *Women in Africa,* ed. Nancy Hafkin and Edna Bay (Stanford: Stanford University Press, 1976), 157–82.

21. Nqudu Rode v. Emma Mayamana alias Ngezana, case 207/43, 24 November 1943, 1/UTA 2/1/1/157; Wilson, *Reaction to Conquest,* 200–201. But see also a dissenting view that the ubulungu cow was a gift to the husband from his in-laws. "Memorandum of the Ubulungu Custom as Laid Down by Chief Dalindyebo [of the Thembu]," ca. 1910 (typescript, one page), S. Pam 572.3925 (6865), The Strange (Africana) Library.

22. Cape of Good Hope, *Commission on Native Laws,* 1:404, 2:33.

23. Wilson, *Reaction to Conquest,* 210–12; Helen Bradford, "Peasants, Historians and Gender: A South African Case Study Revisited, 1850–86," *History and Theory* 39 (2000): 86–110; Daphna Golan, "The Life Story of King Shaka and Gender Tensions in the Zulu State," *History in Africa* 17 (1990): 95–111.

24. South Africa, *South African Native Affairs Commission,* 104–5, 109–11.

25. Martin Chanock, "Making Customary Law: Men, Women, and Courts in Colonial Northern Rhodesia," in *African Women and the Law: Historical Perspectives,* ed. Margaret Jean Hay and Marcia Wright (Boston: Boston University, African Studies Center, 1982), 53–66; Jean Comaroff and John Comaroff, *Christianity, Colonialism, and Consciousness in South Africa,* vol. 1 of *Of Revelation and Revolution* (Chicago: University of Chicago Press, 1991); Deborah Gaitskell, "Devout Domesticity? A Century of African Women's Christianity in South Africa," in *Women and Gender in Southern African to 1945,* ed. Cherryl Walker (Cape Town: David Philip, 1990), 251–72; Gaitskell, "Housewives, Maids or Mothers: Some Contradictions of Domesticity for Christian Women in Johannesburg, 1903–1939," *Journal of African History* 24, no. 2 (1983): 241–57; Ann Stoler, "Making Empire Respectable: The

Politics of Race and Sexual Morality in Twentieth Century Colonial Cultures," *American Ethnologist* 16 (1989): 634–60; Margaret Strobel, "Gender and Race in the 19th and 20th Century British Empire," in *Becoming Visible: Women in European History,* ed. R. Bridenthal, Claudia Koonz, and Susan Mosher Stuard (Boston: Houghton Mifflin, 1987), 375–96.

26. As the resident magistrate of Umtata District, Transkei, put it in 1878, "The great hindrince [sic] to Christianity and civilization are dowry, Polygammy [sic], beer parties, and red clay." RM Umtata District to CMT, 30 December 1878, Annual Report for 1878, 1/UTA 5/1/1/2. Similar remarks are in RM Tsolo District to CMK, 14 January 1888, "Report for Blue Book on Native Affairs for 1887," CMK 1/139.

27. RM Tsolo District to CMK, 22 February 1882, "Approximate Census Tsolo District," CMK 1/98.

28. RM Umtata District to CMT, 6 January 1880, 1/UTA 5/1/1/2, letter 280.

29. Cape of Good Hope, *Commission on Native Laws,* 2:101–2.

30. South Africa, Select Committee on Native Affairs, *Second-Third Reports of the Select Committee on Native Affairs* (Cape Town: Government Printer, 1912), 33.

31. Beer drinks were informal gatherings, often during the harvest period, at which locally-brewed sorghum beer was served, sometimes in great quantities.

32. Cape of Good Hope, *Commission on Native Laws,* 2:34.

33. R. L. Cope, "C. W. de Kiewiet, the Imperial Factor, and South African 'Native Policy,'" *Journal of Southern African Studies* 15 (1989): 486–505.

34. Colin Bundy, "The Emergence and Decline of a South African Peasantry," *African Affairs* 71 (1972): 369–88.

35. Cape of Good Hope, *Commission on Native Laws,* 1:63, 65, 67.

36. South Africa, *South African Native Affairs Commission,* vol. 3, evidence of R. J. Dick; South Africa, *Select Committee on Native Affairs,* pars. 115–23.

37. South Africa, *Select Committee on Native Affairs,* 6–7.

38. RM Nqamakwe District to SNA, 24 October 1932, NTS 1771, file 64/276/5; RM Tsolo District to CMK, 10 January 1887, 14 January 1888, CMK 1/139; RM Engcobo District to CMT, 19 July 1920, CMT 3/612, file 50/11; CMT to SNA, 8 April 1930, NTS 1771, file 64/276/4; Acting RM Umtata District to CMT, 22 December 1891, CMT 3/169, 296; CMT to USNA, 1 January 1892, annual report for 1891, CMT 1/84.

39. CMT to SNA, 6 December 1897, CMT 3/279, letter 902/1897.

40. For a fuller discussion of the insufficiency of the hut tax and other taxes to force Africans into wage labor, see NEC, vol. 15, "Supplementary Evidence to the Native Economic Commission by Professor S. Herbert Frankel on Certain Principles of Taxation—with Special Reference to the Taxation of Natives in the Union." See also the testimonies of Walter Carmichael and Sir Walter Stanford in South Africa, *Select Committee on Native Affairs,* pars. 197–201, 1101.

41. Stoler, "Making Empire Respectable," 634–60.

42. In addition, in eastern Pondoland there was an education rate collected to support schools. NEC K27, file 95, annexures B, E.

43. W. D. Hammond-Tooke, "The Transkeian Council System, 1895–1955: An Appraisal," *Journal of African History* 9 (1968): 455–77; Colin Bundy, "Mr. Rhodes and the Poisoned Goods: Popular Opposition to the Glen Grey Council System, 1894–1906," in *Hidden Struggles in Rural South Africa,* William Beinart and Colin Bundy (Berkeley: University of California Press, 1987), 138–65.

44. South Africa, *Select Committee on Native Affairs,* 117, pars. 1009–10; Bundy, "Mr. Rhodes."

45. See, for example, R. Buell, *The Native Problem in Africa,* 2 vols. (New York: Macmillan, 1928).

46. Saul Dubow, "Race, Civilisation and Culture: The Elaboration of the Segregationist Discourse in the Inter-War Years," in *The Politics of Race, Class, and Nationalism in Twentieth-Century South Africa,* ed. Shula Marks and Stanley Trapido (London: Longman, 1987), 1983.

47. South Africa, *Select Committee on Native Affairs,* 134–38.

48. Harold Wolpe, "Capitalism and Cheap Labour-Power in South Africa: From Segregation to Apartheid," *Economy and Society* 1 (1972): 434.

49. To discuss hut tax, most informants in the Transkei used *irhafu,* a word derived from the Afrikaans word for tax, *opgraaf.* See comments about the hut tax in South Africa, *Select Committee on Native Affairs,* app. A, p. i.

50. RM, Mount Frere District, to CMT, 1 July 1913, CMT 3/629, file 60.

51. Wilson, *Reaction to Conquest,* 135–40.

52. Cape of Good Hope, *Commission on Native Laws,*1:505, 2:app. C, 44.

53. Charles Simkins, "Fertility, Mortality, Migration and Assimilation in the Cape Colony: Evidence from the 1891 and 1904 Censuses," paper presented at Southern African Research Program Workshop, Yale University, 1986.

54. William Macmillan, *Complex South Africa—An Economic Footnote to History* (London: Faber and Faber, 1930), 127–30; Charles Simkins, "Agricultural Production in the African Reserves, 1918–1969," *Journal of Southern African Studies* 7 (1981): 256–83; H. J. Simons, *African Women: Their Legal Status in South Africa* (London: C. Hurst, 1968), 79–80.

55. For information on landlessness in one Transkeian district, see RM Nqamakwe District to SNA, 24 October 1932, NTS 1771, file 64/276/5.

56. Hut tax and land allocation up to the 1890s had been comparatively informal systems, with each magistrate having a fair bit of latitude for making exemptions and allowing unmarried or widowed women to work the land. RM Ngqeleni District to CMT, 3 January 1914, CMT 3/627, file 60; RM Umtata District to CMT, 7 September 1917, CMT 3/1650, file 493.6; RM Umtata District to CMT, 17 February 1920, CMT 3/1650, file 493.6; CMT to SNA, 21 February 1920, CMT 3/1650, file 493.6; Evidence of L. G. H. Tainton, Native Location Inspector King William's Town, 6 November 1903, SANAC, vol. 3.

57. For an example from the Engcobo district see statements from Masikonde Luhana in March 1927, in RM's (Engcobo) office, 1/ECO 6/1/1, file N1/1/5/2. See also SANAC, vol. 3, evidence of Tainton, 6 November 1903.

58. Simons, *African Women,* 261–64.

59. There are numerous magistrates' records documenting male desertion. See, for example, Ngcutshane Ganyoti v. Jongani Ngaleka, case 592/40, 9 August 1940, 1/UTA 2/1/1/153; Alban Magodla to RM Tsolo District, and reply, RM Tsolo District to Magodla, 16 December 1946, 1/TSO 5/1/25, file 2/21/2–51/46; RM Engcobo District to CMT, "Report for the Calendar Year 1936 for the District of Engcobo," 1/ECO 6/1/77, file 17/14/2; RM Engcobo District to CMT, "Report for the Calendar Year 1938," 1/ECO 6/1/77, file 17/14/2.

60. D. W. T. Shropshire, *Primitive Marriage and European Law: A South African Investigation* (London: Frank Cass, 1970), 30–41.

61. Alan H. Jeeves, *Migrant Labour in South Africa's Mining Economy: The Struggle for the Gold Mines' Labour Supply, 1890–1920* (Kingston: McGill-Queen's University Press, 1985), 90, fig. 4.

62. RM Bizana District to CMT, 4 January 1904, CMT 3/55; "Report of the Chief Magistrate" for 1907, CMT 3/681, file 175; CMT, "Blue Book Report for 1911," CMT 3/680, file 175; evidence of Tainton, 6 November 1903, SANAC, vol. 3.

63. In fact, there was no criminal statute for dealing with tax defaulters until the 1920s; until then magistrates had either to sue them in civil court or charge them with criminal vagrancy.

64. It is difficult to prove how many people were not brought to court for defaulting on taxes and why. The evidence is somewhat diffuse: RM Engcobo District to CMT, 25 June 1894, CMT 3/86; RM Engcobo District to CMT, 20 January 1899, Blue Book Report for 1899, CMT 3/90; CMT to All RMs in the Transkeian Territories, 28 November 1921, circular no. 18 of 1921, CMT 3/610; RM Bizana District to CMT, 23 September 1920, CMT 3/612, file 50/11; RM Lusikisiki District to CMT, 20 August 1920, CMT 3/612, file 50/11; SNA to all Civil Commissioners of Divisions of the Colony Proper in which there are locations on Crown Land, 23 April 1907, circular, NTS 2486, file 41/293 (1); Native Commissioner Komgha, H. W. Liefveldt, to Sec'y to Native Economic Commission, 19 February 1932, NEC K26, file NEC 68A; statement by John Guma and Nantiso Kula, representing the Young Men's Agricultural Society, at Engcobo, 20 November 1930, "Records of Statements from the Transkei," NEC K26 15; evidence of R. J. Dick, Special Magistrate, King William's Town, 2 November 1903, SANAC, vol. 3. For case listings of defaulters charged, see also 1/UTA 1/2/1 and successive numbers (the record books for criminal prosecutions for the Umtata magistrate).

65. Examples of independent women succeeding as farmers emerge from various sources: RM Umtata District to Secretary for Social Welfare, Pretoria, 14 August 1940, 1/UTA 6/1/49, file 31/1/3/3 (40); Nomavuta Ndara v. James Fodo, case 164, 12 May 1919, 1/UTA 2/1/1/99; R. v. Billy, case 653, 7 December 1899, 1/UTA 1/1/1/24; Draft for *A Transkei Enquiry,* ca. 1932, A881 Pim Papers, Manuscript Archives, University of the Witwatersrand; Various RMs to CMT, Returns "Agriculture," for 1909 Blue Book, CMT 3/679; "Report of the Chief Magistrate and Chief Native Commissioner of the Transkeian Territories for the Year Ending 31 December 1958," CMT 3/1451, file 38/A; evidence to the Native Economic Commission by Dr. A. B. Xuma, NEC K26 15.

66. W. J. G. Mears, "A Study in Native Administration: The Transkeian Territories, 1894–1943" (DLitt diss., University of South Africa, 1947), 1936.

67. Interview with African woman, approximately 72 years old, Butterworth District, December 1990; Statement by Rev. A. E. Jennings, London Missionary Society, Vryburg, April 1931, records of statements from the Orange Free State, NEC K26 16; Chief Constable Tsolo to RM Tsolo District, 23 January 1904, RM Tsolo District to CMT, 6 January 1904, CMT 3/162.

68. Statements made in the office of the RM Engcobo District, March 1927, 1/ECO 6/1/1, file N1/1/5/2.

69. There are numerous examples of migrant laborers leaving their families in the rural areas: testimony of Sir Walter Stanford in South Africa, *Select Committee on Native Affairs,* 150, par. 1191; evidence to the Native Economic Commission by Dr. A. B. Xuma, MD, NEC K26 15; Native Commissioner Far East Rand (Benoni, Brakpan, Springs) to Sec'y Native Economic Commission, 17 February 1931, replies to questionnaire, NEC K26 25, file 68E; R. v. Qali Mlauti, case 260 of 1933, 19 May 1933, Records of the Resident Magistrate Butterworth District, Cape Archives Depot, Cape Town (hereafter 1/BUT), 1/1/26; statement by Henry Britten, Magistrate Johannesburg, records of Johannesburg statements, NEC K26 12; statement of Superintendent Municipal Native Affairs Dept., Pietermaritzburg, 7 April 1931, records of Durban statements, NEC K26 14; statement of Robert Sello, Junior Vice President of the ICU, and Henderson K. Binda, Provincial Secretary of the ICU, Orange Free State statements, NEC K26 16; evidence of N. O. Thompson, RM Kentani District, 16 March 1904, "Evidence of 3 Transkeian Resident Magistrates, at Butterworth," C 17, vol. 3; quarterly meeting of Chiefs and Headmen, Engcobo, 5 October 1956, Chiefs and Headmen, file 3/4/1, Umtata Archives Depot, Umtata.

70. The only clear-cut exception to this was the property belonging to women herbalists: if a woman could prove that she was an herbalist and that she had earned the property through her practice, her male relatives could not lay legal claim to it.

71. For purposes of marriage, after 1913 African women in the Cape did reach majority at age twenty-one; that is, after a woman turned twenty-one her father could not longer legally prevent her from marrying whomever she wished by denying permission. See Simons, *African Women,* 46; Shropshire, *Primitive Marriage,* 144–55.

72. Dubow, "Race, Civilisation," 85; Buell, *Native Problem,* 1:88–110.

73. Evidence on tax arrears is taken from magistrates' records: CMT to all magistrates in the Transkeian Territories, 9 February 1956, and replies from magistrates, February 1956, CMT 3/1593, file 79B, circular minute no. 16/147/26; RM Bizana District to CMT, 15 August 1957, CMT 3/1593, file 79/1; RM Bizana District to CMT, 5 January 1959, and CMT to RM Bizana District, 15 January 1959, CMT 3/1593, file 79/1; CMT to RM Engcobo District, 15 January 1959, 1/ECO 6/1/54, file 11/1/2; quarterly meeting of Chiefs and Headmen, Engcobo district, 4 October 1953, Chiefs and Headmen 71, file 3/4/1, Umtata Archives Depot, Umtata; Sec'y Divisional Council Uniondale, Cape Province, to RM Umtata District, 3 March 1942, and response, RM Umtata District to Sec'y Divisional Council Uniondale, 10 March 1942, 1/UTA 6/1/84, file 2/5/2.

74. Mears, "Native Administration," 117–18. Mears probably took these figures from the *Report of the Mine Natives' Wages Commission.* Roger Southall has similar figures and cites the *Report.* Southall, *South Africa's Transkei: The Political Economy of an "Independent" Bantustan* (New York: Monthly Review Press, 1983), 81, table 3.3. See also CMT (W. T. Welsh) to SNA, enclosing annual report for 1929, 8 April 1930, NTS, file 64/276/4.

75. Mears, "Native Administration," 288; see also South Africa, *Select Committee on Native Affairs,* 6–7, par. 42. In real terms (adjusting for inflation) the decrease in production per family would be even more dramatic, a result of soil exhaustion, erosion, and the declining size of a flock of sheep.

76. Mears, "Native Administration," 288.

77. "Statements from the Transkei," evidence of C. C. Harris, 20 November 1930, NEC K 15.

78. RM Nqamakwe District to SNA, 24 October 1932, NTS 1771, file 64/276/5. This comprehensive accounting of African rural finances in Nqamakwe District makes the compelling case that in current conditions the district could not provide sufficient agricultural income for those Africans in residence and, additionally, that remittances from migrant laborers were not making up the shortfall in income.

79. South Africa, *Select Committee on Native Affairs,* 150.

80. T. R. H. Davenport, "The Triumph of Colonel Stallard: The Transformation of the Natives (Urban) Areas Act between 1923 and 1937," *South African Historical Journal* 2 (1970): 77–96.

81. Deborah Gaitskell and Judith Kimble, "Class, Race, and Gender: Domestic Workers in South Africa," *Review of African Political Economy* 27/28 (1984): 86–108; Elsa Joubert, *Poppie Nongena* (New York: Holt, 1987).

82. Shula Marks, "Patriotism, Patriarchy and Purity: Natal and the Politics of Zulu Ethnic Consciousness," in *The Creation of Tribalism in Southern Africa,* ed. Leroy Vail (Berkeley: University of California Press, 1989), 225–30.

83. Quoted in Shropshire, *Primitive Marriage,* 30.

84. For other opinions along the same lines as above see statement of Robert Sello, Junior Vice President of the ICU, and Henderson K. Binda, Provincial Secretary of the ICU, Orange Free State statements, NEC K 26 16; evidence submitted by the Kroonstad Joint Council of Europeans and Natives dealing with problems connected with Kroonstad Location, 17 February 1931, records of statements from the Orange Free State, NEC K 26 16; Evidence of the Native Advisory Board, Kroonstad, 17 February 1931, records of statements from the Orange Free State, NEC K 26 16; evidence of Rev. P. K. Kama, Church of England Missionary, King William's Town, 10 November 1903, SANAC 17, vol. 3; written replies to questions by G. W.

Barnes, Protector of Natives, Kimberley, 5 November 1903, SANAC 17, vol. 6; Health Inspector, Municipality of Umtata, Health Dept., to Town Clerk, 23 March 1938, file 50, 3/UTA 66; RM Engcobo District to CMT, 28 March 1892, enclosing various returns re: Native Labour, dated 28 March 1892, CMT 3/86.

85. Evidence of Dr. A. B. Xuma, NEC K 26 15; emphasis in original.

86. This charge was often levied by white municipal administrators who were either ignorant of or unsympathetic to the plight of African women in the rural areas. See for example evidence of Louis Stephanus van der Walt, sergeant in the SAP, stationed at New Brighton, Cape Province, Port Elizabeth statements, NEC K 26 13.

87. Petition signed by Antyi Sobopa and Caroline Sitsila, Engcobo, 20 November 1930, Transkei statements, NEC K 26 15.

88. Alban Magodla to RM Tsolo District, 16 December 1946, 1/TSO 5/1/25, file 2/21/2–51/46.

89. A. Magodla to RM Tsolo District, 16 December 1946, handwritten note by magistrate at top, 1/TSO 5/1/25, file 2/21/2–51/46.

90. RM Tsolo District to A. Magodla, 1/TSO 5/1/25, file 2/21/2–51/46.

91. Keith Breckenridge, "'Money with Dignity': Migrants, Minelords and the Cultural Politics of the South African Gold Standard Crisis, 1920–1933," *Journal of African History* 36 (1995): 290.

92. Philip Mayer, *Townsmen or Tribesmen?* (Cape Town: Oxford University Press, 1961), 162–65; Anne Mager, *Gender and the Making of a South African Bantustan: A Social History of the Ciskei, 1945–1959* (Portsmouth, NH: Heinemann, 1999), 101–4.

93. Mayer, *Townsmen or Tribesmen?* 242.

94. Ibid., 160–62; Wilson, *Reaction to Conquest,* 290–95.

95. Wilson, *Reaction to Conquest,* 316.

96. Ibid., 43.

97. Ralph A. Austen, "The Moral Economy of Witchcraft: An Essay in Comparative History," in *Modernity and Its Malcontents: Ritual and Power in Postcolonial Africa,* ed. Jean Comaroff and John Comaroff (Chicago: University of Chicago Press, 1993), 89–110.

98. Anthropologist W. D. Hammond-Tooke suggested that African women were often the targets of witchcraft accusations because there was a society-wide cognitive dissonance between women's actual power within households and the social ideal of submissive women. Hammond-Tooke, "The Cape Nguni Witch Familiar as a Mediatory Construct," *Man* 9 (1974): 132–35.

99. Redding, "Witchcraft, Women"; John Sharp and Andrew Spiegel, "Women and Wages: Gender and the Control of Income in Farm and Bantustan Households," *Journal of Southern African Studies* 16 (1990): 530.

100. Since it is the argument of this chapter that tax laws had laid the foundation for many of these changes in women's roles, there is an indirect connection to taxation, however.

101. Testimony of Aldin Gwantshu, R. v. Nosengqi Silanga, case 34/1933, 23 January 1933, 1/COF 1/1/1/38.

102. Ibid., testimony of Noorange. The accused diviner was found guilty of making accusations of witchcraft and was sentenced to six months in jail, the first two months of which was to be spent in solitary confinement on a diet of bread and water for two days out of every week.

103. Mayer, *Townsmen or Tribesmen?* 161, 164.

104. Wilson, *Reaction to Conquest,* 474.

105. "The care of cattle, goats, sheep, and horses is the work of men, the *umlaza* (ritual impurity) of women being regarded as dangerous to all stock except pigs and poultry." Wilson, *Reaction to Conquest,* 66.

106. Dyubele Komanisi v. Kwalukwalu Masi, case 401/37, 28 July 1937, 1/UTA 2/1/1/145.

107. Redding, "Witchcraft, Women."

108. Statement by Fina Bobotyana of Ngxaza Location, Tsolo District, 17 June 1943, office of the Chief Magistrate, 1/TSO 5/1/23, file 2/21/2.

109. Anthropologist Isak Niehaus noted a similar phenomenon of naming perceived "collaborators" as witches in parts of the Transvaal province. Niehaus, "Witch-Hunting and Political Legitimacy: Continuity and Change in Green Valley, Lebowa, 1930–91," *Africa* 63 (1993): 498–530; Niehaus, "Witches of the Transvaal Lowveld and Their Familiars," *Cahiers d'études africaines* 25 (1995): 513–40.

Chapter 7: Government Witchcraft

1. Biko was also paraphrasing Aimé Césaire's famous statement made in the 1950s. Biko, "I Write What I Like." In the same essay Biko quoted Césaire directly: "Aimé Césaire once said: 'When I turn on my radio, when I hear that Negroes have been lynched in America, I say that we have been lied to; Hitler is not dead: when I turn on my radio and hear that in Africa, forced labour has been inaugurated and legislated, I say that we have certainly been lied to: Hitler is not dead.'" Biko, "I Write What I Like," 334.

2. Roger Southall, *South Africa's Transkei: The Political Economy of an "Independent" Bantustan* (New York: Monthly Review Press, 1983), 114–35.

3. James Scott, *Domination and the Arts of Resistance: Hidden Transcripts* (New Haven: Yale University Press, 1990), 108–15.

4. Bruce Berman and John Lonsdale, *Unhappy Valley: Conflict in Kenya and Africa*, Eastern African Studies (Athens: Ohio University Press, 1992), 409.

5. Ibid., 380–97; Luise White, "Separating the Men from the Boys: Construction of Gender, Sexuality and Terrorism in Central Kenya," *International Journal of African Historical Studies* 23 (1990): 1–25.

6. Berman and Lonsdale, *Unhappy Valley*, 461–65.

7. Witchcraft beliefs have played a significant role in the recent accounts of rebellion in other parts of colonial Africa, notably Kenya and Zimbabwe, that have emphasized the importance of beliefs in witchcraft and the supernatural generally in motivating struggles against the state. Berman and Lonsdale, *Unhappy Valley*, 344; Clifton Crais, *The Politics of Evil: Magic, State Power, and the Political Imagination in South Africa* (New York: Cambridge University Press, 2002); Norma Kriger, *Zimbabwe's Guerrilla War: Peasant Voices* (Cambridge: Cambridge University Press, 1992); David Lan, *Guns and Rain: Guerrillas and Spirit Mediums in Zimbabwe* (Berkeley: University of California Press, 1985). These beliefs have continued into the postcolonial period and almost invariably have political expressions that have been documented. Cyprian Fisiy, "Sorcery Discourses, Knowledge and the Ambivalence of Power: Access to a Second Pair of Eyes" (unpublished paper, 1994), 1–23.

8. Adam Ashforth, "On Living in a World with Witches: Everyday Epistemology and Spiritual Insecurity in a Modern African City (Soweto)," in *Magical Interpretations, Material Realities: Modernity, Witchcraft, and the Occult in Postcolonial Africa*, ed. Henrietta Moore and Todd Sanders (New York: Routledge, 2001), 206–25; Isak Niehaus, "Witchcraft in the New South Africa: From Colonial Superstition to Postcolonial Reality?" in Moore and Sanders, *Magical Interpretations*, 184–205.

9. Monica Hunter Wilson, *Reaction to Conquest: Effects of Contact with Europeans on the Pondo of South Africa* (London: International Institute of African Languages and Cultures, 1936; London: Oxford University Press, 1961), 319.

10. Govan Mbeki, *South Africa: The Peasants' Revolt* (Harmondsworth: Penguin, 1963), 116–35; William Beinart, "Agrarian Historiography and Agrarian Reconstruction," in *South*

Africa in Question, ed. John Lonsdale (Portsmouth, NH: Heinemann, 1988), 134–53; Beinart, "Soil Erosion, Conservationism and Ideas about Development: A South African Exploration," *Journal of Southern African Studies* 11 (1984): 52–83.

11. Paramount chiefs and subchiefs frequently were direct descendants of precolonial rulers; however, regardless of lineage claims to chiefly authority, the main requirement for becoming a state-appointed chief was a willingness to comply with the state's plans for governing. Chiefs who did not comply were usually deposed and replaced.

12. Anne Mager, "'The People Get Fenced': Gender, Rehabilitation and African Nationalism in the Ciskei and Border Region, 1945–55," *Journal of Southern African Studies* 18 (1992): 761–82; Fred T. Hendricks, "Loose Planning and Rapid Resettlement: The Politics of Conservation and Control in Transkei, South Africa, 1950–1970," *Journal of Southern African Studies* 15 (1989): 306–25.

13. Nancy J. Jacobs, *Environment, Power, and Injustice: A South African History* (Cambridge: Cambridge University Press, 2003), 173–205; Beinart, "Soil Erosion," 52–83.

14. RM Engcobo District to CMT, 25 August 1949 1/ECO, file N2/11/3; RM Tsolo District to CMT, "Report on Native Affairs for the Year 1955," 1/TSO 5/1/136, file 2/9/2.

15. See, for example, minutes of quarterly meetings in Engcobo district between the Magistrate and Chiefs and Headmen, 4 October 1957, 10 December 1957, Chiefs and Headmen 71, file 3/4/1, Umtata Archives Depot, Umtata.

16. Unsigned letter in Xhosa with English translation attached, addressed to Magistrate, 16 March 1959, CMT 3/1593, file 79/1. This was also a comment made frequently by people I interviewed in several districts of the Transkei in 1990: that cattle were routinely seized in the 1950s at the dipping tanks from those who owed back taxes.

17. RM Xalanga District to CMT, 1 May 1961, "Confidential," CMT 3/1471, file 42/1.

18. There was a long history of state officials holding Africans collectively responsible for various crimes, dating back to the old Spoor Laws, which allowed victims of stock theft to collect compensation from any homesteads found near the spoor of stolen livestock.

19. CMT to all resident magistrates, Transkei, February 1956, circular minute no. 16/147/26, CMT 3/1593, file 79B. For other complaints of low rates of tax compliance, see "Report on Native Affairs for the Year Ended 30 June 1952," 1/TSO 5/1/136, file 2/9/2; RM Bizana District to CMT, 15 August 1957, CMT 3/1593, file 79/1; RM Engcobo District to CMT, 36 March 1960, 1/ECO 6/1/2, file N1/1/5/6; CMT to RM Engcobo District, 15 January 1959, 1/ECO 6/1/54, file 11/1/2; replies to CMT's circular, various dates in 1961, "Confidential," CMT 3/1471, file 42/1.

20. CMT to Deputy Commissioner South African Police (SAP), 4 February 1961, CMT 3/1472, file 42/Q.

21. Interview with man, 86 years old (born 1904), Butterworth District, December 1990.

22. Interview with man, 79 years old (born 1911), Bizana District, December 1990.

23. "Report of the Departmental Committee of Enquiry into Unrest in Eastern Pondoland," 9 August 1960, CMT 3/1472, file 42/Q. For similar opinions, see "Minutes of Quarterly Meeting of Headmen and People," at Umtata, 27 June 1957, convened by RM Umtata DistrictChiefs and Headmen 196, file 3/24/1, part 2 (Umtata district), Umtata Archives Depot, Umtata; State v. Mgoduzwa Tshezi, case 946/61, 25 October 1961, 1/LSK 1/1/16; CMT to all Transkeian magistrates, 9 February 1956, circular minute no. 16/147/26, CMT 3/1593, file 79B; replies to CMT circular by Idutywa magistrate, 12 April 1961, "Confidential," CMT 3/1471, file 42/1; letter to RM Bizana District, unsigned, original in Xhosa, translated in Magistrate's office, 16 March 1959, CMT 3/1593, file 79/1. See also Mbeki, *Peasants' Revolt,* 108.

24. "Report of the Committee of Enquiry into Unrest," 9 August 1960, CMT 3/1472, file 42/Q. From 1950 to 1963, Transkeian officials used the titles *magistrate* and *Bantu Affairs commissioner* interchangeably.

25. Quoted in "Report of the Committee of Enquiry into Unrest," 9 August 1960, CMT 3/1472, file 42/Q. See also Mbeki, *Peasants' Revolt*, 95–110; Crais, *Politics of Evil*, 178–80.

26. K. D. Matanzima to CMT, enclosing pamphlet "Issued by the African National Congress, P.O Box 48 New Brighton, Port Elizabeth," pamphlet in English, 9 November 1957, CMT 3/1471, file 42/C; emphasis in original.

27. Wilson, *Reaction to Conquest*, 282.

28. The term *irhafu yempundulu* was used by a seventy-nine-year-old man interviewed in Bizana District in December 1990. Govan Mbeki also notes that General Rate was called an *impundulu*. Mbeki, *Peasants' Revolt*, 107.

29. W. J. G. Mears, "A Study in Native Administration: The Transkeian Territories, 1894–1943" (DLitt diss., University of South Africa, 1947), 130.

30. Superintendent, Native Recruiting Corporation to RM Engcobo District, 3 January 1940, 1/ECO 6/1/77, file 17/14/2; RM Umtata to CMT, 3 June 1953, 1/UTA 6/1/86, file 2/11/2.

31. Reports of Chief Magistrate of the Transkei for 1957 and 1958, CMT 3/1451, file 38A.

32. J. B. Peires, "Unsocial Bandits: The Stock Thieves of Qumbu and Their Enemies," History Workshop, University of the Witwatersrand, 1994, 3–6; W. D. Hammond-Tooke, *Command or Consensus: The Development of Transkeian Local Government* (Cape Town: David Philip, 1975), 105.

33. Quarterly meeting of Chiefs and Headmen, Engcobo District, 29 June 1955, Chiefs and Headmen, Umtata Archives Depot, Umtata.

34. Crais, *Politics of Evil*, 168–69.

35. RM Tsolo District to CMT, 28 March 1957, 1/TSO 5/1/33, file N1/9/2; see also "Report of the Chief Magistrate and Chief Native Commissioner of the Transkeian Territories for the Year Ending 31 December 1956," 6 August 1957, CMT 3/1451, file 38A. Peires notes an increase in stock thefts for Qumbu district. Peires, "Unsocial Bandits," 10–16.

36. Report of Chief Magistrate for 1 July 1950–30 July 1951, 1 August 1951, CMT 3/1451, file 38A; report of Chief Magistrate for 1 July 1951–30 July 1952, 30 September 1952, CMT 3/1451, file 38A; RM Tsolo District to CMT, 24 July 1958, 1/TSO 5/1/133, file N1/9/2; report of Committee of Enquiry into Unrest, 9 August 1960, CMT 3/1452, file 42/Q. W. D. Hammond-Tooke also noted that cattle theft was "a source of revenue to the chief." Hammond-Tooke, *Command or Consensus*, 105.

37. On the use of the word *igqwetha* for lawyer, and what lawyers represented to Africans in court cases in 1903, see evidence of Rev. Mdolamba, Ndabeni Location, Cape Colony, 23 October 1903, Records of the 1902–3 South African Native Affairs Commission, C17, vol. 3, Union Archives, Pretoria Archives Depot.

38. "Report of the Chief Magistrate, Transkeian Territories, for 1st July 1951–30th July 1952," 30 September 1952, CMT 3/1451, file 38/A.

39. Memorandum by Bantu Affairs Commissioner, Bizana District, 11 July 1960, 1/BIZ 6/47, file C9/6/C; testimony of Monaty Mejelo, 12 June 1961, State v. Themba Njolweni and others, case 700 of 1961, 1/LSK 1/1/16.

40. RM Tsolo District to CMT, 24 July 1958, 1/TSO 5/1/33, file N1/9/2; BAC Tsolo District to CMT, 25 February 1961, 1/TSO 5/1/52, file C2.

41. Station Commander, Tsolo to District Commandant, Umtata, copy to the Tsolo magistrate, 23 January 1959, 1/TSO 5/1/52, file C2.

42. RM Tsolo District to CMT, 28 March 1957, 1/TSO 5/1/33, file N1/9/2; see also "Report of the Chief Magistrate and Chief Native Commissioner of the Transkeian Territories for the Year Ending 31 December 1956," 6 August 1957, CMT 3/1451, file 38A; R. v. Mzamo Ntayi and Bekiyeza Bambata, case 602/1954, Criminal Cases 1952–55, 1/ECO.

43. Clifton Crais has also discussed some of the supernatural beliefs that underpinned the Mpondo Revolt. Crais, *Politics of Evil*, 178–212.

44. The origin of the name *makhulu span* is not completely clear. It was suggested to me by an informant in Engcobo District that it meant a team (the Afrikaans word *span*) of many or of the multitude (the Xhosa stem *-khulu*). Peires defines it simply as "big team." Peires, "Unsocial Bandits," 12.

45. RM Qumbu District to Chief Bantu Affairs Commissioner, 4 March 1961, "Confidential," CMT 3/1471, file 42/1. Crais says that Makhulu Span did not emerge until 1956, but the letter cited below, dating from 1955, would indicate otherwise. Crais, *Politics of Evil*, 170.

46. Translation of note in Xhosa (translated in magistrate's office), undated (probably 1955), 1/TSO 5/1/52, file C.4.

47. Peires suggests that in Qumbu district, Makhulu Span members frequently warned suspects in advance of the plans to burn their huts, thus keeping deaths to a minimum. Peires, "Unsocial Bandits," 15. This may have been true in Qumbu, but cases of arson tried in the magistrates' courts of other districts indicate that often people were actually inside the huts when they were set alight. Many arson victims did manage to escape their huts, but often because the barking of dogs or other incidental noises awoke them before the flames were established and escape became impossible.

48. "Report of the Chief Magistrate and Chief Native Commissioner of the Transkeian Territories for the Year Ending 31 December 1956," 6 August 1957, CMT 3/1451, file 38A.

49. Received 13 August 1958, 1/TSO 5/1/133, file N1/9/2.

50. See the opinion expressed by the chief magistrate in "Report for Year Ending 31 December 1959," 17 May 1961, CMT 3/1451, file 38A.

51. Office of the Station Commander to the District Commandant, Tsolo, 22 January 1959, 1/TSO 5/1/52, file C2; see also Hammond-Tooke, *Command or Consensus*, 105–8, 146–48.

52. Anonymous letter to RM Tsolo District, 1958, 1/TSO 5/1/133, file N1/9/2.

53. Ibid.

54. A similar case occurred in 1960 in Butterworth, where two men and their families were ostracized and threatened because they refused to pay ten shillings each to an antigovernment organization. See BAC Butterworth District to CBAC, enclosing statement made by two African men in BAC's office, 9 March 1961, 1/BUT, file C.25.

55. BAC Qumbu District to CBAC, 4 March 1961, "Confidential," CMT 3/1471, file 42/1.

56. Crais, *Politics of Evil*, 172–73.

57. Reply to CMT's circulars by Kentani magistrate, 9 March 1961, reply by Idutywa magistrate, 12 April 1961, and reply by Qumbu magistrate, 10 August 1961, "Confidential," CMT 3/1471, file 42/1.

58. Interview with man, 50 years old (born 1940), professional, Engcobo District, December 1990.

59. BAC Engcobo District to CBAC, 26 October 1962, 1/ECO 6/1/1, file N1/1/5/2; BAC Engcobo District to CBAC, 8 November 1962, 1/ECO 6/1/98, file N1/9/1; BAC Engcobo District to CBAC, 22 February 1963, 1/ECO 6/1/98, file N1/9/1.

60. BAC Engcobo District to CBAC, 18 December 1961, "Confidential," file N1/9/2, 1/ECO 6/1/98. One person who was interviewed also mentioned the plans to bomb the magistrate's office in Engcobo. Interview with man, 50 years old, professional, Engcobo District, December 1990.

61. BAC Engcobo District to CBAC, 6 September 1962, 1/ECO 6/1/98, file N1/9/1.

62. Mbeki, *Peasants' Revolt*, 120.

63. Memorandum submitted by BAC Bizana District to CBAC, 11 July 1960, 1/BIZ 6/47, file C9/6/C; "Report of the Committee of Enquiry into Unrest," 9 August 1960, CMT 3/1472, file 42/Q.

64. Mbeki, *Peasants' Revolt*, 120.

65. In the districts of Qumbu and Tsolo, magistrates tended to associate the Congo movement with the African Political Organisation rather than the ANC, and in Butterworth and Kentani magistrates focused their concern on Poqo, the military wing of the Pan-African Congress. In still other instances, there were rumors of the All-African Convention having had a hand. See Colin Bundy, "Land and Liberation: The South African Liberation Movements and the Agrarian Question, 1920–60," *Review of African Political Economy* 29 (1984): 24–25; Crais, *Politics of Evil*, 180–92.

66. The quotations are from two sources discussing the events in the context of reporting events and testimony given at a trial of rebels. BAC Bizana District to CMT, memorandum, 11 July 1960, 1/BIZ 6/47, file C9/6/C. See also State v. Themba Njolweni, Sotolase Mpangati, Sibodwana Ntlokonkulu, Mqingelwa Fahla, Siboniwe Fulalela, Joko Qasayi, Tshobeni Mzanza, and Mahlaza Qasayi, case 700 of 1961, 12 June 1961, 1/LSK 1/1/16.

67. Church of England, *Report of a Committee Appointed at the Request of the Diocesan Missionary Conference to Enquire into the Question of Witchcraft*, owned by the Strange (Africana) Library, Johannesburg (Umtata: Thompson's Printing Works, 1936).

68. State v. Mgoduzwa Tshezi, case 946/61, 25 October 1961, 1/LSK 1/1/16; Isak Niehaus, "Witch-Hunting and Political Legitimacy: Continuity and Change in Green Valley, Lebowa, 1930–91," *Africa* 63 (1993): 514–29.

69. State v. Themba Njolweni, Sotolase Mpangati, Sibodwana Ntlokonkulu, Mqingelwa Fahla, Siboniwe Fulalela, Joko Qasayi, Tshobeni Mzanza, and Mahlaza Qasayi, case 700 of 1961, 12 June 1961, 1/LSK 1/1/16.

70. John Wesley, *A Collection of Hymns for the Use of People Called Methodists* (London: Wesleyan-Methodist Book Room, 1889), hymn 9, verse 3.

71. The complete text of the constitution as it appeared in the magistrate's records is in CMT 3/1472, file 42Q: typescript, no cover letter, probably originated in Bizana, 19 November 1960.

72. Typescript, 19 November 1960, CMT 3/1472, file 42Q.

73. Ibid.

74. Cf. Gary Kynoch, *We Are Fighting the World: A History of the Marashea Gangs in South Africa, 1947–1999* (Athens: Ohio University Press, 2005).

75. The reference to the Russians at the time of the Xhosa cattle killing of 1856–57 was linked to news reports about the defeat of the British military by the Russian army in the Crimea. These Russians, victorious on the battlefield against the British imperial army, entered into the prophecy of the adolescent Nongqawuse, with the Russians becoming the natural allies of both the soon-to-be resurrected ancestors and the still-living but embattled African population. See J. B. Peires, *The Dead Will Arise* (Berkeley: University of California Press, 1989).

76. Replies to CMT's circulars, various BACs to CMT, dated 1961, "Confidential," CMT 3/1471, file 42/1; CMT to Secretary for Bantu Administration and Development, 25 January 1961, CMT 3/1472, file 42/Q (vol. 1).

77. Engcobo District magistrate (BAC) to CBAC, 18 February 1961, "Confidential," reply to CMT's circular, CMT 3/1471, file 42/1.

78. BAC Umtata District to CBAC, 2 March 1961, "Confidential," reply to CBAC's circular, CMT 3/1471, file 42/1.

79. BAC Butterworth District to CBAC, 17 May 1960, "Confidential," 1/BUT 7/1/88, file C.25.

80. BAC Butterworth District to CBAC, 9 March 1961, "Confidential," enclosing statement of Sonanazi Mtintsilana, 1/BUT 7/1/88, file C.25.

81. BAC Ngqeleni District to CBAC, 21 February 1961, "Confidential," CMT 3/1471, file 42/1.

82. BAC Tsolo District to CMT, 25 February 1961, 1/TSO 5/1/52, file C2.

83. BAC Butterworth District to CMT, 8 March 1963, 1/BUT 7/1/88, file C.25.

84. "Report of the Committee of Enquiry into Unrest," 9 August 1960, CMT 3/1472, file 42/Q.

85. Mbeki, *Peasants' Revolt*, 122.

86. BAC Bizana District to CBAC, 26 August 1960, 1/BIZ 6/61, file N1/9/2/1.

87. Interview with woman, age 53, born 1937, Bizana District, December 1990.

88. BAC Bizana District to CBAC, 4 December 1960, CMT 3/1472, file 42Q; BAC Umtata District to CMT, 2 March 1961, "Confidential," CMT 3/1471, file 42/1; BAC Engcobo District to CBAC, 18 February 1961, 1/ECO 6/1/98, file N1/9/2; BAC Qumbu District to CMT, 4 March 1961, "Confidential," CMT 3/1471, file 42/1; BAC Tsolo District to CBAC, 3 May 1961, 1/TSO 5/1/52, file C2.

89. Mbeki, *Peasants' Revolt*, 124–28.

90. BAC Engcobo District, 18 February 1961, "Confidential," reply to CBAC's circulars, CMT 3/1471, file 42/1.

91. BAC Qumbu District, 25 March 1961, "Confidential," reply to CMT's circulars, CMT 3/1471, file 42/1.

92. CBAC to Secretary for Bantu Administration and Development, 12 January 1961, CMT 3/1472, file 42/Q; "Minutes of Quarterly Meeting of Headmen and People Held at Umtata on 29 March 1963," Chiefs and Headmen 196, file 3/24/1, part 2 (Umtata), Umtata Archives Depot; BAC Qumbu District, 25 March 1961, "Confidential," reply to CBAC's circular, CMT 3/1471, file 42/1.

93. BAC Idutywa District to CBAC, 12 April 1961, "Confidential," CMT 3/1471, file 42/1.

94. BAC Qumbu District to CBAC, 1 May 1961, "Confidential," CMT 3/1471, file 42/1.

95. Kentani District BAC to CBAC, 9 March 1961, "Confidential," CMT 3/1471, file 42/1. See also CBAC to Secretary for Bantu Administration and Development, 25 January, 4 February 1961, CMT 3/1472, file 42/Q (vol. 1).

96. "Magistrate's Court: Bizana," 3 November 1961, CMT 3/1472, file 42/Q. The Flagstaff District BAC reported similar figures.

97. Mbeki, *Peasants' Revolt*, 117.

98. BAC Lusikisiki District, 14 February 1961, reply to CBAC's circular, CMT 3/1472, file 42/Q. Even the Butterworth District Bantu Affairs Commissioner was dismayed by the brutal tactics used by the mobile unit in neighboring Kentani district; he asked that the unit not be sent into his district. BAC Butterworth District to CBAC, 1 March 1961, 1/BUT 7/1/88, file C.25.

99. Mbeki, *Peasants' Revolt*, 131.

100. "Minutes of Quarterly Meeting of Headmen and People at Umtata on 13 June 1963," Chiefs and Headmen 196, file 3/24/1, part 2 (Umtata), Umtata Archives Depot.

101. BAC Engcobo District to CBAC, 26 October 1962, file 3/4/3/2, Chiefs and Headman 71, Umtata Archives Depot; State vs. Dywilise Mnqanqeni, copy of case 95 of 1962, 5 October 1962, 1/ECO 6/1/1, file N/1152.

102. BAC Tsolo District to CBAC, 18 July 1963, "Confidential," 1/TSO 5/1/52, file C.2.

103. BAC Engcobo to CBAC, 22 April 1963, 1/ECO 6/1/98, file N1/9/1.

104. BAC Engcobo to CBAC, 5 September 1963, 1/ECO 6/1/98, file N1/9/1.

105. Mbeki, *Peasants' Revolt*, 117.

106. "Self-government" was a stage on the road to so-called independence.

107. John Lonsdale makes a similar statement about British colonial officials' responses to Mau Mau in Kenya. Berman and Lonsdale, *Unhappy Valley*, 283–86.

108. Karen Fields talks about witchcraft beliefs being part of "the quotidian and the humdrum." Fields, "Political Contingencies of Witchcraft in Colonial Central Africa: Culture and State in Marxist Theory," *Canadian Journal of African Studies* 16 (1982): 584.

109. Philip Mayer, "The Origin and Decline of Two Rural Resistance Ideologies," in *Black Villagers in an Industrial Society,* ed. Philip Mayer (Cape Town: Oxford University Press, 1980), 43–48.

110. Crais suggests rather that it was some white administrators who were mad, made unstable by their authoritarian powers. See Crais, *Politics of Evil,* 196–206.

111. Joan A. Broster, *Amagqirha: Religion, Magic, and Medicine in Transkei* (Goodwood, South Africa: Via Afrika, 1981), 59.

112. Berman and Lonsdale, *Unhappy Valley,* 230–37.

Chapter 8: State Control, Rebellions, and Supernatural Beliefs

1. John Comaroff and Jean Comaroff, *The Dialectics of Modernity on a South African Frontier,* vol. 2 of *Of Revelation and Revolution* (Chicago: University of Chicago Press, 1997), 190.

2. James Scott, *Domination and the Arts of Resistance: Hidden Transcripts* (New Haven: Yale University Press, 1990), 108–82.

3. Steve Biko, "I Write What I Like: Fear—An Important Determinant in South African Politics," in *Steve Biko: Black Consciousness in South Africa,* ed. Millard Arnold (New York: Vintage Books, 1978), 337.

4. In Kenya in the 1950s schoolteacher Karari Njama encountered the need to choose sides several months after taking the initial Oath of Unity with Mau Mau, a fact that suggests that even once rebellion broke out, there was (for a time at least) still multiple "scripts" from which he might choose. See Donald Barnett and Karari Njama, *Mau Mau from Within: Autobiography and Analysis of Kenya's Peasant Revolt* (New York: Modern Reader Paperbacks, 1966), 135–46.

5. Bruce Berman and John Lonsdale, *Unhappy Valley: Conflict in Kenya and Africa,* Eastern African Studies (Athens: University of Ohio Press, 1992), 315–30.

6. Cape of Good Hope, *Report of the Government Commission on Native Laws and Customs, 1883,* facsimile repr., 2 vols. (Cape Town: C. Struik, 1968), 1:479.

7. Ibid., 1:63.

8. CMT to SNA, 3 September 1926, CMT 3/612, file 50/11.

9. Isak Niehaus, "Witch-Hunting and Political Legitimacy: Continuity and Change in Green Valley, Lebowa, 1930–91," *Africa* 63 (1993): 498–530.

10. Glen S. Elder, *Hostels, Sexuality, and the Apartheid Legacy: Malevolent Geographies* (Athens: Ohio University Press, 2003), 116–30; Stephen Ellis, "The Historical Significance of South Africa's Third Force," *Journal of Southern African Studies* 24 (1998): 261–99; Rian Malan, *My Traitor's Heart* (New York: Atlantic Monthly Press, 1990), 223–34; Mahmood Mamdani, *Citizen and Subject* (Princeton: Princeton University Press, 1994), 263–84; T. Dunbar Moodie and Vivienne Ndatshe, *Going for Gold: Men, Mines, and Migration* (Berkeley: University of California Press, 1994), 190–210.

11. The phrase is from Barnett and Njama, *Mau Mau from Within,* 210. On violence within the family see Sean Redding, "Deaths in the Family: Violence and Witchcraft Accusations in Rural Transkei, South Africa, 1904–65," *Journal of Southern African Studies* 30 (2004): 519–37. See also Anne Mager, *Gender and the Making of a South African Bantustan: A Social History of the Ciskei, 1945–1959* (Portsmouth, NH: Heinemann, 1999), 101–18, 127–41.

BIBLIOGRAPHY

Archival Sources

Cape Archives Depot, Cape Town
    Records of the Chief Magistrate of East Griqualand (CMK)
    Records of the Chief Magistrate of the Transkeian Territories (CMT)
    Records of Resident Magistrates of Transkeian Districts
        Bizana (1/BIZ)
        Butterworth (1/BUT)
        Cofimvaba (1/COF)
        Engcobo (1/ECO)
        Idutywa (1/IDW)
        Lusikisiki (1/LSK)
        Qumbu (1/QBU)
        Tabankulu (1/TBU)
        Tsolo (1/TSO)
        Umtata (1/UTA)
KwaZulu-Natal Archives Depot, Pietermaritzburg
    Records of the Chief Native Commissioner, Natal (CNC)
    Records of the Secretary for Native Affairs, Natal-Zululand (SNA)
    Records of Resident Magistrate of Umbulumbulo District, KwaZulu-Natal
Umtata Archives Depot, Umtata
    Chiefs and Headmen Archive
Union Archives Depot, Pretoria
    Records of the South African Native Affairs Commission (SANAC)
    Records of the Native Economic Commission (NEC)
    Records of the Union Native Affairs Department (NTS)
Cullen Library, University of the Witwatersrand
    Howard Pim papers, draft of *A Transkei Enquiry*
Public Record Office, Kew Gardens, London
    Records of the Cape Colony (CO)
Yale University Divinity School
    Records of the Wesleyan Methodist Missionary Society (on microfiche)

Newspapers

Territorial News, Umtata
Daily Dispatch, East London

Interviews

All interviews were conducted by myself with the help of a research assistant (an advanced undergraduate student at the University of the Transkei) during December 1990.

Interviews were conducted in either English or Xhosa, or more often a combination of the two. My knowledge of Xhosa is extremely limited, but my research assistant was fluent in both languages, and most informants were also bilingual to some degree. December 1990 was a turbulent time in South African and Transkeian politics: there was an attempted coup d'état—sponsored by the South African state—against the Transkeian homeland government of Bantu Holomisa in that month, and although the African National Congress had been unbanned by the apartheid government, the future was unknown.

I found that people were far more willing to discuss events (even those that had occurred several decades in the past) if they were guaranteed anonymity. As a result written notes were taken, either by me or my assistant, during the interview (no tape recorder was used), and interviewees were listed only by birth date or approximate age, sex, location, and occupation. (Virtually all the men were farmers when they were interviewed, but most had been migrant laborers—usually at the gold mines—when they were younger). I recognize that this degree of anonymity places real limits on the usefulness of the material. As a result, I confined my use of interview material to information that could either be directly corroborated by other sources or that, in a more general way, accorded with material gained from other sources.

Bizana District
　Man, 65 years old, headman and farmer.
　Man, 79 years old, farmer.
　Woman, born 1916, farmer.
　Man, born 1948, subheadman and farmer.
　Man, 64 years old, farmer.
　Woman, 53 years old, teacher.
　Man, born 1933, headman.
　Man, 61 years old, farmer.

Butterworth District
　Man, 99 years old, farmer.
　Husband and wife, roughly 76 and 72 years old respectively, farmers.
　Man, 66 years old, farmer.
　Man, 86 years old, farmer.

Engcobo District
　Husband and wife, both in their fifties, professionals.
　Man, 79 years old, farmer.
　Man, born 1907, farmer.

Tsolo District
　Man, 72 years old, farmer.
　Man, 74 years old, farmer.
　Man, 99 years old (roughly—could remember rinderpest well), farmer.

Umtata District
　Man, 62 years old, farmer.
　Woman, 79 years old, farmer (widowed for many years).
　Man, 58 years old, farmer.
　Man, 75 years old, farmer.
　Man, 61 years old, farmer.
　Man, 74 years old, farmer.

Man, 67 years old, farmer.
Man, 62 years old, farmer.
Man, 70 years old, farmer.
Man, 56 years old, farmer.

Books and Articles

Ashforth, Adam. "An Epidemic of Witchcraft? The Implications of AIDS for the Post-Apartheid State." *African Studies* 61 (2002): 121–43.

———. "On Living in a World with Witches: Everyday Epistemology and Spiritual Insecurity in a Modern African City (Soweto)." In *Magical Interpretations, Material Realities: Modernity, Witchcraft, and the Occult in Postcolonial Africa*, edited by Henrietta Moore and Todd Sanders, 206–25. New York: Routledge, 2001.

Atkins, Koletso. *The Moon Is Dead! Give Us Our Money! The Cultural Origins of an African Work Ethic, Natal, South Africa, 1843–1900*. Portsmouth, NH: Heinemann, 1993.

Austen, Ralph A. "The Moral Economy of Witchcraft: An Essay in Comparative History." In *Modernity and Its Malcontents: Ritual and Power in Postcolonial Africa*, edited by Jean Comaroff and John Comaroff, 89–110. Chicago: University of Chicago Press, 1993.

Ballard, Charles. "The Repercussions of Rinderpest: Cattle Plague and Peasant Decline in Colonial Natal." *International Journal of African Historical Studies* 19, no. 3 (1986): 421–50.

Barnett, Donald, and Karari Njama. *Mau Mau from Within: Autobiography and Analysis of Kenya's Peasant Revolt*. New York: Modern Reader Paperbacks, 1966.

Beinart, William. "Agrarian Historiography and Agrarian Reconstruction." In *South Africa in Question*, edited by John Lonsdale, 134–53. Portsmouth, NH: Heinemann, 1988.

———. "Amafelandawonye (the Die-Hards): Popular Protest and Women's Movements in Herschel District in the 1920s." In *Hidden Struggles in Rural South Africa*, William Beinart and Colin Bundy, 222–69. Berkeley: University of California Press, 1987.

———. "The Anatomy of a Rural Scare: East Griqualand in the 1890s." In *Hidden Struggles in Rural South Africa*, William Beinart and Colin Bundy, 46–78. Berkeley: University of California Press, 1987.

———. "Chieftaincy and the Concept of Articulation: South Africa circa 1900–50." In *Segregation and Apartheid in Twentieth-Century South Africa*, edited by William Beinart and Saul Dubow, 176–88. New York: Routledge, 1995.

———. "Conflict in Qumbu: Rural Consciousness, Ethnicity and Violence in the Colonial Transkei." 1981. Reprinted in *Hidden Struggles in Rural South Africa*, William Beinart and Colin Bundy, 106–37. Berkeley: University of California Press, 1987.

———. *The Political Economy of Pondoland, 1860–1930*. Johannesburg: Ravan Press, 1982.

———. "Soil Erosion, Conservationism and Ideas about Development: A South African Exploration." *Journal of Southern African Studies* 11 (1984): 52–83.

Beinart, William, and Colin Bundy. *Hidden Struggles in Rural South Africa.* Berkeley: University of California Press, 1987.

———. "The Union, the Nation, and the Talking Crow: The Ideology and Tactics of the Independent ICU in East London." In *Hidden Struggles in Rural South Africa,* William Beinart and Colin Bundy, 270–320. Berkeley: University of California Press, 1987.

Berger, Iris. "Rebels or Status-Seekers? Women as Spirit Mediums in East Africa." In *Women in Africa,* edited by Nancy Hafkin and Edna Bay, 157–82. Stanford: Stanford University Press, 1976.

Berglund, Axel-Ivar. *Zulu Thought-Patterns and Symbolism.* Bloomington: Indiana University Press, 1989.

Berman, Bruce, and John Lonsdale. *Unhappy Valley: Conflict in Kenya and Africa.* Book 1, State and Class; Book 2, Violence and Ethnicity. Eastern African Studies. Athens: University of Ohio Press, 1992.

Biko, Steve. "I Write What I Like: Fear—An Important Determinant in South African Politics." In *Steve Biko: Black Consciousness in South Africa,* edited by Millard Arnold, 331–38. New York: Vintage Books, 1978.

Binns, C. T. *Dinuzulu: The Death of the House of Shaka.* London: Longmans, 1968.

Booth, Alan R. "'European Courts Protect Women and Witches': Colonial Law Courts as Redistributors of Power in Swaziland, 1920–50." *Journal of Southern African Studies* 18 (1992): 253–75.

Bozzoli, Belinda. *Women of Phokeng.* Johannesburg: Ravan Press, 1992.

Bradford, Helen. "Gentlemen and Boers: Afrikaner Nationalism, Gender, and Colonial Warfare in the South African War." In *Writing a Wider War: Rethinking Gender, Race, and Identity in the South African War, 1899–1902,* edited by Greg Cuthbertson, Albert Grundlingh, and Mary-Lynn Suttie, 37–66. Athens: Ohio University Press, 2002.

———. "Peasants, Historians and Gender: A South African Case Study Revisited, 1850–86." *History and Theory* 39 (2000): 86–110.

———. *A Taste of Freedom: The ICU in Rural South Africa, 1924–1930.* New Haven: Yale University Press, 1987.

Breckenridge, Keith. "'Money with Dignity': Migrants, Minelords and the Cultural Politics of the South African Gold Standard Crisis, 1920–1933." *Journal of African History* 36 (1995): 271–304.

Broster, Joan. *Amaqgirha: Religion, Magic, and Medicine in Transkei.* Goodwood, South Africa: Via Afrika, 1981.

Brownlee, W. T. *Reminiscences of a Transkeian.* Pietermaritzburg: Shuter and Shooter, 1975.

Buell, R. *The Native Problem in Africa.* 2 vols. New York: Macmillan, 1928.

Bundy, Colin. "The Emergence and Decline of a South African Peasantry." *African Affairs* 71 (1972): 369–88.

———. "Land and Liberation: The South African Liberation Movements and the Agrarian Question, 1920–60." *Review of African Political Economy* 29 (1984).

———. "Mr. Rhodes and the Poisoned Goods: Popular Opposition to the Glen Grey Council System, 1894–1906." In *Hidden Struggles in Rural South Africa*, William Beinart and Colin Bundy, 138–65. Berkeley: University of California Press, 1987.

———. *The Rise and Fall of the South African Peasantry*. Berkeley: University of California Press, 1979.

———. "'We Don't Want Your Rain, We Won't Dip': Popular Opposition, Collaboration and Social Control in the Anti-Dipping Movement, ca. 1908–16." In *Hidden Struggles in Rural South Africa*, William Beinart and Colin Bundy, 191–221. Berkeley: University of California Press, 1987.

Callaway, Rev. Henry. *The Religious System of the Amazulu*. Springvale, Natal: J. A. Blair, 1868.

Cape of Good Hope. *Blue Book on Native Affairs, 1898*. Cape Town: Government Printers, 1898.

———. *Blue Book on Native Affairs, 1879*. Cape Town: Government Printers, 1879.

———. *Report of a Commission Appointed to Inquire Into the Causes of the Recent Outbreak in Griqualand East*. Cape Town: Solomon, 1879.

———. *Report of the Government Commission on Native Laws and Customs, 1883*. Facsimile repr. 2 vols. Cape Town: C. Struik, 1968.

Carter, Gwendolen, Thomas Karis, and Newell Stultz. *South Africa's Transkei: The Politics of Domestic Colonialism*. Evanston: Northwestern University Press, 1967.

Carton, Benedict. *Blood from Your Children: The Colonial Origins of Generational Conflict in South Africa*. Charlottesville: University of Virginia Press, 2000.

Chanock, Martin. *Law, Custom, and Social Order*. Cambridge: Cambridge University Press, 1985.

———. "Making Customary Law: Men, Women, and Courts in Colonial Northern Rhodesia." In *African Women and the Law: Historical Perspectives*, edited by Margaret Jean Hay and Marcia Wright, 53–66. Boston: Boston University, African Studies Center, 1982.

Church of England. *Report of a Committee Appointed at the Request of the Diocesan Missionary Conference to Enquire into the Question of Witchcraft*. Owned by the Strange (Africana) Library, Johannesburg. Umtata: Thompson's Printing Works, 1936.

Cobbing, Julian. "A Tainted Well: The Objectives, Historical Fantasies, and Working Methods of James Stuart, with Counter-Argument." *Journal of Natal and Zulu History* 11 (1988): 115–54.

Colenbrander, Peter. "The Zulu Kingdom, 1828–79." In *Natal and Zululand from Earliest Times to 1910: A New History*, edited by Andrew Duminy and Bill Guest, 83–115. Pietermaritzburg: Shuter and Shooter, 1989.

Comaroff, Jean, and John Comaroff. *Ethnography and the Historical Imagination*. Boulder: Westview Press, 1992.

—————. *Christianity, Colonialism, and Consciousness in South Africa.* Vol. 1 of *Of Revelation and Revolution.* Chicago: University of Chicago Press, 1991.

—————. *The Dialectics of Modernity on a South African Frontier.* Vol. 2 of *Of Revelation and Revolution.* Chicago: University of Chicago Press, 1997.

Cooper, Frederick. "Peasants, Capitalists, and Historians: A Review Article." *Journal of Southern African Studies* 7 (1981): 284–314.

Cope, R. L. "C. W. de Kiewiet, the Imperial Factor, and South African 'Native Policy.'" *Journal of Southern African Studies* 15 (1989): 486–505.

Crais, Clifton. *The Politics of Evil: Magic, State Power, and the Political Imagination in South Africa.* New York: Cambridge University Press, 2002.

Davenport, T. R. H. "The Triumph of Colonel Stallard: The Transformation of the Natives (Urban) Areas Act between 1923 and 1937." *South African Historical Journal* 2 (1970): 77–96.

Delius, Peter. "Migrant Organisation, the Communist Party, the ANC and the Sekhukhuneland Revolt, 1940–58." In *Apartheid's Genesis, 1935–1962,* edited by Philip Bonner, Peter Delius, and Deborah Posel, 126–59. Johannesburg: Ravan Press, 1993.

Douglas, Mary, ed. *Witchcraft Confessions and Accusations.* London: Tavistock, 1970.

Dubow, Saul. "Holding 'a Just Balance between White and Black': The Native Affairs Department in South Africa, c. 1920–33." *Journal of Southern African Studies* 12 (1986): 217–39.

—————. "Race, Civilisation, and Culture: The Elaboration of the Segregationist Discourse in the Inter-War Years." In *The Politics of Race, Class, and Nationalism in Twentieth-Century South Africa,* edited by Shula Marks and Stanley Trapido, 71–94. London: Longman, 1987.

—————. *Scientific Racism in Modern South Africa.* New York: Cambridge University Press, 1995.

Edgar, Robert R. "The Fifth Seal: Enoch Mgijima, the Israelites, and the Bulhoek Massacre, 1921." PhD diss., University of California, Los Angeles, 1977.

—————. "Garveyism in Africa: Dr. Wellington and the American Movement in the Transkei." *Ufahamu* 6, no. 3 (1976): 31–57.

Edgar, Robert, and Christopher Saunders. "A. A. S. le Fleur and the Griqua Trek of 1917: Segregation, Self-Help, and Ethnic Identity." *International Journal of African Historical Studies* 15, no. 2 (1982): 201–20.

Elder, Glen S. *Hostels, Sexuality, and the Apartheid Legacy: Malevolent Geographies.* Athens: Ohio University Press, 2003.

Ellis, Stephen. "The Historical Significance of South Africa's Third Force." *Journal of Southern African Studies* 24 (1998): 261–99.

Elphick, Richard. "Africans and the Christian Campaign in South Africa." In *The Frontier in History: North America and Southern Africa Compared,* edited by Howard Lamar and Leonard Thompson, 270–307. New Haven: Yale University Press, 1981.

Etherington, Norman. "Christianity and African Society in Nineteenth-Century Natal." In *Natal and Zululand from Earliest Times to 1910: A New History*, edited by Andrew Duminy and Bill Guest, 275–301. Pietermaritzburg: Shuter and Shooter, 1989.

———. "Postmodernism and South African History." *New Contree* 40 (1996): 28–41.

———. "The 'Shepstone System' in the Colony of Natal and beyond the Borders." In *Natal and Zululand from Earliest Times to 1910: A New History*, edited by Andrew Duminy and Bill Guest, 170–92. Pietermaritzburg: Shuter and Shooter, Ltd., 1989.

Evans, Ivan. *Bureaucracy and Race: Native Administration in South Africa*. Berkeley: University of California Press, 1997.

Fields, Karen. "Political Contingencies of Witchcraft in Colonial Central Africa: Culture and State in Marxist Theory." *Canadian Journal of African Studies* 16 (1982): 567–93.

Fisiy, Cyprian. "Sorcery Discourses, Knowledge and the Ambivalence of Power: Access to a Second Pair of Eyes." Unpublished paper, 1994, 1–23.

Fisiy, Cyprian, and Peter Geschiere. "Sorcery, Witchcraft and Accumulation: Regional Variations in South and West Cameroon." *Critique of Anthropology* 11, no. 3 (1991): 251–78.

Fuze, Magema M. *The Black People and Whence They Came: A Zulu View*. Pietermaritzburg: University of Natal Press, 1979.

Gaitskell, Debbie. "Devout Domesticity? A Century of African Women's Christianity in South Africa." In *Women and Gender in Southern African to 1945, edited by Cherryl Walker, 251–72. Cape Town: David Philip, 1990.

———. "Housewives, Maids or Mothers: Some Contradictions of Domesticity for Christian Women in Johannesburg, 1903–1939." *Journal of African History* 24, no. 2 (1983): 241–57.

Gaitskell, Deborah, and Judith Kimble. "Class, Race, and Gender: Domestic Workers in South Africa." *Review of African Political Economy* 27/28 (1984): 86–108.

Geschiere, Peter. *The Modernity of Witchcraft: Politics and the Occult in Postcolonial Africa*. Charlottesville: University of Virginia Press, 1997.

Gillings, K. G. "The Bambata Rebellion of 1906: Nkandla Operations and the Battle of Mome Gorge, 10 June 1906." *South African Military History Journal* 8, no. 1 (1989): 1–15.

Golan, Daphna. "The Life Story of King Shaka and Gender Tensions in the Zulu State." *History in Africa* 17 (1990): 95–111.

Guest, Bill. "Colonists, Confederation and Constitutional Change." In *Natal and Zululand from Earliest Times to 1910: A New History*, edited by Andrew Duminy and Bill Guest, 146–69. Pietermaritzburg: Shuter and Shooter, 1989.

Guy, Jeff. "Analysing Pre-Capitalist Societies in Southern Africa." *Journal of Southern African Studies* 14 (1987): 18–37.

———. *The Destruction of the Zulu Kingdom*. London: Longman, 1979.

———. "Gender Oppression in Southern Africa's Precapitalist Societies." In *Women and Gender in Southern Africa to 1945*, edited by Cherryl Walker, 33–47. Cape Town: David Philip, 1990.

———. *The View across the River: Harriette Colenso and the Zulu Struggle against Imperialism.* Charlottesville: University of Virginia Press, 2001.

Hadebe, Moses M. "A Contextualization and Examination of the Impi Yamakhanda (1906 Uprising) as Reported by J. L. Dube in Ilanga Lase Natal with Special Focus on Dube's Attitude to Dinuzulu as Indicated in His Reportage on the Treason Trial of Dinuzulu." Master's diss., Program of Historical Studies, University of Natal, Durban, 2002.

Hamilton, Carolyn. "'The Character and Objects of Chaka': A Reconsideration of the Making of Shaka as Mfecane Motor." In *The Mfecane Aftermath: Reconstructive Debates in Southern African History,* edited by Carolyn Hamilton, 183–212. Johannesburg: Witwatersrand University Press, 1995.

———. *Terrific Majesty: The Powers of Shaka Zulu and the Limits of Historical Invention.* Cambridge, MA: Harvard University Press, 1998.

Hammond-Tooke, W. D. "The Cape Nguni Witch Familiar as a Mediatory Construct." *Man* 9 (1974): 128–36.

———. *Command or Consensus: The Development of Transkeian Local Government.* Cape Town: David Philip, 1975.

———. *The Roots of Black South Africa.* Johannesburg: Jonathan Ball, 1993.

———. "The Transkeian Council System, 1895–1955: An Appraisal." *Journal of African History* 9 (1968): 455–77.

Hellmann, Ellen. *Rooiyard: A Sociological Survey of an Urban Native Slum Yard.* Rhodes-Livingston Papers, no. 13. Cape Town: Oxford University Press, 1948.

Hendricks, Fred T. "Loose Planning and Rapid Resettlement: The Politics of Conservation and Control in Transkei, South Africa, 1950–70." *Journal of Southern African Studies* 15 (1989): 306–25.

Hexham, Irving. *Texts on Zulu Religion.* Lewiston, NY: Edwin Mellen Press, 1987.

Hill, Robert, and Gregory A. Pirio. "'Africa for the Africans': The Garvey Movement in South Africa, 1920–40." In *The Politics of Race, Class, and Nationalism in Twentieth-Century South Africa,* edited by Shula Marks and Stanley Trapido, 209–53. London: Longman, 1987.

Horrell, Muriel. *The African Reserves of South Africa.* Johannesburg: South African Institute of Race Relations, 1969.

Houghton, D. Hobart. *The South African Economy.* 3rd ed. Cape Town: Oxford University Press, 1973.

Hyden, Goren. *Beyond Ujamaa in Tanzania.* Berkeley: University of California Press, 1981.

Innes, Duncan, and Dan O'Meara. "Class Formation and Ideology: The Transkei Region." *Review of African Political Economy* 7 (1976): 69–86.

Isaacman, Allen, and Barbara Isaacman. "Resistance and Collaboration in Southern and Central Africa." *International Journal of African Historical Studies* 10 (1977): 31–62.

Jacobs, Nancy J. *Environment, Power, and Injustice: A South African History.* Cambridge: Cambridge University Press, 2003.

Jeeves, Alan H. *Migrant Labour in South Africa's Mining Economy: The Struggle for the Gold Mines' Labour Supply, 1890–1920*. Kingston: McGill-Queen's University Press, 1985.

Johns, Sheridan. "Trade Union, Political Pressure Group, or Mass Movement? The Industrial and Commercial Workers' Union of Africa." In *Protest and Power in Black Africa*, edited by Robert Rotberg and Ali Mazrui. New York: Oxford University Press, 1970.

Joubert, Elsa. *Poppie Nongena*. New York: Holt, 1987.

Kertzer, David. *Ritual, Politics, and Power*. New Haven: Yale University Press, 1988.

Kinsman, Margaret. "Beasts of Burden: The Subordination of Southern Tswana Women, ca. 1800–1840." *Journal of Southern African Studies* 10 (1983): 17–39.

Kjekshus, Helge. *Ecology Control and Economic Development in East African History: The Case of Tanganyika, 1850–1950*. Berkeley: University of California Press, 1977.

Kriger, Norma. *Zimbabwe's Guerrilla War: Peasant Voices*. Cambridge: Cambridge University Press, 1992.

Laband, John. *The Rise and Fall of the Zulu Nation*. London: Arms and Armour Press, 1997.

Laband, John, and Paul Thompson. "The Reduction of Zululand, 1878–1904." In *Natal and Zululand from Earliest Times to 1910*, edited by Andrew Duminy and Bill Guest, 193–232. Pietermaritzburg: Shuter and Shooter, 1989.

Lambert, John. "From Independence to Rebellion: African Society in Crisis, c. 1880–1910." In *Natal and Zululand from Earliest Times to 1910*, edited by Andrew Duminy and Bill Guest, 373–401. Pietermaritzburg: Shuter and Shooter, 1989.

Lan, David. *Guns and Rain: Guerrillas and Spirit Mediums in Zimbabwe*. Berkeley: University of California Press, 1985.

Landau, Paul. *The Realm of the Word: Language, Gender, and Christianity in a Southern African Kingdom*. Portsmouth, NH: Heinemann, 1995.

Legassick, Martin. "South Africa: Capital Accumulation and Violence." *Economy and Society* 3 (1974): 251–91.

Levi, Margaret. *Of Rule and Revenue*. Berkeley: University of California Press, 1988.

Maclean, John. *A Compendium of Kafir Laws and Customs*. Mt. Coke: Wesleyan Mission Press, 1858.

Macmillan, William. *Complex South Africa—An Economic Foot-note to History*. London: Faber and Faber, 1930.

Mager, Anne. *Gender and the Making of a South African Bantustan: A Social History of the Ciskei, 1945–1959*. Portsmouth, NH: Heinemann, 1999.

———. "'The People Get Fenced': Gender, Rehabilitation and African Nationalism in the Ciskei and Border Region, 1945–55." *Journal of Southern African Studies* 18 (1992): 761–82.

———. "Youth Organisations and the Construction of Masculine Identities in the Ciskei and Transkei, 1945–60." *Journal of Southern African Studies* 24 (1998): 653–68.

Mahoney, Michael. "The Millennium Comes to Mapumulo: Popular Christianity in Rural Natal, 1866–1906." *Journal of Southern African Studies* 25 (1999): 375–91.

Malan, Rian. *My Traitor's Heart.* New York: Atlantic Monthly Press, 1990.

Mamdani, Mahmood. *Citizen and Subject.* Princeton: Princeton University Press, 1994.

Marks, Shula. "Class, Ideology and the Bambatha Rebellion." In *Banditry, Rebellion and Social Protest in Africa,* edited by Donald Crummey, 351–72. London: James Currey, 1986.

———. "Patriotism, Patriarchy and Purity: Natal and the Politics of Zulu Ethnic Consciousness." In *The Creation of Tribalism in Southern Africa,* edited by Leroy Vail, 215–40. Berkeley: University of California Press, 1989.

———. *Reluctant Rebellion: The 1906–8 Disturbances in Natal.* Oxford: Oxford University Press, 1970.

———. "The Zulu Disturbances in Natal." In *Protest and Power in Black Africa,* edited by Robert I. Rotberg and Ali A. Mazrui, 213–57. New York: Oxford University Press, 1970.

Mayer, Philip. "The Origin and Decline of Two Rural Resistance Ideologies." In *Black Villagers in an Industrial Society,* edited by Philip Mayer. Cape Town: Oxford University Press, 1980.

———. *Townsmen or Tribesmen: Conservation and the Process of Urbanization in a South African City.* Cape Town: Oxford University Press, 1961.

Mbeki, Govan. *South Africa: The Peasants' Revolt.* Harmondsworth: Penguin, 1963.

Mbembe, Achille. "Prosaics of Servitude and Authoritarian Civilities." *Public Culture* 5, no. 1 (1992): 123–45.

———. "Provisional Notes on the Postcolony." *Africa* 62, no. 1 (1992): 1–37.

Mears, W. J. G. "A Study in Native Administration: The Transkeian Territories, 1894–1943." DLitt diss., University of South Africa, 1947.

Moodie, T. Dunbar, and Vivienne Ndatshe. *Going for Gold: Men, Mines, and Migration.* Berkeley: University of California Press, 1994.

Moore, Henrietta, and Todd Sanders. "Magical Interpretations and Material Realities: An Introduction." In *Magical Interpretations, Material Realities: Modernity, Witchcraft, and the Occult in Postcolonial Africa,* edited by Henrietta Moore and Todd Sanders, 1–27. New York: Routledge, 2001.

Natal Colony. *Further Correspondence Relating to the Trial of Dinuzulu and Other Natives in Natal.* London: His Majesty's Stationery Office, 1909.

Ngubane, Harriet. *Body and Mind in Zulu Medicine.* New York: Academic Press, 1977.

Niehaus, Isak. "Witchcraft in the New South Africa: From Colonial Superstition to Postcolonial Reality?" In *Magical Interpretations, Material Realities: Modernity, Witchcraft and the Occult in Postcolonial Africa,* Henrietta L. Moore and Todd Sanders, 184–205. New York: Routledge, 2001.

———. "Witches of the Transvaal Lowveld and Their Familiars." *Cahiers d'études africaines* 25 (1995): 513–40.

———. "Witch-Hunting and Political Legitimacy: Continuity and Change in Green Valley, Lebowa, 1930–91." *Africa* 63 (1993): 498–530.

Packard, Randall M. "Industrialization, Rural Poverty, and Tuberculosis in South Africa, 1850–1950." In *The Social Basis of Health and Healing in Africa*, edited by Steven Feierman and John Janzen, 104–30. Berkeley: University of California Press, 1992.

———. "Social Change and the History of Misfortune among the Bashu of Eastern Zaïre." In *Explorations in African Systems of Thought*, edited by Ivan Karp and Charles Bird, 237–67. Bloomington: Indiana University Press, 1980.

Parry, R. "'In a Sense Citizens, but Not Altogether Citizens . . .': Rhodes, Race and the Ideology of Segregation at the Cape in the Late Nineteenth Century." *Canadian Journal of African Studies* 17 (1983): 384–91.

Peires, J. B. *The Dead Will Arise*. Berkeley: University of California Press, 1989.

———. *The House of Phalo*. Berkeley: University of California Press, 1982.

———. "Unsocial Bandits: The Stock Thieves of Qumbu and Their Enemies." History Workshop, University of the Witwatersrand, 1994.

Phoofolo, Pule. "Epidemics and Revolutions: The Rinderpest Epidemic in Late Nineteenth-Century Southern Africa." *Past and Present* 138 (1993): 112–43.

Pim, Howard. *Introduction to Bantu Economics*. Fort Hare: Lovedale Press, 1930.

Ramdhani, Narissa. "Taxation without Representation: The Hut Tax System in Colonial Natal." *Journal of Natal and Zulu History* 11 (1986): 12–25.

Ramphele, Mamphela. *A Bed Called Home: Life in the Migrant Labour Hostels of Cape Town*. Athens: Ohio University Press, 1993.

Ranger, Terence O. "Connexions between 'Primary Resistance' Movements and Modern Mass Nationalism in East and Central Africa." *Journal of African History* 9 (1968): 437–53.

———. "Taking Hold of the Land: Holy Places and Pilgrimages in Twentieth-Century Zimbabwe." *Past and Present* 117 (1987): 159–94.

Reader, D. H. *Zulu Tribe in Transition: The Makhanya of Southern Natal*. Manchester: Manchester University Press, 1966.

Redding, Sean. "African Women and Migration in Umtata, Transkei, 1880–1935." In *Courtyards, Markets, City Streets: Urban Women in Africa*, edited by Kathleen Sheldon, 31–46. Boulder: Westview Press, 1996.

———. "A Blood-Stained Tax: Poll Tax and the Bambatha Rebellion in South Africa." *African Studies Review* 43 (2000): 29–54.

———. "Deaths in the Family: Violence and Witchcraft Accusations in Rural Transkei, South Africa, 1904–65." *Journal of Southern African Studies* 30 (2004): 519–37.

———. "Government Witchcraft: Taxation, the Supernatural, and the Mpondo Revolt in the Transkei, South Africa, 1955–63." *African Affairs* 95 (1996): 555–79.

———. "Legal Minors and Social Children: African Women and Taxation in the Transkei, 1880–1950." *African Studies Review* 36 (1993): 49–74.

———. "Sorcery and Sovereignty: Taxation, Witchcraft, and Political Symbols in the 1880 Transkeian Rebellion." *Journal of Southern African Studies* 22 (1996): 249–70.

———. "Witchcraft, Women, and Taxes in the Transkei, South Africa, 1930–63." In *Stepping Forward: Black Women in Africa and the Americas,* edited by Catherine Higgs, Barbara Moss, and Earline Rae Ferguson, 87–99. Athens: Ohio University Press, 2002.

Richards, Audrey. "A Modern Movement of Witchfinders." *Africa* 8 (1935): 439–51.

Robinson, Ronald. "Non-European Foundations of European Imperialism: A Sketch for a Theory of Collaboration." In *Studies in the Theory of Imperialism,* edited by Roger Owen and Bob Sutcliffe, 117–42. London: Longman, 1976.

Saunders, C. C. *The Annexation of the Transkeian Territories.* Archives Yearbook for South African History. Pretoria: Government Printer, 1978.

———. "Tile and the Thembu Church: Politics and Independency on the Cape Eastern Frontier in the Late Nineteenth Century." *Journal of African History* 11 (1970): 553–70.

———. "The Transkeian Rebellion of 1880–81: A Case Study of Transkeian Resistance to White Control." *South African Historical Journal* 8 (1976): 32–39.

Scott, James. *Domination and the Arts of Resistance: Hidden Transcripts.* New Haven: Yale University Press, 1990.

———. *Seeing like a State.* New Haven: Yale University Press, 1998.

———.*Weapons of the Weak.* New Haven: Yale University Press, 1985.

Sharp, John, and Andrew Spiegel. "Women and Wages: Gender and the Control of Income in Farm and Bantustan Households." *Journal of Southern African Studies* 16 (1990): 525–49.

Shropshire, D. W. T. *Primitive Marriage and European Law: A South African Investigation.* London: Frank Cass, 1970.

Simkins, Charles. "Agricultural Production in the African Reserves, 1918–69." *Journal of Southern African Studies* 7 (1981): 256–83.

———. "Fertility, Mortality, Migration and Assimilation in the Cape Colony: Evidence from the 1891 and 1904 Censuses." Paper presented at Southern African Research Program Workshop, Yale University, 1986.

Simons, H. J. *African Women: Their Legal Status in South Africa.* London: C. Hurst, 1968; Evanston: Northwestern University Press, 1968.

South Africa. Union Native Affairs Department. *Report of the South African Native Affairs Commission (SANAC).* Cape Town: Government Printers, 1903–5.

———. Select Committee on Native Affairs. *Second-Third Reports of the Select Committee on Native Affairs.* Cape Town: Government Printer, 1912.

South Africa. Native Economic Commission. *Report of the Native Economic Commission, 1930–1932.* Pretoria: Government Printer, 1932.

Southall, Roger. *South Africa's Transkei: The Political Economy of an "Independent" Bantustan.* New York: Monthly Review Press, 1983.

Stoler, Ann. "Making Empire Respectable: The Politics of Race and Sexual Morality in Twentieth-Century Colonial Cultures." *American Ethnologist* 16 (1989): 634–60.

Strobel, Margaret. "Gender and Race in the Nineteenth- and Twentieth-Century British Empire." In *Becoming Visible: Women in European History*, edited by Renate Bridenthal, Claudia Koonz, and Susan Mosher Stuard, 375–96. 2nd ed. Boston: Houghton Mifflin, 1987.

Stuart, James. *A History of the Zulu Rebellion, 1906, and of Dinuzulu's Arrest, Trial, and Expatriation*. London: Macmillan, 1913.

———. *James Stuart Archive of Recorded Oral Evidence Relating to the History of the Zulu and Neighbouring Peoples*. Edited and translated by Colin Webb and John Wright. 5 vols. Pietermaritzburg: University of Natal Press, 1976–92.

Sundkler, B. G. M. *Bantu Prophets in South Africa*. 2nd ed. London: Oxford University Press, 1961.

Swanson, Maynard. "The Sanitation Syndrome: Bubonic Plague and Urban Native Policy in the Cape Colony, 1900–1909." *Journal of African History* 18 (1977): 387–410.

Taussig, Michael. *The Magic of the State*. New York: Routledge, 1997.

Van Onselen, Charles. "Reactions to Rinderpest in Southern Africa, 1896–97." *Journal of African History* 13 (1972): 473–88.

Wesley, John. *A Collection of Hymns for the Use of People Called Methodists*. London: Wesleyan-Methodist Book Room, 1889.

White, Luise. "Separating the Men from the Boys: Construction of Gender, Sexuality and Terrorism in Central Kenya." *International Journal of African Historical Studies* 23 (1990): 1–25.

———. *Speaking with Vampires: Rumor and History in Colonial Africa*. Berkeley: University of California Press, 2000.

———. "Tsetse Visions: Narratives of Blood and Bugs in Colonial Northern Rhodesia, 1931–39." *Journal of African History* 36 (1995): 219–45.

Wilson, Monica Hunter. *Reaction to Conquest: Effects of Contact with Europeans on Pondo*. London: Oxford University Press/International Institute of African Languages and Cultures, 1936. 2nd ed., London: Oxford University Press, 1961.

Wolpe, Harold. "Capitalism and Cheap Labour-Power in South Africa: From Segregation to Apartheid." *Economy and Society* 1 (1972): 425–56.

Wright, John. "Control of Women's Labour in the Zulu Kingdom." In *Before and After Shaka: Papers in Nguni History*, edited by J. B. Peires, 82–99. Grahamstown: Rhodes University, 1983.

Wright, Marcia. "Justice, Women and the Social Order in Abercorn, Northeastern Rhodesia, 1897–1903." In *African Women and the Law: Historical Perspectives*, edited by Margaret Jean Hay and Marcia Wright, 33–50. Boston: Boston University African Studies Center, 1982.

INDEX

Page references in italics denote illustrations.